BATTLE FOR
MONTE
NATALE

For Sister Pat, who gave me great encouragement to write this book about our father. Sadly, she died before it was published

BATTLE FOR MONTE NATALE

FIRST-HAND ACCOUNTS OF THE CROSSING OF THE RIVER GARIGLIANO ON THE GUSTAV LINE

JOHN ERNEST STRAFFORD

Pen & Sword
MILITARY

AN IMPRINT OF PEN & SWORD BOOKS LTD.
YORKSHIRE – PHILADELPHIA

First published in Great Britain in 2024 by
Pen & Sword Military
An imprint of
Pen & Sword Books Ltd
Yorkshire - Philadelphia

ISBN 978 1 03610 818 2

A CIP catalogue record for this book is available from the British Library.

Typeset by SJmagic DESIGN SERVICES, India.

Printed and bound in the UK by CPI Group (UK) Ltd.

Pen & Sword Books Limited incorporates the imprints of Archaeology, Atlas, Aviation, Battleground, Digital, Discovery, Family History, Fiction, History, Local, Local History, Maritime, Military, Military Classics, Politics, Select, Transport, True Crime, After the Battle, Air World, Claymore Press, Frontline Publishing, Leo Cooper, Remember When, Seaforth Publishing, The Praetorian Press, Wharncliffe Books, Wharncliffe Local History, Wharncliffe Transport, Wharncliffe True Crime and White Owl.

For a complete list of Pen & Sword titles please contact:

PEN & SWORD BOOKS LIMITED
George House, Units 12 & 13, Beevor Street, Off Pontefract Road,
Barnsley, S71 1HN, UK
E-mail: enquiries@pen-and-sword.co.uk
Website: www.pen-and-sword.co.uk

or

PEN AND SWORD BOOKS
1950 Lawrence Rd, Havertown, PA 19083, USA
E-mail: uspen-and-sword@casematepublishers.com
Website: www.penandswordbooks.com

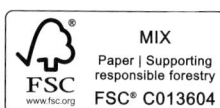

MIX
Paper | Supporting
responsible forestry
FSC® C013604
FSC
www.fsc.org

Contents

Acknowledgements and Thanks

I would like to particularly thank Frank de Planta for clarifying various points with his special military knowledge and expertise. I have been on two battlefield tours in Italy superbly organised by Frank. They were informative, educational and at times amusing. Frank has a great sense of humour which he is able to combine with the serious nature of the subject, and I am most grateful to him.

The one survivor of the Battle of Monte Natale that I met was Geoffrey Winter, who was a Lieutenant in 1 York & Lancaster at the time of the battle. He gave me great encouragement in my research and gave me many of the personal accounts. Sadly, he has now died, but I hope this book will serve as a fitting memorial to him.

In 1995 Ernest Shaw, 1 York & Lancs. was interviewed by the Imperial War Museum. Extracts from the interview are included in the book. I am most grateful to the Imperial War Museum.

Three others require special mention. My son Peter has done an enormous amount of research finding items that I would never have dreamed of pursuing. This has been a great help. My sister Pat had a few memories of our father Ernest. I know this book meant a lot to her and I thank her for all her support and encouragement. My wife Caroline has been a source of strength, organising our travel and making suggestions which I am sure have enhanced the narrative.

Finally, I am particularly grateful to Marcel Eberlein for letting me have the German contributions to the book. I am responsible for the translation into English with some help from Peter Strafford.

Alfred Eberlein, the grandfather of Marcel Eberlein, was killed near the River Garigliano. Here is his story: Corporal of the 194th Pioneers of 94 Infantry Division, deployed on the Gustav Line on the Garigliano front was only 24 years old when his life was cut short during the German counterattacks on 21 January 1944, trying to repel the offensive Operation 'Panther' on the River Garigliano.

Alfred left his young wife and small children and he'll never know that his wife was expecting a baby girl during his last posting. The young wife, after a first communication stating Alfred was missing in battle, will live the next two years with the hope of hugging her husband again, hope shattered by the definitive communication that Alfred had fallen on the field of battle.

Later, a friend of Alfred's roommate, will give the young woman Alfred's handkerchief soaked in his blood. The young woman, now alone in a devastated country, will have to provide for her young children, among thousands of other difficulties. Alfred Eberlein rests in the German Cemetery in Cairo (Cassino).

Army Film and Photographic Unit
Brockman, Patricia Ann
de Planta, Frank
Eberlein, Marcel
Inniskillings Museum
Imperial War Museum
Gieseler, Wolfras. Lt. 3 Battalion, 274 Grenadier Regiment
Lepone, Antonio
Mendico, Mario Mirco
The National Archives
naval-history.net website
Norton, Geoffrey. Retd. Lt. Col. York & Lancaster Regiment
Schumann, Herbert. Cpl. 3 Co., I Battalion, 267 Grenadier Regiment
Schünemann, Ernst. II Battalion, 274 Grenadier Regiment
Shaw, Ernest. 1 York & Lancs. Imperial War Museum
Sheffield City Archives
Sheffield, O.F., *The York & Lancaster Regiment, Volume 3*
Sheffield Telegraph
Stefanelli, Gerardo, Mayor of Minturno
Strafford, Caroline J.M.
Strafford, Guy P.C.
Strafford, Peter M.A.
US National Archives
Wikipedia
94 Infantry Division – German Army

Preface

This story is not just another story about the Second World War. It is a story about a battle which took place over a period of three weeks in January–February 1944 in Italy. My father, Ernest Strafford, was killed in this battle.

How did this book come to be written? In the early evening, about 6pm, on 10 November 2011, I was in London passing Westminster Abbey. All the Royal British Legion crosses were laid out in the Field of Remembrance. As I had time to spare, I thought I would look at the plot of the York & Lancaster Regiment, which was my father's regiment. I found the plot but because it was dark and there were so many wooden crosses, I could not read any names. I had my camera with me, so using its flashlight I zoomed in on the plot. Immediately, one name – Ernest Strafford – came out and hit me. It was as if he was saying 'I'm here'! This was one of the most emotional moments of my life. Tears welled in my eyes and then streamed down my face. For the first time in my life, I thought about my father. I could not help thinking 'What might have been? What was he like'? How different my life might have been if he had lived. I had so many questions to which there was not and could not be any answer, but there were some questions for which perhaps, I might be able to find an answer.

I never knew my father. How did he get killed? Where did he get killed? Was he on his own or with others? On 20 January 1944 he was seriously wounded by a mortar bomb. On 22 January he was **REPORTED MISSING, (Believed Wounded)**.

Westminster Abbey – Field of Remembrance, 10 Nov 2011. (John Strafford)

Left: Westminster Abbey – Field of Remembrance. Photo, 10 Nov 2011. (John Strafford)

Below: Ernest Stafford's War Record, Ministry of War.

On 4 February it was recorded **Body recovered, identified & buried by British Troops**. He died sometime between 20 January and 4 February 1944, but which was the date he died? In investigating his death there was a historical challenge to writing about it. The fog of war descends over the battlefield as it is being fought. Afterwards when it is being written about, each participant only sees part of the picture. War is messy and most accounts lose many of the human consequences, both at the time and thereafter by simplification. Bringing together all the differing accounts of the battle the reader can make their own judgement about what happened.

The Strafford Family

The Straffords lived and worked in the same area of Sheffield for at least 250 years. They were scissor manufacturers and in the 1760s had a workshop in Meadow Street. My father, Ernest Strafford, was born in Sheffield on 26 October 1913, and before his marriage lived with his parents in Midland Street.

Edith and Ernest Strafford were married on 28 August 1937. A year later, on 18 September 1938 their daughter Pat was born. My name is John Ernest Strafford. I am the only son of Ernest Strafford. I was born on 13 September 1942.

On marrying, Edith and Ernest Strafford settled in Hunter Hill Road. It was a two up, two down house with an attic and the toilet was at the bottom of the garden. During the war we had a 'bomb shelter' in the garden. A tin bath was on a hook outside the back door.

Ernest Strafford joined the York & Lancaster Regiment Territorial Battalion on 24 June 1940 and the regular army on 14 October 1943. He was not conscripted, he volunteered. Why?

He was a printer's compositor with the *Sheffield Telegraph*. This was a reserved occupation, so Ernest did not have to join the army. Did he volunteer because of peer pressure? After all some of his fellow workers signed up including the son of Lord Kemsley, the proprietor of the *Sheffield Telegraph*. Just after the end of the war perhaps on the unveiling of the plaque 'In Honoured Memory of Those of The *Sheffield Telegraph* Who fell in the Second World War 1939–1945' Eliza Strafford (Ernest's mother) took myself and my sister Pat to the offices of the *Sheffield Telegraph*. Lord Kemsley told Eliza

Edith and Ernest Strafford, 28 Aug 1937. (Family photo)

xi

John and Pat Strafford, 1945. (Family photo)

that there would always be a job at the *Sheffield Telegraph* for myself and my sister! Did Lord Kemsley influence his staff to join the services and feel a particular link with those who had died, in view of the fact that his own son was one of the casualties?

There was a military background to my family. Ernest's grandfather was one of the longest serving members of the Sheffield Artillery Volunteers which used to meet at the Drill Hall. His father was also a member. On Edith's (Ernest's wife) side two of her father's brothers, Stanley and Maurice Waterfall, served in the York & Lancaster Regiment during the Great War. Sadly Maurice Waterfall was killed at Havrincourt in France on 27 September 1918 just before the end of the First World War. With this background it was only natural that Ernest would feel some pressure to volunteer for the Territorial Army in 1940 and then as a regular in October 1943.

In addition, there were further pressures. Two of Ernest's brothers-in-law were in the army. John Webb (Edith's sister Bessie's husband) was with the Royal Marine Commandos and Arthur Townsend (Edith's sister Gladys's husband) was with the Royal Engineers. Another of Edith's sisters Winnie, was engaged to Len Hill who was also with the Royal Engineers. All three men were in Italy when Ernest arrived there in October 1943. It may have seemed to Ernest that he was not doing his duty by avoiding active service. We will not know what motivated him to join the regular army, but what we do know is that Edith, his wife, was opposed to it and was very upset, as any woman would be, seeing her husband go off to war, particularly if he could legitimately have avoided doing so.

Above left: Ernest Strafford's grandfather, John Strafford. *Yorkshire Telegraph & Star*, 15 April 1929.

Above right: John Strafford at DYRMS, 1959. (Family photo)

Ernest was an only child. His father, Ernest Stafford Sr, died in 1949. His mother, Eliza, died in 1957.

In 1954, I went to the Duke of York's Royal Military School (DYRMS), a boarding school for the sons of soldiers. A tradition of the school was that on parade you wore the badge of your father's regiment. I was the only boy at the school to wear the badge of the York & Lancaster Regiment.

Ernest Strafford's War Record

Ernest Strafford joined the York & Lancaster Regiment Territorial Battalion on 24 June 1940 and the regular army on 14 October 1943, when he embarked on a Landing Ship bound for Italy.

Convoy KMF 25 was the convoy that took Ernest Strafford to Italy. It was the only convoy to Italy at that time. There were eighteen ships in the convoy plus fourteen escort ships, eleven of which had Torpedo Defence Systems. Included in the convoy was SS *Champollion* carrying 2,155 troops. There were two Landing Ships Tank, HMS *Boxer* and HMS *Bruiser*, both the same class of Landing Ship Tank. Loaded, they could each take 13 Churchill tanks, 27 other vehicles and 193 troops. It is likely Ernest Strafford was on one of these. He embarked on 14 October 1943. The convoy sailed from Liverpool on the 16th. Its ultimate destination was Alexandria in Egypt via Gibraltar and Italy. It arrived in Italy on 25 October when Ernest Strafford disembarked and the two cruisers, HMS *Orion* and HMS *Spartan*, ceased escorting the convoy. HMS *Boxer* and HMS *Bruiser* arrived at Alexandria on 31 October.

When Ernest Strafford disembarked he was registered with No. 1 IRTD (Infantry Recruit Training Depot) on the X List (iv). This list comprises all unposted reinforcements and incoming reinforcement drafts. Reinforcements in transit between the base and a unit remain on the X List (iv) until they reach the unit and have been taken on its strength. In Ernest Strafford's case his unit was 1 York & Lancs.

HMS *Boxer* at Salerno, Italy, Sep 1943. (naval-history.net website)

Abbreviations

ADC	Aide-de-Camp
ADS	Advanced Dressing Station
AFPU	Army Film & Photo Unit
Bde	Brigade
BEF	British Expeditionary Force
Btn	Battalion
Cameronians	2 Battalion Cameronian Regiment
Cheshires	7 Battalion, Cheshire Regiment
Coldstream Guards	3 Battalion, Coldstream Guards
C-in-C	Commander-in-Chief
CO	Commanding Officer
Comd	Command
Col	Colonel
Coy	Company
CSM	Company Sergeant Major
CWGC	Commonwealth War Graves Commission
DSO	Distinguished Service Order
DUKW	Wheeled amphibious truck
DYRMS	Duke of York's Royal Military School
FDS	Forward Dressing Station
Fus	Fusilier
Gdsm	Guardsman
GOC	General Officer Commanding
GR	Grid Reference
Green Howards	1 Battalion, Green Howards Regiment
Grenadier Guards	6 Battalion Grenadier Guards
Inniskillings	2 Battalion, Royal Inniskilling Fusiliers Regiment
IRTD	Infantry Recruit Training Depot
IWM	Imperial War Museum
KOYLI	1 Battalion, King's Own Yorkshire Light Infantry Regiment
LCT	Landing Craft Tank
Lt	Lieutenant
MC	Military Cross
MM	Military Medal
MMG	Motor Machine Gun
NCO	Non-Commissioned Officer

Northants	2 Battalion, Northamptonshire Regiment
PIAT	Projector, Infantry Anti-Tank (Grenade)
Pte or Pvt	Private
RA	Royal Artillery
RAMC	Royal Army Medical Corps
RAP	Regimental Aid Post
Royal Scots Fusiliers	2 Battalion, Royal Scots Fusiliers Regiment
'S' mines	Shrapnel mines
Schmeisser	German equivalent of British Tommy-gun
Scots Guards	2 Battalion, Scots Guards
Seaforth's	6 Battalion, Seaforth Highlanders Regiment
Tac	Tactical
TNA	The National Archives
Tommy Gun	British sub-machine gun
TSMG	Tactical Support Machine Gun – Vickers MMG
York & Lancs.	1 Battalion, York & Lancaster Regiment
Wiltshire's	2 Battalion, Wiltshire Regiment

Introduction

This is not just another story about the Second World War. It is a story about a battle which took place in Italy over a period of three weeks from 17 January to 7 February 1944. The battleground covered an area of approximately 9km^2.

This description of the Battle of Monte Natale brings together contemporary accounts showing war, not only at the strategic level involving Corps, Division, Brigade and Battalion, but also the individual level, by extensive use of War Diaries, personal accounts, missing person reports and awards for valour. This is a story of those who fought and died in the Battle of Monte Natale. Minute by minute, hour by hour, day by day, it shows what happened in these three weeks, the mistakes that were made and the individual heroism and acts of courage and includes German views of the battle. Few books about the Second World War show a battle in such detail.

The Battle of Monte Natale was part of the first battle of Monte Cassino. Monte Natale is 25km (15 miles) from Monte Cassino. It is 156m high, 750m in length and 300m wide, with outstanding views of the surrounding area. At this time Minturno, Tremensuoli and Monte Natale were the main battle objectives of 5 Infantry Division and were part of the German winter defensive position known as the Gustav Line.

A small part of this story relates to my father, Ernest Strafford who died during this battle. He was with 1 York & Lancs. On 20 January 1944 a witness reported that he saw Pvt. Ernest Strafford 'wounded in the head when a mortar bomb burst among us during our attack. I believe his wounds were serious.' On 4 February the body of Ernest Strafford was 'recovered, identified & buried by British Troops'. What happened to Ernest Strafford between these two dates?

Allied objectives in Italy were to draw German troops from the Russian front and particularly from France, where an Allied offensive was planned for the following year. Progress through Southern Italy was rapid despite stiff resistance, but by the end of October 1943, the Allies were facing the Germans at the Gustav Line, which stretched from the River Garigliano in the West to the River Sangro in the East.

The River Garigliano was crossed on 17 January 1944. This book describes the Allies build-up of their forces to this date and what happened to 5 Infantry Division in the Southern sector of the Gustav Line in the three weeks after the River Garigliano was crossed.

A beachhead at Anzio was established on 22 January 1944. By early February the Allies were in serious difficulties in maintaining the Anzio beachhead. A decision was taken to halt the advance of X (BR) Corps across the Gustav Line with the exception of Monte Cassino, so that some Battalions could be transferred to the Anzio beachhead. With strong support from the Americans, advance in the Southern sector of the Gustav Line did not begin again until 11 May 1944.

1 Battalion, York & Lancaster Regiment was part of 15 Infantry Brigade, which was part of 5 Infantry Division, and took part in the Allies invasion of Sicily on 10 July 1943. After the Sicilian campaign, on 3 September, the Allies invaded the Italian mainland – the invasion coinciding with an armistice made with the Italians who then re-entered the war on the Allied side. Allied objectives were to draw German troops from the Russian front and more particularly from France, where an Allied invasion was planned for the following year. The York & Lancaster Regiment were among the first troops into Italy and for a time was the leading unit of the Eighth Army moving up the East coast. Progress through Southern Italy was rapid despite stiff resistance, but by the end of October, the Allies were facing the German winter defensive position known as the Gustav Line.

1 KOYLI at Rionero. They are climbing a steep slope. Photo 5 Nov 43. (Sgt Dawson, No 2 Army Film & Photographic Unit, TNA 8508)

A patrol of 1 KOYLI setting out towards Rionero, a village on the upper reaches of the River Sangro. 1 York & Lancs. were at Rionero at the same time, 5 Nov 43. (Photo IWM)

Ernest Strafford joined 1 Battalion York & Lancs. in early November 1943. By this time, the Battalion was battle hardened. They had fought their way through Sicily, taken part in the invasion of Italy and moved up Italy as part of Eighth Army, so Ernest Strafford was joining a Battalion experienced in battle. At the beginning of November 15 Infantry Brigade was in the mountain sector in the centre of Italy around Isernia. During the next fortnight the Brigade, in spite of very bad weather, made considerable progress. On 16 November 1943 1 York & Lancs. arrived at Rionero, near the upper reaches of the River Sangro. Whilst at Rionero the house used as the Battalion Orderly Room received a direct hit by a shell which killed four men. At the same time, the Battalion Second in Command, Major C.H. Nicholson MC was wounded.

The advance of the Eighth Army in the east of Italy brought it roughly to the line of the River Sangro beyond which the Germans had constructed a very strong defensive position. The main attack on this was launched on 20 November 1943 by V (BR) Corps in the coastal sector, which had been reinforced with a vast amount of artillery for the purpose. It attempted to make the enemy believe that the real attack was coming in the mountain sector. V (BR) Corps, in one of the bloodiest battles of the war, fought in appalling weather, crossed the River Sangro, pierced the Gustav Line, and by the end of the year had reached the general line of Ortona-Orsogna.

After a spell in the hills and mountains, 1 York & Lancs. moved East to a line between Orsogna and Ortona, arriving at Crecchio on 10 December. Shortly before Christmas the weather became worse than ever and virtually brought all major operations to a standstill. Just before this, 5 Infantry Division had been moved from the mountain sector to the coastal zone, and 1 York & Lancs. relieved a unit of 8 Indian Division, in the line on 22 December. 1 York & Lancs. then moved on to Lanciano on the 31st. For three weeks it had remained in the line, but few attacks could be carried out owing to the weather. Constant patrolling, however, was maintained.

Whilst in the hills between Orsogna and Ortona Geoffrey Winter of 1 York & Lancs described how his Platoon rushed a German machine-gun post, captured two wounded prisoners and their guns, wounded four more Germans, and put the rest to flight.

Lieut. Geoffrey Winter, 1 Yorks & Lancs. writes
'We were going forward with the company to take a series of hill features. While we waited to go into action we saw one of our planes swoop on a hill and five enemy machine guns opened up on it. We were half-way to the hill when bombs began to fall around us. We sprinted forward for about three hundred yards. We saw bare headed Germans on top of the hill. The position was taken at bayonet point when we reached the top. There we found a mortally wounded German Sergeant-major and a soldier hopping about saying in English "I'm wounded, I'm wounded". The remainder of the Germans had fled leaving their guns but taking four wounded men with them.

'Rain, snow, slush, deep mud, plus hostile Germans. I was then a 21 year old infantry Platoon commander in a forward position west of Ortona. Things were fairly quiet at the time, and it was decided that each Company would be taken out of the line to some farm buildings to the rear out of enemy view, for Christmas dinner. Our turn came. There were three officers in the company, down from the usual five. Our bedrolls were brought up from "B" echelon so for one night we would be able to sleep under a roof in comparative comfort. Sitting in our barn that evening we heard cries for help.

Outside there was nothing to be seen but the cries continued. Then the soldier in distress shouted out his name and his location. It was down a well! Later it emerged that he had been returning to his overnight shelter after a jolly evening with my Platoon when he encountered a low stone wall which he had vaulted with ease only to fall down the well, which was encircled by the wall.

Rescue was the problem. No rope was available. However, officer's bedrolls were secured by long leather straps with buckles. These fastened together were long enough to reach the shivering soldier and we managed to haul him out. If he had been well lubricated before his involuntary descent, he was stone cold sober when he was pulled out.

The following morning, we left and plodded through the slush and mud to our forward positions. For many of the men I knew in the 1st Battalion, the York & Lancaster Regiment, Christmas 1943 was to be their last.'

An alternative version of the 'well' story is given by Ernest Shaw:

Ernest Shaw, 1 Yorks & Lancs. Christmas 1943

'In Italy there was no official truce or anything like that, but we did get a couple of days when neither side fired at each other and that was Christmas day and Boxing day. We were in a little village, and we had had a bit of a sing song and a do in what might have been the village hall and we had come away, Ted Rimmer and I, to go back to the billet. There was a well in the village square and we heard a splash. It was an MT (motor transport) driver, Five feet four inches Ernie, I can't remember his second name at the moment, it will come back to me, but Ernie fell over the wall. He was down the well. We heard the splash, and we ran. It was quite deep. I should think it was 12–14 feet deep to the water line. One of the natives, one of the local people, ran away and came back with a ladder. We got Ernie out and they said he had had a few drinks. He had been drinking vino, the Italian vino and one or two thought he was drunk but he wasn't drunk when he came out of that well, he was sober as a judge. The cold water done him good, but he was a bit of a lad for the ladies was Ernie. There were rumours later that it was an irate Italian husband that chucked him down the well. Whether there is any truth in that I don't really know, but he wouldn't admit to anything like that.'

Ernest Strafford was 5ft 5in tall. He might have been an MT driver as he had not been with the Battalion very long. Could it be that it was Ernest Strafford who fell down the well? In 1944 Ernest was not a common name! Christmas 1943 was Ernest Strafford's first and last Christmas abroad.

Also at Lanciano were 1 Green Howards. Private Roy Hamilton recorded in his diary:

Pte. Roy Hamilton, 1 Green Howards

'The further North we got the difficulties increased. The weather deteriorated and the country became more mountainous. Supply by wheeled transport became extremely difficult and in places impossible because of lack of roads. Ammunition and food had to be carried by mule or even as manpacks. It was very cold and always wet. It was really grim, especially during the night when the wet snow and cold became even more intense.

Christmas Day 1943 was just another very cold, very wet, very grim day here. For dinner we had corned beef hash and the inevitable, so-called rice pudding. As it had been brought forward in containers to us, it was barely warm. Still, we did manage to say: "Happy Christmas" to each other.'

Albert Roper, formerly a butcher, made sure that his platoon had a roast on Christmas Day. He recalled:

Albert Roper, Private Diary, 1 Green Howards, Christmas Day 1943

> 'I went outside this shell battered farmhouse on Christmas Eve and saw by the light of a full moon that in the branches of the tree there were guinea fowl roosting. My mate wanted to get his rifle and shoot one down, but I knew guinea fowl better. They can be so docile and trusting. I just shinned up the tree, caught hold of one by the legs and brought it down. Then I went up again for a few more. We spent the next hour or so plucking them and on Christmas Day got the farm oven heated and had a fine old roast dinner – guinea fowl and biscuits washed down with red vino from a huge demijohn we found in one of the out houses'.

C. Whiting and E. Taylor, *Fighting Tykes*, Christmas Day 1943

'1 KOYLI spent the Christmas of 1943 up in the mountains beyond the little town of Luciano. They ate a miserable Christmas dinner which consisted of cold bully beef, luke-warm tea and hard ration biscuits. There was none of the traditional beer and very little Italian vino, for the supply routes were virtually impassable save for what could be brought by mules. On that day three foot of snow fell. Drifts of up to ten feet were common. They broke down the timber roofs of the dugouts. Men shivered on underground sheets or gas capes in freezing temperatures. Signallers had to sit at their sets in their dugouts up to their knees in icy water. Their flesh became wrinkled and pasty. Sometimes their boots had to be cut off them. To remove them otherwise would tear off the dead flesh. And all the time the men were under constant fire.

German tanks started to appear and 1 KOYLI had few anti-tank weapons. Appeals for help were sent to Brigade Headquarters. Anti-tank gunners volunteered to bring up their cannon, each of which weighed 22 hundredweight. The guns were dismantled and then each gun was carried by means of porters up to the line. Ten men were needed to carry the barrel alone. On Boxing Day some of the men were taken out of the line for a few hours to watch the divisional concert party, The Low Gang, sitting shivering in their overcoats in an unheated opera house at Luciano where the back of the stage had been removed by a Herman shell to let in a freezing draught. But it was a welcome relief from the line, despite repeated German air attacks which had some of the performers leaving the show to man their guns'.

Antonio Lepone writes about the local situation near Minturno at Christmas 1943:

Antonio Lepone

'Without gifts and without dinners, between bombs and pain.

It is Christmas 1943, among the ruins, pains and hopes. The fighting is fierce along the Gustav Line which cuts the Aurunca area in two. The centres of Sud Ponti are half-empty, the families going to the nearby countryside and hills to escape shell fire and air raids. It is not a time for dinners and gifts, but an attempt is made to remember the religious event with the hope of an early peace.

The Church of the Immaculate Conception of Scauri. At the end of the Mass of Mezanotte, celebrated by Dom Stephen, the unmistakable notes of "Silent Night" are heard in the small church of SELVACAVA not far from Spigno Saturnia, proposed by a group of Polish soldiers, stationed in the area, united with the faithful present, desiring to overcome the selfishness of war.

The Church shows the signs of the war: the roof has collapsed, and the bell tower is gone. The workers of the "Sieci" brick factory, led by the director Umberto Pasquini, Master Giuseppe Forte and Antonio Gagliardi, take days to rebuild the roof of the church using the "Marseillaise tiles" recovered from the walls damaged by the bombing.

Above: New Year's Day, 1 Green Howards near Lanciano, Italy. 1 Jan 44 (Photo TNA 10626)

Left: The Commander-in-Chief, Allied Armies in Italy, General Sir Harold Alexander, Commander 15 Army Group. (Photo Capt A.R.Tanner, IWM, TR 1777)

A stone's throw away in a stable in Spigno, some families who had escaped from Scauri, surround the Scaurese factory and live with a Protestant group. This prophetically ecumenical group celebrate Christmas, in tendering at midnight the song "Tu scendi dalle stelle" and sharing sweetened bread.'

5 Infantry Division History

Early in the New Year it was decided that the offensive by Eighth Army would be halted for the time being. As a result, the relatively intact 5 Infantry Division was available elsewhere and reinforcements from it were transferred from the Eighth Army, now under Lieutenant-General Sir Oliver Leese, to join Lieutenant-General Richard McCreery's British X (BR) Corps. X (BR) Corps was stationed along the River Garigliano and was part of Lieutenant General Mark W. Clark's US Fifth Army at the time. No. 5 Infantry Division was commanded by Major General G.C. Bucknall who was about to hand over command to Major-General Philip Gregson Ellis and had the veteran 201 Guards Brigade under its command. 5 Infantry Division was withdrawn from the line on 9 Jan 44 and moved in great secrecy across Italy to a concentration area behind the United States 5th Army's front near the mouth of the River Garigliano, arriving there on 15 Jan 44.

As at 17 Jan 44 the Supreme Commander for the Allied forces in the Mediterranean was General Dwight D. Eisenhower. He was responsible among other things for 15 Army Group commanded by General Harold Alexander, which consisted of the British Eighth Army under Lieutenant General Oliver Leese and the US Fifth Army under Lieutenant General Mark Clark. X (BR) Corp consisted of 5 Infantry Division, 46 Infantry Division, 56 Infantry Division and 7 Armoured Division.

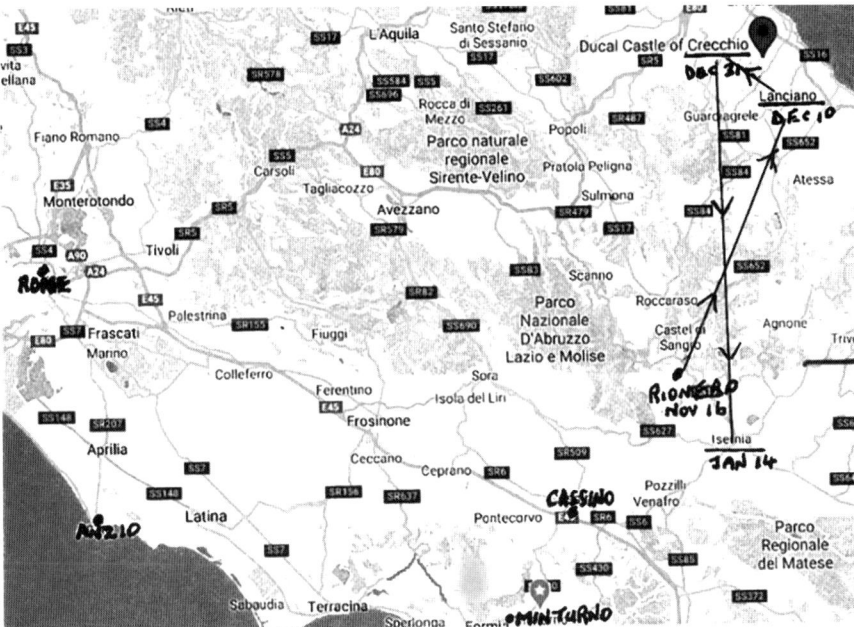

1 York & Lancs. Route through Italy. 16 Nov 43 to 14 Jan 44.

1 York & Lancs. was moved with the rest of 5 Infantry Division across Italy away from the Orsogna–Ortona line on the Adriatic coast, arriving at Isernia on 14 Jan 44 in readiness to attack across the River Garigliano and capture the Ausonia valley beyond the town of Minturno.

The Battle of Monte Natale involved 5 Infantry Division and took place around four small towns/villages. They were Minturno, Santa Maria Infante, Tufo and Tremensuoli. All suffered extensive damage. The people of Minturno suffered greatly, finding themselves under German occupation and positioned on the very edge of the German Gustav Line. The population of Minturno had to endure persecution and reprisals by the Germans and also famine. In addition, the local villages endured heavy land and naval bombardments by the Allied forces, which resulted in catastrophic damage, and the deaths and casualties of many innocent civilians. Many Minturnesi were forced to flee to the mountains and surrounding countryside.

Minturno, 2km west of Tufo and 5km beyond the River Garigliano was a prime Allied objective as it lay on one of the principal roads leading through the Aurunci mountains to the X (BR) Corps objective, Ausonia. The town fell to 1 Green Howards of 15 Infantry Brigade on 19 Jan 44.

W.A. Elliott, 2 Scots Guards, *Esprit de Corps*

'Eventually, because of heavy casualties, the Allied Military Government forced the evacuation of the whole population of the little town of Minturno, that was now in the middle of no man's land. This led to its wholesale looting by those of our troops who had motor transport. But this did not include the Infantry Companies.'

A Grenadier officer expressed the atmosphere of Minturno in early 1944:

Capt. Nigel Nicolson, *The Grenadier Guards in the War of 1939-1945, Volume II*

> Time to start,
> And with five anxious men behind me I will creep
> Full of cold fear down the old muddy track
> Past the burned tank outside the town, through the wet
> Vineyard where our forward sentries stay, wondering if we'll come back.
> A peak-capped figure rises, falls:
> Hell wakes the night,
> A wounded German calls.
> Now forward! End the fight. And back!
> Back to a dim light in Minturno.
> A candle flickering on a cellar floor,
> Glazed eyes, tired faces, sleeping shapes, signallers making tea.
> A weary Major, murmuring over maps and message forms, and we,
> Pushing aside the muddy blanket covering the door.
> Are now at home again, out of the night's inferno.

On 11 May 44 the Allies' object was to capture the village of Santa Maria Infante. This was to be a particularly bitter and bloody battle which lasted for 60 hours without

Minturno town. 16 Oct 2012. (Photo John Strafford)

Santa Maria Infante before the war.

Tremensuoli from the top of Point 141, Monte del Duca. (Photo Peter Strafford)

interruption. The village was finally liberated on 14 May 1944, and this proved to be a defining moment as at long last the Gustav Line was breached, forcing a German retreat.

The village of Tufo lies 4km north of the River Garigliano, on high ground. 2 Wiltshires of 13 Infantry Brigade captured the village early on 18 January 1944 after a short fight. However, the town suffered heavily in the subsequent fighting.

The ruined and empty village of Tufo, perched on top of a hill, is in the front line. Infantrymen here try to clear a road through the rubble, a job made more difficult by constant enemy shellfire, 25 Jan 44. (Photo Sgt. Weber, APFU, TNA 11431)

Chapter 1

The Gustav Line

The Winter Line

The Winter Line was a series of German and Italian military fortifications constructed during the Second World War commanded by Field Marshal Albert Kesselring. The series of three lines was designed to defend the Western section of Italy, focused around the town of Monte Cassino, through which ran the important Highway 6 which led uninterrupted to Rome. The primary Gustav Line ran across Italy from just North of where the River Garigliano flows into the Tyrrhenian Sea in the West, through the Apennine Mountains to the mouth of the River Sangro on the Adriatic coast in the East.

The Gustav Line

The plan was for the French Expeditionary Corps to attack on the right in the mountain sector to the North of Cassino on 12 Jan 44, X (BR) Corps to force a bridgehead over the River Garigliano in the coastal sector on 17 Jan 44 and for II (US) Corps to attack in the Liri valley just below Cassino on 20 Jan 44. The attacks were designed to draw German reserves away from the Rome area so that on 22 Jan 44, VI (US) Corps including a British Division could land at Anzio and threaten the rear of the Gustav Line. It was hoped that this threat would force the Germans to withdraw their troops from the Gustav Line and back to a new defence line North of Rome. 1 York & Lancs. were on the extreme left of the British Corps front by the sea near Minturno.

X (BR) Corps History
By the end of the second week of January 1944, the US Fifth Army had reached the main defences of the German Winter Line. The process of closing up to the Winter Line had begun on the coast at the beginning of November and had been completed so far as X (BR) Corps was concerned and brought almost to a conclusion during the latter part of December and early January with the capture of two of three hills blocking the entrance to the Liri valley. US Fifth Army's next task was to complete the assault on the main defences of the Winter Line.

   Rivers and mountain masses made the Winter Line, on which the Germans elected to stand for the Winter, one of the most favourable to defend and most unfavourable to attack in all Italy. In this sector it was anchored in the North to the mountain massif Monte Cairo, and it continued across the Liri Valley behind the River Gari to the foothills of the Aurunci range on the West bank of the River Garigliano with the Southern flank

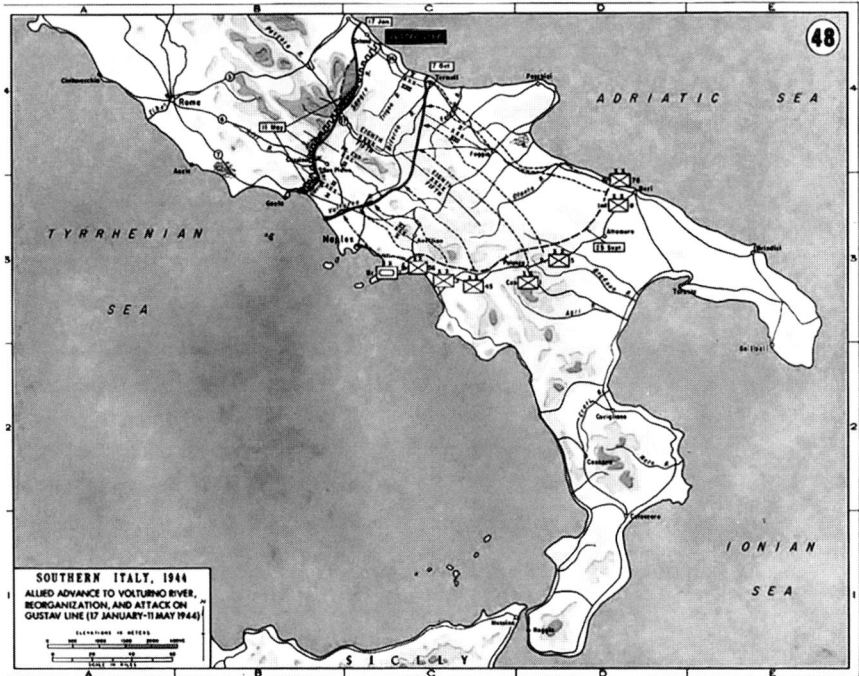

Map of Southern Italy 1944 – The Gustav Line. (United States Military Academy)

resting on the sea. The US Fifth Army had first to cross the river obstacle presented by the Rapido-Gari-Garigliano in the face of an enemy established in commanding positions in the mountains and then to launch a frontal assault against the mountain positions, which the enemy had over two months to prepare their defence.

The US Fifth Army plan for X (BR) Corps was that on 17 January they would attack and force the crossing of the River Garigliano in the Minturno area so as to secure the Lateral road East of the Aurunci foothills and proceeding along it to enter the Liri Valley behind the River Gari and having established a bridgehead employ the maximum amount of armour to exploit West and Northwest.

The sector chosen for X (BR) Corps main attack was a nine mile stretch of the River Garigliano [from Castelforte to the Tyrrhenian sea]. It was defended at the beginning of January by a new and comparatively inexperienced German horse-drawn Infantry Division [the 94 Infantry Division]. Although only a proportion of the enemy reserves were likely to appear in any one sector, it was likely that the two to one superiority, which X (BR) Corps enjoyed initially, would disappear as the battle progressed [and German reserves were rushed down from Rome].

94 Infantry Division consisted of :

- '94' Fusilier Battalion
- '267' Grenadier Regiment
- '274' Grenadier Regiment

- 276 Grenadier Regiment
- 194 Infantry Regiment

X (BR) Corps – History

The flat alluvial plain of the lower River Garigliano begins where the river emerges from a short gorge between the Monte Camino massif and the Northern shoulder of the Aurunci foothills and follows a winding course to the [Tyrrhenian] sea. As the river approaches the sea the plain broadens rapidly and reaches a width of about ten miles at the coast. In winter, the low ground on both banks of the river is intersected by numerous water courses, streams, and ditches, which form an effective obstacle to mechanised movement. Only a few un-metalled tracks lead down to the East [river] bank, many of them impossible in bad weather, whilst the two railway lines, which also cross the river, were so demolished as to be unusable. The river itself was nowhere fordable, its banks were three to four hundred feet apart and normally about fifteen feet high and the stream itself was wide, deep, and fast flowing at that season. Sites for bridging or for rafting vehicles were thus limited to the Minturno bridge and to the few good tracks. These were well known to the enemy and the exits on the West bank had been extensively mined.

The hills which the enemy held centred on the villages of Minturno and Castelforte. The Southern group of hills, centring round Minturno-Tufo, was not formidable, rising nowhere above six hundred feet.

X (BR) Corps Plan

Since the flat land between the river [Garigliano] and the (German) enemy-held hills was nowhere more than two miles wide, the enemy enjoyed excellent close observation of the river line. It was therefore important initially to secure a bridgehead on the commanding ground of the Minturno-Tufo hills to deny the enemy this observation at an early stage so that supporting weapons and vehicles could be rafted across the river by surprise at the outset, there appeared to be a good prospect of achieving this objective. X (BR) Corps Plan was to launch [two Infantry Divisions across the Garigliano at the same time, 5 Infantry Division on the left focused on the Minturno-Tufo feature and 56 Infantry Division on the right on the Damiano-Castelforte feature]. 5 Infantry Division to secure a firm bridgehead round Minturno, then to swing Northwards up the Ausente valley towards Ausonia (15 kilometres distant from the River Garigliano) and capture the rear of the River Liri valley defences.

Although engineer operations and the movement of vehicles would be hampered by enemy minefields and by the poor approaches and exits to the river it was hoped by the comparatively lavish use of rafts to ensure that the infantry would be well supported by getting their support weapons and more ammunition across early in the assault.

Frank de Planta, battlefield expert, 46 Infantry Division

'X (BR) Corps had a third Infantry Division which was 46 Infantry Division. It did not take part in the X (BR) Corps assault because it had been withdrawn by HQ US Fifth Army on 19 Jan 44. In support of the planned II (US) Corps assault in the Liri valley on 20 Jan 44 46 Infantry Division was to cross the River Garigliano and seize the hill feature and village of Sant Ambrogio. This was intended to ensure that II (US) Corp's left flank

Above: The River Garigliano plain looking east – the sea on the right. (John Strafford)

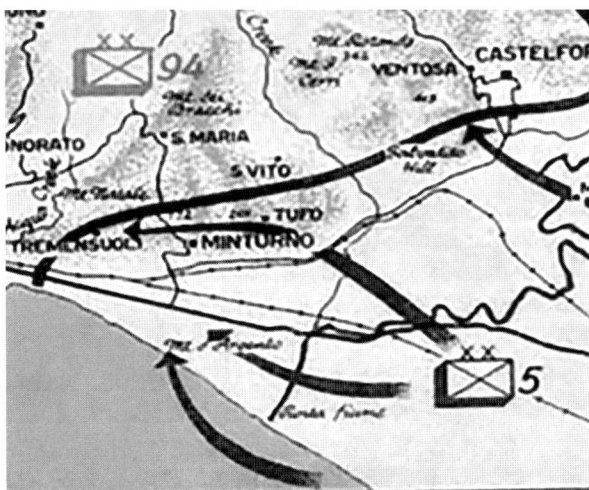

Left: X (BR) Corps Attack across the River Garigliano. 17 Jan 44, (*The Battles for Monte Cassino*, J. Plowman, P. Rowe. (After the Battle 2011). Battle of Britain International Ltd.)

was not exposed to German observation during the assault in the Liri Valley. The impact of taking 46 Infantry Division away from X (BR) Corps was that X (BR) Corps Command had no reserve formation to use in exploitation if a gap in the German line was made.

The plan to help II US Corps did not go at all well. 46 Infantry Division attack was launched by 128 Hampshire Brigade but their attempts to cross the River Garigliano near Sant Ambrogio were unsuccessful. They were due to cross on the night 19-20 Jan 44 but the Germans on that day, opened the sluices of a dam higher upstream on the River Liri, so that the River Garigliano was higher and flowing faster than predicted.'

Richard Doherty, *Monte Cassino: Opening the Road to Rome*
'The speed of the current swept away assault boats on the first attempt. At the next attempt, using a cable, the line broke after only five men had crossed. A third attempt saw about thirty men of 2 Hampshires cross at the mouth of the Peccia stream but the swift

current made it impossible for the boats to return and the isolated Platoon was overrun. Dense fog hindered operations, forcing the assaulting Battalions to return to their former positions. The failure of the Hampshire Brigade meant that the left flank of II US Corps would be exposed as it made its subsequent efforts to cross the Gari to the North.'

The consequence of this were very serious, particularly for the US forces. 36 Division of II US Corps failed to cross the River Gari [the upper reaches of the River Garigliano] suffering 1681 casualties: 143 dead, 663 wounded and 875 missing. After the War ended there was a US Congressional enquiry into this attack.

In 5 Infantry Division it was apparent that even if their operation went well, there would inevitably be some delay before (Bailey) bridges capable of carrying the all-important armour could be built across the River Garigliano. Moreover, the only suitable site for a Class 30 bridge was the demolished bridge crossing on Route 7 and this would certainly be registered by the enemy artillery. To prevent a delay arising in consequence of this, X (BR) Corps engineers planned to establish fourteen rafts to ferry guns and vehicles across as soon as the assaulting Brigades had crossed.

Preliminary Operations

To conceal the attack 5 Infantry Division was not put into the line until two days before the attack was due to begin. Its sector, which ran from the railway bridge to the coast was held by a light screening force formed from the divisional troops of 6 Infantry Division [1 King's Dragoon Guards from 23 Armoured Brigade]. Under cover of this screen 5 Infantry Division carried out its reconnaissance of the river line and finally took over the sector on the night of 15–16 Jan 44. Engineer reconnaissance was carried out intensively during the period and parties of Sappers working without infantry escort were able to patrol the river line and determine the best crossing places. Much equipment assault boats rafts, and bridging material were needed for the crossing and careful measures to conceal any recognisable equipment carrying vehicle were done so that surprise would not be lost. The task of moving X (BR) Corps Artillery and building up the large dumps of ammunition required for the attack had to be carried out at night, since the gun positions, although partially protected from view by olive groves were generally on forward slopes under observation from the hills across the River Garigliano; moreover, they were served by a single road, along which all guns, ammunition and normal maintenance traffic had to pass. Over and above the normal artillery of the assaulting Divisions more than nine Regiments were assembled to support the attack; nevertheless, their movement appears to have escaped the notice of the enemy and the weight of the opening barrage took him by surprise. The enemy was cleared from the whole of the East bank of the river though a few outposts remained on the West bank of the river itself and at the railway bridge. Those were left to be dealt with by the assaulting Brigades so that the enemy should not be forewarned of the impending attack.

In the initial plan of 5 Infantry Division the successive objectives were:

a) To capture the area San Vito – Monte Natale.
b) To advance astride the road Minturno – Ausonia with the object of capturing the defile [and debouching into the Liri valley].

The assault was to be made at night. 5 Infantry Division, on the left with a long approach march to the river line, was to make a silent crossing. The principal change in the order of battle for the attack was the transfer of 201 Guards Brigade to 5 Infantry Division in order to provide the necessary reserve for that Division to exploit Northwards out of the bridgehead in the second phase. The [fighting element of the] order of battle was:

5 Infantry Division

> 13 Infantry Brigade
> 15 Infantry Brigade
> 17 Infantry Brigade
> 201 Guards Brigade
> 40 Royal Tank Regiment [less two squadrons]
> Belgian Troop, 10 Commando

Divisional artillery plus one Field [self-propelled] and one Medium Regiment.
The gun areas, on the forward slopes leading down to the river were dispersed in the thickly wooded and broken country around Leure.

Air and Naval Support

Air and naval support played a disappointing part in the battle. It had been hoped that naval and air bombardment would have practically isolated the battle area during the first days of the assault but some of these resources were required elsewhere and very bad weather interfered with both sea and air operations, however, with the result that after the enemy had recovered from the initial surprise, he was able to move reserves into the battle area practically unimpeded.

HMS *Orion* Naval History
15 Jan 44
Bombarded Gaeta by HM Cruiser SPARTAN and HM Destroyers FAULKNOR, JERVIS, JANUS and LAFOREY.

HMS *Orion, a similar ship to the cruiser* HMS *Spartan.* (naval-history.net web site)

Frank de Planta, battlefield expert
'For their attack X (BR) Corps decided to use 14 rafts in the early crossings, including two strong enough for tanks. Sappers would not try to install any bridges until the German artillery Observation Posts had been cleared of the bridge sites. They had to use the existing road approaches to the river because winter flooding had made the fields on both sides too soft to carry a large number of military vehicles in wet weather, and these roads were certainly registered by German guns. All the early parts of the operation went well using the one good road.

On 16–17 Jan 44 Allied aircraft bombed '94' Infantry Division positions and they were supported by two cruisers and five destroyers firing from offshore. 17 Infantry Brigade were accompanied by a Naval Gunfire Control Officer who was able to direct the fire of one of the cruisers. The Brigade were to have tanks from 40 Royal Tank Regiment in support [about 60 Sherman tanks].

7 Cheshires had a support role in the attack. 'A' Company was allocated to 17 Infantry Brigade, 'B' Company to 13 Infantry Brigade, 'C' Company to 201 Guards Brigade and 'D' Company to 15 Infantry Brigade in Division reserve. 7 Cheshires was organised with a Battalion HQ, an MMG Company of three Platoons, an Anti-Aircraft Company of four Platoons and a Mortar Company of two Platoons. MMG Company had 12 Vickers MMGs – four per Platoon which moved in carriers. Anti-Aircraft Company had 16 20mm Oerlikon quick-firing guns each pulled by a 15cwt truck. Mortar Company eight 4.2-inch barrels – four per Platoon and each carried in a 15cwt truck.

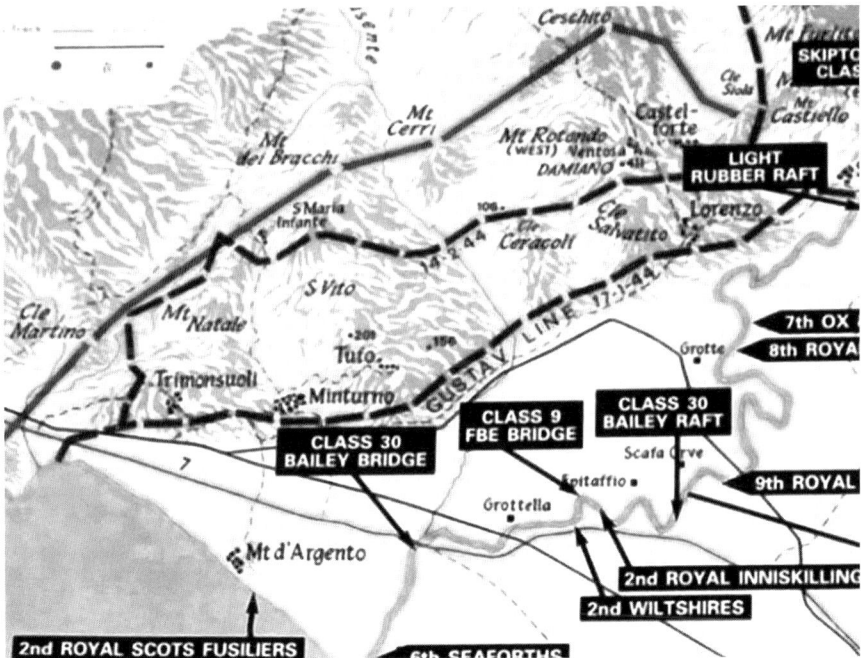

X (BR) Corps attacks across the River Garigliano, 17 Jan 44. (*The Battle for Monte Cassino*, J. Plowman. P. Rowe. (After the Battle 2011). Battle of Britain International Ltd)

Chapter 2

17 January 1944 – Crossing the River Garigliano

5 Infantry Division Order of Battle
13 Infantry Brigade
    2 Battalion, Cameronians
    2 Battalion, Royal Inniskilling Fusiliers
    2 Battalion, Wiltshire
    13 Infantry Brigade Support Company

15 Infantry Brigade
    1 Battalion, Green Howards
    1 Battalion, King's Own Yorkshire Light Infantry
    1 Battalion, York & Lancs.
    15 Infantry Brigade Support Company

17 Infantry Brigade
    2 Battalion, Royal Scots Fusiliers
    2 Battalion, Northants
    6 Battalion, Seaforth Highlanders
    17 Infantry Brigade Support Company

Divisional Troops
7 Battalion, Cheshires [Machine Gun Battalion]
5 Reconnaissance Regiment, Royal Armoured Corps
91 Field Regiment, Royal Artillery
92 Field Regiment, Royal Artillery
156 Field Regiment, Royal Artillery
52 Anti-Tank Regiment, Royal Artillery
18 Light Anti-Aircraft Regiment, Royal Artillery
245 Field Company, Royal Engineers
252 Field Company, Royal Engineers
38 Field Company, Royal Engineers
254 Field Company, Royal Engineers
18 Bridging Platoon, Royal Engineers
5 Division Signals Regiment, Royal Corps of Signals

Frank de Planta, battlefield expert
'An Infantry Division consists of approx.: 20,000 personnel; a Brigade 5-8000; Battalion 821; Support Co.281; HQ Co. 80; Rifle Co. 115 being Three Platoons & Co. HQ. Platoon 34'.

5 Infantry Division History
5 Infantry Division's battle objectives lay in the group of hills around the village of Minturno. Their original plan was for 13 Infantry Brigade to cross the River Garigliano about two miles above the Minturno bridge and secure the Eastern shoulder of the Minturno-Tufo hills and for 17 Infantry Brigade to cross between Minturno and the sea, landing a Battalion of infantry with tanks near Monte d'Argento and swing Northwards to capture the Western portion of the Minturno-Tufo ridge. When the bridgehead was secured 201 Guards Brigade would exploit along the coast towards Monte Scauri and 15 Infantry Brigade was to make the attack up the Ausente valley towards Ausonia.

5 Infantry Division's attack achieved a considerable measure of surprise, helped by the artillery bombardment on the Cassino front which focused enemy attention away from the coastal sector. But, while 13 Infantry Brigade on the right made a most encouraging start and swiftly secured its first objectives, 17 Infantry Brigade attack on the coast met many unexpected hazards and was for the most part unsuccessful. It stalled.

The Germans held the high ground at Castelforte, Monte Argente and the Minturno-Tufo ridge. 2 Royal Scots Fusiliers, 'B' Company of 6 Seaforths and 'A' Company of 7 Cheshires, part of 17 Infantry Brigade were to land on the beach North-East of

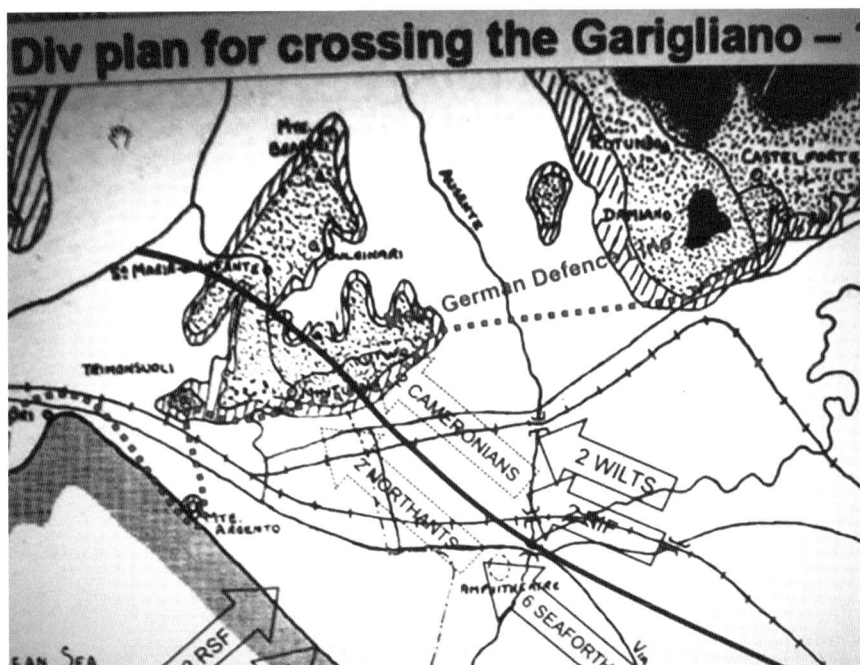

5 BR Infantry Division plan for crossing the River Garigliano, 17–18 Jan 44. (TNA)

the River Garigliano, and just South of Monte Argente. 2 Cameronians (13 Infantry Brigade) and 2 Northants (17 Infantry Brigade) are to lead the attack on the Minturno-Tufo ridge followed by 2 Royal Inniskillings Fusiliers and 2 Wiltshires of 13 Infantry Brigade and 6 Seaforths of 17 Infantry Brigade. In reserve, just across the River Garigliano are 201 Guards Brigade and 15 Infantry Brigade.

17 Infantry Brigade

Total strength of the Brigade at the time the attack began consisted of: 2 Royal Scots Fusiliers
6 Seaforth Highlanders
2 Northants
1 York & Lancs. (on loan from 15 Infantry Brigade).
One Company 1 Green Howards (until forward move of 15 Infantry Brigade).
'A' Company 7 Cheshires.
'D' Company 7 Cheshires
One Platoon 42 Field Company, Royal Engineers
One Troop 98 Field Regiment, Royal Artillery
One Section 52 Anti-Tank Regiment (17 pounders), Royal Artillery
'A' Squadron 40 Royal Tank Regiment
In Support:
38 Field Company, Royal Engineers
245 Field Company, Royal Engineers

Intention
17 Infantry Brigade will secure the high ground Point 172 [between Tufo and Monte Natale] to Point 156 [Monte Natale] and the Tremensuoli feature and destroy any enemy found there. 156 Field Regiment, Royal Artillery will support 17 Infantry Brigade.

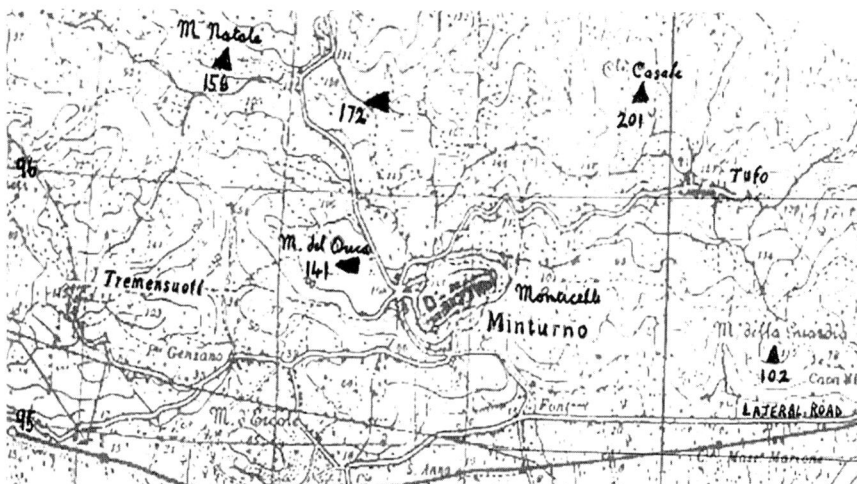

Main objectives of attack were Minturno, Tufo, Tremensuoli and Monte Natale.

10

Method
Operation in four phases:

> PHASE I Establishment of bridgehead across the Garigliano – thence along road Route 7 to about 780940 – Monte d'Argento.
> PHASE II Capture by 2 Royal Scots Fusiliers and 6 Seaforth Highlanders of Point 172 and Point 156
> PHASE III Capture by 2 Northants of the Tremensuoli feature.
> PHASE IV Advance by 1 York & Lancs.

Rate of Advance
100 yards in 5 minutes

Start Time
0300 hours

Exploitation
1 York & Lancs. will be prepared to move to assembly area 779952 on orders by Brigade Command when this area vacated by 2 Northants.

Assault Boat Group
1 York & Lancs. will be prepared to move forward from midnight 17 Jan 44 and on reaching the river will take over all boats from 2 Northants except three manned by crews of 2 Northants which will continue to run the ferry service.1 York & Lancs. will leave all boats on the South side of the river under the direction of the Non-Commissioned Officer in Charge Boats, 2 Northants, and will use ferry service provided by 2 Northants to pass over the last of their crews. 2 Northants will hand over all boats to 201 Guards Brigade as soon as head of 201 Guards Brigade column arrives.

164 Field Ambulance War Diary
17 Jan 44 – 1530
At 1430 left Main Dressing Station following warning order at 1100. X and A Sections proceeded to 2 Wiltshires assembly area at Mondragone and Y and B to 2 Inniskillings assembly area at Falciano.

Royal Inniskillings Regimental Museum records
17 Jan 44 – 2100
2 Inniskillings role:
   Zero hour 9pm for the crossing and clearing of the ground a mile beyond the River Garigliano.
   'D' Company, Major Bill Bradley: operate the boats and clear and guard the far bank.
   'A' Company, Major Martin Grant: cross next and clear the cluster of farms which lay on the plain.
   'B' and 'C' Companies, Majors John Nixon and Percy Blake: cross last, move through 'D' and 'A' Companies and form up for the final attack on the ridge.

11

Most of the boats had not arrived before zero hour. The delay meant that the artillery barrage opened up before the Companies could cross, thus alerting the German defences. When boats arrived, they were shelled during 'A' Company's crossing, many men being wounded, killed or drowned. The Battalion had suffered greatly before the battle had begun.

13 Infantry Brigade War Diary
17 Jan 44 – 2100
13 Infantry Brigade attack with two Battalions up front in the two loops of the river above the Minturno bridge.

2 Royal Inniskilling Fusiliers crossing on the right ran into the overlay of the enemy's fire on 56 Infantry Division front. They met mortar fire from the North bank of the river before their first Company was completely across the River Garigliano and lost their boats.

Sir David Cole, 2 Inniskillings, *Rough Road To Rome*
'"D" Company seized the first boats, rushed them forward to the river and began at once to launch them. This was no easy task. The boats were heavy and awkward. As soon as the first boats had been launched, the leading sections of "A" Company bristling with all their equipment, embarked in them, and paddled out into the stream.

It was obviously for this that the Germans, no doubt warned by their machine-gun crew near the bank, had been waiting. Immediately, with a chorus of curt but devilish screeches, their artillery opened up on us with deadly accuracy and dreadful force. There were angry, rending crashes as the first shells landed in and along the river at our crossing-place. Two boats were hit and began to sink at once in mid-stream. Burdened with their full equipment, thick clothing, and heavy boots, most of the men, already wounded, had little chance of survival as they sunk into the icy muddy water surging towards the sea. Their cries, faint against the tumult of the gunfire, were heart-rending. A few, who struggled within reach of the bank, were pulled out. Despite this hideous misfortune and the further recurrent salvoes of shells, we continued to load men into the remaining boats and take them across. More boats were sunk and when "A" Company had completed the crossing, over thirty of their men and two officers had been lost – killed, drowned, or wounded.

Of our twelve boats, four had been sunk and seven had been damaged beyond repair. With the last one "D" Company had been rescuing survivors and operating a ferry service for "A" Company.

The CO., Lieut. Col. O'Brien-Twohig made a new plan which he cleared at once on the field-telephone with the Brigadier. The rest of the Battalion would cross at the Wiltshires' crossing place a mile or so to our left, as soon as the Wiltshires could spare some boats. To that end "B" Company was to be taken down the road to begin crossing as soon as possible.'

2 Wiltshires War Diary
17 Jan 44 – 2100
Carrier Platoon covering party and taping party move down to the crossing place, 834940.

17 Jan 44 – 2145
Battalion arrives at forming up place.

17 Infantry Brigade HQ War Diary
17 Jan 44 – 2145
6 Platoon of 7 Cheshires landed from DUKWs and proceeded to consolidate but found that infantry had not taken the objective.

17 Jan 44 – 2200
4 Platoon of 7 Cheshires landed and both Platoons took up positions on the beach. 6 Platoon engaged the enemy.

2 Cameronians War Diary
Operation Orders:
Warn all ranks.

(a) No-one except a stretcher bearer or a wounded man helps a wounded man out of action.
(b) Silence is vital. Noise will cost lives. No coughs. Tools and equipment padded. No light. No smoking.
(c) German tactics are to evacuate position and then put in immediate counterattack with grenades and tommy guns.
(d) It is fatal to halt when mortared. Once you are in among his troops he will stop mortaring.
(e) Dig or die?
(f) 17 Jan 44 – 2200

'D' Company were behind time with the boats for the night crossing.
17 Jan 44 – 2215
'A' and 'D' Companies have completed the delivery of the boats.

2 Wiltshires War Diary
17 Jan 44 – 2330
'C' Company erect boats and carry them down to the crossing place. Delay due to late arrival of boats.

Sir David Cole, 2 Inniskillings, *Rough Road To Rome*
17 Jan 44 – 2330
'The moon had fully emerged from behind the hills and revealed all too clearly the havoc wrought by the German bombardment – the ugly craters, the lifeless bodies, and the acrid fumes drifting low above the ground. From across the river in front of us came the angry chatter and crack of machine-gun and mortar fire. A brief wireless message from Major Martin Grant (Company HQ) told us that he had encountered Germans and was attacking with all his remaining men. It was the last time I ever heard his voice.

All "A" Company's officers and senior NCOs were now dead or wounded and command was taken over by Lance Sergeant John Banton who, with only twenty survivors out of a Company of almost 100 men, had cleared the last of the houses.'

Royal Inniskillings Regimental Museum

'A' Company, despite terrible losses caused by German machine gun fire sweeping across the open fields, was clearing the farm at Massa Rossi. It was here that Major Martin Grant was killed by a mortar bomb, which also killed German prisoners in his charge. Losses were so high that command of the Company devolved to Lance Sergeant John Banton. Banton led a bayonet charge which took the farm for which he was awarded the Military Medal.

A critical moment in the entire battle had arrived. The attacks on either side of the Brigade were held up. Three quarters of the Inniskillings had not yet crossed, but under Lieut. Col. J.P. O'Brien-Twohig's inspired leadership the two attacking Companies, 'B' and 'C' were ferried across, along with Battalion HQ.

2 Royal Inniskillings Fusiliers Citation: Military Medal for Lance Sergeant John Banton

17–18 Jan 44

On the night 17-18 Jan 44, L/Sgt. John Banton was Second in Command of 'A' Company, 2 Royal Inniskilling Fusiliers. The Company task was to clear enemy posts East of the Epitaffio track.

During the crossing and shortly afterwards all the officers and NCOs senior to L/Sgt. John Banton were killed and wounded. L/Sgt. John Banton collected the remainder of the Company, reorganised them and carried on with his task.

The leadership, personal bravery and initiative displayed by this NCO throughout 18 Jan 44 was outstanding and it was due to him that the remains of his Company carried out their task and re-joined the Battalion that evening.

164 Field Ambulance

17 Jan 44 – 2330

Sgt. Smith's party moved with 2 Inniskillings to the ferry, having evacuated 20 casualties. 2 Inniskillings gave up attempts to cross at 847937. Sgt. Smith took charge at 834940 as Capt. Birkes had crossed the river and joined up with A Company. Casualties were occurring at both sides of the river. Those from the far side were ferried back on assault boats and carried from the South bank of the river to the Ambulance beach head, 600 yards away. 30 casualties were brought back in this manner.

Mathew Parker, 2 Royal Inniskillings Fusiliers, *Monte Cassino*

'Jack Williams was a stretcher bearer with "A" Company of the Fusiliers. His Platoon Sergeant told him the next day 18 Jan 44 that as he was swimming towards the bank he could feel hands desperately grabbing at his feet from below.

"We got out of the boats", Williams continues, 'and straight away we had to get up to our objective, which was a farm on the right. We had to get down there immediately, we couldn't hang about on the bank. We could hear the shouts and screams of the people, who were thrashing about in the water, who had been hit. It was a bit of a do at the time, and everyone was panicking."

The farm was cleared by grenade and bayonet, and prisoners taken, but during the engagement Williams's Company Commander was killed by mortar fire along with four German prisoners he had captured. The next morning, says Williams, "It was just a question of finding people from your Battalion, as everyone was scattered. Everyone was looking for their mates, to see if they had survived. Everybody was in a state of panic, after such a bad experience the night before. We wondered what we were going into."

In fact, the Company, with nearly eighty casualties, was unable to take part in further battles until the losses were replaced. The only NCOs left were a Sergeant and a Lance-Corporal.

2 Wiltshires War Diary
17 Jan 44 – 2400
First boatload of 'A' Company – Bridgehead Company – crosses. They meet no opposition and remainder of Battalion start crossing. Enemy mortar and machine gun fire starts but casualties are light. This was coming from a post in houses and 'B' Company quickly dealt with it, taking five P.O.W.s.

Information was received from Brigade HQ that 2 Cameronians were now to move forward along Route 7 to the crossing place followed by Tac HQ and 'D' Company

13 Infantry Brigade War Diary
17 Jan 44 – 2400
2 Wiltshire Regiment on the left with 2 Cameronians in reserve crossed without difficulty. 2 Royal Inniskilling Fusiliers after losing several casualties were moved to the Wiltshire's crossing to follow behind 2 Wiltshires in that Battalion's boats.

17 Infantry Brigade HQ War Diary
17 Jan 44
Tac HQ reduced to Brigadier, Information Officer, one Corporal, one signaller without communications, moves across river on foot and goes forward to look for Seaforths and Royal Scots Fusiliers.

Tac HQ finds 6 Seaforths and 2 Royal Scots Fusiliers at X roads 790927. 6 Seaforths report Battalion scattered after encountering mines across the river, position of Companies uncertain. 'D' Company known to be attacking Amphitheatre [outskirts of Minturno]. Remaining Companies just South of Route 7. Estimated 70 casualties with high proportion of Officers.

1 Royal Scots Fusiliers report Battalion split up due to disorganised landing of DUKWs, some of which broke down and others landed South of the river. There were minefields behind the beach. Monte Argente still held by enemy.
State of Battalions makes it impossible for timed attack on Minturno ridge to take place.

2 Royal Scots Fusiliers War Diary
17 Jan 44
Priorities of transport were arranged for crossing the river immediately after the initial stage of the operation. Each Company was allotted one Carrier for equipment, tools etc/four Anti-tank guns were to be towed into position by Carriers fitted with special towing hooks, four Carriers Mortars were given their normal loads while 9 canteens were loaded with miscellaneous stores and equipment. These vehicles were to cross on night of 17/18 Jan 44.

John Ellis 2 Royal Scots Fusiliers, *Cassino the Hollow Victory*
'2 Royal Scots Fusiliers had a particularly grim time. They were to take Monte d'Argento, a large mound near the seashore from which the Germans could enfilade a considerable stretch of the River Garigliano. Two Companies of Fusiliers were to land from the sea in DUKWS [six-wheeled amphibious trucks] and capture it, after which the other two were to pass through and drive on to Minturno. The first stage went badly awry and was not without its farcical elements. One Company's DUKW was ineluctably drawn out to sea and eventually floated alongside a Cruiser. They were about to hail her to ask for directions when a submarine suddenly popped up immediately to port. Uncertain of its nationality the Fusiliers manned their PIAT and were about to sink it when a head popped out of the conning tower and shouted:

"Who the hell are you?" "Royal Scots Fusiliers" was the prompt and somewhat relieved reply.

"Never heard of you", was the even prompter rejoinder as the hatch closed and the submarine submerged.

Peter Caddick-Adams, 2 Royal Scots Fusiliers, *Monte Cassino. Ten Armies in Hell*
'The overnight amphibious landing foundered when some troops were beached South of the River Garigliano (on the "home" side), others landed on the correct side, but were dispersed, and landing craft became disoriented and returned with their cargoes of tanks and artillery. This left too few on the beaches, their weapons clogged with muck, and under mortar fire; the operation cost 2 Royal Scots Fusiliers 140 casualties'.

John Ellis, 6 Seaforths, *Cassino. The Hollow Victory*
'The boats had been brought up to within a mile of the river. It was an awkward back-breaking job carrying the boats forward. With each boat were about 20 men in all, all helping to carry but all encumbered by their own personal loads.

On the edge of the river the first mines were met. Lt. John Holcroft was walking back on his way to contact the boats coming up when he stood on a mine. His left foot was blown off. Major Low and Major Mackenzie were moving up to join him and were both blinded by the explosion. Major Low ordered the boats to go in. Lt. McKee was in charge of the leading boat, with half of 7 Platoon. He stepped on a mine right underneath the guidance tape. Lt Cargill took over and the boats moved out. Near the water he stood on a mine. The survivors managed to get across and reach the main road just South of Minturno. At first light, however, they were discovered by the Germans and counterattacked by tanks and infantry. "A" Company was forced to withdraw, after which the Germans turned their attention to "C" and "D" Companies. The former was virtually encircled by tanks – they had but one PIAT and the ammunition for that was at the bottom of the river – when an artillery observer joined them and was able to bring down a pinpoint "stonk" [artillery bombardment] that compelled the armour to pull back. "D" Company was not so lucky. Their attackers gradually closed in and, after the failure of an attempted breakout, they decided to make a stand in the positions they had captured.

They fought there for hours against tank and infantry attacks., being steadily mortared and without support from their own guns. They were reduced to a handful and still they fought on. Eventually the Company Commander gave the order for each man

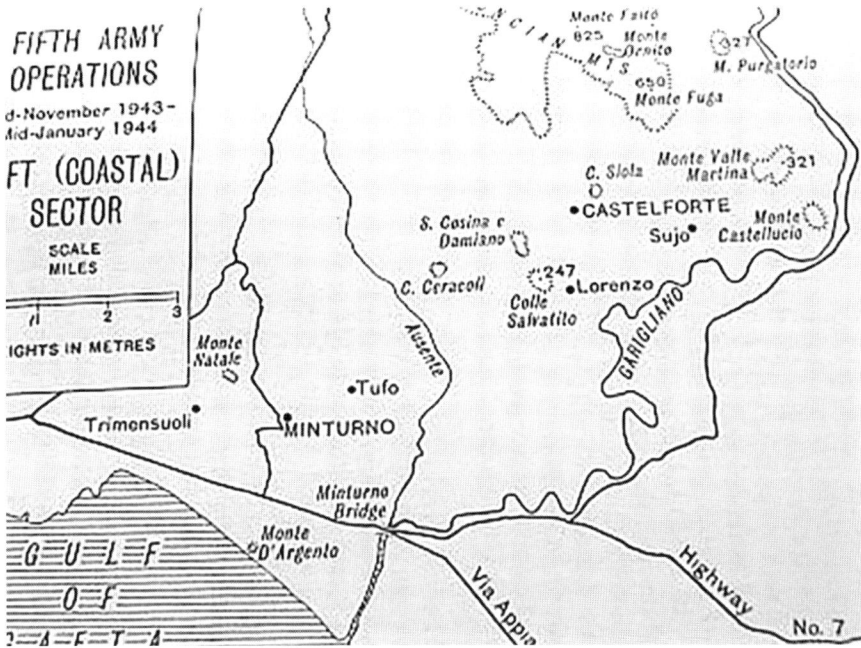

FIFTH ARMY
OPERATIONS
d-November 1943-
Mid-January 1944

FT (COASTAL)
SECTOR

SCALE
MILES

IGHTS IN METRES

5th Army Operations, mid-Nov 43 – mid-Jan 44. Shows Monte D'Argente and Highway 7.

to make a break for it and try to get back as best he could. A few minutes later he was killed by machine gun fire. Only one man got back.'

6 Seaforths War Diary
17 Jan 44 Midnight
At this stage contact had been lost with 'D' Company. which had last reported being heavily attacked by enemy tanks and infantry. The exact whereabouts of 'B' Company were unknown, and personnel of 'A' Company were with 'C' and 'D' Companies. All efforts to contact 'D' and 'A' Companies were in vain. and personnel of 'A' Company were ordered to report back to the river crossing place to be reformed.

What happened to 'A' Company of 7 Cheshires and their part in the operation? A Report was submitted later on 19 Jan 44.

German views of 17 Jan 44
Lt. Wolfgang Wiedemann, II Battalion, 267 Grenadier Regiment
'In Formia. The usual thunder of the guns swelled up to a huge bombardment in the evening of 17 Jan 44. The enemy batteries on the land front and the heavy ship's guns fired from all directions. The First Cassino battle had begun. At 2100 the British Divisions of the X (BR) Corps attacked the River Garigliano.

We were on high alert everywhere. We had to wait for orders. Our Command Post in the farmhouse was moved to the prepared dugout about 200 metres further North when the alarm began.'

17

Lt. Wolfras Gieseler, III Battalion, 274 Grenadier Regiment

'On 17 Jan 44 after dark, an unusual bombardment unexpectedly started on the entire land front of our Division. We hurriedly moved our Command Post to the already prepared bunker, which was in a hollow next to our farmhouses in Santa Maria Infante. In this foxhole, which consists of only two small rooms, we were to spend a few extremely restless and eventful days. Our small community consists only of the Commander, the Adjutant, Schmidt, Sergeant Selle, the two intelligence men Private Gerhard Glausch and Pallmann, and me. Thousands of shells hit our Regiment on the first night, when the Cruisers and Destroyers on the high seas fired their broadsides at us.

If the large shells hit directly next to our bunker, it is like sitting in a submarine. Then the miserable lighting goes out, table and chairs fall over or slide against the walls. We ourselves remain silent for a long time, stretched out in the niches of the room, without losing our indestructible sense of humour. The bunker, built only from old railway sleepers and only covered with a layer of earth about 2 metres thick, is of course no match for a direct hit. Several times the entrance is filled up and even more often the telephone lines to the Battalions and Companies are broken. Then our well-behaved signals communication men must try to repair the damage in a lull in the bombardment.'

Ernst Schünemann, II Battalion, 274 Grenadier Regiment

'We, an eight-man strong crew of "l" Company 274 Grenadier Regiment experienced the shell fire in the shelter, which was well developed against artillery fire, during the night from 17 Jan to 18 Jan 44. From our position we had a good view into the valley. As soon as it got light, we guessed, will the enemy come into the valley near the Roman amphitheatre [the ancient ruins of Minturno on the Via Appia], or will he choose the way over the hedges? Then he would attack us from behind. We did not need to think long. Suddenly the Company Commander appeared, he shouted: "Get out of here". Several bunker crews from 1 Platoon were surprised and captured by Tommy in the dark. Under the road, in a dried-up stream my comrades found cover. I secured the road with my machine gun.

After a short time, our Regiment Commander Lt. Colonel Reich appeared behind me with a rifle in his hand. I was incredibly surprised because Captain Krege, our Battalion Commander had a machine pistol in his hand. Two other soldiers were there [one of these men could have been Lieutenant Gieseler].

"What's going on here?" the Commander asked me. He had no radio communication. Colonel Reich told us all: "Come on, counterattack immediately along the road to Tufo." Before I had picked up my machine gun and hand grenades, the Lieutenant Colonel stormed ahead towards Tufo. There he came to the first close combat with a Tommy. Behind a hedge, the Commander shouted "Hands up!" In the immediate change of thrust our Lieutenant Colonel was the faster one. Corporal Kloth shouted loudly "Go immediately along the wall!" He had just taken care of a wounded Tommy. Captain Krege ordered me to fire into the houses. The battle went on, house by house. We saw that the enemy was retreating. In the meantime, my Company Commander had fallen out. It had already become

Crews of some Priest self-propelled guns at work preparing them for the river crossing. 17 Brigade Garigliano area, 17 Jan 44. (Photo TNA 10922)

morning. Some reinforcements reported to us. We were assigned a new Company Commander.

The house fighting went on. We saw the enemy retreat on the slope opposite us. Another unit of ours pushed back the "Tommies". I saw a German officer with a pistol in his hand. They were jumping down olive groves.

The retreating enemy received reinforcements. Our progress was getting worse. There were close fights up to 4-5 metres away. At noon it caught me, when I saw a Tommy lying in a garden in the attack. I was trying to take this guy out with a machine gun, firing it from the hip. Only one shot came, it did not hit. I dropped to the ground and tried to charge through. He was the fastest gun in the world, and he got a shot off. Tommy had taken a second look at me, but he did not fire. With his finger he pushed up his slipped steel helmet and nodded.

Proud and gloating I ran back. The fight went on. It was only in the afternoon that comrades Ingelmann and Godecke stopped me. I had a gunshot wound. In Tremensuoli I received medical care. Here I learned that Tufo was to be abandoned after all. My commander, Captain Krege, died the same day in close combat.

I must say that without the decision of Lieutenant Colonel Reich to lead this decisive counterattack on Tufo with only a few brave fighters, the necessary relief in this important section of the front would not have come about. Lieutenant Colonel Reich embodied the image of an officer who was not only a daredevil, but also an exemplary infantryman, who could lead classic hand-to-hand combat with his weapon in his hand.'

Philip Brutton, *Ensign in Italy*
17 Jan 44
'Lt. General Richard McCreery's X Corp crossed the Garigliano at its mouth and established a bridgehead. Upstream, adjoining the flank of the American 36th Division, of which only one Company got across. The high ground remained in German hands. The banks of the upper Garigliano, which were mined and barbed wired, are anything from five to ten feet high and the fifty-foot-wide river was in flood with an ice-cold current running at eight miles an hour. The approach was swamp. The field of fire of the German artillery was unimpeded and the whole sector was part of the Gustav Line defensive position where the natural defences had been reinforced by concrete pillboxes built by the Todt organisation. The American 36th Division attack on 20 Jan 44 failed after three days with 1681 casualties.'

Map references
When the British invaded Italy they took the Italian Army maps produced in 1936, translated them into English and devised a different grid for them. At times this caused confusion for some maps still had the Italian grid. On the Italian map, Point 156, 776966 Monte Natale is shown as Point 145, i.e., it is actually 11m lower than shown by the British. This might have caused gunnery problems particularly when conducting a barrage. Each square on the map is 1km in width and length

Reference Points

GR 787961	Griggs Hill
GR 805955	Point 102
	102m above sea level
GR 774985	Point 127
	127m above sea level
GR 785956	Point 141, Monte del Duca 141m above sea level
GR 781959	Point 141 141m above sea level
GR 789971	Spur Point 141, 1.2 Km NW Cemetery 141m above sea level
GR 795963	Point 151 151m above sea level
GR 781967	Cemetery
GR 775967	Point 156
	Monte Natale 145m above sea level
GR 774969	Reverse slope Point 156 130m above sea level
GR 782979	Point 165 165m above sea level
GR 785963	Point 172 172m above sea level

GR 795956	Minturno Ridge 180m above sea level
GR 793999	Point 195 195m above sea level
GR 799967	Point 201, Colle Casale 201m above]
	sea level
GR 807953	Quarry

17 Jan 44

At the end of day one it became clear that the Germans had dug in and were prepared. Their defences were pretty good considering the weight of resource against them.

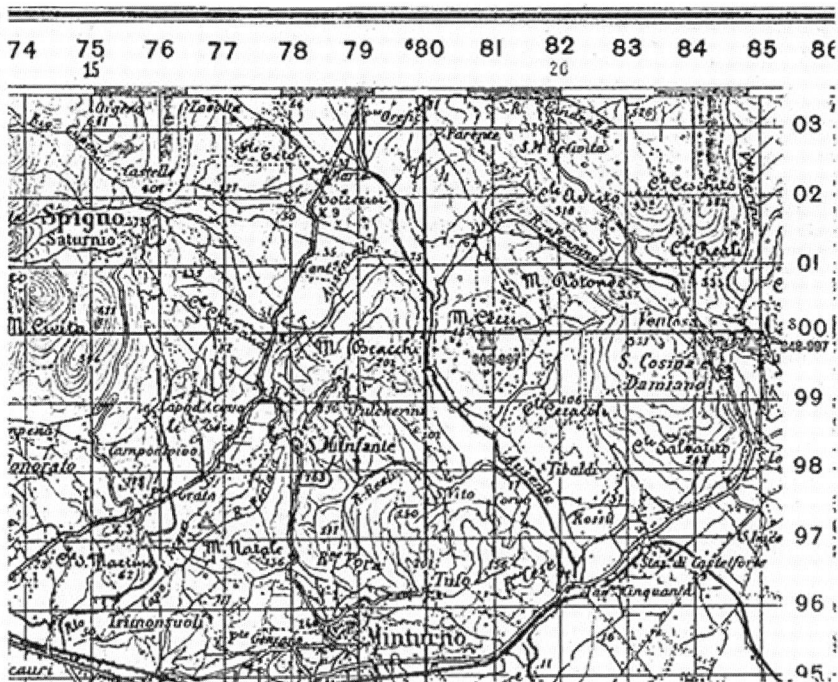

Map of the Minturno area, each square is one km in width and length. This is the grid used by HQ 5 Infantry Division. Some units used slightly different grids. (Map TNA)

21

Chapter 3

18 January 1944 – Securing the Bridgehead

X (BR) Corps:

    5 Infantry Division:
        13 Infantry Brigade
        15 Infantry Brigade
        17 Infantry Brigade
        201 Guards Brigade
        40 Royal Tank Regiment
    46 Infantry Division
    56 Infantry Division

In total, about 50,000 men.

Frank de Planta, battlefield expert

'By first light 2 Northants, less "B" Company, who were running the ferries, were on the far bank and up with 2 Royal Scots Fusiliers and 6 Seaforths. However, the minefield in front of 17 Infantry Brigade proved a very extensive obstacle and many 6 Seaforths had to be retrieved and evacuated which further eroded the Brigade momentum. In addition, any attempt to bring up stores and vehicles was immediately subject to fire from German artillery and pockets of infantry on the flat lands. This further slowed momentum.'

As day broke on 18 Jan 44, the bridgehead was subjected to heavy German artillery fire from Observation Posts in the hills to the North. 17 Infantry Brigade were in the most exposed position, pinned down by minefields and artillery fire on the flat ground around Monte d'Argento, and so a smokescreen had to be put down to shield the position from view. Whilst they were across the River Garigliano, the whole of 17 Infantry Brigade had suffered so many casualties that they were hard pressed to hold onto the triangle of ground that they had secured around Monte d'Argento.

By first light 2 Wiltshires reached the Minturno-Castelforte road and pushed on into the foothills heading for Tufo. Throughout 18 Jan 44 the Germans mounted counterattacks against both 13 Infantry Brigade and 17 Infantry Brigade using some tanks, but all were repulsed largely using defensive artillery.

What caused delay to further sustained progress was the inability to establish permanent crossings of the River Garigliano that were out of range of German guns and observation from German artillery Observation Posts on Monte Scauri.

158 Field Ambulance War Diary

A Medical Station was set up with two Field Surgical Units and one Field Transfusion Unit, and both 'A' and 'B' Companies were employed for the evacuation of casualties during the initial stage of the crossing of the River Garigliano. 'A' Company provided two Sections which landed by DUKW and one Section which crossed the river in assault boats, whereas 'B' Company established a Light Advanced Dressing Station 800 yards South of the river with a pool of trucks working forward to the river.

It was originally intended that the two Sections in DUKWs should land North of the river, clear the casualties, and form a Casualty Embarkation Point and return the casualties on returning DUKWs and Landing Craft. Unfortunately, the DUKWs carrying these Sections ran aground on a sandbank in the mouth of the river and all personnel and equipment had to be taken off by assault boats. After a few days the Advanced Dressing Station moved across the river and was established in the area South of Minturno.

15 Infantry Brigade War Diary

18 Jan 44

GOC 5 Infantry Division Major-General Philip Gregson Ellis, now decided that he could do no more until the original objectives of 17 Infantry Brigade around Minturno and Tremensuoli had been secured. This he could only achieve by using the Reserve Brigade. Accordingly, he planned that 15 Infantry Brigade should cross the river that night at 2200, pass through 2 Wiltshires positions and advance Westwards in the early hours of 19 Jan 44.

The Minturno Sector Dec 43 – Mar 44 showing the three main objectives of 5 Infantry Division: Minturno, Tremensuoli and Monte Natale. (TNA)

At first light on 18 Jan 44 a Staff Officer from 5 Infantry Division arrived to say the battle had not gone quite according to plan the previous night and that 15 Infantry Brigade instead of being held back to pass through 17 Infantry Brigade and directed up the Ausonia valley, would now be at one hour's-notice to move up behind 13 Infantry Brigade, prepared to pass through them probably 18 -19 January and attack Minturno from the East, thus relieving the pressure on 17 Infantry Brigade who were still pinned down in a small triangular parcel of land just beyond the river.

15 Infantry Brigade Command went straight to HQ, 5 Infantry Division, to get back 1 York and Lancs., who had been placed under command 17 Infantry Brigade for the first phase with a view to passing through to secure Monte Bracchi. 1 York & Lancs. had not crossed the river and were accordingly ordered back to their original area, Pizzone, having marched about 20 miles and been on their feet all night. They arrived at Pizzone at about 1500.

15 Infantry Brigade Command spoke to the three Commanding Officers of their Battalions on the telephone from Division about 1300 and ordered all three Battalions to move forward in troop carrying vehicles to the debussing area immediately after dark. 15 Infantry Brigade HQ to move, if possible, before Battalions moved. These moves were carried out without incident.

15 Infantry Brigade now consisted of:
1 Green Howards
1 Kings Own Yorkshire Light Infantry

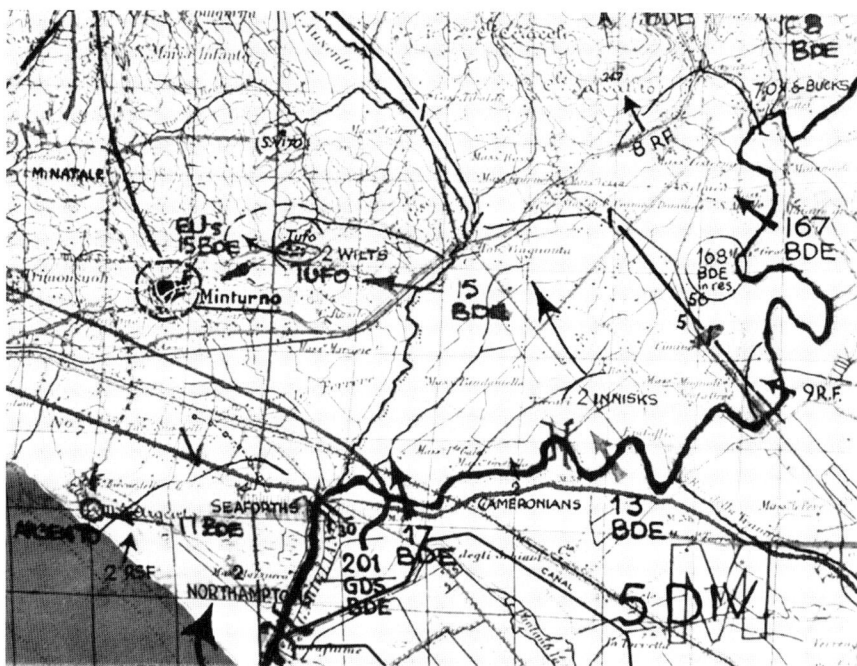

5 Infantry Division Revised Plan of Attack showing 15 Infantry Brigade moving ahead to take Tufo and Minturno. 13 Infantry Brigade are to the right of them. No area was safe from mines. 10 Corps War Diary. (TNA)

1 York & Lancs.

The new orders from HQ 5 Infantry Division were:

1 Kings Own Yorkshire Light Infantry to clear Tufo by 1000 hours 19 Jan 44.

1 Green Howards to advance at 1000 hours on 19 Jan 44 under heavy barrage directed on Minturno and Point 141. 1 Kings Own Yorkshire Light Infantry to advance under same barrage and secure Point 201. Start line to be through West end of Tufo.

1 York & Lancs. to remain in Brigade area of road and track junction as reserve.

From 2200 18 Jan 44 the Battalions were to cross river by ferry; order of march, 1 KOYLI, 1 Green Howards, 1 York & Lancs. Tactical Brigade HQ would also cross during the night.

Brigade HQ would remain at present location and be mainly responsible for calling forward unit transport as soon as bridge was open.

All three Battalions crossed the river without incident and reached their concentration areas, guides being provided by 13 Infantry Brigade. 1 KOYLI were unlucky enough to encounter 'S' mines [Schrapnel mines – when triggered, these mines are launched into the air and then detonated at about 1 metre from the ground] and suffered some 20 casualties, all from one Company. No vehicles were able to cross the river during the night owing to bridging difficulties.

15 Infantry Brigade consisted primarily of Yorkshire men, for all three Regiments were based in Yorkshire. This gave them a County identity as well as a Regimental identity.

1 KOYLI War Diary

18 Jan 44

It was difficult and unpleasant. Mines were a very real danger and a single-line track had been marked across country with tapes by the Royal Engineers. This may well have been good enough for men in daylight, but for heavily laden men in the dark it was a nightmare, despite the new moon.

Owing to the slow progress, the sappers [Royal Engineers] were prevented from bridging by daylight and the move of 201 Guards Brigade was postponed for 24 hours. 56 Infantry Division crossed opposite Castelforte, but 46 Infantry Division failed to get a bridgehead across the River Garigliano.

2 Cameronians War Diary

The CO. went forward to 2 Inniskillings crossing place and found that all their assault boats had been either sunk or holed and that only part of the leading Company had managed to get across the river. Their crossing place had been subject to heavy mortaring and small arms fire. 2 Wiltshires crossing had been successful, and it was agreed between the two COs. that 2 Inniskillings would cross at 2 Wiltshires crossing place, which they did. The CO. was ordered to send only two Companies across the river following 2 Inniskillings.

Lieutenant D.H. Deane, 2 Scots Guards writes

18 Jan 44 Tuesday

'Early reveille, move off in trucks with our hearts in our mouths. Along dreary roads passing very ominous blood wagons coming back the other way. Turn off to debussing area, and wait – wait interminably it seems, no one knows what for. At last, move off and march for an equally long period – troops absolutely whacked, cross the River Garigliano in sinister silence. A very pretty American girl lashing up coffee to the ambulance drivers. I wonder if we look heroic filing away into the darkness. More marching in all about ten miles and arrive in a field with damn all shelter from the cold.'

Frank de Planta, battlefield expert:
18 Jan 44 – 0100
'2 Wiltshires crossed one and a half hours late. The remainder of 2 Inniskillings followed immediately and then 2 Cameronians crossed, still in the boats of 2 Wiltshires.'

2 Wiltshires War Diary
18 Jan 44 – 0115
Leading Companies start their advance.

18 Jan 44 – 0130
Advance is halted at the first objective. This is due to the failure of 2 Inniskillings crossing and the situation of 17 Brigade on our left.

Sir David Cole, 2 Inniskillings, *Rough Road To Rome*.
18 Jan 44 – 0200.

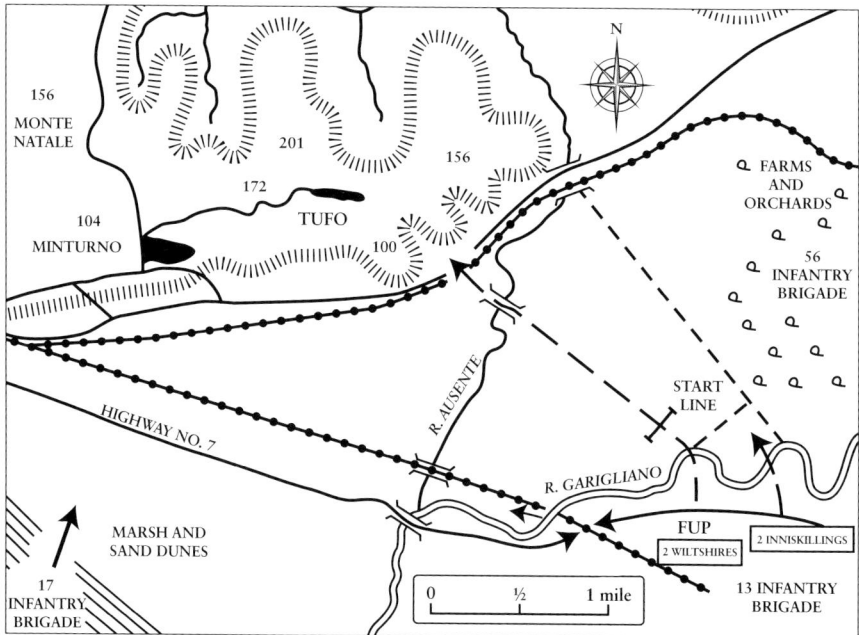

2 Wiltshires and 2 Inniskillings – line of attack. (Map John Strafford)

'Initially the Wiltshires were still using many of their boats so that only three were available for us. Now the whole of "B" Company were over the river and had set off across the plain, now strangely silent, towards the forming-up place for the final assault. "C" Company and Advanced HQ crossed next.'

Royal Inniskillings Regimental Museum
'A' and 'C' Companies were reassembling. As Lt. Col. J.P. O'Brien-Twohig said, 'If you are lost, make for the sound of firing'. The attacking Companies: 'B' and 'C', pushed on towards their objectives protected by creeping artillery fire.

The heavy artillery was on the western slopes of the mountains leading down to the Garigliano plain.

Spike Milligan, 'D' Battery 56 Heavy Regiment Royal Artillery, *Mussolini: His Part in My Downfall*
18 Jan 44 – 0220
'Awakened by someone screaming, coming from the guns, pulled back the blackout and could see the glare of a large fire, at the same time a voice in pain was shouting "Command Post, for God's sake somebody, where is the Command Post?" It was someone with his hair on fire, coming up the path. He was beating it out with his hands. I jumped from my bed, sans trousers and ran towards him, it was Bombardier Begent. I helped beat the flames out. His face and hands were badly burnt. I helped him up the ladder to the Command Post and I blurted out to those within: "There's been a direct hit on the guns." I realised then that I was late with the news, wounded gunners were already being attended to. Everybody looked very tense. Behind me flames were leaping twenty feet in the air. I rushed back to my dug out and dressed in a flash. Took my blankets back to the Command Post to help cover the wounded. I then joined the rest of the Battery, who were all pulling red-hot and burning charge cases away from those not yet affected. They were too hot to pull by hand, so we used pickaxes wedged in the handles. Lieutenant Stewart Pride was heaping earth on them with his hands. Gunner Devine seemed to be enjoying it. He was grinning and shouting. "This is the first time I've been warm today". It never occurred to me that some of the boxes that were hot might still contain unexploded cordite charges. Fortunately, they didn't go off and that's why I'm able to write this diary today.

It was a terrible night. Four Gunners die and six were wounded. All suffered burns in varying degrees. The work of subduing the fire went on until early dawn. It was terrible to see the burnt corpses. There was little Gunner Musclewhite, he'd been killed sitting up in bed. He was burnt black, and his teeth showed white through his black fleshless head. Sgt Jock Wilson too, Gunner White and Ferrier.'

17 Infantry Brigade War Diary
18 Jan 44 – 0245
Brigade Command orders 6 Seaforths to patrol Highway 7 and 2 Royal Scots Fusiliers to secure left flank by capture of Monte Argente. 2 Northants to attack Minturno in daylight.

6 Seaforths War Diary
18 Jan 44 – 0300
All approaches and tracks towards the railway were impossible owing to extensive mine field.

17 Infantry Brigade War Diary
18 Jan 44 – 0330
17 Infantry Brigade to consolidate in present position and 15 Infantry Brigade to take Minturno Ridge by passing through 17 Infantry Brigade.

6 Seaforths Citation: Bar to Military Cross for Major A.E. Low
Major A.E. Low's Company was the leading Company in the assault crossing of the River Garigliano on the night of 17–18 Jan 44. When moving forward to the riverbank, two of his subalterns and three of his Platoon Sergeants were seriously wounded by 'S' mines. He himself was also wounded, but he carried on and led his Company across the river under heavy shell fire and machine gun fire. His calm courage and forceful leadership under most difficult circumstances were a magnificent example to his men and assured the subsequent success of the whole assault crossing by the Battalion. In spite of being in great pain from the wound which had affected his sight, Major Low led his Company, now much depleted by casualties, forward from the river and continued to engage the enemy until the success of the operation. Throughout the night and until about mid-day on 18 Jan 44, when he was ordered to hand over his Command and have his wounds attended to, this officer displayed magnificent courage and devotion to duty.

6 Seaforths Citation: Bar to Military Cross for Captain G.A. Falconer
When the assault crossing of the River Garigliano began on the night 17-18 Jan 44, Capt. Falconer was Second in Command of 'C' Company. His Company Commander was severely wounded, and Capt. Falconer took command and got his Company across the river under intense enemy shell fire. By first light 18 Jan 44 his Company had secured its first objective, and the first enemy counterattack which took place soon after dawn was successfully repulsed. Shortly afterwards the enemy brought up three tanks and counterattacked again. In this engagement Capt. Falconer was himself wounded and his Company suffered many casualties. He continued in action however and conducted a successful withdrawal to more advantageous positions covering the bridgehead. As a result of his fine leadership the enemy counterattack was successfully held. Capt. Falconer's courageous leadership was a magnificent example to his men and the success of the assault crossing was in no small measure due to this officer's skill and courage.

Sir David Cole, 2 Inniskillings, *Rough Road To Rome.*
18 Jan 44 – 0400
'Most of us were now across the river and wireless messages told us that "B" Company, having ejected such German opposition as it had encountered along the way, had reached its ordained position in front of the Minturno Ridge ready for the final assault. "C" Company then started to move forward from the river.'

Advanced HQ paused for a moment near the edge of the last orchard. Men ahead of us were falling, struck by flying shrapnel. Then in a single second everything became instantly silent and dark. I was floating gently in the air. I landed in slow motion, feeling nothing. I had heard no sound and seen no flash. My eyes seemed loath to open. In the blackness my first dazed sense was one of disaster. Sprawled on the ground, I slowly passed a hand over my body. On my haversack and map case I encountered lumps of what seemed like suet pudding. Below my knees my battledress was soaked with blood. God, I've lost a leg, I thought. I felt on and found my boots. I moved my legs. I breathed. Acrid fumes entered my throat. Any sounds I could hear seemed to be miles away. My eyes opened. All this in seconds.

In the dim light I found myself cast like refuse amongst a heap of mangled bodies. In the eddying smoke of the exploded shell, I saw men reeling away, nursing wounded arms or legs. In the middle was a pile of shattered corpses. Besides me that heroic and happy warrior, to whom I had just been talking, lay in pieces. Part of somebody's brains was attached to my haversack. Half of another indistinguishable body lay at my feet, oozing intestines. Its blood had been squirted over my legs. On my left side was a boot with a foot in it and some other miscellaneous objects. I felt no nausea. I felt nothing at all. I was in a state of deep shock. Any momentum that I immediately thereafter developed must have been instinctive or pre-programmed, – the product of training so often repeated that it could influence me even in my sleep.'

Royal Inniskillings Regimental Museum
'Then, suddenly the whole nerve centre of the Battalion was practically wiped out when a shell landed in the middle of Battalion HQ. O'Brien-Twohig himself was wounded. Strenuous efforts by the wireless Officer, Captain David Cole, quickly restored order and communications.'

2 Royal Inniskillings Fusiliers Citation: Military Cross for Captain David Lee Cole
17–18 Jan 44
On the night 17-18 Jan 44, 2 Royal Inniskilling Fusiliers carried out a crossing of the River Garigliano and an attack on the high ground, 8196, *(Eastern edge of Minturno-Tufo ridge)*. Enemy Direct Fire killed the Battalion HQ '18 Set' signallers while in the assembly area. Capt. Cole with great coolness and bravery moved about organising fresh signallers, under fire. On the other side of the river the HQ '18 Set' signaller was injured by a shell which also knocked down and severely shook Capt. Cole. He managed to get the 'Set' working again and communication with the forward companies being absolutely vital, Capt. Cole personally led a line forward to make a connection. One of his party was wounded crossing an enemy mine field, but in spite of this and continuous shell fire, Capt. Cole succeeded in getting a line to the forward companies. This line was of immense value in arranging the Direct Fire.

Throughout the night and next day, Capt. Cole displayed complete disregard for his personal safety and his constant work on communications had the most direct result on the success of the attack.

13 Infantry Brigade War Diary
18 Jan 44 – 0430
Owing to the delay in crossing by the Battalions the Divisional Command allowed zero hour for Phase III to be postponed to 0430 hours.

2 Wiltshires War Diary
18 Jan 44 – 0430
Barrage starts and the Battalion begins to advance. During the advance two of our guns shoot short and fall amongst our Companies, but casualties are slight.

2 Royal Scots Fusiliers Citation: Military Cross for Major A.F. Whitehead
Major Whitehead's Company landed on the beach on 17 Jan 44 about 600 yards South of Mount d'Argento which was found to be firmly held by enemy mortars and machine guns strongly dug in, inside caves. Major Whitehead speedily organised two attacks on this feature, the first immediately on landing, and the second after having arranged covering fire from Vickers Machine Guns which landed later. A third attack with artillery support was launched at 0445 on 18 Jan 44. In the three attacks the open beach was the only possible line of advance. Major Whitehead exhibited the greatest courage and leadership throughout the three attacks which he led personally and pressed home with the utmost determination in the face of enemy fire and the presence of 'S' mines. His energy and fine personal example were an inspiration to all ranks. The attacks by his Company were undoubtably instrumental in preventing the fire of the enemy on Monte d'Argento being brought to bear on the rest of the Battalion landing further South.

17 Infantry Brigade War Diary
18 Jan 44 – 0455
Enemy still hold Monte Argente and 2 Royal Scots Fusiliers call for artillery against them.

6 Seaforths War Diary
18 Jan 44 – 0500
'C' Company reach main road and dig in 100 yards from road.

18 Jan 44 – 0530
Owing to congestion at beach head and enemy shelling of area, 12 Platoon, 'B' Company were unable to cross river. Three Sections of 'A' Company under Lt. Phillips contact Major A.J. Low MC with two Sections and proceed to main road. An enemy Scout Car appeared and halted by this party. On fire being opened up the Scout Car made off.

Sir David Cole, 2 Inniskillings, *Rough Road To Rome*.
18 Jan 44 – 0530
'"B" Company crossed the River Ausente then ran into a deep minefield near the railway line. The need for them to advance fast across open ground in the brightening twilight had limited the usefulness of mine-detectors and within a few minutes the Company had lost 17 men, all dreadfully wounded, on mines. Further progress straight into the minefield would have been suicidal so they had to find a way round.

"C" Company cleared the mines and cut their way through the barbed wire along the riverbank of the River Ausente. They swept on across the railway line where the forward German machine-gun crews, dazed by the bombardment and the steadiness of the soldiers advancing towards them, climbed out of their trenches and ran. A few minutes later the leading Platoons of "C" Company were dashing across the Lateral road at the foot of the ridge and into the tangle of barbed wire beyond. In the full light of day, they could now see how steeply the ground rose up to the German defences.

2 Inniskillings arrive at the forming up place ready for the assault just in time to catch their own barrage. Determined to keep close to the barrage as it crept forward, with bayonets fixed, they walked steadily forward out of the trees on to the last stretch of open grassland at the foot of the Minturno Ridge. "B" Company came out of the gully in which it had been waiting to join the attack.

The speed of "C" Company's assault close behind the barrage deprived the enemy of the opportunity to resist. In a matter of minutes, the forward German defences had been overrun. "C" Company swept up the final steep slopes where the enemy defences were thickest and most sophisticated. Many of the Germans were caught as they climbed the precipitous steps of their dugouts, their eyes blinking in the smoky light. Others were shot as they tried to re-align their machine guns or throw grenades. Some hovered in their trenches, raising their hands and shouting "Kamarad". Some simply bolted. Within a few minutes the summit of the ridge was taken and occupied. "B" Company followed "C" Company up the ridge.'

2 Cameronians War Diary
18 Jan 44 – 0530
'A' and 'B' Companies had crossed the river. The remainder of the Battalion was to remain in the assembly area during daylight and cross at night.

The CO. was ordered by the Brigade Commander to cross with the remainder of the Battalion as the crossing in the left sector by 17 Infantry Brigade had not gone according to plan and to send two Companies to the assistance of 2 Wiltshires.

6 Seaforths War Diary
18 Jan 44 – 0540
Major Low and party are shelled by enemy and withdraw to a position 200 yards from road, leaving Lt. Phillips and six men to watch the road armed with one P.I.A.T. An enemy tank approached and halted 20 yards from the position and opened fire. The P.I.A.T. was fired but the bomb failed to explode, although having made a direct hit on the tank. The party was then ordered to withdraw through a vineyard where contact was finally made with Battalion HQ.

2 Cameronians War Diary
18 Jan 44 – 0545
The CO. ordered 'A' and 'B' Companies to move towards the Lateral road at 815958 to come under the command of 2 Wiltshires. By this time 'D' Company started crossing the river. It had now become light but fortunately there was a ground haze restricting enemy observation.

52 Anti-Tank Regiment Royal Artillery War Diary
18 Jan 44 – 0600
206 Battery: Section of 17 pounders from Landing Craft Tanks landed South of river in error. Landing lights were placed on wrong side of river which resulted in complete disorganisation of landing party. Lieutenant Allen and Troop Sergeant landed successfully near Monte d'Argento.

17 Infantry Brigade War Diary
18 Jan 44 – 0600
DUKWS party reported stranded on sand bar at river mouth.

2 Cameronians War Diary
18 Jan 44 – 0630
'D' Company crossed the river and took over 'A' Company's position. Battalion HQ then crossed followed by 'C' Company and moved forward.

Sgt. Raymond Hawtree, A Company 164 Field Ambulance, Private Papers.
18 Jan 44 – 0600
'Dawn was about to break, and we had travelled about a mile and a half across the fields heading towards a railway track, according to our map.

We came across Captain Essex dealing with his 2 Wiltshires men at his Regional Aid Post and doing a fine job with his treatments. He had found a small house to treat his wounded, under cover, which was a good thing in my estimation. Here we were extremely exposed, as it was getting lighter every minute. Evacuation was out of the question here. Normally, according to all training, we would at this stage be evacuating our wounded to the Main Dressing Station, operated by our Headquarters Company. But in this instance we could not go back to cross the river as we had no transport whatsoever to carry out the job. All we could do was to treat the wounded the best we could with the materials available and carry them forward to some suitable place to be picked up at a later stage. This was indeed a hazardous operation for us, now fully exposed to the enemy, in the light of day.'

2 Wiltshires War Diary
18 Jan 44 – 0700
Forward Companies start to meet opposition and two P.O.W.s are taken.

Sir David Cole, 2 Inniskillings, *Rough Road To Rome*.
18 Jan 44 – 0730
'"B" Company now firmly established on their objective. They occupied the German trenches to face their front, rear and, not least, left flank, where the Germans held the ridge which went to the strongly held towns of Tufo and Minturno, still uncaptured by the British.'

6 Seaforths War Diary
18 Jan 44 – 0730
'C' Company report counter attacked by three tanks and infantry with machine guns. Attack was driven off and casualties sustained on both sides.

92 Field Regiment Royal Artillery War Diary
18 Jan 44 – 0735
Left Observation Post reports Tufo practically obscured by smoke from Direct Fire Plan, not from generators.

18 Jan 44 – 0740
Smoke clears. 2 Cameronians have been ordered to take Minturno owing to delay by 17 Infantry Brigade. Fire Plan will probably be required in support of 2 Cameronians and 2 Inniskillings. Batteries warned barrage may have to be shot again and instructed to keep 200 rounds per gun dumped.

18 Jan 44 – 0750
365 Battery reports heavy anti-aircraft or medium rounds falling short on 2 Wiltshires and causing casualties. HQ Royal Artillery informed.

HMS Orion Naval Record
18 Jan 44
Repeated bombardment from Gulf of Gaeta by HM Cruiser Spartan and HM Destroyers Faulknor, Jervis, Janus and Laforey.

HMS Faulknor Naval Record
18 Jan 44
Bombarded Terracina in support of 5th Army advance across Garigliano River. Enemy shore gunfire was ineffective.

HMS Laforey Naval Record
18 Jan 44
Under air attacks and fire from enemy shore batteries.

13 Infantry Brigade War Diary
18 Jan 44 – 0750
By about first light the two forward Battalions were estimated on their objectives. 2 Inniskillings had Battalion HQ and one Company on the contour. 2 Wiltshires had Companies on Point 102, Point 201 and in Tufo. Heavy casualties had been suffered by both Battalions from enemy small arms fire, mines, mortars, and artillery fire. The enemy positions had been overrun but there were sections of infantry and snipers still in the area.

2 Royal Inniskillings Fusiliers Citation: Military Medal for Sergeant Robert Boak
17–18 Jan 44
Sgt. Boak, as Pioneer Sgt. with 2 Royal Inniskilling Fusiliers, was ordered to move with a fighting patrol ahead of the Battalion to give warning of mine fields and, if possible, to clear paths for the Battalion.

Owing to the break-down of the original crossing this party reached the start line well ahead of the Battalion. Sgt Boak reconnoitred a route forward across the River Ausente a tributary of the River Garigliano, and, with the greatest personal bravery, remained in the riverbed during the opening of our barrage, which fell on the river, so as to clear forward the road, ahead of the attacking troops.

It was due to the outstanding courage and devotion to duty of this NCO that the right attacking Company got through the enemy mine fields without a single casualty.

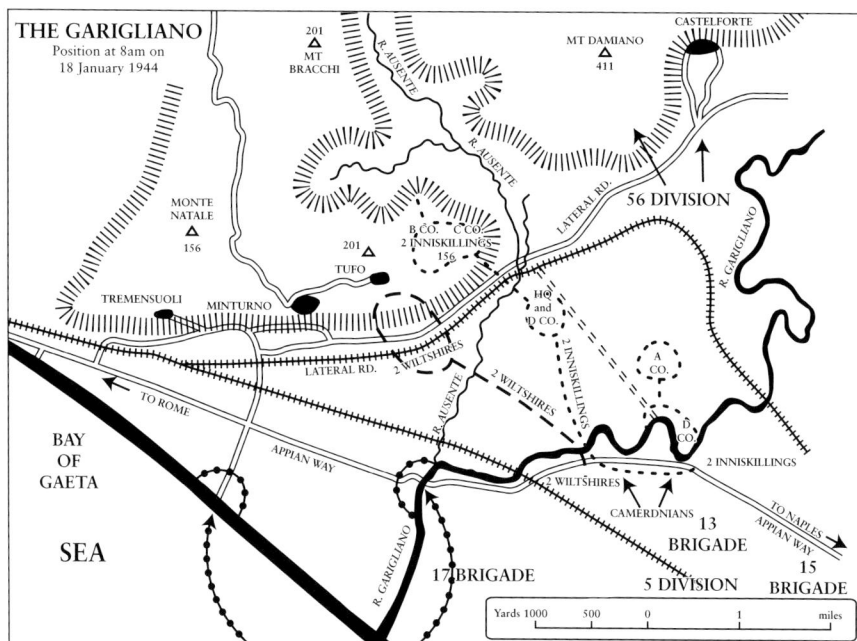

The Garigliano. Position at 8am on 18 Jan 44 showing routes taken by 2 Inniskillings, 2 Wiltshires and 2 Cameronians. (Map John Strafford)

The left company suffered a number of casualties in the mine fields and Sgt. Boak at once moved to their assistance and was of the greatest help to the Company Commander in getting his Company through the mines. Sgt. Boak's *sang froid* had a most tonic effect on the Company, and but for him it would undoubtably have lost time and dropped behind the barrage.

5 Infantry Division History
18 Jan 44 – 0800
Supported by the Division Artillery, 2 Wiltshire's reached the Lateral road from Castelforte to Minturno by first light and crossed it into the foothills soon afterwards.

92 Field Regiment Royal Artillery War Diary
18 Jan 44 – 0810
365 Battery Observation Post reports slight opposition around Tufo. Battalion now dealing with this.

18 Jan 44 – 0830
Message from Brigadier, 13 Infantry Brigade, to Commanding Officer 2 Wiltshires passed to 365 Battery for onward transmission : 1) watch left flank. 2) two Companies 2 Cameronians on way now, to come under Command, Commanding Officer 2 Wiltshire's on arrival, and protect left flank.

34

2 Cameronians War Diary
18 Jan 44 – 0830
The Battalion was now across the River Garigliano without suffering any casualties. 'A' and 'D' Companies, when moving across the open ground to join 2 Wiltshires experienced considerable trouble from enemy sniper and machine gun fire and several casualties were incurred.

2 Wiltshires War Diary
18 Jan 44 – 0830
'B' and 'D' Companies reach East end of Tufo, and 'B' Company push on through the village and penetrate half-way into the enemy positions on Point 201, 795972. Hand to hand fighting takes place. Enemy are too strong for 'B' Company who withdraw to East end of Tufo and form a defensive locality with 'D' Company. During this fighting Major Clark, OC. 'B' Company had the first of two miraculous escapes from the enemy. Going forward to find one of his Platoons he ran into some enemy and took cover in a house where he was surrounded. He fought his way out with his pistol. 'S' Company capture Point 102, 805955. 'A' Company relieved from bridgehead come up into Battalion reserve.

6 Seaforths War Diary
18 Jan 44 – 0830
'C' Company again counter attacked by three or four tanks and infantry. Left flank was forced back. 'C' Company counter attacked and drove off the enemy.

The right flank was then attacked, and Company then withdrew to line of canal where defensive positions were taken up, 603928. The enemy then withdrew, and no further attacks were made.

Frank de Planta, battlefield expert
18 Jan 44 – 0850
'As the situation of 17 Infantry Brigade front was deemed unlikely to improve in time for the original plan to be carried out, the General Officer Commanding 5 Infantry Division decided at about 0850 to bring 15 Infantry Brigade across the river behind 13 Infantry Brigade and pass it through them to clear the remainder of the Minturno-Tufo ridge. 17 Infantry Brigade was told that no further advance was required of it, but that Monte d'Argento, which was strongly held by enemy machine-gun posts must be captured.'

6 Seaforths War Diary
18 Jan 44 – 0900
Stretcher bearer parties were sent out to collect dead and wounded including many of 'D' Company, though up to this time no information had been received regarding their whereabouts.

5 Infantry Division
18 Jan 44 – 0930
A conference at Division HQ was attended by Commander 15 Infantry Brigade and Commander 201 Guards Brigade. Decided: Monte d'Argento must be taken. Monte

d'Argento [just South of Minturno] was now known to be held by at least six machine gun posts firing from caves in the rock.

17 Infantry Brigade HQ War Diary
18 Jan 44 – 0930
6 Seaforths report two tanks seen on main road and are being counter attacked by enemy infantry. Urgent orders to Main HQ to send forward ammunition and 6 pounders. 206 Anti-tank Battery to deploy two 17 pounders on South bank of river.

164 Field Ambulance War Diary
18 Jan 44 – 0930
Message from Brigade stating that 8 casualties were awaiting evacuation. Major Ross went across river with four men and brought 12 cases back in assault boats.

92 Field Regiment Royal Artillery War Diary
18 Jan 44 – 0950
365 Battery Commander instructed to warn 2 Wiltshires of suspected enemy counterattack forming up West of Tufo at request of 13 Infantry Brigade.

Royal Inniskillings Regimental Museum
With great verve, inspired by Sergeant Robert Boak, the leading platoons of 'C' Company, advancing closely behind the barrage, drove the Germans out of their trenches. 'B' Company ran into a deep minefield and suffered heavy casualties. Led by Major Percy Blake 'C' Company pushed on, capturing prisoners and German dugouts. Within 15 minutes a breach had been made in the main defences of the Gustav Line. 'B' Company found a way round the mine field and established its objective. By 10am the two Companies had occupied the German trenches on 800 yards of the Gustav Line. They were the first Regiment to breach the Line.

17 Infantry Brigade HQ War Diary
18 Jan 44 – 1000
6 Seaforths report counterattack beaten off but forced to give ground slightly.

156 Field Regiment Royal Artillery War Diary
18 Jan 44 – 1005
Officer Commanding P Battery called for fire on enemy tanks which were counter attacking 6 Seaforths. Two tanks destroyed.

52 Anti-Tank Regiment Royal Artillery War Diary
18 Jan 44 – 1015
207 Battery: Information received that four German Mark IV tanks had counterattacked 6 Seaforths in area Minturno Ridge which would have been covered by a section of 17 pounders from 206 Battery had our Landing Craft Tanks landed in the right place.

17 Infantry Brigade HQ War Diary
18 Jan 44 – 1015

2 Royal Scots Fusiliers Carrier ferried across river with ammunition. Ferry sunk after discharging Carrier. Ammunition divided between 2 Royal Scots Fusiliers and 6 Seaforths.

18 Jan 44 – 1030
Monte Argente reported still held by enemy. Approx 6 machine guns in caves.

5 Infantry Division History
18 Jan – 1100
The Divisional Commander realising that 17 Infantry Brigade could go no further in the circumstances and that Minturno would have to be attacked from the right, ordered 2 Cameronians, who had two companies in reserve to close up more to the left towards Minturno in support of the hard pressed 2 Wiltshires fighting for Tufo. Much had now to be done to retrieve the position. On the left in 17 Infantry Brigade area, a smoke screen was quickly generated. 2 Wiltshires in the centre made special watch of their open left flank and everything possible was done on both sides of the river to meet the inevitable counterattack. The first one appeared at about 1100 hours after it had been observed to be coming up to the West of Tufo about an hour previously. It was not a well-coordinated attack and was easily broken up by the Battalion and the Divisional Artillery. Meanwhile sporadic incidents occurred all over the front. The Gunners soon claimed direct hits on some tanks that tried to infiltrate around 2 Wiltshires. 2 Wiltshires, during that attack, received two enemy ambulances which reported to their Regimental Aid Post in error and were detained.

164 Field Ambulance War Diary
18 Jan 44 – 1100
Ambulance Dressing Station X and A Sections evacuated to house 300 yards West of original site owing to enemy fire and lack of accommodation. Two captured enemy ambulances put into use. Both Dressing stations under continuous shell and mortar fire throughout the day.

   Sections X and A under command of Capt. Mill-Irving received 71 casualties on 18 Jan 44.

Sgt. Raymond Hawtree, A Company 164 Field Ambulance, Private Papers
18 Jan 44 – 1100
'Our Section kept moving forward with the wounded until we came across a low brick wall. We took cover behind the wall, and I saw that we were alongside the railway lines. The white tape was still visible, over the wall and across the Railway tracks, a road alongside and into the woods the other side.

   I told the men to remain still and under cover of the wall and went ahead to investigate. I heard transport coming from my left side and looked ahead to see, what appeared to be ambulances coming along. However, to my dismay they belonged to the German Army Medical Corps. There were two of them and the first one in front came to a halt by the white tape. The German Medical Officer got out of the Ambulance, walked to the white tape, and then looked at his map, looking all confused. I approached him at the same time, telling my men to be ready for any eventuality unforeseen.

At this moment I decided to take responsibility for my next action. I said to the Officer that he was now my prisoner, along with his men and relieved him of his Luger revolver [*sic*] and his maps. I told the others to fall in with their Officer. The driver of the second Ambulance, at that moment tried to turn his Ambulance around and go back. He received a shock, for as he was turning he went too far from the ditch and hit a mine, which blew the front near side completely away. No injuries from this incident.

We examined the Ambulance cars, as the men joined by this time to assist, by backing up my action. There were no wounded in the Ambulances but full of useful equipment. Capt. Mill-Irving then came forward as I shouted to anyone in the woods to come forward to take the prisoners from us. Sgt. Blackman in charge of the R.A.P. saw our plight and came from out of the woods with a Thompson Machine Gun. I did laugh at him for the nozzle was covered in mud. He took the prisoners away to Brigade Headquarters, followed by Capt. Mill-Irving.

Being now on the road we checked our map reference again and worked out that the Quarry, our rendezvous, was a few miles along to the right to where we were standing. Bearing in mind that we had dealt with the enemy Medical bods perhaps, nevertheless, we felt we had to be cautious along this road to the Quarry. We found it all right and formed a Medical Post, keeping busy with the wounded, coming in at a steady pace from the R.A.P. of 2 Wiltshires.

The captured German Officer and his six men, together with Maps, Luger and other useful paraphernalia were handed in at Brigade Headquarters, proved most useful to our cause on this operation. Interrogation of the prisoners also proved helpful to us in the future advancement of our troops.'

Driving German captured Ambulance along river road, previously marched by us, heading for the Main dressing Station. This we found and I was greeted most enthusiastically by Officers and Other Ranks, all ready to deal with the expected wounded.

I gave my report to the Commanding Officer, name escapes me, and he ordered that the Ambulance be filled with equipment as requested by me. Then Halpin and I went back to the Quarry with the Ambulance loaded, and quickly filled up the Ambulance again with more wounded for the second journey to the Main Dressing Station.

We did this journey until the 160 casualties we had dealt with had been evacuated by Jack Halpin and me, under extreme war conditions; shot and shell etc.

Having cleared the casualties, I then took up my usual position with my Section at the Advanced Dressing Station, still to deal with the wounded, British and enemy coming into us.'

Frank de Planta, battlefield expert
18 Jan 44 – noon
'2 Royal Inniskilling Fusiliers launched Phase 2 at 0530 and after sustaining enormous casualties had, by noon, gained an 800 yards foothold in the bridgehead.'

2 Cameronians War Diary
18 Jan 44 – 1430
2 Wiltshire had not yet taken their objective of Tufo and Point 201, 798966. 'A' and 'B' Companies in reserve until they were ordered to attack Point 201 from the East end of Tufo. 2 Wiltshires had entered Tufo but were still meeting heavy resistance at the West

end. Major Mitchell ('B' Company) assumed control of the attack under the direction of 2 Wiltshire's Second in Command. The attack was started with 'A' Company to the left and 'B' Company to the right. By moving down into the valley between the East end of Tufo and Point 201 'A' Company was subject to heavy machine gun fire coming from the West and North-West. The ground was open and consisted of small terraces down to the valley. 'A' Company suffered many casualties including the Company Commander, Major Wishart and the Second in Command Captain Long. Major Wishart died the following day from his wounds.

2 Wiltshires ordered the two Companies back and to take up a position on the ridge at 805962 [Eastern edge of Tufo]. While 'A' and 'B' Companies were digging their positions the enemy heavily mortared them and many casualties were suffered. Up to this point 'A' and 'B' Companies had approximately 60 casualties. As their position appeared unsuitable, 'A' and 'B' Companies were ordered back to 806958 [200m South-East of Tufo], by the Officer in charge 2 Wiltshires and there they spent the night 18-19 Jan 44.

2 Wiltshires War Diary

18 Jan 44 – 1500

During the evening two Companies of 2 Cameronians, were placed under the command of the Battalion and attacked Point 201 but failed to take the feature. 'B' and 'D' Companies were counterattacked twice during the night. Both attacks were beaten off mainly by good fire direction of Artillery Observation Post with 'B' and 'D' companies.

18 Jan 44 – 1630

Three Enemy tanks and infantry come along road from Minturno just below Tufo and attack Battalion HQ on rear slopes Point 102. Attack beaten off. One tank hit by PIAT and turret damaged.

Sgt. Raymond Hawtree, A Company 164 Field Ambulance, Private Papers

18 Jan 44 – 1630

'Three small German tanks were seen approaching the A.D.S. and, having been accumulating arms from the wounded, we did not wish to be caught with them, so they were quickly stowed under the staircase out of sight.

We heard a loud bang outside and actually saw the turret of the first tank literally disappeared from its housing. The two tanks following decided to beat a retreat, turn and disappeared. The lad that fired the PIAT gun at the tank came into the medical room, with a huge bruise on his shoulder, having fired the gun. He was later congratulated by one of his Officers, when he came in also for treatment.'

17 Infantry Brigade HQ War Diary

18 Jan 44 – 1630

Monte Argento shelled by Navy. Position has been twice attacked by 2 Royal Scots Fusiliers.; is heavily mined and booby trapped.

18 Jan 44 – 1700

Brigade Commander orders no further landing or ferrying until beach area is clear of mines.

Phone message to Main HQ that GOC insists on capture of Monte Argente. Naval support offered. Later considered unsafe and plan arranged for 2 Royal Scots Fusiliers night attack.

164 Field Ambulance War Diary
18 Jan 44 – 1700
Major Ross seriously wounded near ferry by a mortar bomb.

2 Wiltshires War Diary
18 Jan 44 – 1800
'C' Company ordered back to Point 102.

D. Woolard, attached to 2 Wiltshires, *My Day, 18 January*
'We moved up into Tufo and then we were sent out into Companies, two detachments to each Company if they needed any mortar support. Jobber Brown's detachment and ours, Gibb Mullins were sent to "D" Company at the top of Hill 102. After breakfast we drew rations on our way up to the new positions and as soon as we got there, we started to dig our two gun-pits and set the mortars in. We prepared the bombs ready to range when ordered. Our Observation Post was in a house close to the gun-pits, it had been hit many times by shells and had to be entered through a shell-hole on the opposite side to the enemy positions. When inside you went up to an attic which had a small window from which you could see quite an area of enemy held territory. As this house was under constant observation by the enemy, it was dangerous to use binoculars during daylight if it was sunny, or to move about too much.

Apart from a few enemy shells and mortar bombs at intervals, the Germans intensified shelling towards sunset. Our detachment dug deep slit trenches behind two straw stacks so that any shrapnel from exploding shells would be slowed down or stopped from falling into our trenches. The other detachment dug their slit trenches in a bank and covered them with old doors, wood, and branches. In the afternoon we did some ranging with smoke bombs but were not called on to do any real task. Again, we gathered some straw to put in our slit trenches to keep us a little warmer at night. We slept in full equipment ready to stand to the mortars during the night if ordered to do so. We even kept our steel helmets on as several shells fell quite close that night and shrapnel fell extremely near to our slit trenches. When it was my turn to go on guard, I could see the flash and glow of exploding shells and mortar bombs.'

Sir David Cole, 2 Inniskillings, *Rough Road To Rome.*
18 Jan 44
'The evening of 18 January was cold and grey, with a sparse wintry mist hanging low above the ground and a few stars twinkling feebly in a darkening sky. "B" Company were savagely attacked from three sides. First they knew of it was when in the gathering darkness they heard the Germans, obviously in large numbers, shouting and cat calling from amongst the scrub and trees below. The Germans, visible only from time to time as black shapes flitting between the trees, were not only swarming up the ridge in front; they were streaming across the exposed left flank where the ridge ran along to Tufo and soon afterwards they were also heard shouting and trampling about on the slope behind "B" Company.

To begin with, our men not only held on, but in many places climbed out of their trenches and counter charged the Germans with Brens and Tommy-guns. For example, Sergeant Anderson, having seized a German Spandau, charged the enemy with it, and killed many of them at close quarters. As he said laconically afterwards: "I had the Spandau and I had the ammunition, and the Germans were there." But our losses were also heavy and soon Section Commanders could be heard shouting one after another, that their ammunition was running low. About the same time another Spandau opened fire from the Company's right flank, a menacing portent that the Germans would soon complete their encirclement.

Eventually it became clear that the much-reduced Company was being further and seriously depleted, was all but surrounded by a much larger force and had almost exhausted its ammunition. It was decided, therefore that rather than be completely overrun they would try to withdraw the remnants of the Company to continue the fight elsewhere. Orders were given for a general withdrawal towards "C" Company. They withdrew across the rear side of the ridge through the narrow gap still unblocked by the Germans. When "B" Company finally assembled the battered survivors of the Company totalled about 35. Within twenty-four hours over sixty men had been lost and the Company had been reduced to little more than a Platoon.

With the Germans thus re-established just along the ridge, "C" Company was now obviously on the chopping-block next. The Company was then re-organised using the remnants of "B" Company to guard the now highly vulnerable left flank. Vickers machine gunners from 7 Cheshires were placed astride the track leading to the area just recaptured by the Germans.'

Royal Inniskillings Regimental Museum
'B' Company found itself under attack from three sides by overwhelming numbers. As ammunition began to run out and hand to hand fighting developed, the decision was taken to withdraw. Only the bravery of men like Sergeant Thomas Vincent Anderson, Corporal Stephen Hughes, and Fusilier John Stranex enabled the Company to withdraw to 'C' Company's position.

Expecting further counterattacks, Major Percy Blake ['C' Company], organised his Company and the remnants of 'B' Company. When the attack came, elements of practically the whole Battalion fought a ferocious battle to keep the Germans at bay. Eventually sustained British artillery fire halted the attack.

2 Royal Inniskillings Fusiliers Citation: Military Medal for Sergeant Thomas Vincent Anderson
18 Jan 44
'B' Company, 2 Royal Inniskilling Fusiliers was in position on its objective 809964 [East end of Minturno-Tufo ridge]. The Company Sergeant Major had been wounded and Sgt. Anderson was acting as CSM. The Germans counter attacked the Company and a party got into the position. Sgt. Anderson, who had armed himself with a German machine gun, rushed the German party firing his machine gun from the hip. He killed several of the Germans and the remainder were thrown into confusion and dealt with. The ammunition situation in the Company became acute towards evening and 'B' Company was forced by another attack to fall back on 'C' Company's position about

814964 [500m downhill, East of the end of the ridge]. Sgt. Anderson remained behind covering the withdrawal with his German machine gun, and it was due to his outstanding personal bravery and coolness that the majority of 'B' Company was withdrawn in good order. In re-organising 'B' Company in its new position Sgt. Anderson's behaviour in moving about under close range enemy fire put fresh heart into his Company after a difficult time and brought their morale back to the highest level.

There is little doubt that but for the initiative and cool calculating bravery of this NCO a great part of his Company would have been killed or captured.

2 Royal Inniskillings Fusiliers Citation: Military Medal for Corporal Stephen Hughes
18 Jan 44

Corporal Hughes was in command of a Section attached to 'B' Company, 2 Royal Inniskilling Fusiliers, in position on the Minturno-Tufo ridge when a heavy German counterattack developed against 'B' Company, its main thrust being against the Platoon with which Cpl. Hughes Section was part of. With great determination Cpl. Hughes held the fire of his Section until the enemy were only 25yards away. The effect of this was to kill a number of Germans and to defeat that attack.

When the remainder of his Platoon ran out of ammunition Cpl. Hughes continued to hold the enemy off until he was the only one left with ammunition. The enemy had by now infiltrated round both flanks of his Section. Cpl. Hughes with great personal courage moved forward alone and attacked the enemy on the right flank allowing his Section to withdraw. Cpl. Hughes himself, worked through the enemy and by engaging them with his Thomson sub machine gun from their rear, held up their attack and caused them confusion.

His personal bravery throughout the action was a fine example to all in his vicinity.

2 Royal Inniskillings Fusiliers Citation: Military Medal for Fusilier John Stranex
18 Jan 44

Fusilier Stranex was Platoon runner of 10 Platoon, 'B' Company, 2 Royal Inniskilling Fusiliers which was in position about 809964 [East end of Minturno-Tufo ridge].

The Germans delivered a number of determined counterattacks in one of which they over ran a Section Post. The Platoon Commander was with another Section and Fusilier Stranex at once led the other two Fusiliers in the Platoon HQ forward, drove the enemy back from the Post, they had captured with the bayonet and successfully held it.

But for the personal bravery and quick wits of Fusilier Stranex there is no doubt the Germans would have succeeded in taking the remainder of the Platoon from the rear.

17 Infantry Brigade HQ War Diary
18 Jan 44 – 1900

First Carrier (2 Royal Scots Fusiliers) to leave beach blown up on mine 20 yards along track. No casualties, but all ammunition destroyed.

18 Jan 44 – 2010

5 Seaforths report Company in Amphitheatre out of touch. Uneasy situation.

2 Royal Scots Fusiliers War Diary

18 Jan 44

Seven Carriers eventually got across river by ferry but two of these were destroyed by mines.

Weather mainly very good with warm sunshine and good visibility, apart from early morning mist caused mainly by smoke screen on river.

2 Cameronians War Diary

18 Jan 44 – 2100

The first transport across the river arrived at Battalion HQ consisting of two carriers.

1 Kings Own Yorkshire Light Infantry War Diary

18 Jan 44 – 2230

The Battalion crossed the river entirely on a marching basis. Everything had to be carried as so far, no vehicles had crossed the river. The Battalion crossed the river, 22 Officers and 450 other ranks in strength.

The march from the river Northwards to the Assembly area behind 13 Infantry Brigade was difficult and unpleasant, mines were a very real danger and a single line track had been marked across country with tapes by the Royal Engineers. This may well have been good enough for single men in daylight – but for heavily laden men in the dark – it was a nightmare despite the new moon. It was like marching across a mined Romney Marsh, deep dykes and ditches every few hundred yards. If the front halted as it often did, the whole long single file column across the plain halted as well. What a target it was if the enemy had availed themselves of it. Luckily, they did not.

X (BR) Corps History

Enemy Counterattacks

On 18 Jan 44 the Germans, who from information given by some of the prisoners taken in the assault, had evidently been taken by surprise and had no strong force for a counterattack. They were nevertheless able to mount two immediate counterattacks from the resources of 94 Infantry Division, supported by tanks, and by attacking the exposed left flank of the bridgehead were able to regain some lost ground.

The counterattacks of 18 Jan 44 were the first of a long series. Although the enemy was caught with no reserves immediately available, he contrived to resist stubbornly and put in repeated local counterattacks. Forced at first to rely on its own resources 94 Infantry Division fought a costly delaying action, in which sappers and rear echelon troops were used as infantry. In the following four days while X (BR) Corps brought its reserve brigades across the River Garigliano and strove to enlarge the bridgehead, the enemy hurried from every part of the front to build up for a counter offensive.

The X (BR) Corps Commander's intentions at the end of 18 Jan 44 were for 5 Infantry Division to launch 15 Infantry Brigade through 13 Infantry Brigade's positions to clear the rest of the Minturno ridge.

The enemy flung into a hasty counterattack on the night 18/19 Jan 44 was mauled by our defensive fire. Heavy though his losses were, the enemy achieved his object of holding our advances in check while he massed large reserves for a counter-offensive.

The situation on the front of 5 Infantry Division improved during the night 18/19 Jan 44 when 17 Infantry Brigade succeeded in taking Monte d'Argento. Build up and maintenance continued to be a problem, however, as the river had not been bridged and the Class 5 ferry had been sunk during the afternoon of the 18 Jan 44 by a direct hit.

7 Cheshires Citation: Military Cross for Lieutenant P.C. Harris

Lieut. Harris was in command of a machine gun Platoon and landed on the beach at Monte d'Argento at about 2145, 17 Jan 44. Shortly after landing, his Company Commander was wounded, and Lieut. Harris took over the Company. Under heavy enemy fire he took his Sections up to within 150 yards of the enemy, along a completely exposed beach, and neutralised the enemy machine gun posts at short range. At first light on 18 Jan 44 Lieut. Harris moved his Platoons to fresh positions so as to avoid heavy casualties during the daylight. On the evening of 18 Jan 44 he again moved his Platoons up to within close range of the enemy in order to support an attack. Throughout the whole period the beach was under heavy enemy fire. Throughout this operation Lieut. Harris showed outstanding qualities of courage and leadership.

5 Infantry Division History

In the late afternoon 2 Cameronians made an unsuccessful bid to take over Point 201 but received very heavy mortaring which spread along the whole front and heralded a further and probably more organised counterattack. This series of counterattacks lasted for almost an hour and a half, from 1800 to 1930, and was finally beaten off when the enemy had nearly overrun Observation Posts and forward positions. Most credit must go, as it had already done, and will continue to, to the solid steel wall of defensive Artillery fire that was invariably put round our positions when they were being counterattacked. No infantryman in the Division need feel ashamed or would be unprepared to acknowledge that the gunners probably held the small River Garigliano bridgehead when called to do so at frequent intervals. So frequent were these demands for this that the Divisional Artillery fired practically unceasingly for many days.

An enemy wireless message was intercepted at that time from 274 Infantry Regiment of 94 Infantry Division who reported to their Division: 'Enemy in Tufo and we are being shelled intensively. Request objective counterattack.' This message was timed for 1700 and throws increasing light on the highly centralised control exercised by the Germans.

Again, our Gunner communication was used by Brigadier Campbell to instruct 2 Wiltshires to hold on at all costs and if pushed off the ridge to get back on again. 2 Wiltshires spent most of the afternoon of 18 Jan 44 in hand-to-hand fighting in the village of Tufo. Two reserve companies of 2 Cameronians went through them to try and hold Point 201 but were driven back by heavy and accurate mortar fire.

2 Royal Inniskillings Fusiliers Citation: Military Cross for Major Percy Joseph Blake

17–18 Jan 44

2 Royal Inniskilling Fusiliers made an assault crossing of the River Garigliano and attacked the high ground in 8196 [East end of Minturno-Tufo ridge].

44

A group of
German prisoners
awaiting
interrogation,
18 Jan 44. (Photo
Capt R.F. Gade,
2 AFPU, IWM
TR 1526)

Major Blake was in command of 'C' Company, the right attacking Company. Owing to enemy fire, boats on the Inniskilling crossing were destroyed and 'C' Company were put over lower down the river. It was 0430 before Major Blake was in a position to leave the riverbank with two Platoons for the start line 3000 yards away, arriving at 0530. The drive and leadership of this officer in the subsequent advance and attack were beyond praise. His Company took their objective and were almost at once counterattacked. Major Blake's coolness and courage were again outstanding, and he personally led his small reserve in hand-to-hand action and destroyed German parties who had got a foothold in his area.

When 'B' Company, owing to lack of small arms ammunition were forced to fall back on 'C' Company's position, Major Blake organised the active defence of his position so well that further attacks pressed home against it failed, and when he was wounded in repulsing the final attack early on 19 Jan 44 the position was secure.

During 18 Jan 44 and the night 18-19 Jan 44 the Inniskillings were the most advanced British troops and but for Major Blake's great personal bravery and soldierly qualities in holding on, the position of much more than the Inniskillings would have been endangered.

German views of 18 Jan 44
18 Jan 44
Private Wilhelm Prinz, 274 Grenadier Regiment
'On the night of 18 Jan 44, the artillery bombardment began again, so we had to go into our bunker, on the steep slope behind our house, as it was unreachable by enemy grenades, in a blind spot to the enemy.'

Lt. Wolfgang Gieseler, III Battalion, 274 Grenadier Regiment
18 Jan 44
'The long-awaited major attack of the enemy with its far superior forces is now here. Incoming reports state that our resistance groups, which are spread far apart and are also cowering in bunkers bravely hold out and survive the strong fire to some extent.

When the dawn comes the artillery-fire swells up again to a hurricane to creep in weakened form into the hinterland. We now know that the enemy is about to attack for the machine guns have taken over in the meantime. In front of us on the heights near Minturno [Point 201], a bitter close combat fight is already raging, where the Command Post of the III Battalion lies. This time it is still decided in favour of the defenders; but the brave Battalion Commander falls among many others.

Major Haarbrucker, who would have already relinquished his Battalion and was about to return to Germany takes over the orphaned III Battalion, where he falls into English captivity the very next morning, badly wounded, in fierce close combat at the heights of Minturno. The remnants of the Battalion must vacate their positions and retreat to the height of our Regiment Command Post. The enemy has succeeded in a deep penetration.

Even the field replacement Battalion that was brought in for relief on the second night can no longer change the situation. The losses to officers and men are extremely high.'

Private Wilhelm Prinz, 274 Grenadier Regiment
18 Jan 44
'In great haste we had brought the mail bags into the house, when a small Peugeot truck drove up. The very excited driver called on us to help unload and explained that he had loaded dead comrades who had fallen at Garigliano in the morning and were to be buried in our Regimental Cemetery, which had just been set up, just outside Minturno. That was quite a shock for me, after the quiet weeks in the military hospital, but it got even worse: full of consternation I recognized the first dead body I lifted with Karl Weiser was our doctor, Dr. Fries. The artillery fire that had just started again left no time for pity and so we quickly ended our macabre work. The trucks had to be taken out of the danger zone.'

Lt. Wolfgang Wiedemann, II Battalion, 267 Grenadier Regiment
18 Jan 44
'In Formia. We listened to the strong, undulating shell fire. It had started very early. Officially there was little information. In the afternoon there was a lot of fighting and heavy losses. Captain Krege, Commanding Officer of III Battalion, 274 Grenadier Regiment was killed in close combat at Minturno. Large parts of 274 Grenadier Regiment were already destroyed.

The German leadership recognized how the main points of attack were now: Minturno and Castelforte. Now it was a matter of using the last ounce of strength to prevent a breakthrough that would have meant the end of the Cassino Front.'

Katriel Ben Arie, *The Battle of Monte Cassino 1944*
18 Jan 44

'Field Marshal Kesselring immediately recognized the danger and once again proved his ability to fight land wars, especially in defence. He immediately gave the order to throw II Battalion 267 Grenadier Regiment from the coast (II Battalion secured the coastal section from

Gaeta to Scauri) to the front line and to deploy all personnel including drivers of 94 Infantry Division.

However, these measures were not sufficient. The Commanding General of XIV Panzer Corps. General Fridolin Von Senger und Etterlin, contacted Kesselring directly and urgently requested the deployment of Reserves from Army Group C, namely 29 and 90 Panzer Grenadier Divisions. General Vietinghoff supported his request, since neither the Corps nor the Army had any further reserves'.

Mathew Parker, *Monte Cassino*
'Von Senger was the man Field Marshall Albert Kesselring charged with the task of preventing the Allies getting past Cassino. An enigmatic figure far removed from the popular conception of a Nazi General, he had been a Rhodes Scholar to St. John's College, Oxford, in 1912 and remained an Anglophile thereafter. Intellectual, sophisticated, and anti-Nazi, he was also a devout Roman Catholic and as a young man had become a lay Benedictine and visited many Benedictine monasteries in Germany.'

Lt. Wolfgang Wiedemann, II Battalion, 267 Grenadier Regiment
18 Jan 44
'In Formia. Lieutenant Gieseler told me, as Lieutenant Colonel Reich had done all day long, how he had cheered up his company in Minturno and Tufo with a rifle in his hand and personally led several counterattacks with only a few remaining men. His example and his bravery ensured that the fighting spirit of the surviving Grenadiers remained who was part of the crew of their shelter. Only a few hours ago, a shell killed him when the shelter was destroyed as he repaired a shot-up telephone line.'

Private Wilhelm Prinz, 274 Grenadier Regiment
18 Jan 44
'Lieutenant Gieseler and I immediately made friends. We were on the same wavelength. Gieseler was by profession a forester in East Prussia. Lieutenant Colonel Reich was also from East Prussia. We only had a few minutes to exchange some personal points of view. His hand was bandaged. Only a few hours ago, when he and his Commander cheered up the Companies, he was injured by shrapnel. It was a slight wound, and admission to a military hospital was out of the question. Gieseler did not let down his Regiment and especially his Commander. I respected this brave and decent officer. One could feel his honest patriotism burning in his heart. Gieseler became a civilian after the Polish campaign in 1939. It was not until the end of 1942 that he became a soldier again.'

Lt. Wolfgang Wiedemann, II Battalion, 267 Grenadier Regiment
18 Jan 44
'In Formia. Finally, I received the order from the Regiment Commander to deploy 2 Company. About 2 km South-East we had to close a big gap in the front Northwest of Tufo. We had to link up the left and the right. We knew nothing about our left flank. The right flank was supposed to be at the Cemetery at the back of Minturno, on the Santa Maria Infante-Minturno road but it could be occupied by "Tommy".

Lieutenant Colonel Reich had the iron will to hold the positions of his Regiment at all costs. This pale, sleepless man bid me farewell with the usual "soldier's luck". He winked at me with an encouraging wink. A short handshake ended the receipt of orders. And already I stood in front of the dugout and listened where the next grenades would land. It was the second day of the great battle. The outlook was bad for me. Black night, completely unknown, quite mountainous terrain. Nobody really knew where the enemy were. There was enormous artillery fire from the sea and from the land front. I thought of my Company, which was waiting for me in trenches and tunnels somewhere nearby. Now I had to know what to do next.

Characteristic for this 2nd day of action was the seemingly endless artillery fire, the general disorientation, the nature of the wounded and the chaotic conditions during the transport of the wounded. Food and ammunition carriers went for miles through heavy artillery fire. Often, these poor people were left dead or wounded with their loads on the steep mountain slopes.'

Chapter 4

19 January 1944 – The Battle for Tufo

5 Infantry Division Recce Intelligence Report

Enemy Situation

Taken completely by surprise all along the line the enemy has only been saved from complete destruction by the thick maze of mines (mostly wooden box) spread between the River Garigliano and the Minturno Ridge. The coastal belt may almost be described as a mine marsh through which the secure paths can now be traced with the aid of the original plans which we captured.

Up to this point the enemy does not seem to have recognised the weight of our attack on his left which has made good progress. With the loss of Tufo he became very conscious of his danger and counter attacked here with three tanks of which one was knocked out with a PIAT during the afternoon 18 Jan 44. All through the late morning and afternoon Minturno had been the scene of much enemy activity and a succession of counter attacks against Tufo appeared to have their source there. Accordingly, our artillery and air force were able to inflict heavy casualties on the enemy preparing for these attacks. The last counterattack from the North and East, on Tufo seems to have been carried out by 194 Field Reinforcement Battalion which consists of a mixed lot of men, as may be expected.

5 Infantry Division War Diary

On 17 Infantry Brigade front Monte d'Argento has been taken during the night by 2 Royal Scots Fusiliers but the mine situation in the Brigade area was still profoundly serious and badly hampering the build-up and push forward.

The plan of 15 Infantry Brigade was to advance through 2 Wiltshires positions with 1 KOYLI on the right and 1 Green Howards on the left, the latter directed on to Minturno itself. 1 York & Lancs. were in reserve and there was an extraordinarily strong artillery barrage moving from East to West, arranged in support from 0956 to 1130. This was to include all the guns of the Corps Artillery that could be brought to bear.

In outline 15 Infantry Brigade's plan for the day was as follows. Phase I: 1 KOYLI to clear Tufo by 1000. Phase II under cover of a barrage, 1 KOYLI right and 1 Green Howards left from a start line North and South through Tufo onto these objectives: for 1 KOYLI, Point 201, 799967, then the Cemetery exploiting to Point 156, 775967 [Monte Natale]. 1 Green Howards on an axis South of Tufo were directed on to Minturno town and then to Point 141, 781959 [Monte del Duca]. Phase III: 1 York & Lancs. pass through to capture Tremensuoli spur.

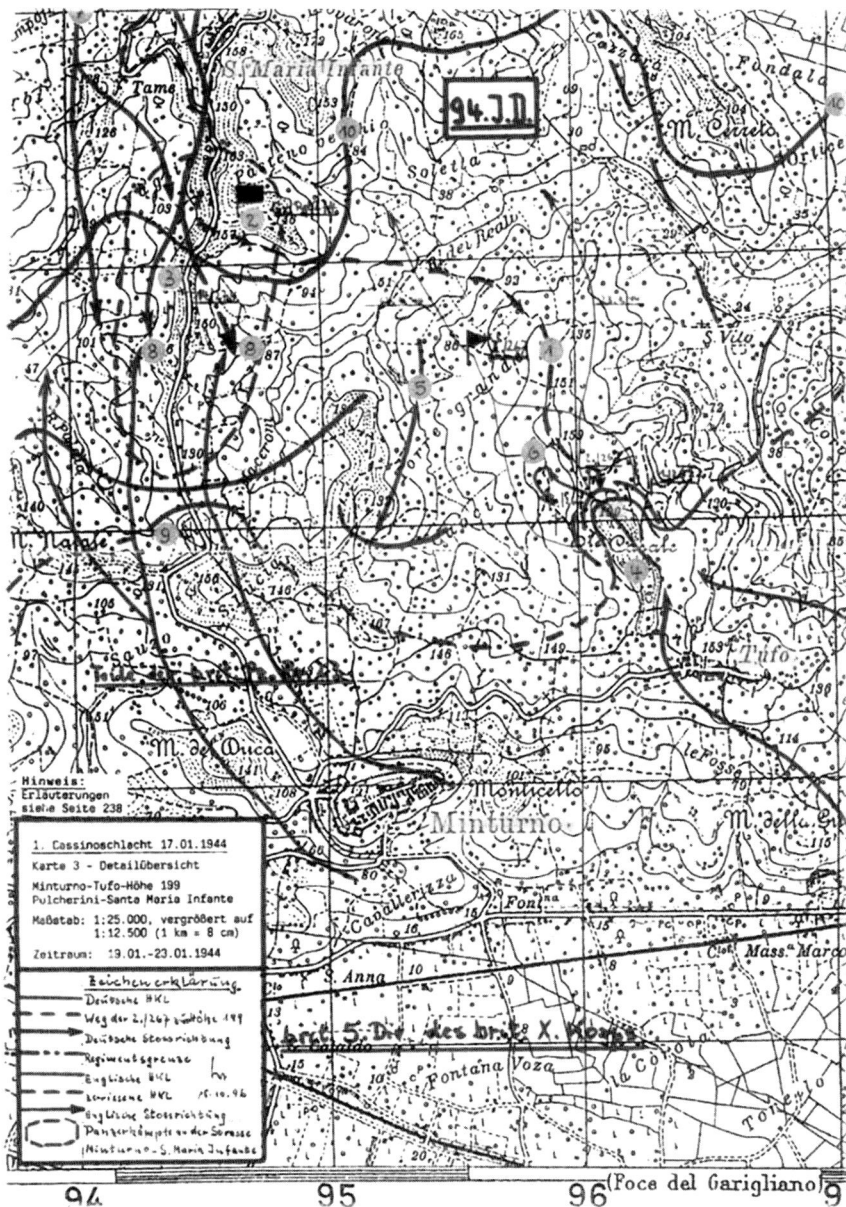

German Position 19-23 Jan 44 as the Germans saw it.

After fighting which lasted until last light, we were secure with a foothold on Point 141, Monte del Duca. The intention for 20 Jan 44 is to pass 1 York & Lancs. through Point 172 onto the Cemetery and onto Point 156.

50

Cemetery, Minturno Santa Maria Infante and Tufo. (Photo US National Archives)

Sir David Cole, 2 Inniskillings, *Rough Road To Rome*
19 Jan 44 – 0001
'We first became aware of the military build-up behind us about midnight when five of our own Bren Carriers, laden with ammunition, weapons, water, telephone cable, wireless batteries and other essentials suddenly came rattling up the track on our right. Unfortunately, the Germans hearing the commotion, threw across a bunch of shells that screeched down amongst our trenches, killing, or wounding several men and setting fire to one of 2 Cameronians carriers just behind.

Later, as we sat cold and tense in our trenches, watching the frosty dew settle not only on the grass but on ourselves and waiting for the inevitable to happen, we were suddenly startled by a symphony of crunches, rumbles, rattles, and squeaks on a really philharmonic scale. The first of our own tanks were arriving. They had been rafted across the river by the Sappers and were laagering just behind us.

The Brigadier of our Reserve Brigade. the 15th, emerged out of the night at Battalion HQ and settled down in a trench for a talk with the CO. It appeared that 15 Infantry Brigade instead of going through the remnants of 17 Infantry Brigade to attack Minturno frontally, were being ordered to move up through our-selves and 2 Wiltshires and attack it from the right. This plan would not materialise if, during the next few hours, "C" Company and the remains of "B" Company were driven off their lonely position on the ridge. "B" and "C" Companies were on the edge of the Minturno ridge East of Tufo. The night was turning into a cold and frosty morning.'

51

17 Infantry Brigade HQ War Diary
19 Jan 44 – 0001
2 Royal Scots Fusiliers report the capture of Monte Argente. Mine situation serious. 100 have been picked up on road leading to Route 7.

1 York & Lancs
In the early hours of 19 Jan 44, 1 York & Lancs. crossed the river by a bridge and boats, although there were only 6 boats available, most of the boats having been sunk.

After a stay in Isernia, 1 York & Lancs. had started to move in preparation for the crossing of the River Garigliano. On 15 Jan 44 they moved to Pizzone. On 17 Jan 44 – 1015 they moved by motor transport the 35 miles from Pizzone to Mondragone, a town on the coast about ten kilometres from Minturno, arriving there at 1200. At this point in time 1 York & Lancs. were a reserve Battalion for 17 Infantry Brigade so at 1700 they had to march to 17 Infantry Brigade's Harbour assembly area for the attack across the River Garigliano. After a three-hour march they arrived at their destination at approx. 2000. At 0600 on 18 Jan 44 they were pulled back a mile from the Assembly area and at 1200 marched the further two miles back to Mondragone. All of this was in full battle kit so would have been quite tiring. From Mondragone 1 York & Lancs. were taken back to Pizzone by motor transport arriving there at 1530.

Now back with 15 Infantry Brigade, 1 York & Lancs. moved off from Pizzone at 2000 and arrived at the debussing area at 2100 at 870912 [about 9km South-East of Minturno]. They marched to the crossing point for the river getting there at 2359.

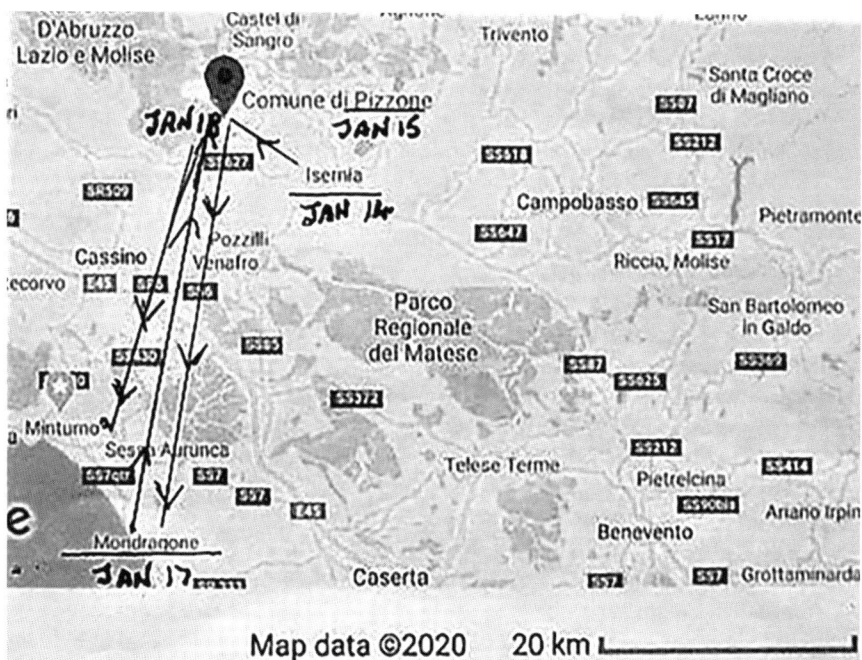

Route of 1 York & Lancs. 14–18 Jan 44. (Google)

At 0100 19 Jan 44 1 York & Lancs. were ready to cross the River Garigliano having marched approximately five kilometres from the debussing point. By 0615 the Battalion was at the assembly area just below the hill to Tufo having crossed the Lateral Road.

Ernest Shaw, 1 York & Lancs., Crossing the Garigliano
'When we got there we found the crossing was established. There was a terrific amount of firing going on, both directions. We were getting mortar bombs from the Germans dropping in the river and around the river. The big guns were firing just behind us. Their shells were coming over us. There were loads of tracer bullets, arcs of tracer fire going up and they lumped us on these ducks [DUKWs] to take us across the river and I didn't like the idea. I reckon it was about 80 yards wide there and it was raging winter water flowing down. I thought well if this gets a mortar bomb when we were in the middle we shan't have much chance as we carried about a hundred weight with your arms and ammunition and god knows what, but we got across.

It was such a raging torrent, winter storm water sort of thing, black, cold. I imagine it was cold anyway. I know I was very pleased to get ashore even though it was regarded as enemy territory. There were mortar bombs in and around the area without being accurate enough to cause us any casualties. Once ashore on the other side we weren't long before they led us walking in single file away from the river. Then it was quiet. They were shelling and mortaring the river area and we were in front of that underneath the fire. It was so dark you had your right hand stuck out in front of you in the centre of the man in front's back, otherwise you would bump into him. We were walking along this open road and 10 Platoon who were in front leading, Company HQ were second and then it was 12 and 11 Platoons at the rear.

We must have walked three quarters of a mile and suddenly the Germans put a load of parachute flares up over us. 10 Platoon and Company HQ were getting towards the lee of a hill. These flares were accompanied by mortars and 12 Platoon caught the shelling and the bombing behind us. We reached the lee of the hill. 12 Platoon took quite a number of casualties. There are about 30 men in a Platoon. I think they lost about 15, but they weren't all killed. 11 Platoon were behind them. They were in the clear.'

Frank de Planta, battlefield expert
'Throughout 18 Jan 44, 2 Royal Scots Fusiliers brought artillery down on Monte d'Argento and were ordered to attack on the morning of 19 Jan 44. Fortunately for them, a patrol sent out on the night of 18-19 Jan 44 found that Monte d'Argento [two miles South of Minturno], had been abandoned and, at 0100, "D" Company and a Platoon of MMG from "A" company 7 Cheshires, went forward to occupy the feature and 'B' Company moved up to a position between the feature and Route 7.'

Roger Chapman, *1 Green Howards History*
19 Jan 44 – 0100
'The Battalion advanced on foot to cross the river. 'The enemy had a very strong artillery barrage on the areas he knew we would be using as assembly areas and for us, laid hugging the wet ground, it was hair raising to hear the shriek of the shells coming over and to see the flickering flames of the explosions as they landed. The sound too of flying shrapnel whining in all directions and the soft thuds of great clods

River Garigliano. Royal Engineers in assault boats embark for the opposite bank to repair the last two sections of the pontoon bridge knocked out by enemy fire. 19 Jan 44. (Photo Capt. R.F. Gade. IWM TR 1523)

River Garigliano. A signalman repairs a line on a recently shelled pontoon bridge, 19 Jan 44. (Photo Capt. R.F. Gade, IWM TR 1530)

of earth thrown up, landing around us. I can remember thinking to myself that someone is bound to be hit in all this.

Soon the whistle to advance and we got to our feet and moved forward, trying to ignore the fact that our legs felt like jelly and beating down the almost overwhelming desire to fall flat at every shell sound heard. We did not notice that, although heavily laden with all kinds of kit, we covered the mile to the river at a steady sustained trot. At the river it was even worse. It was like Dante's Inferno. There was a layer of smoke covering the whole area. Jerry was plastering the whole scene with shell and mortar fire. On the river were masses of rubber boats and collapsible boats and even makeshift rafts, all ferrying men and stores across There were quite a few vehicles shattered and fiercely blazing and there was a strong smell of cordite. It seemed complete chaos and yet everyone knew what they were doing.'

Lieutenant D.H Deane, 2 Scots Guards writes
19 Jan 44 – 0100 Wednesday
'Shells started arriving every minute. No one had dug in owing to tired men, so we all had to shovel away, flopping down at odd moments from the bursts of heavy explosives.

In the morning, go up and recce our attack. I am Reserve Platoon and I feel nervous but in a funny way. Came across a lot of Grenadier water carriers crawling on their stomachs, with stuff flying everywhere, tracer, airbursts. Our attack was cancelled, as we had to form up in a mine field which seemed stupid enough. Came down and brought up 15 Platoon to a little knoll we are to hold. Everything is very noisy still and I am quite bewildered. The enemy seem to be all around. Behind are impregnable mountains obviously with armies of Boche.'

1 KOYLI War Diary
19 Jan 44 – 0200
No guides as promised by the higher staff and the assembly area had to be picked on the ground, with the result that 'B' Company walked straight into a minefield. One Platoon was practically wiped out with 20 casualties killed and wounded. The Company halted in the minefield and was extricated by Lieut. T. McCathie and two detachments of Pioneer Platoon using mine detectors. It took the remainder of the night to extract the men from the heavily mined area and by next morning 'B' Company was in a low state and was not really fit to go straight into a difficult attack. There was some shelling in this area at the time.

1 York & Lancs. War Diary
19 Jan 44
Battalion, less platoon, crossed bridge and moved into harbour area. They appeared to have no cover and to be under enemy fire from area Ceracoli and Tufo so Battalion moved under hillside. After mortar fire 'B' Company had moved forward to lee of hill 819961 [East of Tufo, just across the Lateral Road].

1 York & Lancs. A soldier in 'A' Company described the crossing as follows
'We crossed the River Garigliano in the early hours in rubber dinghies and could hear the artillery fire and as it became light, we came across some troops digging themselves in. The chap who was carrying our food rations for the Section deserted and it was late evening before we had anything to eat. They told us not to cross into this field as it was full of mines. However, we were told to keep going and after proceeding about 75 yards the mines started to go off and half the platoon were casualties. There were only about twelve of us who escaped, and we were incredibly lucky. We carried on advancing and prisoners were being taken and we saw enemy transport retreating. We went into a hut and a German was sitting on a chair looking quite normal except a bayonet was sticking into him and porridge was spilt on the floor. He must have been taken by surprise. We then climbed over a wall into another field, about eight of us, and in the corner was a German with his hands on a machine gun, pointing at us. Luckily for us and for him he lifted his hands in surrender.'

Ernest Shaw, 1 York & Lancs
'Gone up hill 150 yards and 10 Platoon was out in front and Captain Ramsay shouted for the runners, that was Ted and me. We went to him, and he said "I want you to go back to the [Lateral] road and one of you to stay there so that if anyone comes up the road they don't go past where we had turned off and the other one to go back

River Garigliano. Royal Engineers in assault boats embark for the opposite bank to repair the last two sections of the pontoon bridge knocked out by enemy fire, 19 Jan 44 (Photo Capt. R.F. Gade. 2 AFPU, TNA 10943)

Ernest Shaw's hill – Tufo to the right. (Photo John Strafford)

and chivvy them along, 11 and 12 Platoon. Major D. Webster was not here, he had gone to a battle conference (either at Battalion HQ or Brigade HQ, I believe it was Brigade HQ,). So, we had to go back. We get down to the [Lateral] road and Ted said he would stay there. I got the short straw. I had to go back along this section that had been mortared and I got to the same area and up go these parachute flares again. I flung myself down. It was a horrible feeling. I felt as though all the German ruddy army could see me – I lay there a while and gradually the light was dimming as they were going out and eventually I rolled over and there were two left, and one went out almost immediately, but the other bloody thing looked as though it was going to burn

56

forever. course, then I could not see, total blankness. I staggered along until eventually my eyes did clear enough to make my way, perhaps another couple of hundred yards and I was challenged in English, thank God. It was 11 Platoon – Lieutenant Corfield was the Platoon Commander and I told him he had roughly 600 yards to go, and he would find Private Rimmer waiting at the position to turn off. They went on and I continued going back to find out what I could of 12 Platoon, not knowing, to find out how many casualties there were. I got back to the Advance Dressing Station. There were a crowd of them. 8 were wounded and assisted them and carried them back. The Platoon Officer and senior NCO Sergeant had been wounded. There were a couple of Lance Corporals. I do not know whether there were any full Corporals. There were 8 or 9 guys, perhaps 10 or 11, a small group of them and they wondered what to do where to go and they fastened on to me. I led them back and took them back to the Captain and he took over. He told them where to go and said to me "you or Rimmer must stay here at the road-side, there may be stragglers, and the other one come with me to Company HQ and dig in and be available".

Well Ted had the entrenchment tool, and he was carrying it, so I went off down to tell him. I do not mind digging and I knew he did not mind digging. I thought I would go back and said, "You stop here" but he turned around "No" he says, "you take the bloody entrenchment tool". So, I took it from him, and we stood talking a minute or two and there were shells whistling over the top of us over our heads at the time. Our artillery was shelling the top of this hill probably a hundred to a hundred and fifty yards ahead of our chaps and it was a real barrage. You could hardly hear yourselves talk. I suppose our lads up front would be grovelling; it would be going over their heads.

A guy comes staggering up the road and Ted challenges him. At the time we had two American Sergeants attached to us, apparently they were supposed to be sorting out the British way of waging war. They had been attached to us a couple or three days at that stage, and Hiram arrives and after Ted's challenge Ted said "150 yards up the hill you will find the Captain". He goes to start up the hill and he goes twenty-five, thirty yards and there was the hell of an explosion. These shells were still flying overhead, and we thought it was what we called a "fall short". The older 25 pounder, if the barrel was worn, occasionally dropped one short. Ted and I thought it was a fall short. Ted shouted and swore at the artillery, said "Bloody swines". I shouted to Hiram and asked him if he was alright? "I'm OK buddy" he said in proper American style.

After a couple of minutes, I followed Hiram and we get back up to Company HQ and I get digging. I could not get down more than six inches of soil and you are down onto rock. I thought to hell with it, and I got my head down. I suppose I could have been charged for disobeying orders. I must have had a couple of hours sleep. When you are in the front line and you relax, you can drop off to sleep.'

Sir David Cole, 2 Inniskillings, *Rough Road To Rome*
19 Jan 44
'Very lights speckled the sky above "C" Company angrily ripped by tracer bullets. The crucial counterattack had begun.

Up on the ridge the moonlight, though interspersed by wood and scrub, had greatly improved the visibility, and in the shafts of silver light between the trees, the exhausted survivors of "B" Company, struggling to keep alert in their trenches, suddenly glimpsed large groups of Germans moving quietly towards them. In an instant the rustic moonlit ridge became an inferno.

Then the German infantry, abandoning any attempt to conceal their approach, came trampling forward through the trees and grass, shouting and firing.

The Germans were led by an officer of remarkable courage who, ahead of all his men, dashed straight down the track towards our trenches, firing his Schmeisser and shouting to his men to kill the "Schweinhunder Englander". Miraculously he escaped being riddled by the first of our Vickers machine guns, though he ran right past its muzzle. Yelling and cursing, he dashed on, shot one of the crew of the second Vickers and, seizing the gun, dragged it down the track in an effort to position it to fire back at our trenches. But by then another of the Vicker's crew had drawn his pistol and, all but placing the muzzle against the German officer's head, shot him dead. Most of the Germans were by now lying in the grass, only thirty yards away, firing their machine guns, throwing stick grenades and howling intimidatory abuse. 2 Inniskillings gave no ground.

Meanwhile our artillery barrage had started and hundreds of our shells were raining down on the ridge. The barrage not only killed and wounded many of the German's vanguard, as their anguished cries testified, but drove their follow up troops completely to ground.

After our artillery fire was stopped and, in the drifting smoke and dim light of the early dawn, 2 Inniskillings could see that the only Germans still in front of them were dead or wounded. The night was turning into a cold and frosty morning. The cold dawn rapidly blossomed into a beautiful day with a clear blue sky, a gentle sun and limpid visibility.'

Roger Chapman, *1 Green Howards History*
19 Jan 44 – 0400
'Now established in the positions from which to launch the attack on Minturno, some four miles ahead. Lieutenant- Colonel Patrick George Bulfin gave his orders to his Company Commanders: "C" Company [Major Radcliffe] to lead and capture the Southern part of the town, "A" Company [Major Gosden] to follow close behind and capture the North-East portion while "B" Company [Major A.R.M. Tanner] was to pass through and capture Point 141 [Monte del Duca]. "D" Company [Captain Parkinson] was to be held in reserve.

Zero hour, 1000.'

17 Infantry Brigade HQ War Diary
19 Jan 44 – 0400
6 Platoon 7 Cheshires remained in their position on the beach, then they moved to Monte Argente after its capture by 2 Royal Scots Fusiliers and consolidated.

X (BR) Corps History
19 Jan 44 – 0500
Before 15 Infantry Brigade started its attack, 2 Inniskillings [13 Infantry Brigade] were again counterattacked, but after hand-to-hand fighting, drove the enemy back and went on to capture Point 136, 805960, [East end of Tufo], which they had yielded the previous day.

1 KOYLI War Diary
19 Jan 44 – 0500
Battalion received orders to occupy Tufo.

1 York & Lancs. Ernest Shaw
19 Jan 44 – 0600
'I was woken by the sound of troops coming up the hill. It was just breaking dawn. We were supposed to be going over the top at dawn. It must have been put back. This turned out to be "C" Company and they were coming to join us for this attack. Their lead platoon was no more than twenty, twenty-five yards below me and suddenly there was a helluva explosion two, three, four, one after the other. They were in a mine field. I was so flabbergasted. I thought "They can't be". I had been up and down the ruddy hill 4-5 times. Their Sergeant-Major took charge and shouted and got them to stand still rather than running in panic in case they set more off. I twiddled my fingers. I had been up this hill across this mine field five times.

It was not long before the Royal Engineers came with mine detectors, and they swept a track to the road and taped it with white tapes. Eventually they got the wounded away and the dead laid out. I always remember seeing a legless torso, the arms had gone as well, up in a tree. This chap must have trod on the mine himself. There was a little stunted tree. He was dragged up there with his shirt wafting in the wind, terrible. I was talking to the R.E. Sergeant. I said to him "I was so flabbergasted with it all". He said, "Have you been hit, you are shaking". I said "I've not been hit. I do not know why I have not because I have been across it 5 times". "You can't have" he repeated. I said "The Company came up. My mate down on the road has been up it twice. I have been up and down four times and finished back up here". He asked me to point out where I had been. It was right through the ruddy middle, so I must have "fairy feet". He said, "Well you are the luckiest devil I have ever met".

They are Teller mines. These mines (anti-personnel) are wired together. A Teller mine is dinner plate size, probably an inch and a half thick full of high explosives and extremely sensitive. The anti-personnel mines are like a big tin of fruit more or less and they had prongs out, when they were activated they used to jump or leap three or four feet in the air before they exploded, and they were full of scrap and ball bearings as such – they could catch someone 30 to 40 yards away. In fact, Captain Ramsay got a piece of shrapnel from an anti-personnel mine in his ankle, and he was evacuated with the "C" Company casualties. I could not believe it. They were coming to look at me. The Sappers could not believe it. One said: "My mate hit one the other day and lost his foot." From then on, I started thinking about it. Hiram had set a bloody mine off. He should have known it was a mine. He must have trodden on a trip wire or activated one that was not right under him or else he would have gone up. He activated one that was not wired up. I missed walking on a mine.

Ted and I weren't entirely blameless because we immediately decided it was a "fall short" and yet when you hear a shell landing beside you or within twenty or thirty yards there is a helluva high pitched scream and this was just a dull crump, so really we ought to have known and should have suspected it was a mine as well as the American chap. 10 Platoon and Company HQ had gone through it and Ted, and I had come back through it. I had been up and down through it several times. I suggested to the Sergeant the advance of the Company skirted it and that is when he said, "Well can you show me the route?" By then it was light enough to see Ted down at the bottom and I said, "Well my mate is down there, and I have been between here and him six times." The Company itself really got away with it. Felt rattled in my head almost like a bag of peas rattling. I was angry after it at Hiram, and even Ted and myself. I felt it was our fault to an extent that these lads had been killed and yet all the time Ted and I were together down there the shells were roaring overhead. We had got a good excuse. I never saw Hiram again that day to talk about it and I never brought the subject up with him later.'

1 York & Lancs. War Diary
19 Jan 44 – 0615
Move completed just as it was getting light. 4 killed, 6 wounded by mines in orchards. Captain Hewitt (Officer Commanding 'C' Company) and Captain Ramsay (Second in Command 'B' Company) wounded from shelling of road during move of Battalion.

252 Field Company Royal Engineers War Diary
19 Jan 44 – 0630
Lt. Talbot and one Section clearing minefield near road at map reference 811955 (600m East of Point 102). Unable to finish owing to enemy interference. Sappers Ellender and Traxler killed in action. Sapper Bacon admitted to hospital wounded. Sappers Noad and Fleming wounded but remained on duty.

2 Cameronians War Diary
19 Jan 44 – 0630
'D' Company carrier was blown up when over several wooden mines and the crew of two were killed.

19 Jan 44 – 0700
'C' and 'D' Companies were put at one hours-notice to move forward.

2 Wiltshires War Diary
19 Jan 44 – 0700
'D' and 'B' Companies dug in East and West of Tufo. A noisy night.

164 Field Ambulance War Diary
19 Jan 44 – 0730
Message from C.O. 2 Wiltshires via staff Captain that across the river were over 150 wounded awaiting evacuation and that there was urgent need of stretchers and blankets.
    All available ambulance cars were sent up to the bridge.

2 Scots Guards War Diary
19 Jan 44 – 0730
Once again, the Battalion has spent the day in a state of readiness and waiting with their troop-carrying lorries, for the order to move. However, the River Garigliano bridges were not ready, so there was a further delay of twenty-four hours.

The Hill to Tufo. (Photo John Strafford)

2 Northants War Diary
19 Jan 44 – 0750
Battalion mopping up operations. Some enemy equipment was captured, one 2-inch Mortar, six rifles, one automatic rifle, also some of 6 Seaforths equipment.

164 Field Ambulance War Diary
19 Jan 44 – 0800
The Advance Dressing Station Commander informed Capt. Guest that in the quarry south of Tufo there were over 100 cases, approximately half of them lying cases under the care of Capt. Miller and A Company.

Evacuation being impossible over the bridge owing to mines and shell fire. He decided to use the ferry at 847937.

19 Jan 44 – 0830
First cases arrived for evacuation in two captured German Ambulance cars.

6 Seaforths War Diary
19 Jan 44 – 0900
Collection of wounded and dead continued and the final concrete information regarding 'D' Company was obtained one man having reported seeing many of the Company being taken prisoner by the enemy.

1 KOYLI War Diary
19 Jan 44 – 0900
At first light 'D' Company set off to clear the village of Tufo but owing to the unexpected difficulty of the ascent did not reach the village until 0900 hours, which they had been instructed to leave again at 0930 hours owing to the start line of the barrage running through the village. On the outskirts of the village, we contacted the depleted Battalion of 2 Wiltshires [13 Infantry Brigade].

61

19 Jan 44 – 0930

The barrage duly started far too close to our selected start line to be pleasant. Whether the gunners knew exactly where we were or not, I don't know, but all we knew was the line on which the barrage was to start –a grid line on a map – and the time it started.

So, after a long tiring night and early start and a scramble up a steep hillside, the Battalion was just – but only just, ready to attack Point 201 by 1000 hours as the barrage moved forward. The plan was simple, it had to be, time did not allow for anything else. 'C' Company was to go into the village previously reported clear by 'D' Company and swing right-handed across the ridge to Point 201. 'A' Company was to leave the village of Tufo from the back or East end and on to Point 201 on the right, keeping the ridge between themselves and 'C' Company. 'D' Company was then to re-enter the village and hold the forward edge leaving a somewhat depleted 'B' Company in reserve with Battalion Head Quarters in the rear of the village. 'C' Company found some unexpected enemy machine gun posts in the village which had to be cleared up before attacking Point 201. This was done successfully. This was preceded by a Corps artillery barrage and the attack put in with 'C' Company on the left and 'D' Company on the right.

15 Infantry Brigade War Diary
19 Jan 44 – 0930
1 KOYLI having passed through 2 Wiltshires of 13 Infantry Brigade, succeeded in clearing the Eastern half of Tufo collecting two Prisoners of War.

91 Field Regiment Royal Artillery War Diary
19 Jan 44 – 0933
Regiment puts supporting fire on Point 201 prior to attack.

Sgt. Raymond Hawtree Hitchcock, 'A' Company 164 Field Ambulance
19 Jan 44 – 1000
'We had at least 100 casualties, all treated and bedded down, but we were requiring more stretchers, blankets, and medical equipment generally.

At this stage I decided to ask drivers in my Section if they would drive the German Ambulance with the wounded to try and evacuate them across the river. Pvt. Jack Halpin said that he would do so if I agreed to go as well. I intended to do so anyhow. In fact, I drove the Ambulance on its first trip to the river, through the enemy lines under shot and shell from both sides it seemed.

With my full load, we found our way to the river and by that time the Royal Engineers had rigged a pontoon to ferry transport across the Garigliano. What a relief.'

164 Field Ambulance, Citation: Military Medal for Sgt. Raymond Hawtree Hitchcock
During the attack by 13 Infantry Brigade on Tufo, Sgt. Hitchcock was the senior N.C.O. in his Section of the Field Ambulance attached to 2 Wiltshires and was working in his Collection Post at the Quarry 809953. On the morning of 19 Jan 44 it became obvious that the evacuation of casualties was in a critical state since it was not possible to bring Ambulance cars across the river in daylight, the road from the ferry being under accurate and observed shell and mortar fire.

Sgt. Hitchcock with Pvt. Halpin volunteered to attempt the evacuation of the more severely wounded in a captured Ambulance car and at 1000 succeeded in driving the Ambulance car to the ferry point under heavy fire. He then returned and repeated this journey despite the extremely exposed and dangerous position.

By his cool determination, his complete disregard for his personal safety and his devotion to duty, he was instrumental in saving many lives, which otherwise would have been lost, and in restoring his position with regard to evacuation.

1 Green Howards War Diary
19 Jan 44 – 1000
Advance begins.

1 KOYLI War Diary
19 Jan 44 – 1000
Our initial task was to clear the village of Tufo, standing high on a ridge above the assembly area and then to push on to Point 201 to the North of Tufo. A large barrage of all the Corps Artillery plus a Medium Regiment had been laid on to support the attack. Unfortunately, this barrage had been decided upon before the infantry plan had been fixed and it did not in fact quite fit the ground as seen from the ground and not from a map. The attack as it was put in had the barrage on the left flank to start with, gradually moving away as the attack progressed. Not only this but the attack had to go in at 1000 hours to fit the barrage which did not in fact give the Battalion enough time for preparation, recce and forming up. Whilst directing the barrage Captain K. Ashdown, 92 Field Regiment Royal Artillery, who was the Forward Observation Officer was hit by one of his own shells and subsequently died of his wounds.

15 Infantry Brigade War Diary
19 Jan 44 – 1000
Both Battalions, 1 KOYLI right and 1 Green Howards left, then advanced behind the barrage onto their respective objectives. 1 KOYLI secured Point 201 without much difficulty capturing six prisoners of war, many enemies being seen to retire towards the North. Two companies were immediately put in to hold the 201 feature, the remainder of the Battalion being concentrated in and around Tufo itself. Simultaneously 1 Green Howards advance moved well towards Minturno.

Private Wilhelm Prinz, 274 Grenadier Regiment: *My worst days in World War II. Have there been failures?*
'Height 199 at Tufo [Point 201].

My Company was waiting for me. My first question to the Company Commander was "Have there been casualties?". Despite the heavy artillery bombardment, we had no wounded and no dead. How much longer should we be lucky? I informed the Platoon Commander about our combat mission – for better security I did not tell everyone. A messenger from Lieutenant Gieseler had informed me, how to get us into the right position. After 200 metres we were to take the road that goes to Minturno, veering to the left and drop into a deep valley. South East was our direction of travel. After crossing the valley, as Lt, Gieseler had described it, we would reach the North slope of Point 201.

Point 201 and Tufo from the plain. (Photo John Strafford)

We went into combat with the units at almost full target strength at the beginning of this First Cassino battle. I guess each unit had about 130-135 men, divided into 3 Grenadier Platoons.

Powerful explosions tore me away from my thoughts. The first ones wounded, shouted for the medical orderly. I did not want to take my men into this danger zone. I soon discovered that there were danger zones everywhere. There were no oases of relative safety.'

X (BR) Corps History
19 Jan 44 – 1030
The first bridge across the River Garigliano two miles above Route 7 at 13 Infantry Brigade crossing was completed at 0200 on 19 Jan 44, but the first vehicle across exploded a deeply buried mine under the far ramp and temporarily blocked the bridge. The bridge was repaired and reopened just before daylight, but the rate at which vehicles could use it was severely limited by the bad approaches and by extensive mine fields on both sides of the river, then at 1030 the bridge was hit by shell fire and had to be closed once more. Despite these difficulties, 15 Infantry Brigade crossed the river and early on 19 Jan 44 concentrated behind 13 Infantry Brigade ready to attack through it towards Minturno

5 Division History
19 Jan 44 – 1030
The crossing and advance through 2 Wiltshire's positions went without incident and 1 Green Howards reported that the forward elements of 'C' Company (Major Radcliffe) were entering Minturno against only moderate opposition and that their casualties had been slight. 'A' Company (Major Gosden) followed close behind and took over the

64

North-East corner of the town, 'B' Company bringing up the rear. At the same time 1 KOYLI had reached Point 201, their objective, and were in the process of completing a 'job of mopping up'.

The advance continued slowly with 1 Green Howards moving towards Point 141 [Monte del Duca] and 1 KOYLI reporting: Tufo clear after fighting, small counterattack now beaten off, few casualties. Damage to enemy not yet known. Both Battalions were helped or hindered by a heavy mist over the whole front, caused partly by the warmth of the sun over the river, and partly by the haze of cordite from the intensive shell fire of the past few hours. That the latter was effective was confirmed by both Battalions who reported 'quite a number of enemy dead after barrage'.

1 Green Howards War Diary
19 Jan 44 – 1050
Leading elements of 'C' Company entering town [Minturno] followed shortly by 'A' Company. 'B' Company passed through to Point 141. Meet opposition, eventually getting one Platoon onto the feature. Remainder of Company held up by machine gun and mortar fire. Battalion HQ and 'D' Company to area 789960 [just North of Minturno] 'A' Company sent Platoon to assist Platoon of 'D' Company on Point 141 and get established.

15 Infantry Brigade
1 Green Howards forward troops were on the outskirts of Minturno town encountering only slight opposition and taking 11 Prisoners of War. Their own casualties had been light.

Sir David Cole, 2 Inniskillings, *Rough Road To Rome*
19 Jan 44 – 1100
'After half an hour's shell fire from our guns "D" Company dashed off along the ridge towards the Germans. This was a route that had already been used twice for attack and counterattack and it was, in a way strange that the Germans were taken by surprise, but they were. "D" Company overran many of the German defences and took a number of prisoners without a shot being fired. There was some bitter fighting along the crest of the ridge where the enemy blazed away with their machine guns, before jumping out of their trenches and trying to escape through the trees, a gamble against our Brens in which some of them were lucky and others not.' Several "B" Company men, who had been captured or isolated during the enemy attack the previous night found their way back to our lines. In particular a man who had been wounded on the track between the two forward companies and had lain there all night was brought in by the stretcher bearers. He described how the German officer with the Iron Cross who had led the counterattack against "C" Company had, on the way, stopped beside him and spoken to him in perfect English. He had told him not to worry and that, when the attack was over, he would arrange personally for him to be carried to safety.'

2 Royal Inniskillings Fusiliers Citation: Military Medal for Lance Corporal Harry Langford Bell
19 Jan 44
'D' Company, 2 Royal Inniskilling Fusiliers was ordered to recapture 809966 [East end of Minturno-Tufo ridge]. L/Cpl Bell was commanding a Section in 'D' Company.

Private J. Blundell and Gunner J.R. Howarth in their slit trench at a Regimental Aid Post, 19 Jan 44. (Photo Capt. R.F. Gade, IWM TR 1528)

During the attack his Platoon was held up by a German machine gun post to their right flank. L/Cpl. Bell at once dashed forward, though his rifle was hit by a burst of fire from the machine gun, he killed two of the crew with a grenade and took three others prisoner.

But for the immediate bravery of L/Cpl. Bell his Platoon would have lost the benefit of the artillery fire, and other German posts which were captured would have been allowed time to come to life and defeat the attack.

Ernest Shaw, 1 York & Lancs.
19 Jan 44 – 1100
'We were in the lee of this hill. Half-way up this hill. We stayed there until 10.30am to 11am (late morning 19 January) when advance was put on again. In the meantime, the Major re-joined us, but we had lost Captain Ramsay of course.'

6 Seaforths War Diary
19 Jan 44 – 1100
Battalion informed by Brigade HQ that 12 Platoon 'B' Company had been landed at Naples. Their craft had caught fire, but personnel had been picked up by a destroyer and conveyed to Naples. They were now on their way to join the Battalion.

158 Field Ambulance
19 Jan 44 – 1200
Two Ambulance cars crossed River Garigliano about mid-day. Great delay owing to pontoon bridges breaking down. Commanding Officer went up to Advanced Dressing Station. Contacted 201 Guards Brigade regarding requirement of Stretcher Bearers. News received of deaths in minefield of Privates Dando, Ward, West, and wounding of Private Johnson. Officer Commanding 'A' Company sustained a traumatic amputation of foot during the crossing of the River Garigliano.

17 Infantry Brigade HQ War Diary
19 Jan 44 – 1200
2 Northants report pay books of eight 6 Seaforths found in house 804928.

2 Northants War Diary
19 Jan 44 – 1245
'A' Company established Platoon at Route 7 over river and standing patrol at railway bridge 300 yards North of road bridge. Commanding Officer ordered contact patrol West along Route 7 to meet 6 Seaforths.

Contact patrol for 6 Seaforths out for one hour. Made no contact. Enemy equipment found at Road Bridge 807934 [1,500m South of Lateral Road]. Some six Seaforth bodies lying in area. 'A' Company now in position at road crossing and railway crossing.

X (BR) Corps History
19 Jan 44 – 1300
1 Kings Own Yorkshire Light Infantry in the lead recaptured Tufo village and took Colle Casale, Point 201. A small hill overlooking the village to the North-West of Minturno.

1 KOYLI War Diary
19 Jan 44 – 1300
Two Companies were established on their objectives having suffered themselves few casualties and taking 3 prisoners and probably inflicting many casualties on the enemy. After a stiff little battle Point 201 was ours and a Forward Observation Post established

1 KOYLI 'A' & 'C' Cos. on Point 201. 'B' Co. and HQ in Tufo. All 1 York & Lancs. Cos. in Tufo. 1 Green Howards 'A' and 'B' Cos. at Point 141 Monte Del Duca. 'C' and 'D' Cos. and HQ in Minturno. The main road going to the right is the Lateral Road which links up with Castelforte in the East.

on it. Shortly after Point 201 was occupied, a sharp, but not very heavy counterattack was put in from the East of the village of Tufo and was directed mainly against 'B' Company and Battalion Headquarters. An interesting point of this counterattack was that the enemy artillery support was given from guns due West of Tufo whilst the attack came in from the East. During this attack several men were killed in Battalion HQ. and it was decided to move immediately. Battalion HQ accordingly moved nearer the village in the hope of getting out of enemy shelling. These hopes were not successful as the Battalion HQ was shelled heavily during their stay in this area.

No heavy counterattack was put in by the enemy against the Battalion HQ in this new area, although on more than one occasion small groups of enemy which were forming up on the Northern slopes of Point 201 were broken up by artillery fire and small arms fire. The night was uneventful – local activity only between patrols.

Accordingly, by the night 19-20 January the Battalion was firmly established on the Tufo – Point 201 ridge. No rations or supplies of any kind could reach us and by that night we had been 24 hours on one haversack ration and had only what we carried with us for the night.

13 Infantry Brigade
19 Jan 44 – 1324
2 Inniskillings re-occupied far end of ridge east of Tufo.

Royal Inniskillings Fusiliers Regimental Museum
By the afternoon, the assault phase of the battle was over for 2 Royal Inniskilling Fusiliers. During a forward patrol, Lance Corporal John Doherty's gallantry was awarded the Military Medal. The Battalion had been in almost 40 hours of continuous combat. For two further arduous weeks, before being relieved, the Battalion, much depleted in officers and men, clung to the positions it had gained.

This was the Battalion's most bloody single battle of the war. 53 killed and hundreds wounded.

2 Royal Inniskillings Fusiliers Citation: Military Medal for Lance Corporal John James Doherty
19 Jan 44
Lance Corporal John James Doherty's Platoon was under command of 'C' Coy. 2 Royal Inniskilling Fusiliers and was holding the area 814964 [500m downhill East of the end of the Minturno-Tufo ridge].

The Germans discovered a covered line of approach on the flank of L/Cpl. Doherty's Section from the cover of a terraced wall. On no less than three occasions L/Cpl. Doherty left his trench and went forward with his Bren gun to this wall. L/Cpl. Doherty succeeded each time in driving the enemy back, though in order to engage them he had to stand fully exposed on the top of the wall. The outstanding courage and skill displayed by this NCO was responsible for maintaining his Section in position and defeating the German attack.

2 Royal Inniskillings Fusiliers Citation: Bar to Distinguished Service Order for Lieut. Col. J.P. O'Brien-Twohig
'On the night of 17-18 Jan 44, the 2nd Battalion, The Royal Inniskilling Fusiliers, commanded by Lieutenant-Colonel J. P. O'Brien-Twohig, were ordered to force a

crossing of the River Garigliano and to capture the East end of the Minturno ridge. The operation involved crossing the river in assault boats, traversing a broad expanse of plain held by German machine-gun posts and finally taking the ridge itself, which was very steep and woody, protected by deeply dug entrenchments and covered by extensive minefields.

When the first company of the Inniskillings was crossing the river an unlucky burst of shellfire holed all the boats except one, which later sank, and caused numerous casualties. Almost at the same time another salvo fell in the Battalion Assembly Area, while a third destroyed the reserve boats. Undismayed by these set-backs Lieutenant-Colonel O'Brien-Twohig led his Battalion to another crossing a mile lower down the river, getting them across in the boats of another Battalion and having his two leading Companies on the start line in time to advance behind the barrage. In spite of heavy casualties, the Inniskillings stormed the ridge and captured their objectives. A counterattack drove them off one of them, but Lieutenant-Colonel O'Brien-Twohig personally re-organised them on the remaining high ground which he held firmly until he was able to organise a further attack which finally routed the enemy.

Throughout this long and difficult action Lieutenant-Colonel O'Brien-Twohig gave an inspiring example of gallantry and leadership. With complete disregard of danger, he personally organised and encouraged his men and produced a complete recovery from a succession of setbacks which might well have proved fatal to the success of the operation.

During the advance, a shell fell beside him, killing two officers and four signallers. Although painfully wounded and considerably shaken, he refused all offers of assistance and evacuation and insisted on continuing to command and lead his men.

The successful completion of the task was very largely due to his personal example and encouragement, and he gave an outstanding example of courage and leadership at a time when such qualities were most urgently required.'

2 Northants War Diary
19 Jan 44 – 1325
Ten 6 Seaforths wounded in 'A' Company area were brought in by stretcher bearers to Regional Aid Post. One of the wounded had interesting information which could not be passed by wireless.

17 Infantry Brigade HQ War Diary
19 Jan 44 – 1349
2 Northants report enemy equipment and 6 Seaforth bodies found at 807934.

15 Infantry Brigade
19 Jan 44 – 1400
1 Green Howards reported Minturno clear and their forward Company in contact with the enemy on Point 141. Total prisoners of war were at least 36. During afternoon Brigadier J.Y. Whitfield (Commander 15 Infantry Brigade), and Lieutenant Colonel Kirwan, (Officer Commanding 92 Field Regiment) made a Fire Plan to launch 1 York & Lancs. onto (a) Point 172 (b) Cemetery (c) Point 156 (Monte Natale), whilst 1 Green Howards were to attack and hold Tremensuoli ridge. 1 KOYLI meantime remained secure on Point 201.

[A Fire Plan sets out the plan for the artillery, showing the times of fire, objectives, and length in time the bombardment will last, together with the calibre of rounds used. With a rolling bombardment this is essential.]

Roger Chapman, *1 Green Howards History*
'All went according to plan, except capturing Point 141, which was vital to the consolidation of the main position covering the town. "B" Company ran into strong opposition. The leading Platoon Commander was killed, and the Platoon faltered, Captain E.S. Roberts, the second in command, ran forward and took over.'

1 Green Howards Citation: Military Cross for Capt. E.S. Roberts
On 19 Jan 44 1 Battalion Green Howards were ordered to capture Minturno (787956). Captain Roberts was Second in Command of 'B' Company whose objective was Point 141, Monte del Duca, 785957, which was vital to the consolidation of the main position. The leading Platoon came under heavy fire, and it appeared the objective would not be taken. Captain Roberts immediately took command of the Platoon and by his own energy and example he urged the Platoon across about 350 yards of open ground, under heavy machine gun and mortar fire, finally reaching the objective with 14 men.

For four hours Captain Roberts held this position under continuous fire, driving off two enemy attacks, until reinforced under cover of darkness. His initiative, determination and outstanding courage were directly responsible for the success of the operation and were an inspiration to his men.

1 Green Howards Citation: Military Medal for Lance Sergeant J.R. Maddox
Throughout the attack and capture of Minturno on 19 Jan 44, L/Sgt Maddox showed outstanding courage and initiative. Early in the advance the leading Company came under accurate machine gun fire from the flank. L/Sgt. Maddox, realising that any delay would deprive the Company of the vital close support of the barrage, immediately detached his Section and with great dash and utter fearlessness led it into the assault. In this action L/Sgt. Maddox personally accounted for two machine gun posts, killing or wounding twelve enemy with grenades and TSMG (Tactical Support Machine Gun).

Later in the same operation his Platoon came under heavy and accurate machine gun fire. L/Sgt. Maddox was wounded in the leg, his Platoon Commander was killed, and the remainder of the Platoon were pinned to the ground. Despite his wound, L/Sgt. Maddox immediately took over his Section Light Machine Gun and by his accurate fire enabled the remainder of his Platoon to extricate themselves in the daylight, subsequently bringing his own Section out about two hours later in the dusk. His courage, leadership and fearlessness were of the highest order and had a marked effect on all who saw him.

1 York & Lancs. War Diary
19 Jan 44 – 1500
Officers went to Tufo to see ground for tomorrow's operation. No adequate viewpoint of even the first objective. Battalion spent uneventful day in slit trenches in a concentrated area South-East of Tufo. The weather was fine and warm during the day, but dry and cold at night. No hot meal, blankets and greatcoats left South of the river.

HQ 17 Infantry Brigade War Diary
19 Jan 44 – 1710
2 Northants patrol contacted 1 York & Lancs. at 810953 [just South of Tufo].

2 Scots Guards War Diary
19 Jan 44
The Commanding Officer crossed the river to join the Brigadier of 15 Infantry Brigade at Minturno, with the intention of doing a recce at last light, but this proved impossible, because the town had not been cleared of the enemy. The Commanding Officers spent the night at TAC Brigade HQ, which was installed in a quarry, about a mile back from Minturno.

1 Green Howards War Diary
19 Jan 44 – 1800
Situation: 'C' Company 790956 [600m North-East of Point 141, Monte del Duca], 'D' Company 789960 [just North of Minturno]. Two Platoons 'A' Company and one Platoon 'B' Company on Point 141. Remaining Platoon of 'A' Company on North edge of town. Two Platoons 'B' Company at Battalion HQ as mobile reserve. Approx. 40 – 50 Prisoners of War taken.

15 Infantry Brigade War Diary
19 Jan 44 – 1900
Lt. Col. Kirwan returned to Main Brigade and gave the timings on the operations for 20 Jan 44 which were: 0700; 1 York & Lancs. to attack their three objectives in turn supported by a barrage. 1100; 1 Green Howards from West end of Point 141 to go for the Tremensuoli ridge. This operation would also be supported by a barrage.

7 Cheshires War Diary
19 Jan 44 – 2000
Adjutant went up to contact 'B' Company's rear HQ. and saw Company Second in Command, little news from forward HQ but understood that there were approximately twenty-three casualties.

1 Green Howards War Diary
19 Jan 44 – 2100
Patrol under Sergeant Coleflax leave for Point 172 to check if occupied or not.

19 Jan 44 – 2250
Patrol returned. Intermittent shelling and mortar fire during night

19 Jan 44, German view of the day: Private Wilhelm Prinz, 274 Grenadier Regiment
19 Jan 44
'Wednesday – The British continued their offensive with their main effort on Minturno-Tufo, after which the whole sector became foggy with phosphorus smoke grenades. 274 Grenadier Regiment had an entire anti-tank Platoon for Minturno in position: several light Italian anti-tank guns, 47 mm calibre, served as flank protection.

During a lull in the barrage, I went with the Technical Sergeant Hemm to have a look at a captured gun and to consider its operational readiness. Thank goodness, there had been no losses so far. Once again there was shelling, which forced us to move double quick in the direction of the Company Command post. Almost simultaneously, we met our Company Officer, Lieutenant Kensy, without his motorbike, again. He had gone late on foot to Minturno and in the direction of the anti-tank Platoon to get an overview of the battle situation. His driver, Private Vache, had arranged to wait for him. As Lt. Kensy started on the way back towards our artillery, machine guns fired on him from the English attackers, who had gone around behind our anti-tank platoon. He could only avoid impending capture through a rapid escape. He had been taken by surprise.

Totally by surprise, a runner arrived from a trapped anti-tank Platoon with a cry for help. It was Private Pielok, a slender youngster, who with his child's face did not look like a nineteen-year-old. With much skill he had previously escaped encirclement and been awarded a distinguished honour [Iron Cross Second Class]. He had escaped from being a prisoner of war.

Now Private Pielok went rather dramatically along the Santa Maria Infante – Minturno road, on the route to the Regimental HQ. I came to the dugout shelter of the Command Post. At this entrance a comrade lay, just fallen. It was Private Gerhard Glausch, from the Signal Platoon of 274 Grenadier Regiment who straight after going to the telephone maintenance man, a shell exploded nearby. In my time in the Battalion as a runner I came to know comrade Glausch as a signalman. He ate quietly at the time and was very easy going, His messmate Bernard Pytel reported that among others things Glausch often did not have any rations in his bread bag, though the books written by the poet Friedrich Holderlin were always at hand. His early death shook all who knew him. However there was no time for long and profound contemplation, the action demanded our total attention.

Meanwhile Minturno, despite all our efforts was just hardly held. At one point our energetic Commander, Lieutenant Colonel Reich, carbine rifle in hand, gathered every soldier along the track and with this small group led a counterattack on the enemy occupied high ground by Tufo town.

Tufo and Minturno involved heavy losses in fighting over the course of 19 Jan 44 and were finally lost. The material and personnel superiority of the attackers was simply too much. The English succeeded in advancing as far as the Parish Cemetery of Minturno, so that even our Regimental Cemetery lying opposite became inaccessible. The support, one armoured unit, with some Panzer IV tanks intervened and contributed significantly to the stabilisation of the position. We, part of 274 Grenadier Regiment, were a complete anti-tank Platoon, with all enlisted personnel, three artillery guns, vehicles etc. We had 14 casualties. We could never make up the losses. We were standing in front of our dugout, when a fighter bomber dropped its bomb on us, and it went off. With a quick reaction we leapt into the dugout and were under the structural supports when a heavy blast made the earth shake. Suddenly we saw daylight, the shaking made the wall on the side of the valley hill subside and that made our shelter tumbledown and become unusable. Then we half spilled out. Once freed we saw the mess: the fighter bomber attack had aimed for the stationery Panzer IV tank in our proximity, however it remained undamaged. Instead, the heavy bomb had made a large crater, half a street and half of our houses. Even so, we remained uninjured.'

5 Infantry Division History

By the end of 19 January, the Minturno-Tufo ridge was secure against anything but the most formidable counterattack from a reinforced enemy. The casualties sustained by the Division in getting so far were however, by no means light, and even with the assistance of 201 Guards Brigade, as yet uncommitted, there appeared to be little possibility of achieving the planned exploitation up the Ausente valley. By dusk, 15 Infantry Brigade had not met all its original objectives but did have a foothold on Point 141. The intention for 20 Jan 44 was to pass 1 York & Lancs. through 1 KOYLI to Point 172 to the Cemetery and to Point 156. The night of 19 January was spent in planning and preparing for the further attack by 15 Infantry Brigade on the following day, and in active patrolling to gain information for that attack.

Major General P.G.S. Gregson Ellis OBE and his Aide-de-Camp, Lieutenant Sir Peter Wills Bt. Grenadier Guards arrived at 5 Division. He is to take over Command of the Division.

D. Woolard, attached to 2 Wiltshires, *My Day, 19 January*

'Very little out of the ordinary happened. Just the usual intermittent shelling, mortaring, and a little small arms fire from time to time. That night we decided to sleep in an old out house. Enemy shells came over for a while in the evening, but by stand down it was quieter. As soon as the first two lads were on guard, we flung our gas capes and greatcoats, which came up that day, onto the floor which was littered with dry maize straw and tried to sleep. Some of the lads were soon asleep as I could hear their heavy breathing and most unmelodious snoring, but as tired as I was, I could not sleep. I felt itchy and thought the straw was lousy with fleas. I lit several matches to see if I could see anything and smoked no end of fags. I caught and killed dozens of the little blighters, but I found out later they were not fleas or bugs but were a kind of maize weevil, which did not bite and were quite harmless. I was extremely glad to get on guard that night, the shelling had almost ceased, when I went out, but our own Royal Artillery were still sending a few shells over on enemy targets. When I finished my turn on guard I went in and lay down again and pulled the greatcoat over my head and fell fast asleep.'

1 York & Lancs. Missing Person's Report by Corporal Waddington

'On 19 January 1944 during the action at Minturno my Platoon had reached their objective about 600 yards North-East of Minturno. I saw Private Stanley Holland wounded, about half an hour later whilst laying in the open he was fired on by a German Machine Gun and killed. During the afternoon of the same day, I personally assisted to remove Private Holland's body to the rear of my Platoon's position. I cannot say where he was buried but it would be in the area occupied by my Company on that date.'

German views of the day: Lt. Wolfras Gieseler, III Battalion 274 Grenadier Regiment

19 Jan 44

'Private Glausch is killed on the morning of 19 Jan 44 right next to the bunker, when he has just stepped outside the door. He had already witnessed the fighting in Stalingrad. He wanted to become a journalist when he was only 21 years old. As a last legacy he left us with an evocative account about his "experiences and thoughts in France and Italy". The death of Glausch shakes us who must hold out in the bunker very much.

The third morning of the attack arrives after more strong shellfire in the night, our small bunker crew sits in foxholes on the small hill just ahead of us, waiting for the Allies early attack. The machine gun operated by Sergeant Selle is ancient. Lt. Colonel Reich and the rest of us have our rifles at the ready. Artillery fire is silent at dawn. And then they come slowly towards us at a distance of about 200 metres in several rows of gunners, about 40 men each in a row. It looks as if large caterpillars or the legendary worms are moving through the rubble. The effect of our suddenly starting defensive fire is astonishing. The English throw themselves to the ground and crawl back quickly, leaving dead and wounded behind. It is probably assumed that our height is occupied by stronger German forces. In any case, the attack has been defeated and will not be repeated this day or in the following days, despite further heavy artillery fire.'

Lt. Wolfgang Wiedemann, II Battalion, 267 Panzer Grenadier Regiment

'At noon I received the order to gather the Company together. A convoy of trucks was to pick us up around 3 p.m. There was no relief and the coastal section remained without security. We informed the groups which had the longest way to go to get to us as soon as possible. There were special problems only with one group that held their positions on a rocky outcrop. It could only be reached by boat. We did not have any means of communication. Little by little the NCOs and their groups met in the vineyards, near the Company Command Post. The Platoon and Section leaders checked the weapons, ammunition, and hand grenades.

Because of the acute danger of aircraft, the trucks kept large distances between each other. The transport column provided the "Hermann Göering" Panzer Division. A Sergeant commanded the Unit. He had the order to take my Company immediately – without any loss of time – to Transport Regiment 274. The Command Post of this Regiment was at Santa Maria Infante. It was the first time I heard that name. If heavy artillery fire made it impossible to continue, we would have to fight our way through on foot.

When the Company was complete, I gave the order to mount. I put two men on each truck as aerial observers. We drove at full speed towards Gaeta Formia. We kept to the timetable. The cloudless sky worried us. Still, we did not see any bomber aircraft. When we saw the Gulf of Gaeta in front of us, we immediately noticed several Allied warships. They lay peacefully in the gulf and stopped firing.

I did not have a map of that battle zone. That was usually the case when spontaneous action was ordered. The Sergeant who led the convoy of trucks knew where we were going. He had also informed me that we would take the coastal road for about 12 kilometres and then turn inland. Soon we reached Formia. On the Via Appia we went East. With serious faces, the men stared at the sea. What would the warships do? They had to see us. The road was often damaged by artillery and bombs. Our driver could not drive very fast. Well-placed volleys of these heavy ship's guns had left us in great distress. Everyone felt it like a miracle, no aircraft in the sky and the flashing of the ship's artillery did not happen.

The fleet that kept the Battalions of our Division under heavy fire for days were 2 Cruisers [HMS *Orion* and HMS *Spartan*] and five Destroyers. We knew almost nothing about the enemy. We heard from the Hermann Goering people that they were 'Tommies'. Our enemies were British units.

The Allies had two armies in Italy, which were part of the 15th Army Group under General Alexander. The British 8th Army fought in the Northern part of the front, towards the Adriatic Sea under Lieut. General Oliver Leese.

The Southern part of the front towards the Tyrrhenian Sea was occupied by the American 5th Army under Lieut. General Mark Clark. On the left side of this Army was British X (BR) Corps under Lieut. Gen. Richard McCreery and they were directly in front of 94 Infantry Division. The area around Minturno was attacked by the British 5 Infantry Division, and the area around Castelforte/Sujo by the British 56 Infantry Division. The British 46 Infantry Division was further North.

The tension was enormous. Kilometre by kilometre we went South – without enemy action. At the fork in the road at San Croce, a road sign pointed to the left – "Cassino" was written on it. With full speed we turned off. The Via Appia led straight ahead to Scauri and on to the River Garigliano. Our soldiers soon called this fork in the road "death crossroads": it was a very special attraction for ship and land artillery as well as for the bomber aircraft, who, however, did not manage to close the railway bridge until the end or block the supply road at San Croce. When we passed that critical point, I took a breath. Now in the hills further East we heard the sounds of battle and dying Grenadiers. After a noticeably short time we saw individual houses next to the road. It was a small town or district – Penitro.

Now it started. Shells howled and detonated right and left of the road, which led further, past Santa Maria Infante, to Cassino. The enemy had certainly already occupied a few hills and could see the terrain. I gave the order: "Dismount and take full cover." Santa Maria Infante was about 5 km ahead of us on a bigger hill.

In a few seconds, my men had jumped off and disappeared into cover. The able Hermann Goering men had already turned around and were quickly heading towards Formia. These drivers did not have an easy life. The fire attack by the enemy artillery continued for some time. For many of the men it was the first close encounter with death. With my three Platoon Commanders, I discussed the next steps. The Company had to follow me at a long distance. I searched for the Regimental Command Post. We made slow progress, but the artillery kept forcing us to take cover.

We met several times with fellow countrymen bringing captured Englishmen into the rear area. The Englishmen, with their typical flat helmets, looked exhausted and made sad faces. I think they were glad to have escaped death. When we climbed up the road to Santa Maria Infante, the sun had already disappeared. An Observer from 274 Grenadier Regiment drove us the last distance to the Command Post just as the heavy shells of the two Cruisers made the earth tremble. When we arrived at the Command Post it was pitch dark. In the shelter were only a few men. Candles were burning, the mood I could hardly judge. I reported to Lt. Colonel. Reich. Without a word the Regimental Commander shook my hand, he looked grey and exhausted.

Lt. Colonel Reich had to answer the phone again. Lieutenant Wolfras Gieseler, his Adjutant, was in charge. He was extremely cooperative. The first thing he did was print a map for me. Gieseler informed me about the situation as far as possible. He explained the streets, the terrain, and a few places in the Minturno area. Flickering candlelight, sometimes went out when the impacts of the bombs were very close, he showed me what was assumed to be enemy positions and the main battle line on the map in the evening of 19 Jan 44. I could register only all place names and designations with difficulty. My receptiveness was limited in this tension-loaded hour. Still two or three men were in the shelter. There was chaos – it could not be any different from the days of rough camping. The Commander made one phone call after the other.'

Nigel Nicolson, *The Grenadier Guards*
19 Jan 44

'At the beginning of an offensive the British soldier understood well enough what was the immediate objective for he could see with his own eyes the shell bursts and the clouds of dust which marked the furthest points reached by the converging pincers. But when the battle developed, and the Allied advance poured along a dozen separate channels, the soldier's horizon was apt to be confined by the mountains bordering his own particular valley. More often the men and junior officers were engaged in battles of which they did not know the full significance in relation to the strategic plan. For hours and sometimes days, they would wait patiently in dusty fields while others broke fresh ground ahead of them. Ordered suddenly to put on their equipment and climb back into their lorries, they would be driven off to unknown destinations, lurching along hot by roads all through the day or night, delayed at intervals by blown bridges, long enough to brew a can of tea by the wayside, then on again, down the steep diversions, which the bulldozers had carved out of the stream-banks, or rattling across the loose boards of a Bailey bridge. So, they came once more to their Division, past the tanks, within the range of gun fire, and then heard a shot or the rattle of a machine gun. Where were they? There was no time and no real need to explain the wider situation. Out came the maps, a small isolated, square of Italian soil, a hurried identification of features on map and ground. "The Germans are here and there, perhaps here there too. The bridge is blown, the tanks held up. We must have this ridge by nightfall." Then the Battalion, Company and Platoon plans in increasing detail: "That hedge . . . will be the 2-inch mortar reach? . . . Get them under cover of this farm . . . and No. 3 Platoon on your right . . . in half an hour from now." So, the battle started; a few more fields, another village, abandoned by the Germans, entered by our own men, and so "captured". And this minor skirmish would make its mark upon the great operation maps of rear headquarters and even affect the bulge of the broad, black line published the next day in the newspapers of the world. The exact position of the front line, the line joining the points reached by the leading tanks or sections of a hundred different columns, was always of great importance. Beyond it lay country which looked no different from the country already in our hands but somewhere across that broken stretch of fields lay a curtain dividing friend from foe, guns that would shoot to defend you from guns that would shoot to kill.'

Chapter 5

20 January 1944 – Battle of Monte Natale – the Start Line

X (BR) Corps History

20 Jan 44

1 York & Lancs. were ordered to pass through and capture Monte Natale. The situation at dawn on this day was that the Germans were known to be holding in strength the high ground North of Minturno and the Minturno town Cemetery, as well as Monte Natale which was another 800 yards further on to the West of the Cemetery.

The plan for the attack consisted of two phases. In Phase 1, 1 York & Lancs. 'A' Company under Major A. Wilson on the right and 'D' Company under Major D. Young on the left were to advance behind a barrage along the ridge leading West from Tufo and capture the enemy positions North of Minturno, at Point 172.

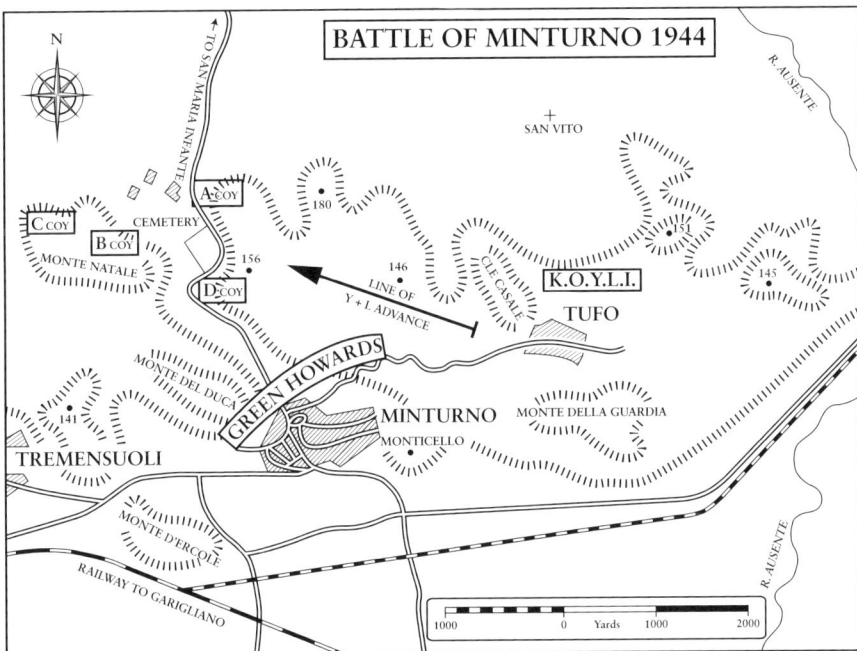

Battle of Minturno 1944. 1 York & Lancs. Plan of attack. (Map John Strafford)

In Phase 2 'D' Company was to hold the position captured in Phase I while 'B' Company under Major D. Webster on the right and 'C' Company on the left were to follow another barrage and capture the Cemetery and Monte Natale, Point 156. 'A' Company was to follow 'B' and 'C' Companies and occupy the area of the Cemetery.

2 Army Group Royal Artillery War Diary

During the advance of 1 York & Lancs. on the Cemetery 781967, enemy infantry, and tanks in area 782984 [Santa Maria Infante] attempted to interfere and were engaged by 69 Medium Regiment and 56 Heavy Regiment in conjunction with 5 Division Artillery. Enemy areas opposite the 56 Infantry Division front were engaged by Group Regiments throughout the day.

1 KOYLI War Diary

20 Jan 44

On the morning of 20 Jan 44, 1 York & Lancs. Were to attack Westwards through us on to Point 172. On the previous day, 19 Jan 44, 1 Green Howards had got on well to the outskirts of Minturno itself. A patrol went out to Point 141, Monte del Duca, at first light made up from the Carrier Platoon under command of Lieut. D.E. Dimbleby.

1 York & Lancs. War Diary

20 Jan 1944 – 0575

Battalion moved from harbour area to Tufo to carry out attack under barrage of Corps artillery. First objective was Point 172. 'A' Company right 'D' Company left. Second objective Point 156 [Point 156 was the hill in front of the Cemetery, but later it came to represent Monte Natale, so the object was to take both]. 'B' Company right, 'C' Company left. Start line at West edge of Tufo. Rate of advance 100 yards in 3 minutes, pause for 15 minutes on first objective. Zero hour – 0700.

1 Green Howards War Diary

20 Jan 44 – 0600

'D' Company moved South of road [Minturno – Tufo] to keep clear of barrage which was assisting 1 York & Lancs.

1 York & Lancs. War Diary

20 Jan 44 – 0650

Battalion formed up for attack on Monte Natale on the West edge of Tufo and Tactical HQ established in house in Tufo. Afterwards the house was discovered to have 12 'Neberwerfer' [*sic*: Nebelwerfer] bombs and 12 cases of high explosives in a room. 1 KOYLI 'A' and 'C' Companies were on Point 201 and 'B' Company and Battalion HQ in Tufo. 1 Green Howards had captured Minturno, 'A' & 'B' Companies. on Point 141, Monte del Duca.

15 Infantry Brigade War Diary

20 Jan 44 – 0700

1 York & Lancs. moved forward to their Start line without incident and their attack commenced as planned.

International Red Cross
A report of an interview by the International Red Cross given by Private Thomas Pryor, 5 September 1944 whilst he was a prisoner of war at Stalag IV B.

International Red Cross interview with Pte Thomas Pryor. 5 Sep 44.
INTERNATIONAL COMMITTEE OF THE RED CROSS
CENTRAL AGENCY PRISONERS OF WAR
STALAG IV B
Concerning No. 4755938 Rank Pte. Name
STRAFFORD, Ernest
Regiment: York and Lancaster Regiment
Statement from Private Thomas Mills Pryor
'I last saw Pte. Strafford wounded in the head when a mortar bomb burst among us during our attack. I believe his wounds were serious.'
Were you an eyewitness? **Yes**
Actual date of incident and place: **20 January 1944 Near Minturno**
Date: 5 Sept 1944
Signature: T M Pryor P.O.W No. 240609

7 Cheshires War Diary
20 Jan 44
Two Platoons from 'B' Company assisted in beating off several counterattacks on Point 201, 798966 fighting in this area again very fierce and bitter throughout the day.

2 Wiltshires War Diary
20 Jan 44 – 0700
'A' Company takes over Point 201. 'B' and 'D' Companies remain West and East of Tufo.

92 Field Regiment Royal Artillery War Diary
20 Jan 44 – 0715
368 Battery Command Observation Post reports 'fire effective.' HQ Royal Artillery informed one gun, probably Medium Regiment firing short.

1 York & Lancs. War Diary
20 Jan 44 – 0745
In Phase I, 1 York and Lancs. passed through Tufo and crossed the Start-line behind a barrage on time. It was soon apparent that the enemy was not too sure from which direction the attack was coming, as his defensive fire did not trouble 'A' and 'D' Companies unduly and they made good progress. After advancing about 800 yards, these two companies attacked the enemy with great dash and determination and, after a brief fight, the Germans surrendered.

'D' Company reported 'have taken 50 prisoners and are on our objective'. They were held up by wire at one point and suffered about 40 casualties. 'A' Company reached their objective with little difficulty. They took 100 prisoners.

Ernest Strafford's body was found on 4 February 50 metres from Point 172 behind the hedge on the right, going up the hill, so it is possible he was one of the

Road: Cemetery–Tufo. Point 172 at top. (Photo John Strafford)

40 casualties, in which case he would have been with 'D' Company. As he was seriously wounded, he may have died at this location. Otherwise, he may have continued with 'D' Company to the slope down to the Cemetery.

Sergeant Fielding, 'D' Company, 1 York & Lancs. Missing Person's Report
20 Jan 44
'Private Holland [Private Stanley Holland, Minturno CWGC Cemetery] was transferred to my Platoon about 15 January 1944 because the Anti-Aircraft Platoon, HQ Company, was being disbanded. He was not with me long enough for me to get familiar with his home life, town, occupation, etc., but his age would be about 25 years, rather sharp features, slim build, fair hair.

At 7am on 20 Jan 44 the Battalion, on a two Company front, "A" and "D" Companies, were ordered to attack hill Point 172, about one mile Northeast of Minturno. I advanced with two Sections forward, Private Holland being in the Right Section. His Section Commander was wounded before reaching the objective. On the top of the hill, I disposed of one Machine Gun position, turned around, and saw my Right Section going for another one. I saw a German throw a stick grenade towards Private Holland, saw Private Holland fall down, and move his legs, and before I could get to him to evacuate him, or dispose of the enemy, he received a full burst of Machine Gun fire from the remaining Machine Gun position. Eventually we consolidated on hill Point 172 and

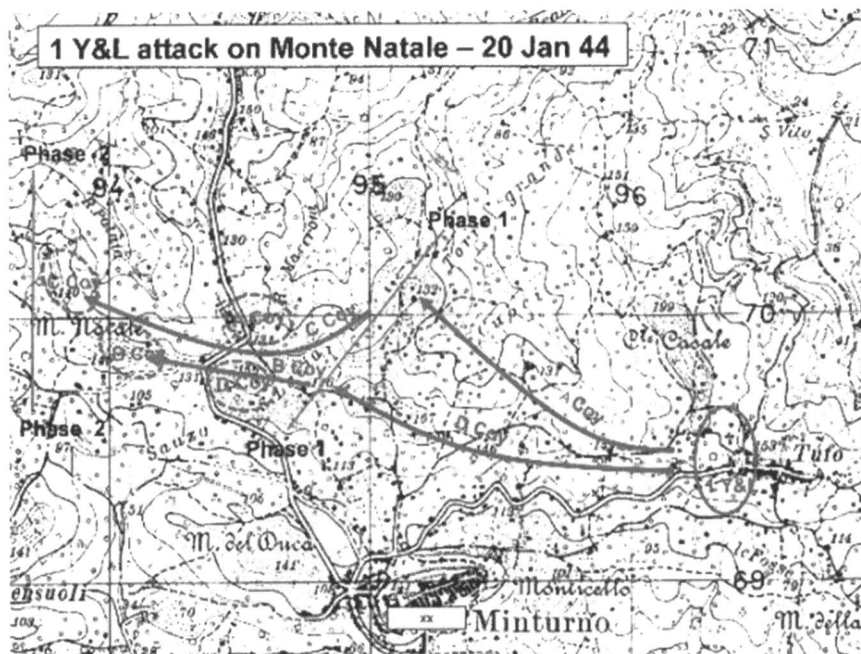

1 York & Lancs. actual route of attack on Monte Natale 20 Jan 44. 'A' Co. on reaching the road turned right in front of the Cemetery and went around the corner to the left. (Map Frank de Planta)

81

being then the Acting Sergeant Major of the Company I called for Platoon casualty slips and detailed Sergeant Waddington, 18 Platoon "D" Company to gather in the dead bodies. We had 12 dead, and 33 wounded out of this action. Private Holland laid amongst the dead. I sent immediately for the Medical Officer of the unit to confirm the lost lives of the bodies. All personnel effects together with one identification disc was taken off, docketed, and forwarded to Battalion HQ. The Company was going to bury the men, but we had orders to move at once and on each man's body was left all particulars on a piece of paper tied to the body, plus one identity disc. Major D. Young will bear out this statement.'

The dead were moved after the action. Ernest Strafford's body was on its own on Hill 172 when buried on 4 February so was not amongst the 12 dead that were moved to Minturno.

This indicates that he was still alive on 20 January and went on to the Cemetery with either 'A' Company or 'D' Company.

A Soldier from 'B' Coy. 1 York & Lancs
20 Jan 44
'We left the long stone wall at Tufo and advanced in open order as best we could for some 500 yards of grape vine wires behind a creeping barrage from our 25 pounders. We came to a clearing where a ginger haired Gerry was draped over his mortar and must have been caught by the barrage. All the rest of his crew were in an adjacent deep bunker screaming "Kamerad". We fetched them out just as we were strafed by Yank aircraft, so they dived back down the dugout. We left one bloke to take them back to Tufo and carried on.'

Start Line – stone wall at Tufo. (Photo John Strafford)

Monte Natale. (Photo John Strafford)

15 Infantry Brigade War Diary
20 Jan 44 – 0800
Point 172 reported as captured with some 100 prisoners of war. The advance pushed on towards the Cemetery, where however, a few enemy tanks and/or self-propelled guns caused a check. It was not possible to resume the advance to Monte Natale, Point 156, and 1 York & Lancs. forward troops re-organised just East of the Santa Maria Infante road. The Prisoner of War total had now risen to at least 150, mostly 274 Grenadier Regiment from 94 Infantry Division.

92 Field Regiment Royal Artillery War Diary
20 Jan 44 – 0830
Second in Command reports 1 York & Lancs. doing well. 50 Prisoners of War taken. Will inform HQ if second part of direct fire programme is to be delayed.

20 Jan 44 – 0900
Smoke screen started.

98 Field Regiment Royal Artillery War Diary
'E' Observation Post 783966 [hill overlooking Cemetery] supporting 1 York & Lancs. Engaged seven tanks and all but two retired Northwards, no direct hits.

1 York & Lancs. War Diary
20 Jan 44 – 0915
Officer Commanding 'B' Company arrived at Tactical HQ to explain situation. 'B' Company passed through 'A' Company position to time but encountered tanks at Cemetery and were badly shot up. Company caught the barrage and saw enemy

running from their dugouts to weapon slits on Point 156, Monte Natale. Company were in position with one Platoon in area of Cemetery, with one Platoon across the road and remainder of Company round buildings. 'C' Company formed up behind 'D' Company.

Ernest Shaw, 1 York & Lancs

'Started the attack and suddenly there were German fighter bombers dive bombing us. I stood watching one and saw the plane and suddenly realised it was going to drop on my head. Ted and I dived into a captured gun pit, about 3 feet deep and about 10 or 12-feet square, I suppose it had had a gun in there.

There was an almighty explosion. I thought my ear had been blown off. I dare not feel for it. Ted must have said "What's up Shaw? Have you been hit? You have gone a funny colour." I stuttered "Is my ear on?" He came over and said, "Of course your bloody ear is on". I thought it had gone. He peered inside my right ear and got a match out and got the tiniest piece of shrapnel out. A pin head would be large beside it and he held it in his hand and said, "If you are looking for Blighty you need something bigger than this" and threw it away. It was not the shrapnel it was the blast that really knocked my hearing about. I could not sleep on that side on my right ear for years after.

We went over the top of this hill, Point 172. Germans had moved out from top of hill, but there were skirmishes.

We had to cross the road [in front of Cemetery]. There were a couple of German tanks on it. They fired and knocked one or two of our lads about, then motored away. We crossed this road and went on probably half a mile onto another hill designated Point 156. During the advance to take hill Point 156, 11 Platoon were away on the left of Company HQ and the Major sent me with a message for Lieutenant Corfield.

I do not remember what the message was now. I was running, loping along, and had got a lot of ground to cross, and Germans must have seen me, and they opened fire

Point 172 – Minturno in distance. (Photo John Strafford)

with a machine gun. I heard bullets through the grass, and I ran like the devil. Jesse Owens was the World Champion, but he would not have caught me that day. I reached 11 Platoon and passed the message to the Lieutenant. Then I saw I had a couple of bullet snags in my left sleeve just above the wrist near the cuff. My tommy gun had lost the forward grip, there was just the bolt that fastened the wooden part to it, the wooden part had gone – it had been shot off. I had not got a scratch. I found a more unobtrusive route back to Company HQ. I had had five narrow scrapes and then this happened.

"C" Company owing to "D" Company meeting wire and opposition on the objective were unable to pass through and lost the barrage. "C" Company had therefore formed up behind "D" Company.'

1 Green Howards War Diary
20 Jan 44 – 0920
Commanding Officer's orders for Company Commanders: 'A' Company to send patrol to Point 141, Monte del Duca, to see if occupied.

Plan.

'B' Company left to capture town [Minturno] and secure all approaches.
'C' Company right.
'A' company move from Point 141 into immediate reserve.
'D' Company to take over Point 141 from 'A' Company.

1 York & Lancs. War Diary
20 Jan 44 – 0930
Commanding Officer went to 'B' Company area by Cemetery to plan advance to second objective.

40 Royal Tank Regiment War Diary
20 Jan 44 – 0940
Received wireless message that enemy tanks were operating in area 7897, just North of Cemetery, and ordered to proceed there.

20 Jan 44 – 0950
Reached cross-roads, 793953 [500m south of Minturno]. Found track to Minturno blocked and mined and waited for Royal Engineers to clear the track.

1 KOYLI War Diary
20 Jan 44 – 1000
All went well and Minturno and the Point 172 ridge were in British hands. We were then told we were in Brigade Reserve and were to occupy and hold Minturno, 1 Green Howards having previously passed through this town – but not cleared it, on the night of 19-20 January.

There was no rest for the Battalion. After 1 York & Lancs. had attacked the Cemetery, 2 Wiltshires re-occupied Tufo and took over Point 201 from us and we returned to our assembly area of the previous day where we had a quick meal and a wash before going on to Minturno.

Left: Sherman tank of 40 Royal Tank Regiment crossing the River Garigliano on Class 30 Bailey pontoon raft operated by 252 Field Company, Royal Engineers, 20 Jan 44. (Photo Sgt. Tyler AFPU. TNA 11066)

Below: A Sherman tank crosses the River Garigliano by Royal Engineers' ferry, 20 Jan 44. (Photo Sgt. Tyler AFPU. TNA 11069)

92 Field Regiment Royal Artillery War Diary
20 Jan 44 – 1010
No change in programme. 1 York & Lancs. nearly on final objective. 150 Prisoners of War taken for loss of two wounded.

1 York & Lancs. War Diary
20 Jan 44 – 1030
'B' Company area dive-bombed, and machine gunned by our own planes.

92 Field Regiment Royal Artillery War Diary
20 Jan 44 – 1040
Second in Command reports second part of direct fire programme may have to be delayed. Concentration required on Point 156, Monte Natale, from 1100-1115. Regiment laid on target and HQ Royal Artillery asks for additional support. 467 Battery Commander reports 1 Green Howards attack going according to plan.

20 Jan 44 – 1050
467 Battery Commander reports being mortared continuously. Bombed by own planes.

1 Green Howards War Diary
20 Jan 44 – 1100
Zero hour. Barrage lifting 100 yards in three minutes.

5 Infantry Division History
20 Jan 44 – 1100
The weather held and it was still possible to take advantage of the early morning mist and the fact that any sun shone directly into the eyes of the German Observation Posts. 15 Infantry Brigade plan exploited Westwards and was carried out in two parts. In Part 1, 1 York & Lancs. attacked towards Monte Natale, all went smoothly, and 150 prisoners were taken for the loss of only two wounded. However, the Battalion was held up continuously in the final stage of the attack. Part 2 of the plan followed at 1100.

40 Royal Tank Regiment War Diary
20 Jan 44 – 1100
Moved to 'T' junction, 783950 [500m South-West of Minturno]. One tank developed engine trouble here and was left in an anti-tank role covering the roads.

20 Jan 44 – 1110
Troop, now consisting of two tanks, moved North to the 'Y' junction at 781955 [just South of Point 141].

98 Field Regiment Royal Artillery War Diary
20 Jan 44 – 1118
471 Battery Commander: 70 prisoners come in, 786964 [by Point 172].

1 Green Howards War Diary
20 Jan 44 – 1120
1 York & Lancs. attack progressed well, and they were around the Cemetery, but held up by tanks from the direction of Santa Maria Infante area.

40 Royal Tank Regiment War Diary
20 Jan 44 – 1120
Reached 787955 [outskirts of Minturno] and encountered a roadblock. This was cleared and the two tanks moved East towards Minturno.

20 Jan 44 – 1130
Reached Minturno and removed mines from the road at 785956 [start of road to Cemetery]. Advanced to village 785958 on Santa Maria road [about 1km South of the Cemetery] and encountered more mines which were removed.

1 York & Lancs. War Diary
20 Jan 44 – 1130
Tactical Head Quarters established at X tracks [just East of Point 172]. C.O. arranged for repeat of barrage on road Minturno – Santa Maria Infante for capture of second objective. This was difficult as although Battalion had Forward Observation Officers from 98 Field Regiment and 102 Medium Regiment, neither were in direct touch with Division Artillery. The wireless set for communication with Brigade did not work although wire had been laid from Brigade HQ. As the Battalion had advanced, wire had been broken by shellfire.

When the barrage re-started, 'B' and 'C' Companies, the latter now under Captain Ivor J. Wedgbury, began their advance against Monte Natale which lay beyond the Minturno – Santa Maria Infante road. After covering about 400 yards, the Companies reached the forward slopes of the hill leading down to the road. At once they came under heavy and accurate fire from enemy tanks in the area of the Cemetery and from a group of houses some 800 yards further North. As a result, the attack was temporarily brought to a halt while the exact positions of the enemy tanks were ascertained.

When two enemy tanks emerged from the Cemetery and moved up the road to join others near the houses, Lieutenant Corfield of No 11 Platoon took his P.I.A.T.[Projector Infantry Anti Tank grenade], team down the hill and engaged the rear one. Although hit this tank was not disabled. Artillery fire was then brought down on the area where the tanks were known to be, and this caused them to withdraw some distance towards Santa Maria Infante.

A soldier from 'B' Company 1 York & Lancs. described what happened
'We went forward again as the barrage lifted and topping a rise came under observation from a Gerry tank near the civvy Cemetery, our anti-tank crew fired two shells at him, one hitting his track guard and the other the turret, without going off. I reckon the second was not primed but it brought the gun round in a hurry and he fired on the Platoon on our right and caused casualties.

Now we were in full sight of the Gerry Aid Post where another tank was loading wounded ready to leave the place, In all three enemy Mark III tanks took off at speed past the Cemetery. At this time a Gerry officer and two wounded men were captured, and we jumped down a high wall onto the road and into the now empty Aid Post leaving the wounded on top of the wall. Two of us searched right round the Aid Post and found nothing but dead, on stretchers. We searched upstairs and found it clear. Now we waited instructions from Company HQ but were rudely interrupted by the whirring of a stick

Forward slopes of the hill in front of the Cemetery. Wall at the bottom. (Photo John Strafford)

Cemetery as seen from the forward slopes. (Photo John Strafford)

German Aid Post seen from forward slopes of the hill. (Photo John Strafford)

grenade which must have come through the window. It must have been a long fuse because seven or eight of us got outside in a hurry and the only casualty was the Gerry officer with a hole in his backside the size of a teacup. The rest of B Coy arrived.'

92 Field Regiment Royal Artillery War Diary
20 Jan 44
1 York & Lancs. joined the fray, and 150 Prisoners of War were taken for loss of two wounded in 'A' Company.

'A' Company attacked to the right of Point 172. If Ernest Strafford had been with 'A' Company and was one of the two wounded, he would either have had to go up a steep hill to get to Point 172 where his body was found or carried on with 'A' Company towards the Cemetery.

A soldier from 'A' Company, 1 York & Lancs. described what happened
'Our objective was some ground outside a town called Minturno. As we were going down a muddy track [Tufo to Cemetery] a German tank was at the bottom. It let off a few shells which caused casualties, amongst them being the chap who went swimming with me at Geneiefa. I spoke to him as he was carried away on a stretcher.'

[Was this man one of the two wounded in 'A' Company? If so, was Ernest Strafford the other one and still with 'A' Company?]

About 10 of us occupied some ground on a slope and we dug ourselves in and the rest of the Battalion dug in different areas. Just above our slope was a road and over the

The valley 'A' Co. 1 York & Lancs. crossed to get to the Cemetery. Monte Natale on the left, Tufo on the right. (Photo John Strafford)

German Aid Post on the road, forward slopes on the right. (Photo John Strafford)

road down the hill was a Cemetery probably about two hundred yards distance from us. At night, from the Cemetery area, we could hear lots of noise and we knew the Germans were there and receiving reinforcements. We also came under very heavy shelling and had to keep our heads down and hope for the best reinforcements. When dawn broke there was no let up and there was firing all over the place.

92 Field Regiment Royal Artillery War Diary
20 Jan 44 – 1145
368 Battery Command Observation Post: 1 KOYLI took a further 10 Prisoners of War this morning. Battery Commander reports 1 Green Howards at 772956 [edge of Tremensuoli] – barrage going well.

1 Green Howards War Diary
20 Jan 44 – 1200
1 Green Howards occupied Tremensuoli. Battalion HQ and 'A' Company moved up, 'B' Company entered town, 'C' Co. was just West of Minturno, 'D' Co. was to take the high ground behind 'C' Co.

40 Royal Tank Regiment War Diary
Heavily bombed and strafed but sustained no damage. Moved to village at 784958 [midway between Minturno and Cemetery].

15 Infantry Brigade War Diary
20 Jan 44 – 1300
1 Green Howards reported their objective secured and 40 Prisoners of War taken. Their own casualties had been light. About mid-day General Officer Commanding 5 Division (Major General G.C. Bucknall) accompanied by the new GOC (Major General P Gregson Ellis) visited Brigade HQ. The Brigadier was informed that a Battalion of 201 Guards Brigade (3 Coldstream Guards) would relieve 1 Green Howards on Tremensuoli on 21 January, 1 Green Howards passing into Brigade Reserve behind Minturno. During the morning 1 KOYLI were relieved on Point 201 by 2 Wiltshires via quarry, where a hot meal was obtained, and withdrawn to the Minturno area.

1 Green Howards Military Cross Citation for Major A.R.M. Tanner
Major Tanner commanded the left forward Company in the attack and capture of Tremensuoli (769957) on 20 Jan 44. Throughout this action he showed exceptionally high standards of leadership in directing and controlling his Company, cleaning up opposition and ensuring the immediate mopping up and consolidation of the objective.

During the whole operation the village was under heavy enemy artillery and machine gun fire and his Company was in close contact with the enemy on the lower slopes. Major Tanner moved continuously from Platoon to Platoon directing operations wherever the enemy fire was heaviest, and by his coolness and untiring energy set a magnificent example, which was an inspiration to his men.

1 York & Lancs. War Diary
20 Jan 44 – 1300
Adjutant arrived at Tactical HQ having brought haversack rations, tools and ammunition to Tufo by Jeep. Jeeps and carriers not so essential as adequate supplies available in many positions, also arms and ammunition.

98 Field Regiment Royal Artillery War Diary
20 Jan 44 – 1315
391 Battery Observation Post in Minturno dive bombed by five enemy bombers. 474 Battery Observation Post also involved in this attack. One man hit.

92 Field Regiment Royal Artillery War Diary
20 Jan 44 – 1325
467 Battery Commander reports Observation Post Officer and two Other Ranks wounded.

52 Anti-Tank Regiment War Diary
20 Jan 44 – 1330
Guns have crossed bridge. Battery Commander met Commander 15 Infantry Brigade who considered main threat would come from North and asked for guns North of Minturno. Battery Commander and Lt. Harman, 'E' Troop Commander, therefore recced area.

1 York & Lancs. War Diary
20 Jan 44 – 1400
'B' Company and Tactical HQ bombed, and machine gunned. Considerable sniping and enemy machine gun fire in 'B' Company area. 'B' Company ordered to withdraw behind 'D' Company.

Tactical HQ at this point were at the crossroads by Point 172, approx. 50m from where Ernest Strafford's body was found. If Ernest Strafford was with Tactical HQ this might have been the time he was wounded by a bomb although in the witness statement it said he was injured 'during our attack', so unlikely he was with Tactical HQ.

1 KOYLI War Diary
20 Jan 44 – 1400
Point 172 occupied by 'A' & 'B' Companies. 'C' Company. in reserve. 'D' Company on the high ground, Tac HQ just behind 'A' Company.

1 York & Lancs. War Diary
20 Jan 44 – 1430
CO. telephoned Brigade from 1 KOYLI HQ. Brigadier ordered 1 York & Lancs. to capture and secure second objective [Point 156, Monte Natale] before nightfall and arrangements were made to give full artillery support.

2 Scots Guards War Diary
20 Jan 44 – 1500
The Brigadier held his Orders Group on Point 141, Monte del Duca, a bare and exposed hill just west of Minturno [the purpose of meeting here was to recce the battlefield and the objectives]. The Commanding Officer held his Orders Group in the same place immediately afterwards, but as it was not possible to get a sufficiently detailed view of

Point 141, Monte del Duca, hill on left, Minturno on the right, taken from South-West. (Photo John Strafford)

the Battalion objectives, the Brigade plan was only given out and a further Order Group fixed for tomorrow at Tremensuoli, which is the next feature to the West.

40 Royal Tank Regiment No. 1 Troop War Diary
20 Jan 44 – 1500
Tried to contact 1 York & Lancs. to support them in their attack on Point 156, Monte Natale, but was unsuccessful.

13 Infantry Brigade War Diary
20 Jan 44 – 1530
Locations:
2 Wiltshires, two Companies on Point 201, Battalion HQ and one Company in Tufo.
2 Cameronians in reserve on hillside of Point 201.

2 Wiltshires War Diary
20 Jan 44 – 1600
Enemy counterattacked Point 201 by estimated one Company [approx. 100 men]. Forward Platoon dislodged but Reserve Platoon counterattacked with the bayonet and enemy were driven off. P.O.W.s were taken.

15 Infantry Brigade War Diary
20 Jan 44 – 1600
1 York & Lancs. attack went in successfully, though in fact only half of Monte Natale was cleared of enemy. 1 KOYLI were ordered to take over Point 172 from 1 York & Lancs. and to patrol forward during the night with a view to occupation the following day.

2 Army Group Royal Artillery War Diary
20 Jan 44 – 1600
Between 1600 hours and 1625 hours 69 Medium Regiment, 74 Medium Regiment and 56 Heavy Regiment took part in a small Fire Plan in support of the attack by 1 York & Lancs. on Point 156, Monte Natale. This support was in the form of concentrations against enemy areas at 776966, 774967, 772969, 764967, 776968 [all points to the North and West of Monte Natale]. Nearly 550 Prisoners of War have been taken since this operation started.

1 York & Lancs. War Diary
20 Jan 44 – 1600
'B' and 'C' Companies advanced to capture second objective at Point 156, Monte Natale, under barrage from road running North from Minturno. Barrage concentrated on road for 5 minutes, then advanced at rate of 100 yards in 3 minutes. Neither Company met any opposition. Two barrages in one day had apparently been too much for the enemy who had withdrawn or surrendered to 1 Green Howards in area Tremensuoli. When 'B' and 'C' Companies had captured their objectives, 'A' Company mopped up and took up position in area of Cemetery – [track to Tufo] junction. 'B' Company consolidated at South end of Point 156 feature and 'C' Company on the North-West end.

'C' Co. 1 York & Lancs. position looking towards Santa Maria Infante. (Photo John Strafford)

The action was described as follows:

'B' and 'C' Companies renewed the advance under heavy artillery support. Thanks to this fire which paid attention to the enemy tanks, the road was crossed without difficulty and Monte Natale captured against relatively light opposition. The position was then consolidated with 'C' Company on the exposed North-West end of the feature, 'B' Company on the main part of the feature itself, and 'A' Company astride the road. Behind this line 'D' Company and Battalion Headquarters occupied the area of the Cemetery, whilst on the right 1 King's Own Yorkshire Light Infantry took over the hill [Point 172] originally captured by 'A' and 'D' Companies in Phase 1. By 1600 hours the objectives had been achieved.

'C' Company's position on Monte Natale gave it a view of the whole valley. It is no wonder that both sides wanted to hold this position.

Ernest Shaw, 1 York & Lancs. reports

'Another lucky escape. On the same track we were going down the side of a road, perhaps 50 yards off the road on the right of the road (just before the Gerry Aid Post). One of our platoons rounded the bend on the road itself and there must have been a German tank with this corner under observation and he let fly at them. There were a couple of casualties before they got off the road. While Ted and I were still behind this corner and still 30 to 40 yards short of the corner but off the road, "A" Company came marching down, a full platoon, not marching but walking in single file. Their Company Commander, I believe his name was Wilson, Major A. Wilson, was not far from the front, perhaps a couple of Sections in front of him and I shouted to him 'Excuse me Sir watch it on the corner, you are under observation, you are better off the road'. But whether he did not hear me properly, he glared and carried on. Next thing the Gerry tank sees these guys going around the corner and lets go again and they scatter. There were a few casualties. I cursed the officer. "Daft Bugger". I had got a piece of schrapnel in my wrist, but again it was only a flea bite, probably a quarter inch long, only just gone under the skin of my left wrist. Rimmer poked it out again and I wrapped my hanky round it and carried on. The advance was held up somehow after that. Then after a couple of hours we were off again, and we got to the start line at Company HQ. We had a Royal Artillery Observation Officer with us, and he had got a radio link with his guns. He was looking for targets for his guns. This was at a farmhouse. Targets were on Hill 156. Gerry saw him first and let go with a Howitzer. This shell could not have cleared us by more than 5 feet and whistled over the top of us and all Company HQ dived under the gable of this farmhouse. I was at the front corner and this next shell hit the corner, must have been 6 to 8 feet above me and buried me in rubble. I had only a couple of bruises and got away with it. Whether they were short of ammo they did not fire again. Fair run of luck. From then on, I worried no more – daft.

Attack on Hill Point 156. We took it. "C" Company and "B" Company combined. "C" Company lost their Company Commander and the Major handled both companies then. Hill 156 was not up and down. It was just a promontory. It was not like a mountain – just like a foothill. From the side we attacked it from, there was not a lot of incline. It fell away down to where the Germans were, where they had already retreated to. They retreated off the hill. We came on level ground to the top. We were on the top and I did not know it. The hill was taken by the forward lads in both "B" and "C" companies, and naturally Company HQ was a little bit behind. They were perhaps 100 yards in front of us, but we could not see them. There was rough ground between us and them. Behind us were "A" Company and also to the right of us. It was here where the Major threatened to shoot some "C" Company members. When the Germans attacked some of "C" Company started to run away from them, and came through us, but he stopped that little schmozzle. We settled down there and held the hill.'

If Ernest Strafford, although wounded, had managed to carry on with 'D' Company or 'A' Company he would now be in the area of the cemetery. Was he with Major Wilson?

1 KOYLI War Diary
20 Jan 44 1600
We were established in a Battalion position with 1 York & Lancs. on our left front and 1 Green Howards on our left rear. All seemed to be going well. The Germans had obviously left in a hurry and left behind any amount of equipment. Prisoners were coming in well – all from 94 Infantry Division. By the night of 20 Jan 44 all objectives had been obtained and it appeared only had to be consolidated.

5 Infantry Division
20 Jan 44 – 1605
1 KOYLI had taken over Point 141, Monte del Duca, from 1 Green Howards and Point 172 from 1 York & Lancs. 1 York & Lancs. were then attacking Monte Natale Point 156.

40 Royal Tank Regiment No. 1 Troop War Diary
20 Jan 44 – 1630
The Troop Leader saw a party of Germans at 781964 [German Aid post on Santa Maria Infante road]. On seeing the tanks, the enemy ran away, but were chased in to 1 KOYLI lines by the Troop Leader.

20 Jan 44 – 1645
Took enemy Non-Commissioned Officer prisoner from house, 782961 [half a kilometre South of the Aid Post].

20 Jan 44 – 1700
Contacted the Commanding Officer of 1 York & Lancs. at his Command Post. The Troop was ordered to take up an anti-tank counterattack role at the Cemetery at 781968 [just round Cemetery corner on Santa Maria Infante road], at first light 21 Jan 44 0630. The Troop was put under the command of the CO. 'A' Company, 1 York & Lancs.

98 Field Regiment Royal Artillery War Diary
20 Jan 44 – 1725
'E' Troop, 471 Battery Observation Post, location 783966 [Hill in front of Cemetery]. Approx. eight German Self-Propelled Guns and Mk. IV tanks in vicinity of road 780970 [Santa Maria Infante].

1 York & Lancs. War Diary
20 Jan 44 – 1750
'D' Company position on point 172 taken over by 1 KOYLI. 'D' Company moved to area in reserve.

If still alive, Ernest Strafford may have remained at the Cemetery with 'A' Company or gone with 'D' Company back close to Point 172.

5 Infantry Division
Location Statement:

- 1 Green Howards   Grid Square   7695 [just West of Tremensuoli]
- 1 KOYLI   Grid Square   7895 [Point 141, Monte del Duca]
- 1 York & Lancs.   Grid Square   7796 [Monte Natale]

15 Infantry Brigade War Diary
20 Jan 44
Position at dusk was that 1 York & Lancs. held half of Point 156 and the Cemetery; the Santa Maria Infante road being included with them, whilst 1 KOYLI held Point 172 as a firm base. On the left 1 Green Howards were secure on Tremensuoli patrolling to the railway station. 1 York & Lancs. were ordered to patrol forward towards Santa Maria Infante both on the axis of the road and the high ground running North from Point 156. Communications were difficult and these orders were never clearly confirmed. A Troop of tanks from 40 Royal Tank Regiment [23 Armoured Brigade] which was placed under command 1 York & Lancs. had been able to get forward during the day and were in support of 1 York & Lancs. The night passed uneventfully.

158 Field Ambulance War Diary
20 Jan 44
Advanced Dressing Station moved up in late evening to Minturno. Visited by Commanding Officer who decided to withdraw elsewhere. The Advance Dressing Station working awfully hard. Casualties heavy. Evacuation occurs in following phases: (a) Hand carry from Regimental Aid Post. This was long and difficult from 1 Green Howards [Tremensuoli] and steep but shorter from 1 York & Lancs. [North of Minturno]. Stretcher bearers becoming very tired.

Jeeps available but not very much used at this stage. 3 Tonner trucks of 'B' Company crossed river in late afternoon.

40 Royal Tank Regiment No. '1' Troop War Diary
20 Jan 44 – 1800
The Troop withdrew to 784958 [1km South of the Cemetery] for the night.

1 York & Lancs. War Diary
20 Jan 44 – 2000
Rations and hot meals were taken forward to Companies. Wireless set arrived for communication with Brigade HQ.

5 Infantry Division
20 Jan 44 – 2135

1 York & Lancs. were established on Monte Natale holding a line from the Cemetery to Point 156. This Battalion had taken a large part of the 244 prisoners of war which were the Brigade's bag for the day, including a Major Haarbrucker, the Commanding Officer of III Battalion 274 Grenadier Regiment.

A counterattack during the afternoon was beaten off by 2 Wiltshires and artillery and machine gun fire caught and killed many of the 150 enemy who made the attack as they were retreating down the hill.

2 Scots Guards War Diary
20 Jan 44 – 2230

The Battalion which had moved forward under the command of the Adjutant, crossed the river Garigliano at 2230 hours. They moved forward to a concentration area by the side of the road [Lateral Road], which passes south of the hill on which Minturno stands; this hill appeared to give a measure of protection, but the road subsequently became a most popular target for harassing fire.

Ernest Shaw, 1 York & Lancs. reports

'Just captured Hill Point 156 and then we had to defend it, because this was a keenly contested area. By the time we had taken the hill it was late afternoon/early evening and being wintertime, it was not long before it was dark. We had 60 of us that evening and the Major [Major Webster] allocated them between B Company and C Company. There were new reinforcements. Some of them had been fighting elsewhere. They were not all straight from Blighty. I did not mix much with them. They were allocated to various Platoons and Sections. That evening the Major and I went on a tour again and we went around every member of every Platoon and spoke to almost every man in the Company and told them we were going to have a hard time the following morning. There will be a counterattack in the morning. He had laid a barrage on with the artillery officer who went back to his unit. They were going to put a curtain fire in front of us. The code name would be, say "Cockatoo". He would call for "Cockatoo" at 5 a.m. and this barrage would come down. I was remarkably close to him when they were sorting this area to shell, when the Royal Artillery officer objected. He said they were too close to your own men, and he insisted and said we will have to take the risk on that. So, the RA officer went away to organise this. The Major called for me and Joe his batman and we went round and spoke to practically every man in the Company and told them we were going to have a harsh time the following morning, but he thought the Germans would have a damn sight harder time than us. Everyone had got to be awake, fully alert, half an hour before daybreak. This is where he inspired confidence in the people. He was a great officer, and this is where he showed it. Dawn was approaching and he called for "Cockatoo". He must have left it on for five minutes. A lot of shells can drop in 5 minutes in a tight area, it might have been only 3 minutes and he called it off. He relied on time of the day. He called the attack off and we could hear the Germans screaming even though I was at Company HQ probably fifty yards behind the forward lines. He gave them time to recover their dead and wounded and called for it again. He called them a second and then a third time. I cannot imagine how many German dead there were that day, so that held them off. The attack was done but Germans reformed.

The night of 20/21 Jan 44 passed quietly, except for considerable patrol activity by both sides. The enemy patrols paid attention to 'C' Company's position.'

Lieutenant Geoffrey Winter, 1 York & Lancs
'Major D. Webster was an undemonstrative man in general, but clearly knew that the men needed to be braced up for the German counterattack. He tended to be aloof not only with the men but also with his fellow officers.'

A soldier 'B' Coy 1 York & Lancs. described the situation. Map drawn by soldier afterwards
'B' Company advanced towards Monte Natale and dug in along a ridge which had a high hedge which was thick enough to be a barrier, but we could still see to our front through the sparse root system. After a while 'C' Company passed through us and dug in about 50 yards to our front. The whole area became quiet except for digging. All night one could hear horse transport on the road in front.

X (BR) Corps History
By the evening of 20 Jan 44, the greater part of the two Divisions taking part in the main assault had been committed. All three Brigades of 56 Infantry Division were in the line and in face of growing resistance had made little progress during the last two days. On the front of 5 Infantry Division, although there were only two Brigades on the Minturno ridge, the third, 17 Infantry Brigade, was still engaged in clearing the minefields in the coastal sector and would not be available for the front for some days. Only one Infantry Brigade, 201 Guards Brigade remained uncommitted. Orders were given that on the night of 21 – 22 Jan 44 the Guards Brigade would be put in on the left to continue 5 Infantry Division's advance and clear the remainder of the Minturno ridge.

1 KOYLI War Diary
All was quiet on the night of 20 – 21 Jan 44 and a second Company, 'A' Company was put up on the ridge to assist 'B' Company at Point 172 and a standing patrol pushed out on to Point 141, Monte del Duca. Local patrols during the night reported that Point 172 ridge and Point 141 were clear and the morning of 21 Jan 44 brought no contact with the enemy. Considerable enemy air activity over Minturno did not disturb the Battalion who were consolidating their positions and 'B' Company moved forward to hold the high ground on the left of Point 172 with 2 Platoons and Company HQ on the reverse slopes. At last light 'A' Company moved up from their rear position on to the right hand of the high ground of Point 172.

1 KOYLI. Citation: Distinguish Service Order for Lt. Col. Peter Ford
On 19-20 January 1944 Lt. Col. Ford was in command of 1 KOYLI which was ordered to attack the Minturno Ridge. This operation which involved the difficult task of clearing Tufo village was successfully carried out in the face of fierce opposition. The Battalion was subjected to a series of bitter counterattacks which lasted almost

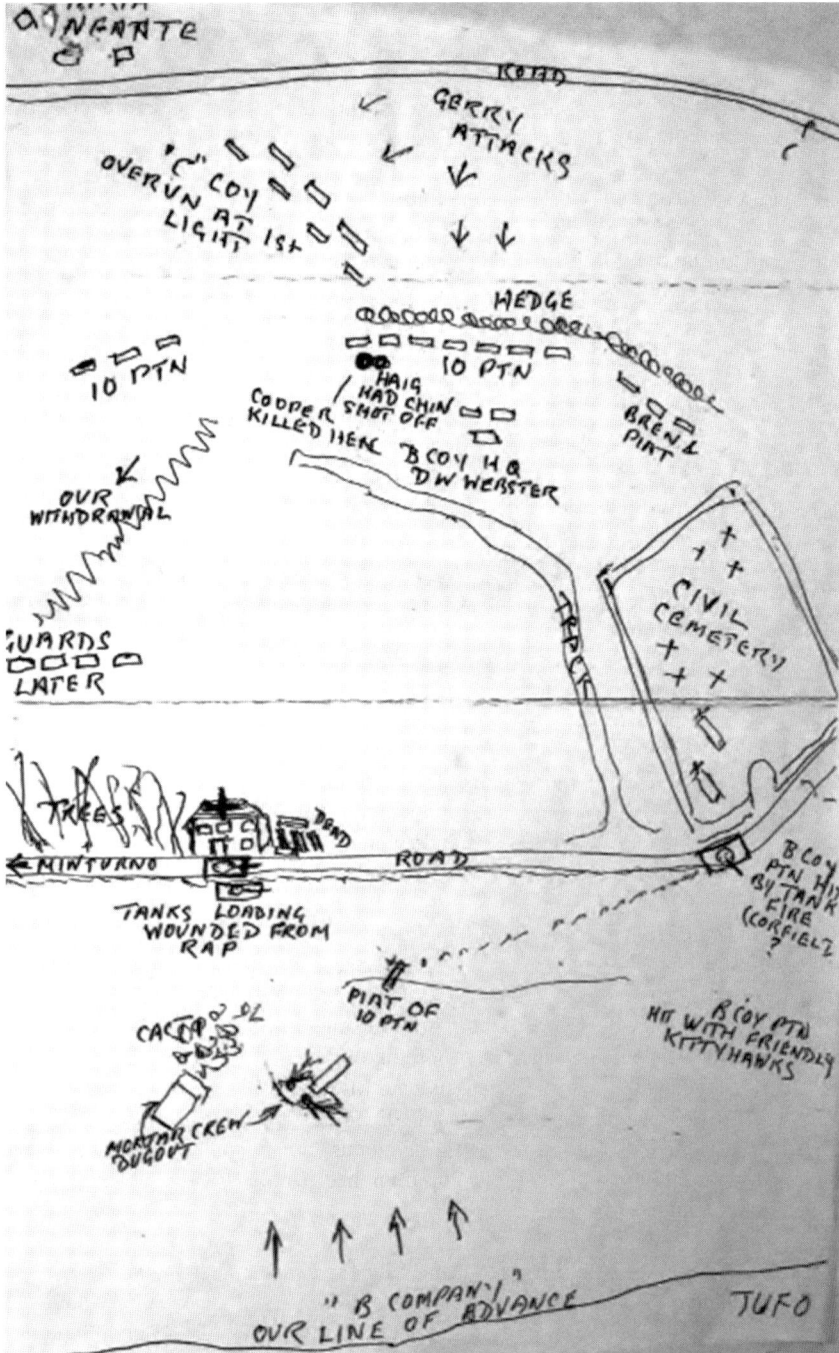

Sketch of battle drawn afterwards by a Private in 1 York & Lancs.

Position of PIAT per sketch. (Photo John Strafford)

Same position 12 May 44 when US Forces arrived. (U.S. National Archives)

Forward slopes of Monte Natale. The German attack came up these slopes. (Photo John Strafford)

continuously for the next 36 hours. Although in a very exposed positions 1 KOYLI held firm and eventually fought the enemy to a standstill. The Battalion was inspired in its difficult and exhausting tasks by the grim determination and confident judgement of its Commanding Officer, whose efforts never relaxed, despite great physical weariness. But for the example of Lt. Col. Ford, it is doubtful if the Battalion could have resisted the determined enemy onslaught for so long.

Roger Chapman, *1 Green Howards History*
20 Jan 44
'After being kept awake by intermittent shelling and machine gun fire during the night Lieutenant-Colonel Patrick George Bulfin went forward at dawn to make a reconnaissance of Tremensuoli, a small village a couple of miles ahead. He had been ordered to capture it this morning with support from 15 Infantry Brigade artillery units.

It was to prove a hard fight, as the artillery barrage did not stop the German machine gun and mortar fire. There were many casualties from splinters including Lieutenant Norman Yardley, who recovered from the wounds and later captained a successful English cricket XI in several Test matches after the war.

As 1 Green Howards consolidated their position in front of Tremensuoli, their elation was dampened by the news that the other units on either side of them had failed to reach their objectives. They were left alone on the salient subject to almost continuous shell and mortar fire throughout the day and night.'

1 Green Howards Citation: Distinguish Service Order for Lt. Col. P.G. Bulfin
On 19-20 Jan 44 Lt. Col. Bulfin was in command of 1 Green Howards when that Battalion was ordered to attack first Minturno and subsequently Tremensuoli. Lt. Col. Bulfin pressed his attacks with vigour and determination and despite intense enemy fire of all kinds, his Battalion gained their objectives and reorganised. Lt. Col. Bulfin's influence was most marked and his presence at points of danger throughout this action were an encouragement and inspiration to all ranks under his command.

View of Tremensuoli from Point 141, Monte Del Duca. (Photo Peter Strafford)

Despite great physical exhaustion Lt. Col. Bulfin's efforts never flagged, and he raised his tired Battalion to great efforts. His cool judgement under fire, his skill in directing his Battalion and his own example of fearlessness showed qualities of leadership which were quite outstanding.

'D' Battery 56 Heavy Regiment Royal Artillery – 56 Infantry Division
20 Jan 44
Lance Bombardier Spike Milligan joined the Royal Artillery at the start of the Second World War and served in North Africa and Italy [after the war he became a famous comedian]. On 20 Jan 44 he was with 56 Heavy Regiment Royal Artillery, having crossed the River Garigliano. The Regiment was equipped with massive 7.2-inch calibre guns, capable of hurling a 202lb shell over nine miles. He suffered from shell shock and was repatriated to Naples. He describes what happened in his book, *Mussolini, His Part in My Downfall:*

'Passing a steady stream of ambulances; one I noticed had schrapnel holes in the sides. All around are dead Jerries. Machine Gun bullets are whistling overhead as we duck and run inside.'

D. Woolard, attached to 2 Wiltshires, *My Day, 20 January*
'A large grave was dug near our gun positions and three Non-Commissioned Officers, and a Lieutenant were buried there. In the afternoon we moved forward, and my mortar and Jobber Brown's ranged with smoke bombs. Towards evening enemy shelling became more intense. Some of the lads slept in a German dugout and the remainder of us slept out in the open behind any cover we could find. I found a blanket left behind in the German dugout and a few bits of wood. I made a rough bed and put it behind a bank of earth. I covered myself up, laid my rifle by my side under the blanket and tried to sleep. I did not sleep at first because there were enemy planes overhead and the Ack-

Ack guns were pumping tracer shells up at them. The Royal Artillery and the Germans were shelling heavily. Suddenly I heard the scream of bombs coming down and they did sound awfully close. Then came a few terrific flashes followed by explosions not far away in Tufo itself. The enemy planes droned on and away and I must have fallen fast asleep because the next thing I remember was Ernie Hayward shaking me for my turn on guard. We whispered about the bombing and wondered what had been hit and if there had been many casualties. Then the conversation turned to more normal things like the food, or the lack of it, good times in the past, relations and friends and about recent events. Our two hours soon went in this manner, and we woke the next two chaps and saw them get up before we got down to sleep again. We were called to stand to just before dawn because the Germans were shelling our positions heavily. I put on my steel helmet, took my rifle, and got into our gun-pit with the rest of our detachment.'

X (BR) Corps History
20 Jan 44

Enemy Position: By dawn on 20 Jan 44 the German 94 Infantry Division had been reinforced by the Reconnaissance Battalion of the Herman Goering Division, and by the end of the day it had succeeded in temporarily stabilising a line and containing the bridgehead. Their success was not achieved easily. The two German Regiments which were holding the Gustav Line at the start suffered heavily.

13 Infantry Brigade continued its advance on 20 Jan 44. 1 Green Howards on the left went on from Minturno and captured the village of Tremensuoli during the afternoon. This fighting yielded two hundred and forty-four prisoners chiefly from the area of Monte Natale; in addition, the enemy suffered further casualties from machine gun and artillery fire in an unsuccessful attempt to recapture Colle Casale, Point 201, the hill above Tufo village, which 13 Infantry Brigade had taken over and held, from which it was supporting the advance of 15 Infantry Brigade.

German views of the day
20 Jan 44

Lt. Wolfgang Wiedermann, II Battalion 267 Grenadier Regiment
20 Jan 44

'The artillery fire always occurred in intervals. We recognized the shells of the ship's guns by their much more powerful explosions. For seconds, the valley was illuminated by the impacts, above all else also by the dreaded phosphorous shells. So, we were able to orientate ourselves a bit. Our bad luck was that we could only use the one narrow path that led to the bottom of the valley. Even during the day, the steep terrain was hardly passable. This path became the fate of many of our men. To the right the terrain dropped steeply. To the left it went up just as steeply. Partly there were large flat steep walls. Due to shelling, tons of earth and debris were loosened in these places, which buried the narrow path. We had these bad experiences during the descent. Half-buried comrades, who were buried or injured by the avalanches, could only be freed with great difficulty. It was despairing – only very slowly we made progress in this terrible, dark night. A way into hell could not be worse. The Sergeants and other NCOs did everything they could to cheer the men up.

Despite these murderous circumstances, there was no panic. The soldiers had rigid discipline. They were mainly 18–20-year-olds who had no experience at the front. Admirably, they passed their baptism of fire. When we reached the valley about 20 men were missing. About a dozen wounded. Eight men had to carry two seriously wounded. It took them several hours to cover a short distance.

By daybreak we were supposed to be in our starting positions because of the enemy's visibility. Orientation was still not possible in the darkness. The opaque situation unsettled us. Friend and foe were colourfully mixed up in the main battlefield.

The Company proceeded cautiously. In the glow of the detonating shells, we recognized the outline of a mountain top. This must be the high ground of Point 201. I assigned the Platoons to the North and West slopes of Point 201. The men had to dig in immediately. The enemy artillery had only short breaks of fire during the night. To prevent the approach of German Reserves, the English shelled every road and path with artillery and mortar fire. This tactic was sufficiently felt when we descended into the valley. At the first morning light in the valley, we recognized right above, at the Santa Maria Infante-Minturno road the wall of the Cemetery. I immediately sent a small troop of three men to investigate whether "Tommy" is sitting there or make connection to the right flank. These men never came back. Maybe they were lying in the shellfire, or "Tommy" had caught them. The attempt to connect with the left flank failed. After many hours, the troop returned completely exhausted. There was no left flank at this point.

In the valley bottom there were layers of yellow fog. The many smoke and phosphorus grenades that exploded here on 17 Jan 44, in addition to the explosive grenades, left behind these poisonous smelling veils. Tree stumps and splintered trees were the result of days of artillery fire.

A small scouting party was assigned to find out if the height Point 201 was occupied by the enemy – before our men reached the top, they received fire. Now I knew that we had to take the height by storm. The English could not see us, because we were in the shadow of the front slope. We were still preparing for the attack. The observation planes of the enemy artillery were hanging in the sky as soon as the brightness began to increase. For sure they could observe us. A quick surprise attack was for us the only chance. Connection to 274 Regiment by radio was lost. Major Frank and I Battalion 267 Grenadier Regiment had not been in contact since San Agostino. Where our Battalion was deployed is unknown. An Advanced Observer from our artillery was not available in the combat section at this time. Maybe he had fallen or been captured. After all, the British units had achieved kilometre-deep infiltration and only small remnants or nothing at all of our Grenadier Companies existed anymore.

Now at a decisive moment I raised my arm and gave the signal to attack. Determined, the Grenadiers jumped up and stormed and climbed up the mountain slope. As we held fire in the upper third of Point 201, I heard the powerful voice of Sergeant Pinkes, as he cheered the men of his Platoon. In these moments of extreme tension, one had to repress feelings. Fighting cries rang out everywhere. 40–50 metres in front of me I saw two English officers in olive uniforms shouting and cheering on their men. They had peaked caps on and small sticks or riding whips in their hands. These officers were extraordinarily brave and contemptuous of death. We were very close to the target. and a veritable fireball went off.

"Tommy" had, in desperate situations we did the same, requested concentrated barrage fire of his own artillery on his own lines. Without cover holes the Company pushed the murderous shellfire mercilessly. The cries of the wounded were drowned in the roar of the bursting shells. Many cried in vain for help. This direct fire had certainly been prepared and drawn by the Observation Posts and Artillery Observers who sat on the surrounding high ground.

The experienced front-line soldier could recognize quite exactly the two sounds of the approaching shells, which kind of artillery it was, or whether shells were firing at us. This time for the first time in Italy I heard projectile noises which I still remember from Russia. On the Eastern Front our compatriots called these weapons of destruction "Stalin organs". I owed my third wound at the beginning of the Stalingrad offensive in the summer of 1942 to this devilish stuff. It was only for seconds that I registered the unpleasant fact.

Before we were struck by the barrage from the English in this weak phase, I gave the order to retreat. Looking for shelter, we reached our starting positions depressed. I immediately ordered the machine guns into position. A fast English counterattack could have had devastating consequences. When we sat in the foxholes offering protection, we were safe from the effect of the artillery fire. Now our concern was for the wounded. Relieved of their injuries, our comrades searched for the way to the First Aid Post, which must be near the 274 Regiment's Command Post. The severely wounded gave me the greatest concern. For each of them we needed four stretcher bearers, who had to wait for hours to return in mountainous terrain. One had to have strong nerves after such a setback.

Among my Platoon Commanders, Sergeant Pinkes, was seriously wounded in the attack. His men called for me urgently. The concentrated barrage had been replaced by heavy disruptive fire. Jumping from cover to cover, I reached the desperate men after about 150 metres. The comrades had pulled the seriously wounded man out of the danger zone in a tent tarpaulin. Pinkes was curled up in the bloody canvas. His pain-distorted, bloodless face, lime-white and without consciousness showed me immediately that it looked bad for him. Only twitching reflex movements indicated that he was still alive. He had many injuries. We could not help. One of these brave men hastily told me: "We were very close to Tommy, and a machine gun burst hit him. Then came the barrage fire and he got some shell splinters." I gave a signal to the four stretcher bearers. Carefully they picked up their brave Platoon Commander and carried him back into the valley. There was little hope for Sgt. Pinkes. This chaos had drained us of all human emotion.

I wanted the Company Commander to check on the strength of the Company, but there was no point in such an effort; changes were constantly taking place. There were not many of us left. No one knew the number of men carrying the wounded away. Suddenly, Sgt. Freygang said, "Here comes a 'Tommy'." He pointed toward the Minturno Cemetery. An Englishman, with a rifle at his hip, was leading a German soldier into captivity. Without a belt, with arms raised, the visibly shaken Grenadier, with his guard coming from behind, ran directly towards us,. In seconds, who will be our prisoner of war, "Tommy?". Our freed comrade was from 274 Grenadier Regiment. He reported that the Cemetery of Minturno was in enemy hands. Whether the liberated man is happy or not, I do not believe it.

The men who had taken away Sergeant Pinkes, who had been shot at, reported to me. They looked exhausted. Their faces were grey. Sgt. Pinkes had not survived the severe wounds. After only a few hundred metres they left their Platoon Commander. Without regaining consciousness, he had bled to death. One of these men had collected his pay book and valuables in the Sergeant's bread bag. Apart from his watch and his wallet I saw his wounded badge. We kept silent in awe. Sgt. Pinkes was an old Russian fighter and a very brave soldier. We did not say anything.

My Company's men keep coming back. They were taking wounded men to the dressing station. They had been on the road for many hours, completely exhausted. I was shocked by the eyewitness report of a group of wounded soldiers. They had experienced how a severely wounded man and his four comrades, who carried him, were buried by tons of earth and rubble. An enemy grenade had hit a steep rock face and triggered a fatal avalanche. Help was not possible. Whether the English, after they had conquered the area, dug up the dead, we never knew.

The man, who had collected Sergeant Pinkes valuables in a bread bag, came back to the scene. He wanted to know who should receive these items. The food carriers should hand over the bread bag to the Sergeant Major. The Sergeant Major sends the contents to the relatives.

"Hopefully, the food carriers will come through the damn door tomorrow night"' the man said dryly. There had been no rations last night. I gave the iron portions freely, hardly anything was eaten.

On the road from Santa Maria Infante to Minturno we heard a heavy battle. Between the Minturno Cemetery and the Southern edge of Santa Maria Infante there was fierce fighting. Machine guns rattled. Strong engine noise reached us. The fighting took place at 1500–2000 metres (as the crow flies). We heard from the sound of shells that tanks on both sides had intervened in the fighting.

With force the English tried to reach Santa Maria Infante and then the road that led from Formia to Ausonia and Cassino. It was clear to us that on the third day of this offensive, 20 Jan 44, the soldiers of 5 British Infantry Division did everything they could to force the breakthrough. Then the German front could be rolled up to Cassino. The Germans tried with their last strength to prevent this objective being achieved.

To the right of us, towards the Minturno Cemetery, we suddenly took hold, we had not received any information in the chaos of those hours. The pioneers of our Division, one Pioneer Company, or at best two Companies, made a desperate attempt to run against the Allies' roll of fire. They wanted to push back the English. "Tommy" had concentrated on the road and the terrain right and left. After only minutes, we could watch, our Pioneer comrades were literally showered with shells of all calibres, including ship artillery. In between, smoke shells and the dreaded phosphorous grenades, it was a single cauldron. We were abruptly denied the pleasure of watching. "Tommy" included our room in the bombing!

Now we were in our holes, hoping to survive. Time did not pass at all. Suddenly there was a short silence. Now came the fighter-bomber Squadrons, which added to that inferno. Only here did I see fighter planes bomb the forward lines. The earth shook, and bombs that hit nearby took our air. The shock waves were terrible. I lay huddled in my foxhole. To observe the spectacle better, I turned on my back. My hope of getting out of here was nil. The descending fighter-bombers fired their cannons.

The tongues of fire were clearly visible. And then I saw the bombs being released. My fingers clawed into the ground. Vibrations and shock waves took our minds for a short time. Phosphorus fumes, the smoke grenades and the blast of explosions prevented us from breathing. It was an unbelievably bad day, but it showed that even if it were only a few infantrymen who were thrown into battle, desperately fighting infantrymen could prevent a breakthrough.

The attacking "Tommies" were as much at the end of their tether as we were. Prisoners we took the next day confirmed this to us. Our losses were extraordinarily high. We could only survive in deep holes. When the day ended, we were only 50 heads left. In 24 hours, the company had lost two-thirds of its men.

Late that night, Sergeant Major Kretzschmann came with the food. The men were impressed by the atmosphere of heavy combat and were shaken by our losses. Everyone got three portions, because our dead and wounded could not receive anything. We all hoped for an improvement the next day. It was to get much worse.'

Corporal Herbert Schumann, a signaller in 3 Company 'I' Battalion 267 Grenadier Regiment
20 Jan 44
'My company was alerted in the night of 19-20 Jan 44. III Battalion 267 Grenadier Regiment had to secure and defend the coastal section between Terracina and Sperlonga. After a night drive on trucks towards Cassino the trip ended Northwest of Santa Maria Infante. On 20 Jan 44 the Company reached Santa Maria Infante around noon. For many young soldiers the artillery raids were the first baptism of fire. The Company waited for the order to deploy into sheltered cellars. At midnight, the Company marched off. Large safety distances were a matter of course. I had a funny feeling in my stomach. We reached the staging area at dawn. We immediately received heavy artillery and mortar fire. The "spotter" aircraft was already in the sky. This machine, a reconnaissance plane, was used primarily by Allied Artillery Observers. We signallers from 3 Company, Knechtel, Schumann. Engel Muller and Brandl, had to link up with the Platoons. I could not find 2 Platoon. The path was exposed and under constant machine gun and grenade launcher [mortar] fire. The first wounded, as far as they could walk, came back. The fire was getting stronger and stronger. When I reached a fork in the road, I saw something very bad. A bull's eye had exploded in the middle of the pack train, just as my comrade Knechtel was arriving. He had splinters in his back. I bandaged up two more of my comrades who had chest wounds. For some men, there was nothing more I could do. I grabbed Private Knechtel somehow and dragged him back. That was all I could do for the moment. The ravine, which led to the height Point 201 and then on to Minturno, had attracted the enemy fire especially. The Officer Kutschera had caught a Tommy. So, we had to pay for our first fire baptism in Italy with a lot of blood of my comrades and superiors.'

Chapter 6

21 January 1944 – German Counterattack

When Pat Strafford (daughter of Ernest) first enquired about Ernest Strafford's death with the York & Lancaster Regimental Museum their records showed that he died on 21 January 1944. This was altered to 22 January 1944 after contact with the Commonwealth War Graves Commission!

X (BR) Corps History
The situation at dawn on 21 Jan 44 was as follows:

On the left of the bridgehead the difficulty of crossing the River Garigliano interfered with 5 Infantry Division's preparations. Although a Class 30 bridge on Route 7 had been completed on 20 Jan 44 it could only be used at night, while the Class 9 bridge two miles upstream could not be used to the full owing to the minefields and bad approaches. 201 Guards Brigade had crossed the river and concentrated South of Minturno, but, as some of its supporting artillery had failed to get across, it was decided to postpone the 201 Guards Brigade attack for twenty-four hours.

Meanwhile the enemy had completed his preparations for a counter offensive. The continuous counter attacks of the past few days flared up on 21 Jan 44 into a general offensive along the entire bridgehead front. X (BR) Corps was forced on to the defensive and had to fight hard and bitterly for two days to hold its position. During the fighting the enemy employed two new Divisions and part of a third in addition to

Italians with pack mules cross the Garigliano river with supplies for our forward troops, 21 Jan 44. (Photo 2 AFPU Sgt Bowman TNA 11240)

Sherman tank near the River Garigliano. 13 Brigade, 5 Division, 21 Jan 44. (Photo 2 AFPU Sgt. Tyler TNA 11115)

the depleted 94 Infantry Division and elements of the 44 Infantry Division which had already been in action.

15 Infantry Brigade War Diary
21 Jan 44
1 Green Howard's patrols during the night [20/21 January] reported Railway Station area strongly held by enemy machine guns and reported enemy digging into their North. 1 York & Lancs. patrols had not been able to get very far forward, whilst 1 KOYLI reported Point 141 edge unoccupied and sent a Carrier Platoon patrol out there to remain, at first light.

5 Infantry Division Counterattack Tasks
One Battalion of the Reserve Brigade will be prepared to carry out one of the following counterattacks:

(a) Counterattack ABLE to recapture Point 201, 7996.
(b) Counterattack BAKER to recapture Point 172, 7896.
(c) Counterattack CHARLIE to recapture Point 156 [Monte Natale] from direction of Point 172.
(d) Counterattack DOG to recapture Point 156 (Monte Natale) from the South.
(e) Counterattack EASY to recapture Spur 764961 – ring contour 762959- Spur 764957.

In the event of an enemy attack from the North or North-East becoming probable, Division Reserve Battalion will be ordered to assemble astride the jeep track-road and track junction 805935-Tufo. Battalion Command will report to HQ Infantry Brigade commanding centre sector. If an enemy attack from West is probable, Battalion will be ordered to assemble in area South of Point 141 781959, Monte del Duca. Battalion Command will report to HQ Infantry Brigade commanding left sector.

German tanks came down this road from Santa Maria Infante. This was 'A' Company 1 York & Lancs. position. (Photo John Strafford)

The outline of each counterattack is given. Detailed arrangements including a simple fire plan will be made when the conditions of the actual operation are known.

There then followed details of the tasks for each counterattack. 1 Green Howards was made the Division Reserve Battalion.

With all this activity around Point 172 was Ernest Strafford there or not? If there alive, he would surely have been attended to, so he was either dead and unseen or not there.

1 Green Howards War Diary
21 Jan 44 – 0200
'A' Company to area 770950 [half a kilometre South of Tremensuoli].

2 Wiltshires War Diary
21 Jan 44 – 0300
'D' Company move into position behind 'A' Company North-West of Tufo. Their previous position is taken over by 'D' Company, 2 Cameronians.

1 KOYLI War Diary
21 Jan 44
A patrol went out on to Point 141 at first light, made up from the Carrier Platoon under the command of Lieut. D.E. Dimbleby.

1 York & Lancs. War Diary
21 Jan 44 – 0700
'C' Company counterattacked from West and driven off North-West end of Point 156 on to 'B' Company's position. No direct fire brought down owing to failure of wireless and Verey Light signals not being seen. No telephone cable available to Company lines

as signals truck stuck South of the river and all cable which could be carried having been used to lay line to Brigade HQ. 'C' Company suffered heavy casualties and lost much equipment. Remainder of 'C' Company came under command of 'B' Company to strengthen their position on South end of Point 156. Enemy has withdrawn to reverse slopes except for observation posts on front slopes.

Major D. Webster was then ordered to take command of all troops on Monte Natale. He reorganised them as a composite 'B/C' Company on a five-platoon basis.

A soldier with 'B' Co. York & Lancs. describes what happened
'Another rude awakening at first light [21 Jan 44] when Gerry put in an attack on 'C' Coy. They were quickly overrun as they had been caught having breakfast. Even at 50 yards you could see our fellows standing with the Gerrys with their hands raised. The Gerrys seemed oblivious to our presence till we picked a couple of them off but with being so close together it was hard to shoot at our own. Anyway, they were marched off to the road and Gerry turned his attention to us. They had a good sniper and Private Cooper's brains [Private William Cooper. Minturno CWGC Cemetery] were running down the tree at my elbow, his legs must have wedged his body in an upright position while leaning back on the tree behind him. Another three shots hit him, and the sniper must have thought he had missed. Why he did not shoot me I cannot start to understand but I soon moved to another position. Then for the rest of the morning Gerry came screaming at us in waves, thank God for the thick hedge and our 25 pounders, which Major D. Webster had given us.'

A soldier from 'A' Co. 1 York & Lancs. described his experience
'When it became dark an enemy tank came up to where we were dug in and sprayed us with bullets but could not see where we were. We were pleased when he went off. Later when it became light two of us carried a box of ammunition to "B" Coy on our left who had been attacked.'

15 Infantry Brigade War Diary
21 Jan 44 – 0700
A minor counterattack developed on 1 York & Lancs. about 0700 hours which they repulsed successfully but the enemy remained on the Northern half of the Natale feature in very close contact with our troops. A few enemy tanks remained lurking in the area. One was claimed knocked out by our Artillery.

40 Royal Tank Regiment No. 1 Troop War Diary
21 Jan 44 – 0720
The disposition of No 1 Troop was as follows – Troop Leader at 781967, 1 disabled tank at 781968 [these are both within 100–200 metres North of Cemetery corner on the Santa Maria Infante road] the third tank at 780966 [by the Aid Post on the Santa Maria road] in a counterattack role.

2 Scots Guards War Diary
21 Jan 44 – 0800
Owing to the slow progress of the last few days and the stiff resistance which had been encountered, the plan for the attack by 201 Guards Brigade had been considerably

Scauri feature. Tremensuoli is in front of it, taken from Minturno. (Photo John Strafford)

modified. 6 Grenadier Guards were still to go for part of the Scauri Peninsula; 2 Scots Guards was to capture Scauri village, and 3 Coldstream Guards were to remain in reserve at Tremensuoli. In accordance with this plan all arrangements and reconnaissance of the area were carried out. The Battalion was sent for to move up to the start line when the whole attack was postponed till first light the following morning. The reason given for this was the discovery of a counterattack forming up in Scauri.

In the early hours of the morning a shell hit a house occupied by Michael Fitzherbert Brockholes, Duncan Cawbridge and about twenty signallers. It burst in a basement and the floor of the room in which the signallers were sleeping collapsed. Four men were killed, and five others wounded.

Spike Milligan, D Battery, 56 Heavy Regiment, Royal Artillery, *Mussolini: His Part in My Downfall*
21 Jan 44 – 0900
'We went forward. We reached the gully. In a ravine to the left were infantry all dug into the side; they were either resting or in reserve. So far so good. We reach the end of the stone gully and start climbing the stepped mountain – each step is six-foot high, so it is a stiff climb. Crump, Crump, Crump, mortars. We hit the ground. Crump, Crump, Crump – they stop. Why? Can they see us? We get up and go on, Crump, Crump, Crump – he can see us. I cling to the ground. The mortars rain down on us. I will have a fag, that's what. I am holding a packet of Woodbines, then there is a noise like thunder. It is right on my head, there is a high-pitched whistle in my ears, at first, I black out and then I see red, I am strangely dazed. I was on my front, now I am on my back, the red was opening my eyes straight into the sun. I know if we stay here, we will all die . . I start to scramble down the hill. There's shouting, I cannot recall anything clearly. Next, I was at the bottom of the mountain, next I am speaking to Major Jenkins, I am crying, I do not know why, he is saying "Get that wound dressed."'

I said, 'What wound?' I had been hit on the side of my right leg.

"Why did you come back?" He is shouting at me and threatening me, I cannot remember what I am saying. He's saying "You could find your way back, but you couldn't find your way to the Observation Post", next I'm sitting in an ambulance and shaking, an orderly puts a blanket round my shoulders. I am crying again, why, why, why? Next, I am in a Forward Dressing Station, an orderly gives me a bowl of hot extremely sweet tea. "Swallow these", he says, two small white pills. I cannot hold the bowl for shaking, he takes it from me and helps me drink it. All around are wounded, he has rolled up my trouser leg. He is putting a sticking plaster on the wound. He is telling me it is only a small one. I do not really care whether it is big or small, why am I crying? Why cannot I stop? I am getting lots of sympathy, what I want is an explanation. I am feeling drowsy and I must have started to sway because next I am on a stretcher. I feel lovely, what was in those tablets . . . that is the stuff for me, who wants food? I do not know how long I am there. I wake up. I am still on the stretcher, I am not drowsy, but I start to shiver. I sit up. They put a label on me. They get me to my feet and help me to an ambulance. I can see really badly wounded men, their bandages soaked through with blood, plasma is being dripped into them.

When we get to one of the Red Cross trucks, an Italian woman, all in black, young, beautiful, is holding a dead baby and weeping; someone says the child has been killed by a shell splinter.'

92 Field Regiment Royal Artillery War Diary
21 Jan 44 – 1115
368 Battery Commander reports that 1 KOYLI killed one sniper and captured another on Monte Natale ridge. Small counterattack repulsed this morning.

98 Field Regiment Royal Artillery War Diary
21 Jan 44 – 1130
Fire Plan from 471 Battery Commander. Battery to fire on line 772967 – 773965 [Western slopes of Monte Natale].

6 Grenadier Guards War Diary
21 Jan 44 – 1140
The Battalion was ordered to move to the Tremensuoli area to hold the line to ridge of the hills, prepared in a counterattack role.

N. Nicholson, 6 Grenadier Guards, *The Grenadier Guards in the War of 1939-1945, Volume II*
'The front line was scarcely four hundred yards North of the river, half-way up the first foothills which led to the massive cliffs of the Aurunci Mountains, and the Grenadiers at Tremensuoli led a troglodyte existence in slit trenches dug between the olive trees and rocky outcrops. The shell and mortar fire were unceasing'.

1 York & Lancs. War Diary
21 Jan 44 – 1230
1 Green Howards relieved by 3 Coldstream Guards and now in Brigade reserve in assembly area Minturno 784953 [half a kilometre South of Point 141, Monte del Duca].

14 Infantry Brigade War Diary
21 Jan 44

During the morning 1 Green Howards were successfully relieved on the Tremensuoli feature and came into Brigade reserve. Casualties unfortunately included the Adjutant and Information Officer wounded. The Brigade Information Officer, Captain H. Gundill was accordingly sent to 1 Green Howards to help them out temporarily and Captain J. Scott called up from 'B' Echelon to take over. ['B' Echelon is the Battalion's administrative area behind the lines where new arrivals are gathered, and stores stockpiled. Normally manned by the Quartermaster and his stores team. Often connected with the Division Admin Area.] He arrived about midday. It then became clear that the enemy was building up for a further counterattack on Monte Natale. 201 Guards Brigade on our left reported infantry debussing from half-track vehicles North-West of Monte Natale. This target was successfully engaged by the guns.

40 Royal Tank Regiment No. 1 Troop War Diary
21 Jan 44 – 1300

The Troop was dive bombed and the disabled tank was hit and set on fire, but the Troop suffered no casualties [tank was just North of Cemetery on Santa Maria Infante road].

52 Anti-Tank Regiment War Diary
21 Jan 44 – 1300

Brigade Commander returned and ordered guns up to Minturno and then proceeded back to the town to do a recce with the Regimental Officers. The ground was found to be very unsuitable for tanks, but guns were deployed in depth covering the road Route 7.

5 Infantry Division History
21 Jan 44 – 1300

A counterattack by 1 York & Lancs. on Point 156 at 0930 forced the Germans to yield about 200 yards but they remained in possession of the main feature. By 1215 1 Green Howards had been relieved by 3 Coldstream Guards [at Tremensuoli and Point 141] but at 1300 the other two Battalions [1 KOYLI and 1 York & Lancs.] were attacked by enemy aircraft and suffered further casualties. An earlier air attack had already been made on Minturno.

40 Royal Tank Regiment No. 1 Troop War Diary
21 Jan 44 – 1330

The disabled tank fire was extinguished, and the tank abandoned. Extensive damage was caused, one engine being out of action, the radiator smashed, the left-hand sprocket smashed and the tracks and suspension damaged.

98 Field Regiment Royal Artillery War Diary
21 Jan 44 – 1352

471 Battery Commander asked for Air Observation Post to observe the following areas: 7697,7696,7797 [areas Northwest of Monte Natale]. West half of road running North-East through 7697. 7697 believed to be area where counterattack is forming up

40 Royal Tank Regiment No. 1 Troop War Diary
21 Jan 44 – 1400
Orders received from the CO. of 1 York & Lancs. to move to protect the left flank.

21 Jan 44 – 1430-1630
We were accurately shelled and the third tank hit. No casualties and the tank still a runner.

1 York & Lancs. War Diary
21 Jan 44 – 1430
Report received of counterattack forming up in area. Artillery concentrations put down in area.

21 Jan 44 – 1435
Brigadier arrived at Tactical HQ to discuss recapture of North-West end of Point 156 by 'D' Company under barrage.

1 Green Howards War Diary
21 Jan 44 – 1435
Battalion moved to rest area 797949 [1km South-East of Minturno].

6 Grenadier Guards War diary
21 Jan 44 – 1450
Report: enemy debussing from half trucks about road junction – known as 'Squiggle' – forming up and attacking 1 York & Lancs. on Monte Natale.

1 York & Lancs. War Diary
21 Jan 44 – 1500
Another enemy counterattack was launched, not only against 'B/C' Company on Monte Natale but also 'A' Company on the road. The enemy put down a light smoke screen from the North to hide their attack on 'A' Company. The enemy suffered severe casualties. Accurate defensive fire by the artillery and the Battalion's 3-inch mortars prevented the Germans penetrating the main positions, but some of the forward posts were lost before the counterattack faded out.

98 Field Regiment Royal Artillery War Diary
21 Jan 44 – 1520
Commanding Officer reports enemy going to 775973 [1km North of Monte Natale].

1 KOYLI War Diary
21 Jan 44 – 1600
The enemy put in a counterattack with his axis along the road Santa Maria Infante – Minturno. It was directed in the main on Monte Natale which had previously been occupied or partially occupied by 1 York & Lancs. However, this counterattack although sharp was not successful and it appeared that the presence of our patrol on Point 141, Monte del Duca, reinforced by the new location of 'A' Company and present position of 'B' Company deterred the enemy from coming in on our front.

Heavy casualties were not suffered although the Germans succeeded in penetrating through the Platoon positions of 'B' Company. An interesting note on German methods was made. On more than one occasion it was reported that Germans were firing their automatics up in the air and generally behaving in a fashion as to indicate that they wished to give themselves up, but later on it was confirmed that the German fires into the air in this manner so as to indicate that he has at that point penetrated defences. Wherever he ran up against our prepared positions he engaged them with direct fire, and it was only when he got in between Sections or Platoon posts that he fired up into the air. Enemy prisoners were identified as the 90 Light Division, who were of a quite different calibre to those the Battalion had previously met. They came in all talking, shouting, and using many English phrases as 'You've had it Tommy' and 'Stick them up Tommy'.

1 KOYLI. Citation: Military Cross for Lieut. D.E. Dimbleby
20 Jan 44 – 1600

On 19 January 1944 the Battalion had reached and occupied the line of the Point 172 ridge North of Minturno. The position was under full enemy observation and continually under shellfire. In front of the ridge is a spur with Point 141 on the extremity, the dead ground beyond this was an ideal area for an enemy counterattack to form up. It was decided to send Lieut. Dimbleby and six Bren guns from the Carrier Platoon, which he commanded, to occupy this Point. A stronger patrol could not be spared. Lieut. Dimbleby occupied the position by first light on 20 January 1944. During the day nothing of importance happened. At about 1600 the enemy could be heard in the dead ground in front of Point 141. Lieut. Dimbleby took his Bren guns forward and found, as expected, the Germans in force forming up for an attack. He let them have all he had from his six Bren guns. Chaos was created amongst them, and Lieut. Dimbleby extracted his small force to prepare positions further back down the ridge to await developments. During the whole of the action the enemy small arms and artillery fire was heavy and continuous. After some delay the Germans came on again down the ridge. Again Lieut. Dimbleby held the fire of his Brens and then gave the enemy all he could at short range. Although out of touch with the rest of the Battalion Lieut. Dimbleby stayed in position until he had fired every Bren magazine in his possession. Only then did he withdraw to his own lines. This very gallant action by Lieut. Dimbleby preventing the enemy counterattack developing.

1 York & Lancs. War Diary
21 Jan 44 – 1630

'A' Company counter attacked under light smoke screen from North. 'B' Company attacked from Northwest. Attacks both very heavy and enemy suffered severe casualties both from small arms and artillery fire. Line communications with Companies broken early on but wireless worked well until 'A' Company's destroyed by shell fire. 'B' Company's set worked well throughout.

52 Anti-Tank Regiment War Diary
21 Jan 44 – 1630

Enemy counterattacks on 1 York & Lancs. positions started, preceded by artillery and mortar concentration on Monte Natale. By last light some penetration had been made and gun detachments stood to, manning small arms. Attack was not continued during the night, but Minturno was shelled regularly. No casualties but several near misses.

40 Royal Tank Regiment No. 1 Troop War Diary
21 Jan 44 – 1640
Enemy commenced a counterattack with tanks and infantry. The leading tank of the Troop engaged an enemy tank which however withdrew under cover of smoke. The Troop silenced several machine-gun posts.

1 York & Lancs. Missing Person's Report by Private Mathews
21 Jan 44 – 1700
'D' Company moved up to Hill 156 to assist the forward Companies who were being counterattacked. '17' Platoon to which Private Franks belonged was ordered to take up position in support of 'A' Company on the right flank and at that time Private Franks was in good health. That was the last I saw of Private Franks.

6 Grenadier Guards War Diary
21 Jan 44 – 1700
A high feature on our right [Monte Natale] was counterattacked successfully by the Germans and in consequence our positions became more important in that they should be held as a firm base.

98 Field Regiment Royal Artillery War Diary
21 Jan 44 – 1726
Counterattack appears to be coming to area 7796, Point 156, Monte Natale.

7 Cheshires War Diary
21 Jan 44 – 1730
Two Platoons 'D' Company rushed into action during a fierce enemy counterattack on Monte Natale. Very rapid action by the Platoons. Guns were in action and firing seven minutes after order had been received. These Platoons had approximately 500 feet of uphill country to cross to reach their positions.

15 Infantry Brigade War Diary
21 Jan 44 – 1735
By 1735, 1 York & Lancs. reported a heavy counterattack coming in on their front and all available artillery support was asked for and accepted. It appeared that the enemy was putting in two main thrusts, one down the Santa Maria Infante Road and the other up the valley between Monte Natale and Tremensuoli ridge.

7 Cheshires War Diary
21 Jan 44 – 1745
One Platoon 'C' Company in action [just West of Point 141, Monte del Duca].

102 Medium Regiment Royal Artillery War Diary
21 Jan 44

One Other Rank killed. One Other Rank wounded in dive bomb attack – Minturno.

At dusk the expected counterattack came in on 1 York & Lancs. To meet any further loss of ground 'F' Company was sent to a defensive position West of Minturno, and 'C' Company to a similar position. Right Flank Company remained in reserve.

2 Wiltshires War Diary
21 Jan 44 – 1800
'A' Company patrols report enemy digging in on forward slopes of Point 201 and a Regimental Concentration of fire is put down on that area. 'A' Company warned to expect strong counterattack and Carrier Platoon sent up to reinforce them.

92 Field Regiment Royal Artillery War Diary
21 Jan 44 – 1805
467 Battery Commander with 3 Coldstream Guards at 769956 [Tremensuoli]. Wireless set broken, new batteries and rations needed. 467 Battery ordered to send replacements immediately.

7 Cheshires War Diary
21 Jan 44 – 1815
One Platoon 'D' Company carried out harassing shoot on enemy position on Point 156, Monte Natale.

92 Field Regiment Royal Artillery War Diary
21 Jan 44 – 1825
Message by wireless from 467 Battery Commander: 'All guns are to raise range 400 yards on Direct Fires and not to fire until further orders'. Message suspected to be bogus!

98 Field Regiment Royal Artillery War Diary
21 Jan 44 – 1830
Hectic hour in which 392 and 471 Batteries each received urgent SOS's and 391 Battery alternated from one to the other in support. Meanwhile Division asked for six Stonks [artillery bombardments] which had to be refused. Ammunition running low.

40 Royal Tank Regiment No. 1 Troop War Diary
21 Jan 44 – 1830
The Troop withdrew to 781966 [Aid Post] to entice the enemy tanks on to their guns, but the enemy did not follow up.

201 Guards Brigade War Diary
21 Jan 44 – 1830
One Platoon of 'C' Company, 7 Cheshires in position 779956 [just West of Point 141] with counter penetration task. Enemy infantry worked forward to gain contact with 3 Coldstream Guards. Enemy Observation Posts and infantry on Monte Natale and the West end of the Tremensuoli spur got the measure of 6 Grenadier Guards and 3 Coldstream Guards. Mortaring and shelling prohibited movement by day and started to cause casualties. The proposed relief of 3 Coldstream Guards by 15 Infantry Brigade

was cancelled because the Monte Natale situation was not cleared up. The attack of 201 Guards Brigade Westwards was also put in abeyance.

15 Infantry Brigade War Diary
21 Jan 44 – 1830
1 York & Lancs. were out of touch with their right-hand forward Company in the Cemetery area ['A' Company] whilst the Monte Natale 'C' Company, was down to 30-40 effective soldiers. The Battalion was at the time organised in three strong Companies and the third was sent to reinforce Monte Natale. Reinforcements were however urgently needed and the Brigade Major in the absence of the Brigadier (who was at 201 Guards Brigade HQ) ordered one Company from 1 Green Howards to move up at once under command of 1 York & Lancs. whilst a second Company was placed at 15 minutes notice to move in reserve. Ammunition was also in very short supply and assistance asked from 201 Guards Brigade and 13 Infantry Brigade were readily forthcoming.

92 Field Regiment Royal Artillery War Diary
21 Jan 44 – 1845
368 Battery Commander orders engagement of target at 785972 [1km North of Point 172].

21 Jan 44 – 1850
368 Battery Commander reports enemy counterattack was preceded by heavy mortaring and shelling of 1 KOYLI positions.

1 Green Howards War Diary
21 Jan 44 – 1900
Battalion standing by to relieve 1 York & Lancs.

15 Infantry Brigade War Diary
21 Jan 44 – 1900
1 KOYLI reported that their right and centre were OK, but they were anxious about their left which adjoined the main road [road to Santa Maria Infante]. Their Carrier Platoon on Point 141 had previously been withdrawn having fired all their ammunition and successfully broken up the counterattack East of the road. Throughout this period Line Telephone communications were disabled, and the Battalion Major was in touch with 1 York & Lancs. and 1 KOYLI by radio telephone. [Some Regiments called their Battalion Second in Command the Battalion Major, whilst others used the term Senior Major.] The Brigade Commander was at 1 York & Lancs. HQ when the counterattack started – later he went to visit 201 Guards Brigade HQ and 13 Infantry Brigade HQ. Control in this period was in the hands of the Brigade Major who had as his Second in Command Major C. Aris, 92 Field Regiment RA who was supervising artillery support.

1 KOYLI Citation: Distinguish Service Order for Major H.L. Robinson
21 Jan 44
Major H.L. Robinson was in Command of 'B' Company, 1 Battalion, The King's Own Yorkshire Light Infantry holding the left of the 172 ridge on 20 January 1944. This position was the key to the Brigade defensive area and had to be held at all costs. At

about 1600 hours whilst just forward of Minturno on the 172 ridge a heavy counterattack developed on our left. Although on his left flank the position was obscure, Major Robinson went up to the forward Platoons and so directed the battle that the enemy were unable to make any headway on his Company front. During the night 20-21 January the Company position was under enemy machine gun and artillery fire, whilst on his left it appeared that they had succeeded in infiltrating through. At first light it was obvious that they intended to drive us from this position. Right from the beginning of this action the left flank of the position was exposed, and the Company was in fact almost encircled. Despite this Major Robinson continued to lead the fighting from the forward positions until such time as the forward Platoons were overrun by Germans. Then fighting his way by grenade and machine gun fire he reached his Company HQ position where he carried on the fight. For a long time, Major Robinson could be seen directing the fire of his automatic weapons and skilfully holding the Germans at bay. When at last his total Company was reduced to some dozen men and it was impossible to hold the position he skilfully withdrew some 300 yards to the Reserve Company locality, where he at once reformed his group of men and engaged the enemy. The Germans never succeeded in penetrating this second line of defence, although a counterattack continued until late evening of 21 January. As a result of this Officer's magnificent example of personal courage, his complete disregard for his own personal safety and his cool, skilled handling of his Company, the enemy never succeeded in occupying the 172 ridge and the key position was held by our forces. The battlefield on Point 172 covered as it is with dead Germans and with the men of Major Robinson's Company bears eloquent witness to the fierceness of the fighting and to the skill and courage of the defenders.

40 Royal Tank Regiment No. 1 Troop War Diary
21 Jan 44 – 1910
Attack finally beaten off, and the Troop withdrew to 785958 [half a kilometre North of Minturno] taking up a counterattack role astride the Santa Maria Infante road where they were shelled throughout the night.

92 Field Regiment Royal Artillery War Diary
21 Jan 44 – 1910
368 Battery Commander reports 1 York & Lancs. having 'a difficult time, but 1 Green Howards are there. Fire was good'.

5 Infantry Division History
21 Jan 44
In the afternoon, enemy artillery activity heralded a further counterattack from the direction of Monte Natale. This was once more effectively broken up by the Divisional Artillery. To what extent was basically described by Major Prior, OC 368 Battery supporting 1 KOYLI, who reported 'The Boche caught no mean packet.' Farther to the North-West of Minturno, however, the depleted 1 York & Lancs. was having a difficult time and 1 Green Howards, only just relieved by 3 Coldstream Guards, sent their 'A' and 'C' Companies to help. The latter Company put in a quick counterattack under Command of 1 York & Lancs. but were forced to abandon it under heavy pressure. All afternoon repeated attempts were made to hammer 1 York & Lancs. positions.

1 York & Lancs. War Diary
21 Jan 44 – 1930
'A', 'B' and 'C' Companies suffered heavy casualties. 'D' Company sent up to reinforce 'A' and 'B' Companies. One Platoon being put under command 'A' Company, two Platoons under 'B' Company. Counterattack beaten off. The enemy withdrew to the reverse slope. HQ was dive bombed during the day.

1 York & Lancs. Military Medal Citation for Sergeant B Smith
On 21 January 1944 when his Company was heavily counterattacked North-West of Minturno and overrun by tanks Sergeant Smith displayed great gallantry and devotion to duty in organising his Platoon in a defensive position when under fire. He led his Platoon under fire, got them into positions and moved from Section to Section with complete disregard for his own safety, encouraging his men to stick to their posts. He set an exceptionally fine example to his whole Platoon and greatly helped to maintain our positions.

1 KOYLI War Diary
21 Jan 44 – 1930
In the evening things began to happen. 1 York & Lancs. on our left were heavily counterattacked and our own front was only protected by the skilful action of our standing patrol on Point 141.

The attack died down at dusk – but by this time it was apparent that the enemy had reinforced, and we were up against 90 Light Division, a well-known hard fighting unit. Things did not look quite so good on the Point 172 ridge and accordingly 'C' Company, previously in reserve, was moved a little closer to 'B' and 'A' Companies.

1 KOYLI Citation: Military Cross for Captain G.E. Pinkerton Royal Army Medical Corps.
Captain Pinkerton RAMC. is Regimental Medical Officer attached to 1 KOYLI. During operations on 21 January 1944 in front of Minturno he displayed an extraordinary devotion to duty in maintaining his Aid Post in a forward position, for the greater part of the time under enemy fire, both small arms and artillery. He dealt coolly and efficiently with many casualties from all areas and other units as well as his own. Early in the battle a Company suffered some 20 casualties through walking into an enemy minefield. Captain G E Pinkerton regardless of his own personal safety and knowing that the area was heavily mined led a rescue party and successfully evacuated the wounded. He remained without rest for some 36 hours, never failing to give continued treatment even though during the intense enemy fire his Regimental Aid Post was hit and pierced by anti-personnel shells on three occasions. This Officer's complete disregard for his own personal safety and his great display of individual courage were a fine example to all ranks.

98 Field Regiment Royal Artillery War Diary
21 Jan 44 – 2000
Stonk 773973 [1km North West of Monte Natale] over period of 15 minutes. 471 Battery Observation Post reports strong counterattack by the enemy.

15 Infantry Brigade War Diary
21 Jan 44 – 2000
The Brigade Major spoke to HQ 5 Infantry Division on the phone and was told that 1 York & Lancs. must hold their ground that night and that not more than one Company, 1 Green Howards should be used as reinforcement unless absolutely essential. This message was passed on to the Brigade Command by the Brigade Information Officer on foot.

5 Infantry Division History
21 Jan 44 – 2030
Just before last light 1 KOYLI and 1 York & Lancs. on Point 156 were again counter attacked, the attack this time was supported by armour, but in the initial stages only, as the failing light soon forced the enemy to withdraw his tanks. By 2030 it was known that 1 York & Lancs. had repulsed the attack and some prisoners had been taken. The enemy however remained in close contact. 1 York & Lancs. were by now very thin on the ground and a Company of 1 Green Howards was moved up between them and 1 KOYLI, a further Company following up as reserve.

1 KOYLI reported that the enemy appeared to hold the Monte Natale feature with many machine guns. Enemy patrols were still active, and it looked as though another counterattack could be expected on the left flank. A small counterattack was later repulsed. 1 KOYLI got up onto Monte Natale, killed a sniper and captured another. 91 Field Regiment, Royal Artillery made a dash for their new area and were able to get in quite a lot of digging before the enemy reacted with counter battery fire.

98 Field Regiment Royal Artillery War Diary
21 Jan 44 – 2100
'E' Battery Observation Post reports reason Stonk stopped was one of our Regiments firing noticeably short. 777973 (approx. 1km North of Monte Natale), should be OK.

15 Infantry Brigade War Diary
21 Jan 44 – 2155
1 York & Lancs. were able to report that they had given no ground at all, viz, they still held a footing on Monte Natale and held the Cemetery as well. Their casualties however had not been light. They were in touch on their right with 1 KOYLI on Point 172.

1 KOYLI War Diary
21 Jan 44 – 2200
Tactical HQ heavily shelled. 102 Medium Regiment RA wireless set destroyed and also one of 98 Field Regiment's sets.

21 Jan 44 – 2300
'C' Company was subjected to a very heavy enemy counterattack and was driven back with heavy loss on to 'B' Company's position. 'C' Company lost much equipment. During the night of 21/22 Jan 44 there was shelling, considerable patrol activity, and moreover heavy enemy motor transport movement was heard.

Two Companies of 1 Green Howards put under command of 1 KOYLI Battalion, one Company arrived 2300 and was used to reinforce 'A' and 'B' companies. The other would not arrive until 0530, 22 Jan 44, then remain in reserve.

17 Infantry Brigade War Diary
21 Jan 44 – 2305
Warning order received from Division that Brigade may have to push through 13 Infantry Brigade if 1 Green Howards fail to restore ground lost by 1 York & Lancs. [Point 156]. Weather: Fine.

1 Green Howards War Diary
21 Jan 44 – 2345
'A' Company moved off to reinforce 1 York & Lancs.

1 York & Lancs. War Diary
21 Jan 44 – 2359
Hold half of Point 156. 1 Green Howards on way to reinforce. 1 KOYLI have a Platoon on Point 141. 6 Grenadier Guards, North and East of Tremensuoli. 2 Scots Guards on Point 141. 7 Cheshires, One Platoon 'C' company in position. 2 Wiltshires: 'A' Co. Point 201, 'D' Co. behind 'A' Co. Battalion HQ in house South of Tufo, 'C' Co. on Point 151, and 'B' Co. West of Tufo.

This was the position at midnight on 21 January 1944. Two Sherman tanks were positioned on the road North of Minturno ready to assist 1 York & Lancs.

X (BR) Corps History
21 Jan 44
On the left of the bridgehead, the attack on Monte Natale was fiercely pressed and, though the attack was held the enemy remained in close contact when night fell on 21 January. GOC 5 Infantry Division planned a preliminary attack by 15 Infantry Brigade to restore its front before launching 201 Guards Brigade to clear the remainder of the high ground.

5 Infantry Division War Diary
It was arranged during the night that as 15 Infantry Brigade had to carry out an operation to restore its front on Point 156 this attack should be made before that of 201 Guards Brigade so that each operation might be given the maximum artillery support.

5 Infantry Division History
In the week ending 21 January 1944 there were 48 deserters from 5 Infantry Division.

The *Sheffield Telegraph* War Correspondent post-battle account – 5 February 1944
'More details can now be revealed of the heroic battle fought by a battalion of the York and Lancaster Regiment defending ground gained during the Garigliano fighting. The battle lasted two days.

The German forces were vastly superior numerically – at one time they had five battalions supported by armour – but the Englishmen only withdrew when ordered to do so. By this time one company was described as a skeleton of its former self but the enemy had paid heavily for his temporary success. When the ground was taken later, hundreds of German bodies were found.

At dawn on the day after a hill with twin peaks had been taken and the two companies of the York and Lancs. holding them were attacked, one company was forced off its height and joined the other company.

For two and a half hours they were heavily in action with their own mortars firing at under minimum range with grave danger of the bombs falling on themselves. But these mortars helped to beat off the morning attacks.

In the afternoon two German Battalions advanced to attack, but the remnants of the two companies held on, aided by heavy artillery support although the enemy were so close that some shells were bound to fall into British positions.

The Germans at one time were within forty yards of the peak but there they were halted. One of twelve prisoners said that almost all his company had been wiped out. Until dark, with ammunition running low the York and Lancs. held off an enemy six times as numerous and at dusk the Germans withdrew to the foot of the hill.

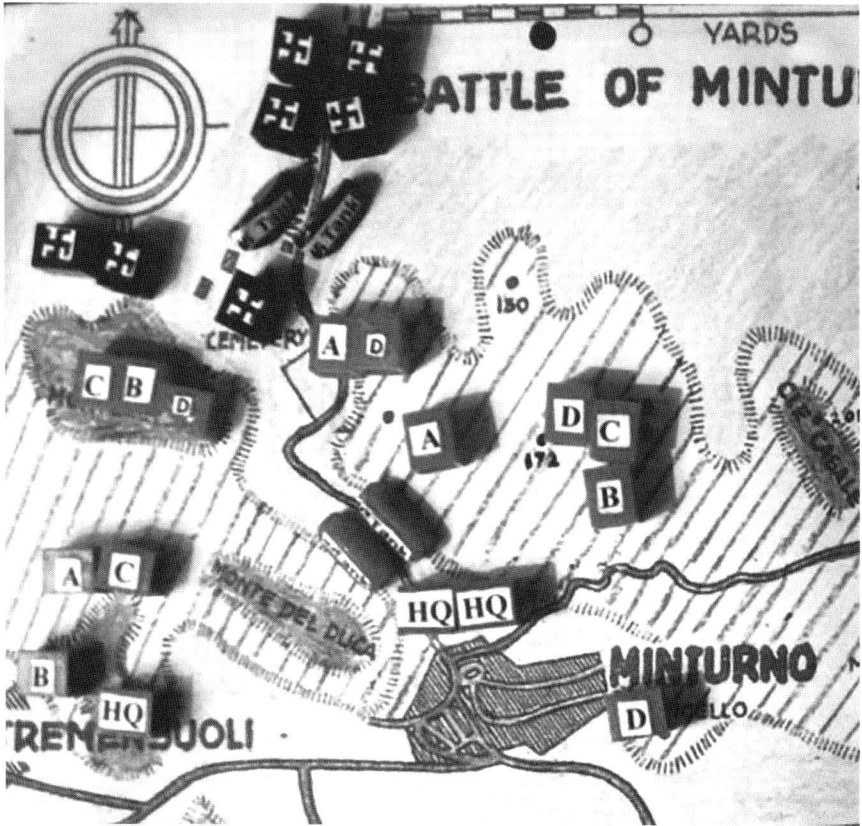

Main dispositions of 1 York & Lancs. 1 Green Howards and KOYLI at midnight 21 Jan 44. 1 York & Lancs. on Monte Natale. 1 Green Howards around Tremensuoli. 1 KOYLI. At Point 172.

6 Seaforths War Diary

21 Jan 44

Strong counterattack afternoon of 21 January by 300 to 400 infantry and six tanks on 1 York & Lancs. position. 1 York & Lancs. forced to give ground slightly.

German views of the day: Lt. Wolfgang Wiedemann, II Battalion, 267 Panzer Grenadier Regiment

21 Jan 44

'The night 20–21 Jan 44 remained restless. The days of the Great Battle had reached their climax. The artillery fire subsided a little at times, but it lasted all night. Totally exhausted, our men slept in their shelters, their rifles, or submachine guns in their arms. The machine-gunners were placed in a safe position. Defensive readiness had absolute priority. At the first beam of light, I jumped from group to group. The danger of an English attack at this early morning hour was very great.'

Corporal Herbert Schumann 'I' Battalion 267 Grenadier Regiment

21 Jan 44

'Today the rest of the Company withdrew to Santa Maria Infante. There I was informed that my comrade, Frederick Knechtel had died of his serious injury. On this mission we lost 50% of our Company strength. Our Company Commander, Lieutenant Kroner was relieved of his post. Lieutenant Horst Castner became our new Commander.'

127

Chapter 7

22 January 1944 – Private Ernest Strafford REPORTED MISSING

5 Infantry Division History

22 Jan 44

The alarums and excursions died down as night fell on 21 Jan 44 but both sides patrolled actively throughout the night. Patrols from 13 Infantry Brigade reported that the enemy was preparing a large-scale attack against the Tufo area and sure enough at first light, preceded by a heavy artillery and mortar bombardment, he launched a sharp attack that overran 'A' Company of 2 Wiltshires, forcing them to give up about 200 yards of valuable ground. The Company Commander [Capt. Clarke] together with his Forward Observation Officer [Capt. Plant of 91 Field Regiment RA] and a Platoon, went forward immediately to restore the position, but they were likewise overrun. Capt. Plant called for Direct Fire on to their positions and most of the party were extricated, but the two Captains themselves were shot and taken prisoner. Whilst they were receiving attention from a German medical orderly a heavy concentration from the Divisional Artillery came down onto Point 201. This forced the enemy to withdraw and abandon their two prisoners who managed to struggle back to the main positions. A successful counterattack was made by 2 Cameronians who secured Point 201 for good.

York Record Office

Private Ernest Strafford: REPORTED MISSING – Believed wounded. (York Record Office)

On the extreme left of the sector 2 Northants, then under command of 13 Infantry Brigade, came into Divisional Reserve and moved up into the foothills of the Minturno-Tufo Ridge to reconnoitre a counterattack on to Point 156. This counterattack plan was later cancelled. They remained dug in and suffered only a few casualties from heavy shell fire. In the evening a few lonely enemy bombers added to their temporary discomfort.

5 Infantry Division Intelligence 22 Jan 44
Enemy situation
II Battalion 200 Panzer Grenadier Regiment came into the Monte Natale area followed by II Battalion 361 Grenadier Regiment into the area of Point 141. In the morning '9' Company, III Battalion, 200 Grenadier Regiment came in between the two other Battalions and attacked down the road past the Cemetery. As we have known before, '9' Company of 90 Panzer Grenadier Division is used both to be carried in half-tracked vehicles and very often used in close cooperation with the tanks of 190 Panzer Battalion. In December 43 they lost their half-tracked vehicles, but the Company may still be used independently. It is therefore by no means established that all of III Battalion 200 Panzer Grenadier Regiment is on our front.

102 Medium Regiment Royal Artillery War Diary
22 Jan 44
Heavy counterattack North-West of Minturno repulsed. Capt. Mirando slight wound – not evacuated. One Other Rank killed [Sgt. Ernest Hughes. Minturno CWGC Cemetery]. 'A' Troop gun position shelled during morning. One Other rank killed. One Other Rank wounded.

1 York & Lancs. War Diary
22 Jan 44 – 0001
7 Cheshires MG [machine gun] arrived and ordered to occupy positions to cover valley South of Point 156, Monte Natale.

92 Field Regiment, Royal Artillery War Diary
22 Jan 44 – 0030
HQ Royal Artillery inform that Fire Plan will be required in support of 1 Green Howards on 22 Jan 44 between 0700 – 0730. Details to follow. X (BR) Corps Artillery to be silent between 1200 – 1300 except in emergency as Reserve Company out making special effort to locate German Heavy Batteries during that period.

5 Infantry Division History
22 Jan 44 – 0200
1 York & Lancs. positions were still very insecure. In the temporary absence of the Brigade Commander who was involved somewhere or other in the thick of the fighting, the Brigade Major F. W. de Butts, alerted and moved 1 Green Howards into a longstop position and tried to get a Battalion of 201 Guards Brigade, facing the same way. This was to be the peak of the enemy's efforts and he was within an ace of achieving his aim.

1 York & Lancs. War Diary
22 Jan 44 – 0300
Two men from 92 Field Regiment arrived to arrange artillery fire in support of counterattack on North-West end of Point 156, Monte Natale. Zero hour at 0900 decided on, consisting of barrage from three Field and two Medium Artillery Regiments in a semi-circle round North-West end of Point 156 arranged. SP [self- propelled gun] Regiments to fire concentrations on localities on Point 156 already registered. Four anti-tank guns in position in 'A' company's area.

15 Infantry Brigade War Diary
22 Jan 44 – 0345
Traffic became hopelessly jammed between Point 172 and the Class 9 bridge over the River Garigliano. However, labour provided by 13 Infantry Brigade managed to clear the debris and about midnight traffic was moving round this very exposed corner OK. The Brigadier now established himself in some buildings just South West of Minturno. and Brigade Main HQ moved up to join him leaving at approx. 0345.

1 Green Howards War Diary
22 Jan 44 – 0400
'C' Company moved off to reinforce 1 York & Lancs.

1 York & Lancs. Missing Person's Report by Sergeant Fielding
22 Jan 44 – 0430
'Private Wibberley was in Lance Corporal Shaw's section of 8 Platoon, "A" Company, 1 York & Lancs. The Platoon had lost its Platoon Commander so Sergeant Durose, Platoon Sergeant, took control. This Platoon was so battered that I had to reinforce it with my "17" Platoon "D" Company. At about 4.30am, 22 Jan 44 I was ordered by Major A. Wilson, Officer Commanding "A" Company, (since deceased) to send Lance Corporal Shaw and his Section, to find out the strength of the enemy at the Cemetery, about a mile and a half North of Minturno, and about 350 yards North of our position. The patrol went out and did not return. I have since heard that Lance Corporal Shaw was wounded. and taken prisoner.'

1 York & Lancs. War Diary
22 Jan 44 – 0530
'C' company 1 Green Howards arrived. The company given orders regarding counterattack.

1 York & Lancs. Missing Person's Report by Corporal Lane
22 Jan 44 – 0530
'At Minturno, North of the River Garigliano I was on a line party with Lance Corporal Packer. It was about 0530. He suddenly cried out that he had been shot and fell to the ground. Very shortly after, a party of Germans appeared and took me prisoner. They would not let me attend to Lance Corporal Packer, but I am certain he was dead. They took me to their lines and that was the last I saw of the body.

Company Sergeant Major Frogget, who was Company Sergeant Major of "A" Company, 1 York & Lancs. and also taken prisoner may be able to substantiate this.'

1 York & Lancs. War Diary
22 Jan 44 – 0545
FOO [Forward Observation Officer] from 98 Field Regiment arrived to go forward with 'C' Company.

1 Green Howards War Diary
22 Jan 44 – 0600
CO [Commanding Officer] with Company Commander 'C' Company, 1 Green Howards and Forward Observation Officer carry out recce for counterattack. One Platoon Commander killed [Lt. John Whiteman. Beds & Herts attached to 1 Green Howards. Minturno CWGC Cemetery], one wounded by own artillery fire.

2 Scots Guards War Diary
22 Jan 44 – 0600
The counterattack of last night was continued at dawn and although successfully held it was felt that the troops who faced it were pretty exhausted. In consequence Right Flank Company was moved up to consolidate on Point 141, West of Minturno known as Monte del Duca, in case of encroachment. This hill is bare and rocky, digging is extremely difficult, and the inevitable result was a gradual wastage of men through harassing fire. The counterattack was held, and the Battalion was not immediately engaged. Lieutenant Victor M. Gordon-Ives [Minturno, CWGC Cemetery] was killed by a shell whilst reconnoitring his Platoon position on Point 141.

The mortar Platoon under Ronnie Jenkinson was supporting 3 Coldstream in Tremensuoli, from mid-day yesterday until this morning. The reason for this was that a 3 Coldstream Platoon had suffered very heavy casualties from one shell and had become disorganised by their loss. Our Platoon was kept busy by engaging opportunity targets, which they did quite successfully, unfortunately six men were wounded before they moved out. The carrier Platoon took up a position between Minturno and Tremensuoli facing West.

Monte Natale formed a bulge facing North-West towards the towering bulk of Petrella, and the Tufo position faced North-East towards the German held village of Castelforte in the hills above the right bank of the River Garigliano. Monte Natale and Tufo were each exposed to fire almost from the rear, from enemy facing one another, and inaccurate rounds aimed at Minturno itself tended to pass over the hill into the area of Battalion Headquarters, Support Company, and 'A' Echelon near the main road.

No. 1 Troop 'A' Squadron 40 Royal Tank Regiment War Diary
22 Jan 44 – 0610
No. 1 Troop moved to area 780965 [Aid Post on road] to assist 1 York & Lancs. to repel an enemy counterattack made by infantry with tank support. The Troop engaged the enemy, but visibility was very poor.

X (BR) Corps Headquarters War Diary
22 Jan 44 – 0615
15 Infantry Brigade: Counterattack launched against 1 York and Lancs. at Point 156, Monte Natale at last light 21 Jan 44 repulsed. Enemy casualties believed heavy.

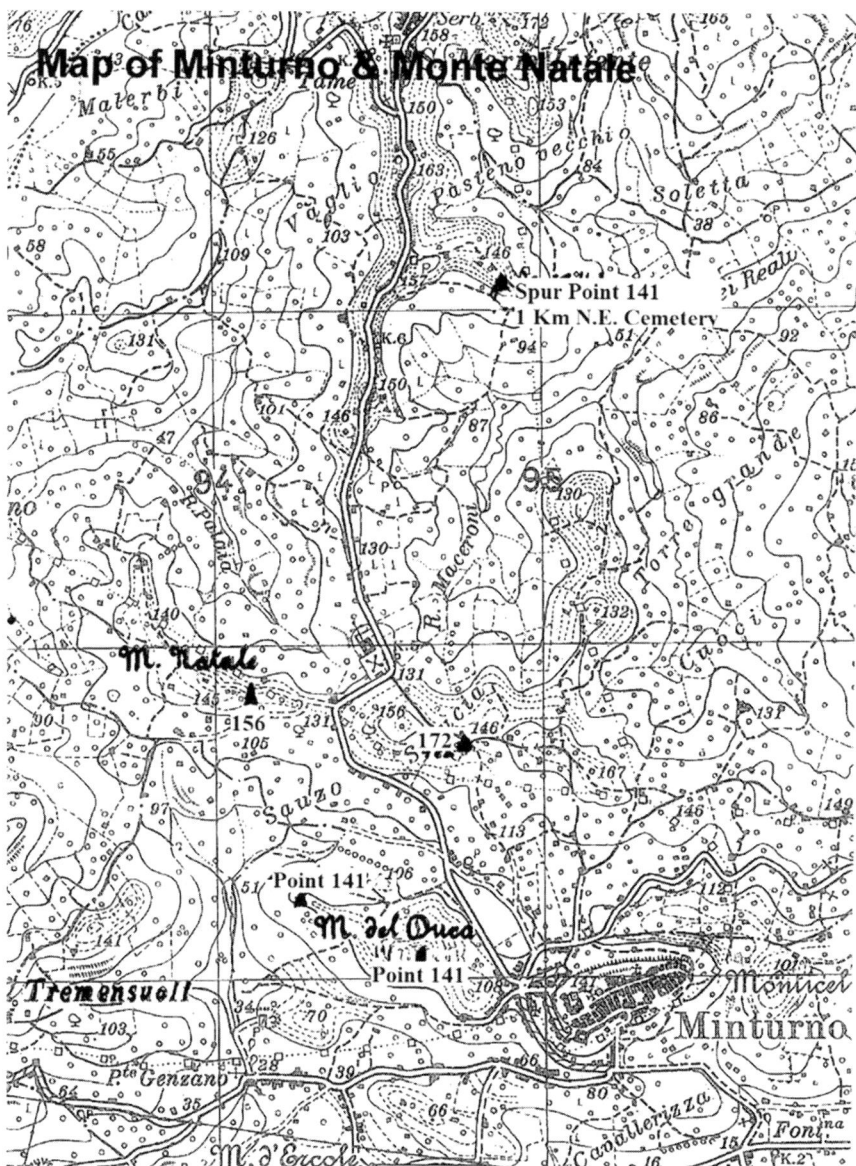

Minturno and Monte Natale. Three separate locations for Point 141: Monte del Duca, Point 141 to the West of Monte del Duca, and Spur Point 141, 1km North-East of the Cemetery.

1 KOYLI War Diary
22 Jan 44
It was with some surprise that at first light the Battalion found they were being attacked far more heavily. An extremely well supported counterattack was directed against the

Point 172 ridge. 1 York & Lancs. had not succeeded in holding the high ground on Monte Natale and 'B' Company positions were almost untenable.

1 York & Lancs. History

22 Jan 44 – 0630

In the morning the full fury of a really heavy counterattack fell on 'B/C' Company, 'A' Company and on 1 Kings Own Yorkshire Light Infantry on the right. The attack was made by a Regiment of Panzer Grenadiers who had been ordered to reach the line of the River Garigliano at all costs.

Enemy counterattacked from the North. The attack was heaviest astride the main road. Owing to casualties a clear picture is difficult to arrive at. Enemy tank knocked out 2 anti-tank guns on main road and penetrated 'A' Company's position. The tank Troop had already been ordered forward but there was some delay in reaching 'A' Company. 'A' Company on the road fought to the last, against an overwhelming force of tanks and infantry and was practically annihilated. Major A. Wilson [Officer Commanding 'A' company] was killed [Maj. Alistair Wilson MC. Minturno CWGC Cemetery] and Captain Cruickshank [Company Second in Command] and Major D. Young [Officer Commanding 'D' Company] attached to 'A' Company were wounded early on. 'A' Company after suffering heavy casualties were over run. Before this occurred the Platoon of 1 KOYLI on point 141 had withdrawn and shortly afterwards 1 KOYLI Company on Point 172 withdrew and the enemy therefore achieved a major penetration of the defences. The enemy were thus able to bring fire to bear behind 'A' and 'B/C' Companies positions making a counterattack on 'A' Company's old position impossible. 'B/C' Company held off all attacks despite heavy casualties and made good use of artillery support. Owing to the Field Regiment wireless set being destroyed communications with them was circuitous but the Forward Observation Officer from 91 Field Regiment provided additional assistance. Direct Fire tasks were called down continuously and inflicted

The German tanks were coming down this road from Santa Maria Infante. 40 Royal Tank Regiment had to stop them getting to this corner of the Cemetery. (Photo John Strafford)

heavy casualties. The Germans were all round the leading Companies all night, and at dawn the counterattack began in earnest.

On Monte Natale itself 'B/C' Company was fortunate in that it had a Regiment of Artillery in direct support. By keeping this Regiment firing continuously for over two hours and by bringing the defensive fire back so that it fell almost on its own positions, the Company which had now been reinforced by two platoons of 'D' Company kept the enemy off the summit of the hill, but only at the cost of heavy casualties to itself. 'B/C' Company inflicted heavy casualties on the enemy by using light machine guns, the fire from which was so intense that some guns seized up.

Later in the morning German tanks advanced down the road to about 783963 [midway up the track between the Cemetery and Point 172] but were held by our tanks and enemy machine guns were established in the houses at 778963 [200m West of the Aid Post]. Patrols were sent out to stalk the tanks and to deal with the machine guns with some success.

1 Green Howards Citation: Military Medal for Sergeant F.M. Roche

On 22 Jan 44, Sergeant Roche was commanding a Platoon which was under Command 'A' Company 1 York & Lancs. in the area of the Cemetery, 781966, with orders to hold his position at all costs.

At about 0620 the Platoon locality was attacked by a Mark IV Tank, which was engaged, the Platoon suffering casualties. At about 0630 the Platoon was attacked by Infantry in strength and the situation became critical, the enemy having infiltrated round both flanks and completely surrounded the locality.

At this juncture Sergeant Roche collected all available grenades and arming the members of his Platoon with T.S.M.Gs [Tactical Support Machine Guns] and extra ammunition went out to attack the enemy. By superb courage and offensive action of the highest order, Sergeant Roche overcame great odds, killing and wounding several enemy and causing the remainder to break up and run.

1 Green Howards Citation: Military Medal for Sergeant H. Sissons

On 22 Jan 44, in the area of Minturno Cemetery, 781966, No. 7 Platoon was heavily engaged. Early on, the Platoon Commander became a casualty and Sergeant Sissons immediately took over.

Casualties were being suffered and the Platoon was soon reduced to two Sections. Sergeant Sissons quite undaunted, was seem moving from Section to Section directing the fire of his Platoon and a number of dead and wounded Germans were lying about 20 yards from his position.

Although Sergeant Sissons was himself wounded in the shoulder, he refused to be evacuated and remained in command of his Platoon, controlling its fire, until it was ordered to withdraw, and he had brought it safely back.

1 York & Lancs. Missing Person's Report by Lance Corporal King

20 Jan 44 – 0630

'I last saw Private Clegg at about 0630 on 22 Jan 44 on Hill 156 forward of Minturno. He was forward of the Company with Sergeant Hayes laying a minefield when we were heavily counterattacked. I have not seen him since.'

2 Wiltshires War Diary
22 Jan 44 – 0630
First enemy attack. This penetrated 'A' Company's position on Point, 201, but was counterattacked and driven off with the bayonet.

3 Coldstream Guards War Diary
22 Jan 44 – 0630
Commanding Officer, Lt. Col. W.A.G. Burns MC and his group left the Assembly area. They went to the Battalion HQ of 1 Green Howards which were in slit trenches behind Tremensuoli. The HQ was under intermittent shellfire and aerial bombardment.

98 Field Regiment Royal Artillery War Diary
22 Jan 44 – 0650
SOS Category continuous: 471 Battery report strong counterattack making progress coming up road 781969 and at 780968 [Santa Maria Infante road, a kilometre North of the Cemetery].

158 Field Ambulance War Diary
22 Jan 44
Some slight difficulty was experienced in re-assembling the Sections to form an Advance Dressing Station. This was however done in the evening of 21 Jan 44. An Advanced Dressing Station was established in a quarry South of Minturno. Later the ADS moved into Minturno, but on orders of the Commanding Officer moved back at first light to a more suitable position just outside the town to a farm under cover of a hill. Shelling less severe in this locality. Arrangements made to send extra Stretcher Bearers to 201 Guards Brigade and to loan two Jeeps for their attack on morning of 22 Jan 44.

X (BR) Corps History
22 Jan 44 – 0700
Before 15 Infantry Brigade could begin its attack, the enemy renewed his attack in strength along the whole line of the Minturno hills using strong forces of infantry supported by tanks.

5 Infantry Division History
On the 15 Infantry Brigade front where 1 Green Howards were planning an attack to restore the position, the enemy forestalled them and launched a counterattack into 1 KOYLI. Shortly afterwards an enemy Self-Propelled gun supporting this attack got into the Northern outskirts of Minturno near the Cemetery and made a nuisance of itself until chased out by our own tanks. The attack was beaten back with losses to both sides.

'A' Squadron of 40 Royal Tank Regiment War Diary
22 Jan 44 – 0700
The Commanding Officer of 1 York & Lancs. ordered No. 1 Troop to advance North along the road from 780965 [Aid Post] but as the leading tank was held up by Anti-Personnel fire, this order was countermanded.

92 Field Regiment Royal Artillery War Diary
22 Jan 44 – 0710
368 Battery Commander reports enemy among 1 KOYLI. Regiment to stand-by.

2 Cameronians War Diary
22 Jan 44 – 0715
While the CO. was visiting 'C' Company, the Battalion Second in Command received a verbal message from Brigade that 2 Wiltshires were being counter attacked on Point 201 and 2 Cameronians were to move another Company to Tufo to support them.

92 Field Regiment Royal Artillery War Diary
22 Jan 44 – 0720
HQ Royal Artillery order fire on 784973 [Santa Maria Infante road, a kilometre and a half North of the Cemetery].

22 Jan 44 – 0722
Target changed by HQ Royal Artillery from784973 to 773968 [half a kilometre North West of Monte Natale]. Regiment engages.

2 Cameronians War Diary
22 Jan 44 – 0725
Battalion Second in Command ordered 'B' Company to move immediately to Tufo area and Officer Commanding 'D' Company to report to 2 Wiltshires Battalion HQ. 'A' Company were warned to be prepared to move to Tufo area but to proceed only on the Commanding Officer's order.

98 Field Regiment Royal Artillery War Diary
22 Jan 44 – 0730
102 Medium Regiment report a York & Lancs. Company overrun in area 780968.
    This is 'A' Company 1 York & Lancs. withdrawing down the Santa Maria Infante road in haste in the area of the Cemetery.

92 Field Regiment Royal Artillery War Diary
22 Jan 44 – 0730
Intercept. 91 Field Regiment ordered to fire on 798966 [Point 201] – counterattack.

22 Jan 44 – 0740
Regiment Second in Command at HQ 15 Infantry Brigade reports heavy armoured attack from left. Self-Propelled Gun in area Minturno rather troublesome, and now being chased by our tanks. Commanding Officer required to visit Commander Royal Artillery at Brigade HQ this morning.

2 Cameronians War Diary
22 Jan 44 – 0815
The CO. having returned to Battalion HQ left for 2 Wiltshires Battalion HQ outside Tufo arriving at 0815. 2 Wiltshires by then had driven off the first enemy counterattack

and was preparing for second enemy attack on Point 201. 'B' Company were contacted, and the CO. ordered 'B' Company to take over the defence of the West end of Tufo to allow 2 Wiltshire's Company to go forward to support the Companies on Point 201.

2 Wiltshires War Diary
22 Jan 44 – 0830
Second enemy attack. Only slight penetration. Beaten off.

92 Field Regiment Royal Artillery War Diary
22 Jan 44 – 0840
368 Battery Commander reports own tanks now moving up, situation quiet now. Counterattack by enemy started in area of Cemetery.

22 Jan 44 – 0845
368 Battery Observation Post reported to have lost wireless set in a skirmish. Line communication being established. Observation Post now established with Battery Commander at 786964 [200m East of Point 172].

17 Infantry Brigade War Diary
22 Jan 44 – 0845
Brigade put at 2 hours-notice to restore situation on 15 Infantry Brigade front.

'A' Squadron, 40 Royal Tank Regiment War Diary
22 Jan 44 – 0900
One tank of No 2 Troop was shelled and set on fire, but the crew were unharmed.

15 Infantry Brigade War Diary
22 Jan 44 – 0900
A strong attack by infantry supported by tanks came in against 1 York & Lancs. position at the Cemetery. 1 KOYLI badly needed thickening up on Point 172 and by arrangement with 201 Guards Brigade a Company of 2 Scots Guards took over Point 141, Monte Del Duca, immediately West of Minturno, enabling the Platoon of 1 KOYLI there to move forward to Point 172 area.

6 Seaforth Highlanders War Diary
22 Jan 44 – 0900
Strong counterattack on 21 January by 300 to 400 infantry and six tanks on 1 York & Lancs. positions. 1 York & Lancs. forced to give ground slightly. Attack repeated this morning. 1 Green Howards to attack and restore situation. 3 Coldstream Guards established West of Tremensuoli. 6 Grenadier Guards East of Tremensuoli. 2 Scots Guards at 777952 [road junction 2km South-West of Minturno) told not to attack Scauri until artillery released from present position. 17 Infantry Brigade at two hours-notice to restore situation on 15 Infantry Brigade front if 1 Green Howards attack unsuccessful.

During 21-22 Jan 44, 40 Royal Tank Regiment had several tanks hit in the area of the Cemetery. In their book *The Battles for Monte Cassino. Then and Now* Jeffrey Plowman and Perry Rowe write: 'A Sherman of the 760th Tank Battalion rumbles past

Gate to the Cemetery, May 44. (Photo U.S. National Archives)

the Cemetery. The knocked-out Sherman beside the Cemetery wall is not one of theirs, but was a casualty from the earlier fighting for the Garigliano bridgehead by British X (BR) Corps. It was most likely disabled on Jan 22 44, the War Diary recording "One tank of two Sherman troops KO'd. Other five tanks North of Minturno. Boche tanks thought unlikely to come further than Cemetery".'

After Ernest Strafford was reported as killed in action, his daughter Pat recalls that an officer of 1 York & Lancs. wrote to her mother. He said that Ernest Strafford was near a tank by a Cemetery, standing near an officer when the officer was hit. Ernest Strafford went to help him when he was hit. The officer may have been either Major A. Wilson or Captain Cruickshank of 'A' Company or Captain D. Young of 'D' Company. In this case Ernest Strafford would have been either with a Platoon of 'D' Company or with 'A' Company. It is thought that the Platoon of 'D' Company and 'A' Company or what was left of them retreated in the direction of Point 172 where Ernest Strafford's body was found. There was also a disabled tank on the Santa Maria Infante road near the Cemetery. One or other of these tanks could have been where Ernest Strafford was hit.

2 Cameronians War Diary
22 Jan 44 – 0915
'B' Company were in position now at the West end of Tufo

X (BR) Corps War Diary
22 Jan 44 – 0922

138

5 Infantry Division: Confirming verbal instructions. Task of 13 and 15 Infantry Brigades will be to remain firm on Minturno ridge. 15 Infantry Brigade to re-establish itself on Point 156 as soon as present situation permits. Will then re-group and have the front held by two Battalions forward, tanks in support and one Battalion in reserve. As soon as Corps and Division artillery can be released from present Direct Fire, 201 Guards Brigade will complete occupation of high ground to East and this side of River Capo d'Acqua to prevent any enemy movement down Route 7 axis or by road North-East from San Croce. Armour and anti-tank position accordingly. Attack on the Scauri feature postponed until present situation is stabilised, and fire support can be made available. Inter Brigade body as at present.

17 Infantry Brigade in Division Reserve will be prepared to move to Minturno area with a view if necessary, to re-establishing the situation on the high ground 7896 [Minturno-Tufo ridge-Cemetery to Point 172] moving from the East through 13 Infantry Brigade. 17 Infantry Brigade at two hours-notice.

2 Cameronians War Diary
22 Jan 44 – 0930
The enemy started a counterattack on Point 201 supported by shelling Point 201 and the West end of Tufo. The counterattack was strong and succeeded in driving back 'A' & 'D' Companies of 2 Wiltshires to the southern section of the hill.

'A' Squadron 40 Royal Tank Regiment War Diary
22 Jan 44 – 1000
Orders received from 5 Infantry Division to place two troops under command 15 Infantry Brigade and two under command 201 Guards Brigade. The two Troops under command 15 Infantry Brigade moved to the area of the Cemetery 781967 and the high ground to the East of the Cemetery, at Point 172, whilst the two Troops under the command of 201 Guards Brigade took up positions at 815957 and 780954 (road 500m West of Minturno).

2 Wiltshires War Diary
22 Jan 44 – 1000
Third enemy attack. This attack was successful and 'A' Company, and the Carrier Platoon were forced back to 'B' Company at the West end of Tufo. During final attack 'A' Company Commander Capt. J. Power was killed [Capt. John Power. Minturno CWGC Cemetery]. It was during this last attack that Major Clark had his second escape from the enemy. He had gone forward to see 'A' Company and was caught in a dugout when the attack came, and a hand grenade was thrown in. When he was out, the waiting Germans were fired at and took cover. Major Clark seized his opportunity and made a successful dash back to our own positions.

1 KOYLI War Diary
22 Jan 44 – 1000
Both 'A' and 'B' Companies were heavily engaged – but fighting stubbornly. 'D' Company was now in a position to support 'B' Company on the ridge. 1 York & Lancs. on the left were in a bad way and rapidly becoming overrun and disorganised.

A soldier from 'A' Company, 1 York & Lancs. described the situation
22 Jan 44 – 1000
In the early hours of the morning, we heard a lot of shouting and screaming and found the Germans had counterattacked one of our platoons and they had all been taken prisoner or killed. At the time we did not know this but hearing the screams as we were not very far away, we guessed something like this was happening. About 10am I was sharing a trench with a man who also came from Sheffield and had not been very long with us, when a German tank appeared in front of us a few feet away. We both crouched as low as we could as he sprayed us with bullets and we both thought it was the end. However, he could not get the barrel of the gun to aim into the trench and the bullets hit the top and then fell on us; there must have been 100 rounds. Then it all went quiet and after about two minutes we looked up and there was no sign of the tank. This must have been a miracle.

Afterwards I heard our Bren gunner shooting away. I said to him [Maurice Jones from Hoyland near Barnsley] 'What are you firing at?' He said he saw some Germans go into a house which was not far away, so I fired my rifle and sent a few rounds into the house. We did not see anyone come out. We were still being heavily shelled when word came that we had to withdraw and split up into two sections as the enemy were all over. My partner went into the other section and was killed, as was Major A. Wilson, our Company Commander. In this battle the Battalion had 300 casualties of whom 60 were killed. There were very few of my Company left so we were added to the few left of 'B' Company and with reinforcements formed another Company. I was now in the same Company as Maurice Farber and Maurice later became a Sergeant. Our Company was commanded by Major D Webster, a Sheffield man who had also served in France and Norway.

15 Infantry Brigade War Diary
22 Jan 44 – 1015
The situation at the Cemetery had deteriorated and the Brigadier ordered the Squadron Commander of 40 Royal Tank Regiment, who had two Troops of tanks with 1 York & Lancs. to act as offensively as possible to relieve the pressure on the infantry. About this time the enemy shelled Brigade HQ area fairly heavily and destroyed two trucks including the 'intelligence truck' containing a number of maps. One man of the Defence Platoon was fairly badly wounded.

2 Cameronians War Diary
22 Jan 44 – 1015
The CO. obtained permission to move 'A' Company to Tufo from Point 102.

15 Infantry Brigade War Diary
22 Jan 44 – 1027
1 York & Lancs. had been obliged to withdraw from the Cemetery and the guns immediately put a 'murder' [heavy bombardment] down on the area North of it.

Lt. Col. Patrick George Bulfin, Commanding Officer 1 Green Howards was ordered to report to Brigade HQ and on arrival ordered to move at once to a defined position on the Northern outskirts of Minturno with a Company of 2 Scots Guards on Point 141 under his command. [This was Right Flank Company who had gone there to take over from a Platoon of 1 KOYLI.] Two Platoons from 207 Battery 52 Anti-Tank Regiment were also in position just at the North end of the town.

13 Infantry Brigade War Diary
22 Jan 44 – 1030
Three enemy counterattacks were put in on Point 201. 2 Wiltshires had been pushed off the top of Point 201 but held the Southern slopes and Point 151 firmly. Artillery put down an immediate concentration of fire.

2 Wiltshires War Diary
22 Jan 44 – 1030
'A' & 'B' Companies amalgamated at West of Tufo.

1 York & Lancs. War Diary
22 Jan 44 – 1030
There was a pause in the enemy counterattack. The new composite 'B/C/D' Company, although almost surrounded, still barred the way to Minturno and was prepared to fight on if need be.

The enemy were thus able to bring fire to bear behind 'A' & 'B/C/D' Company positions making a counterattack on 'A' Company's position impossible. Later in the morning enemy tanks advanced down the road to 783963 [400m South of the Aid Post] but were held up by our tanks. Enemy machine guns were established in the houses at 778963 [200m West of the Aid Post]. Patrols were sent out to stalk the enemy tanks and to deal with their machine guns with some success.

1 York & Lancs. Missing Person's Report by Private Wallis
'On 22 January 1944 we were on the outskirts of Minturno in the area of Hill 156. Two Platoons of 'A' Company and Company HQ were forward and Private Handley was among the forward troops. Heavy counterattacks were made by the enemy on the forward positions, and they were completely overrun by the Germans. I never saw him after the counterattacks, and I think it is probable he will be a prisoner of war.'

We now know that the Germans were close to Ernest Strafford by 10.30am, if he was still with a Platoon of 'D' Company or 'A' Company. Did he retreat up the track leading from the Cemetery towards Tufo which was their line of retreat?

201 Guards Brigade War Diary
22 Jan 44 – 1030
The enemy continued his pressure on the axis of the road Santa Maria Infante – Minturno and on Tufo from the North. 6 Grenadier Guards were ordered to be ready to counterattack on axis North of Minturno towards Tufo.

2 Cameronians War Diary
22 Jan 44 – 1030
The CO. talked to Brigade Commander by line, and it was agreed that 2 Cameronians would counterattack Point 201 immediately and take over 2 Wiltshires position during the day.

92 Field Regiment Royal Artillery War Diary
22 Jan 44 – 1031
368 Battery Observation Post call for fire on 783967 [Cemetery]. 467 Battery to engage.

2 Cameronians War Diary
22 Jan 44 – 1040
The CO. issued orders to Officers Commanding 'B' & 'D' Companies at the West end of Tufo. 'D' Company to counterattack along the ridge of Point 201 at 1130 from a Start line 100 yards short of the South edge of Point 201 which 2 Wiltshires are still holding. Point 201 was a long ridge running North and South and was only about 50 yards wide. 'D' Company were ordered to attack with one Platoon behind the other supporting each other forward. 'B' Company were ordered to support the attack by firing small arms from their position. Artillery was to fire 20 rounds slow rate from 1105 and stonk from 1125 to 1220.

5 Infantry Division Counterattack tasks to recapture Point 201
Instructions were:

Probable Conditions, Tufo and Point 151 still in our hands. [This was the case.]
Forward Assembly Area, Immediately South of Tufo.
Battalion HQ in Forward Assembly Area, With HQ of Battalion already in Tufo.
Start Line, Track North-East-Southwest at 800962.
Formation, One Company front. Leading Company to recover Point 201, Second Company to pass through and clear feature to the North of Point 201. Remaining Companies in reserve.

X (BR) Corps War Diary
22 Jan 44 – 1045
5 Infantry Division: Enemy counterattack on 1 York & Lancs. and 1 KOYLI. and 2 Wiltshires commenced first light, strength estimated at one Battalion. Enemy incredibly determined and fighting at close quarters. One Company 1 York & Lancs. on Point 156, 775968 reported overcome and the remainder of the Battalion had to fall back, also, one Platoon of 1 KOYLI. Point 201 799966 reported in enemy hands.

1 KOYLI were being attacked on Point 172, 785964 just to the North of Minturno village; and on 13 Infantry Brigade front 2 Wiltshires had been driven off Point 201, Colle Casale and on the left 15 Infantry Brigade prepared to defend Minturno. 1 Green Howards were brought into position North of Minturno and two Companies were sent to reinforce 1 York & Lancs. in new positions South of Monte Natale.

2 Northants War Diary
22 Jan 44 – 1045
Brigade gave Commanding Officer orders to concentrate in area Point 102, 805956 [1km South-East of Tufo] and track to Tufo. Company Commander left for recce of Battalion area.

92 Field Regiment Royal Artillery War Diary
22 Jan 44 – 1045
467 Battery repeat fire on 783967 [Cemetery].

22 Jan 44 – 1050
368 Battery Commander reports Guards now in his area to reinforce 1 York & Lancs.

98 Field Regiment Royal Artillery War Diary
22 Jan 44 – 1050
Enemy counterattack down road – occupied Cemetery – some armour with them – situation fluid.

22 Jan 44 – 1053
471 Battery – enemy still counterattacking strongly – some infiltration – situation still fluid.

201 Guards Brigade War Diary
22 Jan 44 – 1100
A request from 15 Infantry Brigade for the loan of one Company from 2 Scots Guards [the Brigade's Reserve Battalion] to hold Point 141, 780968 and come under command of 1 KOYLI. Decision on this was given and 2 Scots Guards ordered to find one Company.

52 Anti-Tank Regiment War Diary
22 Jan 44 – 1100
208 Battery Commander recalled by Brigade Commander and told there was a possibility that 201 Guards Brigade would need some guns in area 7695 [West of Tremensuoli].

1 KOYLI War Diary
22 Jan 44 – 1100
1 York & Lancs. was withdrawing hard pressed, and our 'B' Company had withdrawn what remnants remained through 'D' Company where all three Companies 'A', 'B', and 'D' formed a strong point on the East edge of the Point 172 ridge from which they were never forced to withdraw.

1 KOYLI withdrew from Point 141 and Point 172. By 1100 hours the enemy had been in contact for some hours and the Company Commander had committed his reserve which was the relieving party for the patrol on Point 141. At an early stage in the counterattack, 'C' company was pulled out of their original positions and put into a reserve area about 785960 [400m South of Point 172], and at about 1100 hours 'C' company commenced to occupy the high ground from which 'B' company withdrew.

3 Coldstream Guards War Diary
22 Jan 44 – 1100
The Battalion took over from 1 Green Howards at Tremensuoli under intermittent shell and mortar fire. One enemy mortar bomb landed at what was afterwards known as 'Stonk Corner' amongst the Mortar Platoon and caused 14 casualties. The Battalion area, particularly the village of Tremensuoli, were mortared and shelled during the afternoon.

15 Infantry Brigade War Diary
22 Jan 44 – 1100
1 York & Lancs. reported their remaining troops on Monte Natale were in danger of being cut off and requested permission to withdraw all they could onto the main

position which now ran from Point 141, Monte del Duca, to Point 172. This was agreed to by the Brigadier. The line telephone was disconnected throughout the period and all these orders had to be given by radio telephone.

15 Infantry Brigade Brigadier was ordered to meet 5 Infantry Division Commander at HQ. On return he immediately went up to HQ, 1 KOYLI which was in the North-East corner of Minturno, met all three Company Commanding Officers and coordinated the defence of the sector

The Brigade front was now to be held by 1 KOYLI based on Point 172, though in fact the enemy had a foothold on the top of the feature, with 1 Green Howards in depth behind them stretching across the road. Both Battalions together were about three Companies strong. 40 Royal Tank Regiment had five Sherman tanks available for immediate counterattack. In addition, two Platoons of 'D' Company 7 Cheshires were in action forward plus the two platoons from 207 Anti-Tank Battery from 52 Anti-Tank Regiment and eight 4.2-inch mortars from the Brigade Support Company. In view of the fact that the enemy held the top of Point 172 the Brigadier ordered 1 Green Howards to attack and capture the summit during the afternoon.

5 Infantry Division Counterattack tasks for the recapture of Point 172
Instructions were:

Probable Conditions, Point 201 and Point 151 still in our hands. [They were now.]

Forward Assembly Area, South of Point 151, North of Tufo – Minturno Road.

Battalion HQ in Forward Assembly Area, With HQ of Battalion already in Tufo.

Start Line, Track running South from houses at 792962 [300m West of Point 151] to road Tufo – Minturno.

Formation, One Company front. Leading Company to capture area track junction 786964 [50m from where Ernest Strafford's body was found], Second Company to pass through and capture area 783965 [hill] overlooking Cemetery. Remaining Companies in reserve.

1 York & Lancs. Citation: Distinguished Service Order for Major D. Webster
On 20 January 'B' and 'C' Companies captured Point 156 North West of Minturno. Early on 21 Jan 44, 'B' & 'C' Companies were counter attacked and 'C' Company were driven back on to 'B' Company's position. Major Webster who was commanding 'B' Company was responsible for the re-organisation of the position which he did with the greatest coolness under heavy shelling and small arms fire. On the evening of 21 January 'B' Company were again counter attacked and Major Webster again displayed great coolness controlling his reserve with skill, moving about in the open under heavy fire and bringing down artillery fire by means of his wireless. Through his example to his men and his coolness in a critical situation, the counterattack was beaten off. On the morning of 22 January, the position was attacked once more with even greater determination. 'A' Company which was on 'B' Company's right were over-run but in spite of this 'B' Company beat off the enemy attacks and though they suffered heavy casualties held the position for a further three hours until ordered to withdraw. It was undoubtedly due to the example set by Major Webster's leadership, determination, and courage that his Company held these three counter attacks. He was moving about in the open directing his reserve and encouraging his men to whom his example was an inspiration.

Ernest Shaw, 1 York & Lancs. opinion of Major Webster
'The whole Company looked up to Major Webster. He was a fine officer. He knew what to do in the right manner and put people in the right place. He had an unknown view towards the war. He was a strict disciplinarian. You had not to step out of line very far. The Major outshone them all. There is no doubt about that.'

Lieutenant Geoffrey Winter, 1 York & Lancs. wrote in his book *Winter's War*
22 Jan 44

'The enemy launched an extraordinarily strong counterattack supported by tanks and after very heavy fighting our troops were forced to withdraw behind a position held by 1 Green Howards. In just over two days fighting, the Battalion had about three hundred casualties – 60 killed, the rest wounded or missing. But it would be misleading to express this as a percentage of the total strength (about 800 men) of the Battalion. The brunt of the fighting falls essentially on the rifle companies (some 400 men) who had therefore suffered about seventy-five per cent casualties. In the fighting on Monte Natale, "A" Company was almost annihilated.'

X (BR) Corps War Diary
22 Jan 44 – 1125
5 Infantry Division: 15 Infantry Brigade: Battalion 1 KOYLI has half of Point 172. 1 York & Lancs. forced out of Cemetery and withdrawing to make stand at Battalion Headquarters at 777963 [Southern slopes of Monte Natale approx. 200m from the Aid Post]. Two Companies 1 Green Howards West of Minturno moving forward to reinforce. One Company of 2 Scots Guards under command 1 Green Howards at Point 141, 781959, Monte del Duca. 201 Guards Brigade: 6 Grenadier Guards North-East Tremonsuoli. 13 Infantry Brigade: Reserve Company 2 Cameronians going up to counterattack Point 201. One Company of 2 Scots Guards taking over Point 102 from a Company of 2 Cameronians.

5 Infantry Division War Diary
22 Jan 44 – 1125
1 Green Howards were moving to hold the Northern face of Minturno and 1 York & Lancs., who had been driven off the Cemetery by a powerful enemy thrust down the road were falling back onto them. 1 KOYLI were holding firm on the main positions to the East.

On the 13 Infantry Brigade front 2 Wiltshires were heavily counterattacked on Point 201 at about 0800 and by 1030 the enemy had managed to obtain a footing there.

1 York & Lancs. War Diary
22 Jan 44 – 1130
Orders were received to establish a line connecting with 1 KOYLI at 785962 [200m South of Point 172], and the 201 Guards Brigade [2 Scots Guards Company] on Point 141, Monte Del Duca, 781959. This was already being done by 'C' Company 1 Green Howards.

201 Guards Brigade War Diary
22 Jan 44 – 1130
6 Grenadier Guards saw 60 men coming from Monte Natale – these proved to be the remains of 1 York & Lancs. and 1 Green Howards.

Ernest Shaw, 1 York & Lancs
'The Major was ordered to withdraw. He led us back by a circuitous route. We were not completely surrounded but we did not come out in a straight line. We had to weave a bit to get through to Minturno just behind the line. We were heading towards there and the Guards were coming in to relieve us. We were marching in single file, getting away, and they were coming the other way, passing side by side, and they cursed and swore at us. Terrible, called us "scared bastards" and all sorts. That really, really upset me. We had lost so many lads and we fought to the last man nearly. They can come and they were supposed to be the cream of the army. It was them who were bloody scared weren't it? Any way they took over and we went back into Minturno. [6 Grenadier Guards apologised later.]

1 KOYLI War Diary
22 Jan 44 – 1130
Local patrolling by both sides failed to make any impression and it was, therefore, with some surprise that at first light the Battalion found they were being attacked far more heavily on the same front. An extremely well supported counterattack was directed against the point 172 ridge. 1 York & Lancs. had not succeeded in holding the high ground on Monte Natale and 'B' Company positions were almost untenable.

2 Cameronians War Diary
22 Jan 44 – 1130
'A' Company arrived at Tufo from Point 102 and were put in position at the East end.

2 Wiltshires War Diary
22 Jan 44 – 1140
After heavy artillery preparation, attack started and was successful. 'C' company from Point 151 report enemy badly caught by artillery when retreating and cut to bits by Vickers machine gun fire.

2 Cameronians War Diary
22 Jan 44 – 1145
The Brigade Commander arrived at the West end of Tufo. The Commanding Officer postponed the 'D' Company attack until 1145 as 'D' Company did not have enough time to get on the start line by 1125. The Artillery was warned and continued firing at slow rate on Point 201 until 1140 and put down the stonk from 1140 to 1145.

'D' Company crossed the start line with Lieutenant Johnson's platoon leading. The Commanding Officer was on the Start line and encouraged the Company forward. The leading Platoon marched forward slowly at first and encountered enemy rifle and machine gun fire. One man shouted, 'Come on the Cams' and the whole Company moved forward extremely quickly dealing with the enemy with the bayonet.

146

92 Field Regiment Royal Artillery War Diary
22 Jan 44 – 1145
368 Battery Commander 'Stop firing, rounds falling short.'

1 KOYLI War Diary
22 Jan 44 – 1200
It was not until about 1200 that Officer Commanding 'B' Company was compelled to withdraw from Point 172 to the next high ridge some 300 yards South. By this time, the Battalion was getting thin on the ground. At the same time the attack was developing on our right flank.

The first fierce counterattack was weakening and the Battalion although no longer holding the whole of Point 172 ridge was firmly established with its left on the high ridge about 784963 [just South of Point 172], and its right 'A' company still on the Eastern ridge of the high ground. In the meantime, 1 York & Lancs. had not been able to hold the enemy and were withdrawing in fair order down the road covered by our Company on the high ground at Point 141.

X (BR) Corps War Diary
22 Jan 44 – 1200
By midday, the line had been stabilised; 2 Cameronians had retaken Point 201, Colle Casale, and the forward Battalions of 15 Infantry Brigade, 1 KOYLI and 1 Green Howards were holding firm.

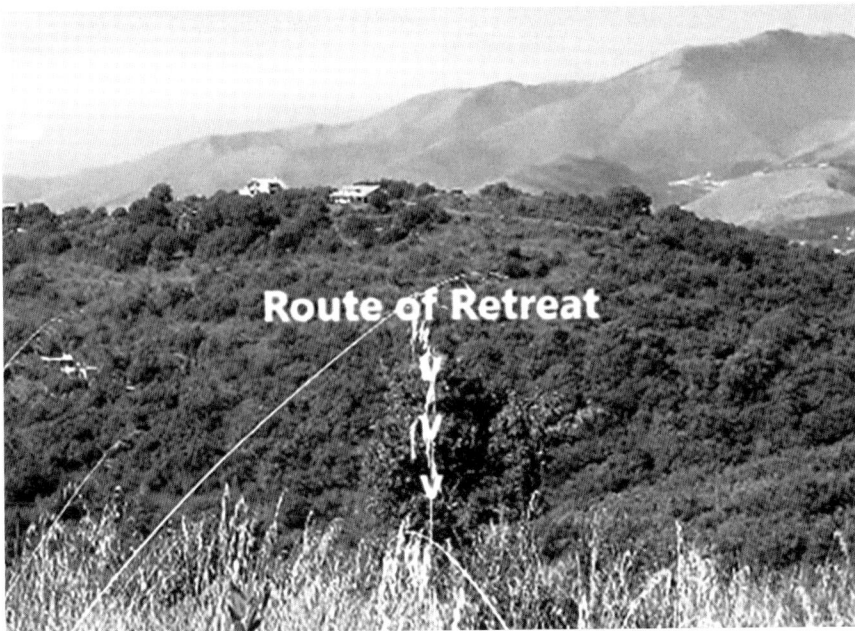

22 Jan 44 1200 1 York & Lancs. 'B' & 'C' Cos route of retreat from Monte Natale as seen from Point 141, Monte del Duca. (Photo Peter Strafford)

13 Infantry Brigade War Diary
22 Jan 44 – 1210

2 Cameronians Company re-captured Point 201, supported by artillery, machine guns and fire from 2 Inniskillings who were two kilometres East of Tufo. The counterattack drove the Germans off the hill and as they ran back the artillery and machine guns inflicted further casualties.

Successful landing of two Divisions South of Rome was announced [Anzio].

15 Infantry Brigade: Enemy counterattacks re-captured Point 172 but later 1 Green Howards were again on top. 201 Guards Brigade held the area Tremensuoli. 2 Cameronians relieved 2 Wiltshires who came into reserve area South-East of Tufo.

2 Cameronians War Diary
22 Jan 44 – 1210

'D' Company had occupied Point 201 and cleared the ridge except for small groups of enemies, who were quickly withdrawing leaving their wounded and equipment behind. 'D' Company's leading Platoon suffered casualties of one killed and three wounded. 11 enemy machine guns were captured, and many enemy wounded were taken. Many enemy dead were found lying in the area. The Carrier Platoon took up position at the South end of Point 201 allowing 2 Wiltshire's Companies to withdraw to a reserve area.

The CO. went forward to 'D' Company and ordered small patrols to be sent out to the East and West of the Northern edge of Point 201. Patrols were to give warning of any enemy counterattack and to return by 1730.

Sir David Cole, 2 Inniskillings, *Rough Road To Rome*
22 Jan 44

'Shortly after breakfast, prodded by the residual instincts of civilisation and a long, hard stare from the Regimental Sergeant Major, I was hacking through a three-day beard when the sound of violent machine-gun fire to our left brought my razor to an abrupt and bloody halt.

Simultaneously Bill Bradley telephoned to say that he could see a fierce battle on Hill 201.

We could see a fierce battle on Point 201. There were Germans swarming up the hill and 2 Wiltshires appeared to be withdrawing. This unpleasant news was quickly confirmed by Brigade informing us that 2 Wiltshires had indeed had to withdraw, that 2 Cameronians were launching an immediate counterattack and that we should give whatever supporting fire we could. Twenty minutes later we watched 2 Cameronians going in. It was a good old-fashioned counterattack of the "up Guards and at em" variety. Legend has it that their CO. was seen leading the way, brandishing a spade! The Scotsmen surged forward so fast and with such indifference to the enemy fire, that when they were still quite distant, the Germans lost their nerve and began jumping out of their trenches and darting down the back of the hill. This was the chance our own machine gunners had been waiting for and they immediately opened fire, visibly knocking down several of the retreating Germans. A few minutes later 2 Cameronians were consolidating on Point 201.'

Lt. Wolfgang Wiedemann, II Battalion, 267 Panzer Grenadier Regiment
22 Jan 44

'A harsh, familiar voice asked for Lieutenant Wolfgang Wiedemann, it was Major Frank. Now our No I. Battalion Grenadier Regiment is here, too. He asked to be briefed on the enemy situation. Then he ordered: "At 7.00 o'clock we attack Point 201. '1' Company attacking on left, '3' Company on your right!" Before I could give the word, the Battalion Commander was gone again. Sergeant Freygang looked at me in amazement, in the short time on the beach of San Agostino I had not really got to know the newly taken over Company Commander. In those days of battle the men got to know each other very quickly. Each knew what to think of the other comrade.

The "lame ducks" [spotter aircraft], and there were usually several of them, appeared again in the sky. Particularly good reconnaissance capabilities enabled our opponent to recognize all movements, especially the approach of reserves, at an early stage and to react accordingly.

The first officer to appear was Lieutenant Friedenberger, a capable officer and Company Commander of 1 Company, I Battalion 267 Grenadier Regiment. He said, "Let them enter. Frank gave you the appropriate orders." I was amazed. I said, "Where's Major Frank?" Friedenberger pointed backwards: "In his Command Post," he answered. I instructed Friedenberger. He moved his men quickly to the left. There had already been a dangerous accumulation at the foot of the high ground of Point 201. Lieutenant Kroner appeared. He ordered the Platoons to close in on my men on the right. He kept one Platoon with him as a reserve. I wondered why he did not follow his Company. His behaviour was different than usual. How could the attack be successful under such difficult conditions without the presence of the Battalion Commander? I was convinced that the Company Officers and the Grenadiers did everything they could for this important high ground. Sgt. Freygang made a scornful remark when we were alone for a moment: "Remote controller!" He looked in the direction of the Battalion Command Post.

When our artillery started the short bombardment, we knew that now it would start. The Companies jumped up. Also, the infantry men on our right attacked. This time they had to succeed. In the middle of my Company's area, a path led to the summit and then on to Tufo. With flares we signalled to our Artillery that the fire should be moved forward. So far everything went according to plan. When Point 201 was almost reached, the (British) spotter planes triggered a firestorm from the Allied Batteries. Like the day before, the shells hit the offensive lines of the English and us. Desperately seeking cover, my men, but especially the Grenadiers of "3" Company and the reserve Platoon were hit, one hit after another, which caused a real bloodbath in the hollow. I had taken cover at the edge of the hollow, behind the remains of a shot-up goat shed. I could hardly lift my head because of the continuous detonating shells. Everywhere the wounded were calling for medics. Only now did I realize that Kroner had also sought refuge amongst the walls, although there was only room for one person. I thought Kroner was wounded; his body was twitching as if he had a fever.

It was useless to run against that roll of fire. When the fire subsided a little, I ordered my Company to move to its initial positions. I found this failure extremely depressing. Lt. Kroner went back with them. He was not wounded. It was only now that I began to feel clearly that something was wrong. He was chalky white, shaking all over, and he could not talk. He was in shock. The force of the fire had broken his will power.

Everything was done to save the dead and wounded. It was horrible in the ravine. I went to the Mintumo-Santa Maria Infante road and could hear a lot of gunfire. At the sound of the tank guns, I heard that a special oath had developed there. As I learned later, units of 90 Panzer Grenadier Division had started a counterattack. They were successful in the attack and the front was stabilized – Santa Maria Infante remained in German hands. The big target for the "Tommies" was to conquer Santa Maria Infante and to reach the Formia-Cassino road. This tactical success had denied them.

Word got around very quickly that the Company Commander of No "1" Company, Lieutenant Friedenberger, had fallen or was wounded and in captivity. Some men of "1" Company saw how it collapsed in front of the English positions in the defenders' fire. Then came the Allied fire wall. It proceeded as it had 24 hours before with Sergeant Pinkes. Friedenberger had serious leg injuries – bullet wounds. The English took him out of the danger zone and gave him a good burial. Hats off to this decent opponent. We lived this fair way of fighting, Englishmen and Americans were equally important in demonstrating their humane attitude.

Kröner was no longer able to lead a Company. He had lost the will and two men of his company led this decent and capable officer to Dr. Hoffmann. The detonation force of the bombs and the cramps had defeated the man Lt. Kröner. When he wanted to return to the Regiment the Regimental Commander laconically stated – no need. A tragic human fate in the great war.

In addition to the fact that the fighting was already raging on the Southern edge of Santa Maria Infante, which was almost behind us, we received orders to set off about 200 metres. From there we had better chances of defending ourselves. Everything was done to get the men upright. Again, we had to dig in. The Grenadiers were totally exhausted. The soldiers shouted with all their strength: "Tommy is attacking!" They had taken us by surprise. Big tall guys were suddenly between our foxholes. It was an absurd situation. "Tommie" wanted to capture us, and we wanted to capture the English. No one used the gun. I cried out in desperation: "Capture them" and "Shoot them." There was great confusion. Everything was open. A few "Tommies" surrendered. I do not think the attackers expected us to be so stubborn. They ran back. Some of them surrendered. In no time, we had about 20 prisoners. There was no close combat. No shots were fired. We had found our opponent simply sympathetic, probably the other way around, too. This time great luck was on our side.

That night we could have been killed. It was our third night in the big fight – everyone was physically exhausted. A tiny rural hut, shelter for shepherds, the ramparts of which were still standing. served as the Company Command post. Communication from the Battalion's Intelligence unit had a line that even worked. The Commander wanted to see me. A voice said "one moment" two or three times. Then it was done, total fatigue had triggered a kind of fainting spell in me – I was no longer in this terrible world. Only when others woke me up did I regain consciousness. The Company was no longer functional. A kind of unconsciousness had seized everyone. Our rations were next to us, and nobody noticed that the food bearers were there. The English were probably also in a state of exhaustion, they were just as poor devils as we were. The only one who got terribly excited was the Commander, and rightly so this time. This day, 22 Jan 44. was a day without end and full of cruelty. Everybody asked himself the question – how could it go on?'

[As the Germans retreated some of the British Prisoners of War were able to re-join their units. However, many were put on trains to Germany and spent the rest of the war in German Prisoner of War camps.]

1 Green Howards War Diary
22 Jan 44 – 1210
'B' company arrived and dug in [Northern outskirts of Minturno]. Minturno being heavily shelled.

5 Infantry Division War Diary
22 Jan 44 – 1210
2 Cameronians counterattacked and at 1210 had restored the position on Point 201 and were holding the feature firmly.

1 York & Lancs. War Diary
22 Jan 44 – 1230
Headquarters withdrew to Minturno.

15 Infantry Brigade War Diary
22 Jan 44
1 York & Lancs. were withdrawn during the afternoon to a semi-rest area on the Lateral Road quite near Brigade HQ about 800952. Their rifle Companies strength totalled only about 120 and they had lost three Company Commanders of whom two were killed.

2 Wiltshires War Diary
22 Jan 44 – 1230
Point 201 firmly consolidated by two Companies of 2 Cameronians. The amalgamated 'A' and 'B' companies are to be known as 'B' company and will be commanded by Major Clark.

92 Field Regiment Royal Artillery War Diary
22 Jan 44 – 1230
Regiment has 20 guns [a Field Regiment normally had 24 guns] only in action now, due to breakdowns. One gun has jammed shell in bore with broken ejector projectile. Arrangements made for new barrel to be fitted on gun site.

Own friendly troops now in area Point 201. Many enemy dead due to artillery fire.

X (BR) Corps War Diary
22 Jan 44 – 1255
13 Infantry Brigade: 2 Cameronians retook Point 201, catching enemy withdrawing with machine guns. Many enemy dead. 15 Infantry Brigade: 1 York & Lancs. bore brunt of attack which is being held by 1 Green Howards. Fighting on Point 172 continues.

1 Green Howards War Diary
22 Jan 44 – 1300
'B' & 'D' Companies moved to 788956 [Northern outskirts of Minturno].

1 York & Lancs. History

22 Jan 44

1 Green Howards had occupied a strong position in rear of Monte Natale and in consequence the survivors of York & Lancs. 'B/C/D' companies were ordered to withdraw. This was successfully done just as a renewed enemy counterattack with tanks from the direction of the road was beginning.

The Battalion had fought its greatest battle of the war, but very few officers and men of the rifle companies reached the concentration area behind Minturno. Nearly 300 casualties, of which 60 were killed, tell their own story of the severity of the fighting on and around Monte Natale. For his able and gallant leadership Major Webster was awarded an immediate D.S.O., while Captain Ivor J. Wedgbury received the Military Cross, Private Seldon the Military Medal and Lieutenant Corfield and Private Hinchcliffe were 'Mentioned in Despatches'.

It became known afterwards that the Battalion and 1 KOYLI had been attacked by a reinforced regiment of 90 Panzer Grenadiers Division, formerly the famous 90 Light Division, and that the Germans had been ordered to reach the line of the River Garigliano at all costs. Had they achieved this the whole X (BR) Corps bridgehead would have been in great danger.

1 York & Lancs. Military Cross Citation for Captain Ivor Wedgbury

On 20 January 1944 'C' Company of 1 Battalion York & Lancaster Regiment was ordered to attack and capture Monte Natale, Point 156, North-West of Minturno.

Captain Ivor J. Wedgbury had just that morning taken over command of the Company in place of the Company Commander who had been seriously wounded. Under his leadership the Company successfully gained its objective. At dawn the following morning, 21 January a heavy German counterattack was launched from the West. All lines were cut, and the wireless destroyed by the preliminary bombardment, and in consequence no artillery Direct Fire was shot. The Company positions were partly over-run and heavy casualties were incurred. Captain Wedgbury, though out of touch with his Battalion HQ throughout this battle successfully resisted this; also, two further attacks that evening. He was constantly up with his forward Platoons, encouraging and inspiring them, and it was almost entirely due to his example and skill that the German attacks were broken up and our positions regained.

At 0630 hours the next day 22 January the heaviest attack of all came in supported by tanks, dive bombers and intense artillery concentrations, and quickly penetrated the positions on Captain Wedgbury's right ['A' Company's position around the corner of the Cemetery on the Santa Maria Infante-Minturno road]. His own Company, however, resisted all onslaughts and he continued to fight the battle for eight hours without respite, although enveloped on three sides by the enemy. He was, when communication had been re-established, ordered to withdraw. He carried out this difficult operation under the continuous fire of the enemy with such skill that he suffered only minor casualties.

Throughout the action and although physically very weary he never allowed his efforts to flag. At all times he was at the point of danger and situations which appeared desperate he restored by his inspiration, determination, and fearless example.

Privates Taylor and Cartwright of 1 York & Lancs. described their experience of the final part of the battle
'Six of us were in a German trench that was so deep we could not see out of it, so we had to crawl out. We were fired at by a tank 300 yards away and then we saw four Germans with a gun coming up the slope. We opened fire with our Bren guns, and they went to ground writhing. When the Company got the order to withdraw, we missed it. There was nobody on our right or on our left or behind us. We half expected to find Gerry in our big trench when we went back to it, but it was empty, and we sat down. Then we saw a German tank with infantry on it coming up the track to get around behind us, so we decided it was time to go. We backed out of the trench with our Bren and Tommy guns pointing in the direction of the tank and walked backwards until we reached the ridge. Then we turned around and went quick.'

52 Anti-Tank Regiment War Diary
22 Jan 44 – 1300
207 Battery: Enemy managed to penetrate a certain distance along ridge around Point 172 but were stopped 800 yards short of the town. Tanks were reported in the area of the Cemetery, but none made their appearance within range of any anti-tank gun.

X (BR) Corps War Diary
22 Jan 44 – 1330
1 KOYLI position improving but Boche still on part of Point 172, 785964. One Company 1 Green Howards has been sent to Point 151, 795963 [400m West of Point 201]. One tank of two Sherman Troops knocked out. Five tanks North of Minturno. Boche tanks thought unlikely to come further than Cemetery.

2 Cameronians War Diary
22 Jan 44 – 1330
The CO. ordered 'A' Company to move from the East end of Tufo and take over the position at 798962 [Point 201] from 'D' Company 2 Wiltshires, who moved to the East end of Tufo into 'A' Company's position.

C in C Mediterranean, General Alexander meets Major Ivor Wedgbury of 1 York & Lancs.in the middle of the town of Anzio to congratulate him on being awarded the Military Cross. (TNA)

22 Jan 44 – 1400
Brigade Commander ordered 'C' Company forward from the position at 821961 to Point 102, 805956.

2 Northants War Diary
22 Jan 44 – 1430
CO. returned to 13 Infantry Brigade HQ where he saw the Brigade Commander regarding the 2 Northants Battalion counterattack role on Point 172 North of Minturno, 785964.

2 Cameronians War Diary
22 Jan 44 – 1430
'C' Company were called forward to recce the position of 'C' Company, 2 Wiltshires at Point 151 795962 [400m West of Point 201].

98 Field Regiment Royal Artillery War Diary
22 Jan 44 – 1430
Air Observation Post on recce but does not see anything. Enemy tanks at 776965, Point 156, Monte Natale.

22 Jan 44 – 1445
471 Battery reports three Sherman tanks previously stuck now OK. Observation Post Officer slight injury. 'E' Troop Observation Post Officer resting with 1 York & Lancs. Battery Commanders jeep disabled.

1 KOYLI War Diary
22 Jan 44 – 1500
The plan was made at about 1500 by the Brigade Commander for 1 Green Howards to come up from the reserve area South of Minturno and attack behind an artillery barrage, the remainder of the Point 172 ridge. In order to enable the barrage to go down the forward Companies tightened up their position and 'A' Company were withdrawn into their original area about 787960 [250m South of Point 172]. One Company of 1 Green Howards who had been attached to 1 York & Lancs. was left on the ground covering the gap between 'C' Company and the road. 'B' Company was pulled out into the same area as 'A' Company and the two Companies were amalgamated to form 'A/B' Company. The total Companies strengths at this time were believed to be approximately 195, split 'A' Company – 50, 'B' Company – 15, 'C' Company – 50, 'D' Company – 80.

In order to enable this operation to take place one Company of 2 Scots Guards was put under the command of the Battalion and occupied the high ground Point 141, Monte Del Duca, 781959. 1 Green Howards attack went in, but they had not sufficient men to push home their attack with thoroughness and were not able to occupy the whole of the Point 172 feature and despite attempts by both sides this feature remained in 'No Man's Land'.

By this time, it is almost certain that Ernest Strafford was at or near Point 172, dead or alive.

1 KOYLI War Diary
22 Jan 44 – 1500
'A' Co withdrawn to 787960 (250m South of Point 172), one Company 1 Green Howards put between 'C' Company and road at Point 172, 'B' Company amalgamated with 'A' Company. One Company 2 Scots Guards occupied Point 141, Monte Del Duca, 781959.

98 Field Regiment Royal Artillery War Diary
22 Jan 44 – 1500
Enemy tanks at 779966 [Aid Post].

1 York & Lancs. War Diary
22 Jan 44 – 1630
Brigadier ordered Battalion to move to 801952 [beside Lateral Road, 1km South of Tufo] to reorganise, where they arrived at 1630.

Battalion arrived at destination South-East of Minturno 801952. Although the Battalion had suffered total casualties of 10 Officers, 247 Other Ranks, during the 3 counterattacks they had severely mauled the enemy.

The final tally of casualties during the battle was:

KILLED – 2 Officers, 47 Other Ranks.
WOUNDED – 8 Officers, 136 Other Ranks.
MISSING – 64 Other Ranks.
The attacking Companies comprised in total about 400 men.

Ernest Shaw of 1 York & Lancs.
'In the early afternoon, the Germans tried a different approach. First of all, they fired smoke shells, surrounded us almost left and right with smoke and then they came in a pincer movement, they went left and right of us. They actually got tanks behind "B" Company and what was left of "B" and "C". I thought we have had it. We saw the Tiger tanks behind us. Huge things, and we could not do much about them. All we had got were rifles and tommy guns.

We went to Minturno and there we were taken back behind the town. We were just in front of our artillery positions. There we were issued with 2-man bivouacs. Whilst fighting going on, 11 Platoon had been knocked about pretty well and Ted had been sent to help them out, not as a runner but as a fighting man. Consequently, as we got back just in front of the artillery camp, I got a tent to myself. It was January and the ground was soggy wet, and after all these episodes I was getting edgy after the bombing, to put it mildly.'

7 Cheshires War Diary
22 Jan 44 – 1640
One Platoon 'D' Company fired at enemy in small wadi South-East end of Point 156, 778966.

1 Green Howards War Diary
22 Jan 44 – 1640
Lt. Col Patrick George Bulfin orders for attack: 'B' and 'D' Companies to capture and consolidate on Point 172, 785964. 'B' Company left. 'D' Company right.

1 Green Howards Citation: Military Medal for Private R. Peel
On 22 Jan 44 'B' Company took part in an attack on the Minturno ridge. Casualties were suffered and early in the advance Private Peel took over the duties of Platoon Sergeant. Although under enemy shell fire, he was seen running from Section to Section, urging the men forward close into our barrage.

Shortly afterwards, in the darkness, Private Peel and part of his Platoon were surrounded and he was taken prisoner. His courage undaunted, he escaped from his escort and re-joined his Company, bringing back valuable information as to the enemy's strength and position which enabled the artillery to be employed with effect.

He next manned the P.I.A.T. [Projector, Infantry, Anti-Tank grenade] and was largely responsible for breaking up a formation of enemy who were assembling in the woods below the Co.'s position. Private Peel's actions this night were worthy of the highest traditions of his Regiment and the British Army.

1 Green Howards Citation: Military Medal for Corporal J. Murphy
On 22 Jan 44 in the area of the Minturno Cemetery, 781966, the situation of No. 8 Platoon became critical; the enemy having infiltrated in some strength and surrounded the Platoon locality.

Having armed himself with all available grenades and extra T.S.M.G. [Tactical Support Machine Gun] ammunition Corporal Murphy went out with his Platoon Sergeant [Private R. Peel] to attack the enemy.

By superb courage and offensive action of the highest order they overcame great odds, Corporal Murphy himself killing six Germans, wounding others, and causing the remainder to break up and run.

X (BR) Corps History
22 Jan 44 – 1700
15 Infantry Brigade passed to the offensive and 1 Green Howards counterattacked, recapturing Point 172.

5 Infantry Division History
1 Green Howards attack on to Point 172. 'C' Company, now only thirty-three all ranks strong, led the way to the Cemetery North-West of Point 172. 'B' Company on the left and 'D' Company on the right followed them. Two German tanks held them up but, after some confused fighting 'D' Company then secured their objective and several prisoners. 'B' Company had to withdraw backed by part of the Carrier Platoons. The Battalion held on where it was, under heavy shelling, for the whole night and all the next day.

For their fine work in this battle 1 Green Howards Battalion Commander, Lt. Colonel Patrick George Bulfin was awarded the Distinguished Service Order. Sergeant F. M. Roche gained a bar to his Military Medal, and six Distinguished Service Medals were also gained by the 1 Green Howards Battalion.

1 Green Howards Citation: Military Medal for Private H.C. Archer
On 22 Jan 44, in the area of the Minturno Cemetery, 781966, Private Archer's Platoon was ordered forward to try and destroy one of three German tanks and to break up the

infantry covering party, which threatened the left flank of the main counterattack on to the Minturno ridge.

The P.I.A.T. attack failed, nevertheless Private Archer rushed forward unhesitatingly, in the face of heavy machine gun fire, to within 30 yards of the enemy tank, and by throwing grenades killed and wounded several enemy in the vicinity and caused great confusion.

The Platoon then moved in order to make a further attack, and again came under very heavy fire and were pinned to the ground. In spite of this, Private Archer continued to crawl forward and by engaging the enemy with his rifle and throwing grenades, personally accounted for another six Germans.

Throughout this action Private Archer showed an extremely high example of bravery and coolness under heavy fire.

15 Infantry Brigade War Diary
22 Jan 44 – 1700

1 Green Howard's operation was successful, and two Companies were established 300 yards apart on the main feature though some enemy pockets were holding out between them. Many enemy dead were found in the area and a few Prisoners of War were taken identifying both Regiments of 90 Panzer Grenadiers Division [200 and 361 Panzer Grenadier Regiments]. The third Company from 1 Green Howards was in position immediately behind the main feature whilst 1 KOYLI now held the old 1 Green Howards position covering the front of Minturno with 2 Scots Guards Company on Point 141, under their Command. 1 KOYLI were made responsible for contact with 13 Infantry Brigade on ring contour 151, 794962 [400m South-West of Point 201].

52 Anti-Tank Regiment War Diary
22 Jan 44 – 1700

Two Companies of 1 Green Howards attacked Northwards along the Point 172 ridge and recaptured the ridge without undue difficulty taking about 15 Prisoners of War.

6 Grenadier Guards War Diary
22 Jan 44 – 1700

Battalion HQ received more hits and moved its position. Lt. Stokes-Roberts in command of No 1 Company [who had survived many more critical situations], was killed by a mortar bomb [Lt. George Stokes-Roberts MC. Minturno CWGC Cemetery].

5 Infantry Division Locations List
22 Jan 44 – 1800
Troops under Command

201 Guards Brigade
      HQ 201 Guards Brigade   806954 Point 102
      6 Grenadier Guards   773958 1km West of Point 141, Monte del Duca
      3 Coldstream Guards   767955 500m West of Tremensuoli
      2 Scots Guards   8095
      40 Royal Tank Regiment

15 Infantry Brigade

HQ 15 Infantry Brigade	807954 Point 102
1 Green Howards	7996
1 KOYLI	7896
1 York & Lancs.	7995
158 Field Ambulance, RAMC	803953 Near Point 102

3 Coldstream Guards War Diary

22 Jan 44 – 1800

Mortars and spandaus [machine guns] opened up on our right flank and fired very heavily for two hours. As it seemed that an enemy counterattack might be coming in, two Platoons of 6 Grenadier Guards were brought up to thicken the Battalion front. However, nothing more happened and apart from occasional shelling it was an uneventful night.

2 Northants War Diary

22 Jan 44 – 1800

Telephone line parties went out to the Companies. Signal exchange set up. [The Signals Exchange was a telephone switchboard that controlled the line calls in and out of Battalion HQ. It was manned by the Signals Platoon.] Battalion dug in the Company positions and settled down for the night. Greatcoats arrived too late to be of use, but rations arrived and were distributed.

164 Field Ambulance War Diary

22 Jan 44 – 1830

One AFS ambulance car overturned on way to collect casualties at Tufo, 803962. Service maintained by jeep.

1 Green Howards War Diary

22 Jan 44 – 1900

'D' Company reached objective, Point 172, and consolidated. 'B' Company was forced to withdraw under cover of 3-inch mortar fire. 'D' Company reinforced by personnel from Carrier Platoon.

2 Cameronians War Diary

22 Jan 44

'C' Company arrived at Tufo and waited until dark before moving forward to take over the position and no movement was allowed at dusk when the likelihood of counterattack was greatest.

2 Wiltshires War Diary

22 Jan 44

'B' company moved back to point 102, 805955 in reserve. 2 Cameronians relieved 2 Wiltshires as left forward Battalion. During the night 'C' Company are relieved on point 151 by a Company of 2 Cameronians and came back to West of Tufo just South of the road with an immediate counterattack role on Point 201. 'D' company moved back to their original position in the East end of Tufo. The first fairly quiet night for five days.

D. Woolard, 2 Wiltshires, *My Day, 22 January*

'It was a hellish stand to, shells and mortar bombs bursting everywhere and Spandaus ripping out long bursts. I could hear Brens firing and grenades bursting somewhere to our left. There was no stand down this morning. In fact, we had truly little rest all day and even less to eat as there was no time to stop for food. As soon as it was light, we were given ranges and deflection and at once started to fire with both mortars. The reinforcement carrying party were sent back to Platoon HQ for more shells. They made several journeys that day carrying shells uphill and over the debris of the previous night's bombing at Tufo. One of our anti-tank guns was mounted behind some of this rubble to give hell to any enemy armour if it tried to break through to Tufo.

At times the carrying party, after struggling uphill with our shells, helped the walking wounded back to the Regional Aid Post. During the morning the shelling increased, and we had to duck down into the gun-pits as shells burst dangerously close. We were showered with flying earth and shrapnel whistled overhead and could be heard bumping into the ground nearby or in the trees around us. I remember one large lump of shrapnel penetrating a tree and cutting it in half. After about two hours of firing, we had to dig out the base plate of the mortar, reset it and then carry-on firing. It was warm work for such a cold morning, and we got very thirsty and hungry, but there was no time to stop until late in the afternoon.

I saw many of our wounded coming back, some walking, others on stretchers, with blood running from arms or legs. Some had head or face wounds, and some were moaning in great pain. Some were cursing and others were very pale and quiet. From the stretcher bearers we learned how the situation was up in the forward positions. A Captain and six men were killed in the first attack. Some men were wounded, and others taken prisoner. Corporal Lush was killed after a fight in which he killed several Germans, his brother was with him but was not wounded [Corporal Lawrence Lush. Minturno CWGC Cemetery]. "A" Company were having a very rough time of it, the Germans put in three strong counterattacks. The final attack was repulsed with help from a Company of 2 Cameronians with heavy machine guns giving close support. In the late afternoon things began to quieten down a little except for shelling and a few small arms duels and we were given the order to cease fire. We opened a few tins of meat and vegetables and a tin of tomatoes. We put them in a dixie and heated it up on a smokeless fire. When it was hot enough, we each had a mess tin full, with some hard biscuits. Lofty collected the water from our water bottles and put it in a stew dixie and dashed to a ruined house near our gun-pits. I can picture him now as shells burst nearby, he just bent his lofty form forward and carried on with the precious dixie of water. When he came back with the tea, it was most welcome.

A report came back to us that Corporal Simmonds who was in one of our Observation Posts had been wounded and taken prisoner. All that was found in the Observation Post was his "38" radio receiver and transmitter which was severely damaged. Sergeant Wallysuch, also of our Platoon was wounded and blinded, but was not taken prisoner. Casualties were high that day on both sides, especially in "A" Company. By nightfall we were all feeling very tired, so we were glad when stand to was over, so that some of us could get down to a few hours' sleep. Apart from a little shelling it was a quiet night and there were no more counterattacks.'

2 Cameronians War Diary
22 Jan 44 – 1900
'C' Company were in position. The Battalion had now completely taken over the Tufo area with 'D' Company on Point 201, 'C' Company on Point 151, 'A' Company at 798962 [West of Tufo] and 'B' Company at 805962 [East of Tufo]. HQ was in Tufo and Main Battalion HQ at 805962. Standing patrols were established throughout the night and day at 792965 [1km West of Point 201], by 'A' Company, 802968 [600m North-East of Point 201], by 'B' Company, 790963 [500m East of Point 151], by 'C' Company and 792973 [1km North-West of Point 201], by 'D' Company. The Padre, Captain Robertson was slightly wounded during the afternoon on the Lateral road.

Point 201 North of Tufo changed hands four times before 2 Cameronians finally took and held it for good.

5 Infantry Division War Diary
22 Jan 44 – 1930
After Medium Artillery concentrations on it, 1 Green Howards attacked Point 172 and by 1950 both forward Companies were digging in on the feature and had taken ten Prisoners of War.

5 Infantry Division Intelligence War Diary
22 Jan 44 – 2100
Fierce and strong counterattacks have been developed by the enemy and unquestionably he had no intention of allowing us to break further through his main position. What he will do now that the threat to his rear has so suddenly arisen, remains to be seen.

He has renewed his attacks but on an apparently smaller scale today, and last night switched his effort so that the main thrust has been against our own front down the axis Santa Maria Infante – Minturno with a subsidiary effort against Point 201. The formation responsible has seemingly been 267 Grenadier Regiment later reinforced by elements of 90 Panzer Grenadiers Division, both Regiments have been identified by us.

Thus, it is clear that 90 Panzer Grenadier Division is to bear the main thrust of the Allied attack now that 94 Infantry Division has almost disintegrated and unless all goes well for him the enemy will not easily be able to withdraw the units hastily assembled to fill the gaps.

Any attack launched from the San Croce area 7395 will almost inevitably keep North of Route 7 and towards Minturno advancing probably by way of the railway station at 764950 [South-West of Tremensuoli[. When held up the tendency will be to shift the weight North-East by way of Martino [now known as Vaglia to the West of Tremensuoli] 7596 towards Monte Natale.

1 Green Howards War Diary
22 Jan 44 – 2100
Battalion HQ established, 785959 [300m South of Point 172].

22 Jan 44 – 2130
'A' and 'C' companies re-joined the Battalion and took up positions: 'C' company,784964 [close to Point 172], 'A' company 787964 [300m East of Point 172]. During the night there was heavy shelling and mortaring.

1 Green Howards Citation: Military Medal for Private E. Gilbert

Throughout 22 Jan 44 'C' Company of 1 Green Howards were subjected to continuous artillery, mortar, and machine gun fire in the area of Minturno, 787966 and there were a number of casualties.

During the entire day Private Gilbert displayed great coolness as a Regimental Stretcher bearer, time and again crossing and re-crossing the open bullet swept ground without regard to his own safety, tending casualties in the open and evacuating them to the Regimental Aid Post.

His devotion to duty in great danger and fortitude in spite of extreme fatigue, was magnificent.

164 Field Ambulance War Diary
22 Jan 44 – 2200
One captured enemy ambulance car hit by shellfire at track junction 794945 [Lateral Road South-East of Minturno], while returning to Aid Post. No casualties.

2 Cameronians War Diary
22 Jan 44 – 2225
'D' Company standing patrol reported enemy digging in the area 796976 [1km North of Point 201] and were ordered to fire on them and they in return brought machine gun fire

22 Jan 44 midnight: The dispositions of 15 Infantry Brigade troops. York & Lancs "B" "C" "D" Cos. and HQ. East of Minturno, KOYLI and Green Howards North of Minturno and Wiltshires around Tufo. (Photo John Strafford)

from the enemy who continued digging throughout the night. At 2225 the area 796976 [1km North of Point 201] was engaged by Artillery.

201 Guards Brigade History
22 Jan 44

Carrier Platoons of all three Battalions with one Troop of 'A' Squadron 40 Royal Tank Regiment lining track from Tremensuoli to Minturno. During the day movement was seen in the whole sector from Monte Natale to Scauri. The enemy was engaged by 3-inch mortars of both forward Battalions and the 4.2-inch mortars of 227 Anti-Tank Battery, also one Platoon of 'C' Company 7 Cheshires. The mortars expended 200 rounds 3 inch and 330 rounds 4.2 inch. As a result, enemy movement everywhere became more circumspect particularly on the road San Croce – Santa Maria Infante. The 4.2 mortars making the road junction and quarries at 755975 [known as Squiggle] particularly unsafe. An enemy ammunition dump was shelled in this area. The road was harassed day and night by all arms whenever movement was seen or heard. On the other hand, 6 Grenadier Guards, 3 Coldstream Guards and one Company of 2 Scots Guards [on Point 141] came in for much shelling which produced a constant flow of casualties, the infantry themselves being able to do nothing to hit back as they did not have the long-range weapons required.

On 22 Jan 44, the same day that 1 York & Lancs. was desperately defending Monte Natale the Americans and British made an unexpectedly easy landing at Anzio and secured a narrow bridgehead there. Although by no means strong in numbers after its recent heavy fighting, the British X (BR) Corps seized the opportunity to attack and try to enlarge its own bridgehead over the River Garigliano.

Lieutenant D.H. Deane, 2 Scots Guards writes
22 Jan 44 Saturday

'Went to link up with some gunners in their Observation Post. And got blown about horribly by mortar stonk which came down very fiercely – there was no room in their trenches, so I had to lie in a crack in a rock until it calmed down – I said goodbye to them over my shoulder and flew back to my own small fortress. Large German shell came over and set four carriers alight killing four from HQ Company. What they call a casa shifter.'

1 KOYLI History
22 Jan 44

The day before the counterattack [21 Jan 44] 1 Green Howards had been withdrawn into reserve and replaced on the ground by 201 Guards Brigade. By midday on 22 Jan 44 the Brigadier 15 Infantry Brigade seeing the situation, ordered 1 Green Howards to take over on the Point 172 ridge from us – while we concentrated on the defence of Minturno – 1 York & Lancs. meantime going back to re-organise. This stage went according to plan, and a comparatively quiet night 22–23 Jan 44 was passed except for the usual shelling. By this time, Battalions were getting a little thin on the ground and also a little jumpy from the incessant shelling and mortaring.

Sir David Cole, 2 Inniskillings, *Rough Road to Rome*

'Meanwhile we in 2 Inniskillings were steadily settling down in our new positions [on the furthest part of the Minturno ridge East of Tufo]. Our various holes in the ground, whether they were Five Star Highly Recommended Dugouts or, like mine, totally unrecommended little slit trenches unfit for even bed and breakfast, became all that for the moment we could call home. Battalion HQ with its Bren-guns and weapon-pits amongst the trees and scrub, seemed a warlike little place, better equipped for a good scrap than for smoking a quiet pipe over an Operation Order. The C.O. and Peter Slane lived in a peculiar trench of Cubist design, surrounded by a few sandbags, and covered with a tarpaulin. Between them and my-self was another trench containing the telephone switch board and control wireless. The Doc, his practice thriving, had his consulting room in a nearby German dugout some fifteen feet underground, which I personally found so claustrophobic that I hoped, even more earnestly than before, not to require his services at the present juncture. Not far away was the Regimental Sergeant Major, Paddy Kilduff, who, though like all of us busy with his various duties and being blown about by the odd shell, emerged every morning from his little trench as smartly dressed as if he were about to take a drill parade; boots shining, gaiters whitened and brass buckles gleaming. With what abracadabra he brought this about I never knew. But in my eyes, he was to good order and military discipline what Einstein was to science. Fortunately, the weather, which Lord God arranged with unsatisfactory impartiality, that we and the Germans should share, remained for the time of year relatively merciful; in particular it never really rained, so we were spared the extra hell of waterlogged trenches and muddy tracks.'

X (BR) Corps History

22 Jan 44

One of the Herman Goering Panzer Division's two Infantry Battalions had already been identified on 20 Jan 44, the other was in action on 22 Jan 44.

With the exception of a single unsuccessful counterattack against 1 Green Howards newly won positions North of Minturno during the night, these were the last of the enemy's attacks against the Garigliano bridgehead. VI United States Corp had landed at Anzio in the early hours of 22 Jan 44 achieving complete surprise and it was now necessary for the Germans to rush reserves nearest to hand Northwards to contain this threat to his lines of communications. During the night 22–23 January therefore the enemy on the X (BR) Corps front went over to the defensive.

5 Infantry Division History

1 Green Howards had approximately two weak Companies on Point 172 and reported that there were no enemy forward of the Cemetery. 6 Grenadier Guards had taken up a new position on a line 775958 – 770959 [a line in front of Tremensuoli facing North].

158 Field Ambulance

22 Jan 44

Aid Post moved back to 783942 [1km South-West of Minturno]. Shelling still very severe. Ambulance drivers and orderlies putting up a magnificent show under heavy and continuous fire.

1 York & Lancs. Military Medal citation for Private H.H. Sheldon
22 Jan 44

During the period 20–22 January 1944 North West of Minturno 'B' Company suffered many casualties. Private Sheldon was the only stretcher bearer left. Although slightly wounded on three separate occasions he worked incessantly to bring in the wounded whilst constantly exposed to shell and machine gun fire, during three determined counterattacks, the last of which lasted five hours. He continued his work under heavy fire until wounded a fourth time when he bandaged himself and walked to the Regional Aid Post.

1 York & Lancs. Missing Person's Report by Sergeant Waddington

'On 22 January 1944 Private Sheldon was in my Platoon. It was reported to me as Platoon Commander that Private Sheldon along with other members of his Section had been wounded. I proceeded to where they were in position and after their wounds had been dressed, I directed him along with others to the Regimental Aid Post, they were all walking cases. I did not see Private Sheldon, but he may have been taken prisoner later in the day when the Germans counterattacked and got in the rear of "A" Company's position. This action took place about 600 yards beyond Minturno.'

German views of 22 Jan 44
Lt. Wolfgang Wiedemann, II Battalion, 267 Grenadier Regiment

22 Jan 44

'The Allied landing at Anzio resulted in the immediate withdrawal of 90 and 29 Panzer Grenadier Divisions, which were Army Group reserves. The brave 90 Panzer Grenadiers had prevented the breakthrough of the English at Santa Maria Infante at the last minute. 29 Panzer Grenadier Division was able to force an equally valuable success at Castelforte. The front stood, if only held by remnants of 94 Infantry Division.

Today propaganda shells rained printed paper on us instead of deadly splinters. Then we could read "Allied landing at Anzio/Nettuno behind the German front".

After a moment of shock, the unshakeable compatriots quickly found their composure again. Those who had survived four days of major combat against such enormous material superiority were probably not to be shaken so quickly. The extremely critical situation of 94 Infantry Division, and this of course applied to the entire XIV Panzer Corps, was made clear by the fact that the coastal defence section from Terracina via Sperlonga – Gaeta – Furia to Scauri, over 50 km long, was completely covered by a thin layer of German troops.

In the night 22/23 Jan 44 the remains of the Companies were left to build up a new front South of Pulcherini and Santa Maria Infante. "2" Company had about 30 men. When we were dead tired, hungry and with our last ounce of strength, our thoughts were with the comrades who had fallen or been wounded in the days of the Great War. The still existing mists of phosphorus in the valley reminded us of those terrible days. In the morning mist, South of Pulcherini, Major Frank awaited us. He announced the boundaries for the Companies.

When I tried to report the Company strength to him, he waved me away uninterested. He made the vicious remark that the Battalion had failed. I pointed out the high number of failures in all Companies. I also observed that the Company took about 20 prisoners. Poisonously, he said, it could have been two or three times more. I had never experienced so much ignorance and malice. What could I do? He was my Superior Officer.'

Lieutenant Wolfras Gieseler III Battalion 274 Grenadier Regiment
22 Jan 44
'Now it is my troubled duty to write to the relatives of 23 fellow soldiers of the Grenadier Regiment, who have died or gone missing in the past few days. Almost as many are wounded or reportedly captured. What suffering has been inflicted on so many families, and it is not easy for me to find the right words. Lieutenant Colonel Reich and we, who survived and remained healthy, mourn the death of many a good comrade.'

Mathew Parker, *Monte Cassino*: 276 Grenadier Regiment, 94 Division
'"To one of our shells, you send ten or twenty to our side"' was a comment made repeatedly by Prisoners of War. "Barrages all day" reads the diary of an eighteen-year-old German soldier who had been given a crucifix by an Italian family. "The Tommies are attacking . . . more barrages. A wounded man lies beside me and ahead of me three dead. I have changed a good deal. I cannot smile now." A letter home from a soldier shows the suffering endured by the Germans in the Garigliano sector; "On the way to Company HQ, a distance of less than 200 metres there are at least twenty German dead – how it happened is all too evident. One tries not to look at them. At night one falls rather than walks over the rocks. The Tommies creep stealthily around. Their snipers shoot only too well. Again, and again head wounds. The mortars fire and the whistle and explosion of shells goes on, day and night. Sometimes for a moment or two there is peace, and then I think of home. Sunlight by day, the night spent on cold stones."'

Chapter 8

23 January 1944 – Attempt to Take Back Monte Natale

5 Infantry Division History

23 Jan 44

It was arranged that 17 Infantry Brigade, now relieved and reassembled, should attack the Monte Natale feature and Solacciano, the spur to the West of it [1km North-West of Monte Natale). The object was to open up the way for an attack on Santa Maria Infante.

The Brigade plan was for 6 Seaforths to go for Spur Point 141, a spur to the North of Point 172, halfway to Santa Maria Infante, from Point 172, and 2 Royal Scots Fusiliers for Point 156, Monte Natale. 2 Northants were to push on to Santa Maria Infante on the following day.

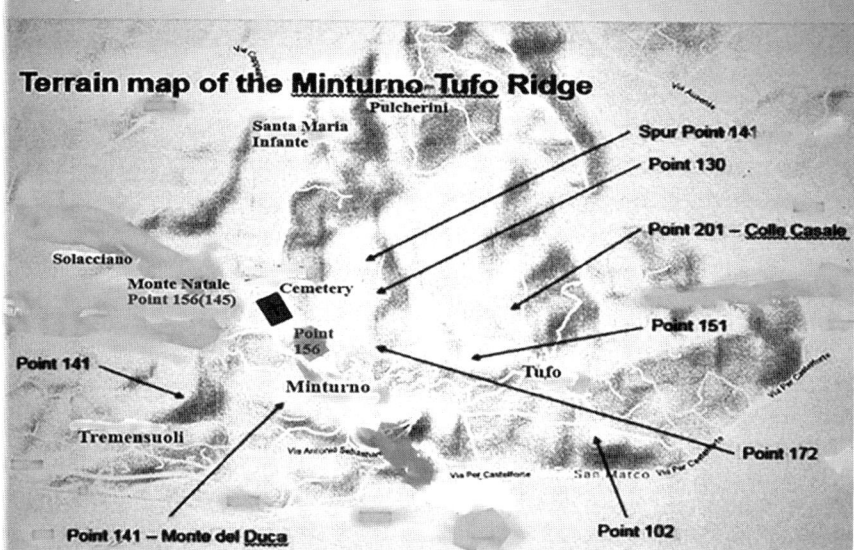

January 1944 – Attempt to take back Monte Natale

Terrain map of the Minturno-Tufo Ridge

Terrain of the Minturno-Tufo Ridge. British troops refer to Monte Natale as Point 156. Exact location to which they refer is Point 145 and shown as such on the map above. Point 156 is a hill in front of the Cemetery. (Map Frank de Planta)

40 Royal Tank Regiment War Diary

23 Jan 44

No 4 Troop was relieved by a troop of the 16/5 Lancers who proceeded to 780954 [400m South-West of Point 141, Monte Del Duca].

16/5 Lancers War Diary

23 Jan 44

Troop, 'A' Squadron were in support of two Battalions, 6 Seaforths and 2 Royal Scots Fusiliers for their attacks on Spur Point 141 and Point 156. Weather still fine.

15 Infantry Brigade War Diary

23 Jan 44 – 0130

Second in Command 1 Green Howards, Major D. Cobden arrived at Brigade HQ having just seen his Battalion and reported that a counterattack had gone in on the Company positions on Point 172 whilst the third Company which had gone forward towards the Cemetery to cover the consolidation of Point 172 had got rather disorganised and a number of men were missing. Heavy stonks were immediately ordered through Division Royal Artillery onto the Cemetery area and the situation remained quietish for the rest of the night with 1 Green Howards not entirely secure on Point 172, but the enemy not making any further attempts to push them off.

X (BR) Corps War Diary

23 Jan 44 – 0200

Counterattack on Point 172. Enemy now on Western end of Point 172 and in some strength from there North-West to Cemetery.

92 Field Regiment Royal Artillery War Diary

23 Jan 44 – 0240

Intercept: 102 Medium Regiment to 91 Field Regiment: Safe to fire on 781968 [next to Cemetery].

7 Cheshires War Diary

23 Jan 44 – 0400

'A' Company reported one Platoon moving to 17 Infantry Brigade concentration area at 801952 [near Lateral Road, 300m West of Point 102. Same location as 1 York & Lancs. was moved to]. Remainder of Company stayed on Monte d'Argento.

1 York & Lancs. War Diary

23 Jan 44 – 0630

Battalion in area 801952 [near Lateral Road, 300m West of Point 102] to reorganise.

15 Infantry Brigade War Diary

23 Jan 44 – 0645

Brigadier J.Y. Whitfield of the Queens Regiment arrived during the afternoon of 22 Jan 44 to take over the Brigade from Brigadier Martin. Brigadier Martin actually left about 1800 on 22 Jan 44, and Brigadier Whitfield was in control for 1 Green Howards operation that evening. The new Brigadier went forward and found the situation better than expected. 1 KOYLI had little to report whilst by daylight 1 Green Howards were able to reorganise their positions. Point 172 was definitely clear of enemy though it was clear he was still holding at the Cemetery and of course Monte Natale. During the day 1 KOYLI collected nine Prisoners of War identifying both German 90 Light Division and 94 Infantry Division.

X (BR) Corps War Diary
23 Jan 44 – 0745
Enemy hold West of Point 172. 1 Green Howards firm on East of Point 172 and in touch with 1 KOYLI, who were on hill in front of Cemetery.

98 Field Regiment Royal Artillery War Diary
23 Jan 44 – 0900
392 Battery Commander with 201 Guards Brigade. Regiment is now entirely in support of 201 Guards Brigade with Batteries affiliated as follows: 391 – 6 Grenadier Guards. 392 – 3 Coldstream Guards. 471 – 2 Scots Guards

23 Jan 44 – 1020
Battery Commander – Enemy tanks reported on road – 781967 [by Cemetery]. Observation Post to engage if he can see.

17 Infantry Brigade War Diary
23 Jan 44 – 1100
Brigadier J.Y. Whitfield, Brigade Commander holds Orders Group at Brigade HQ. He changes the original plan by limiting 2 Royal Scots Fusiliers to securing Point 156 [145, Monte Natale], rather than the more distant Solacciano, Point 140 at the far end of Monte Natale. 17 Infantry Brigade will attack Points 156 [145] and Spur Point 141 and hold this against all counterattacks. 6 Seaforths to attack Spur Point 141 supported by artillery concentrations and 2 Royal Scots Fusiliers Point 156 [145] under barrage. Further Plan: 2 Northants to pass through at first light 24 Jan 44 and capture Santa Maria Infante. 'A' Squadron 16/5 Lancers from 23 Armoured Brigade in support of operation.

6 Seaforth Highlanders War Diary
23 Jan 44 – 1100
'B' Company march to area vacated by 'D' Company 2 Northants and come under command of 2 Northants with a view to possible operations together.

1 York & Lancs. War Diary
23 Jan 44 – 1100
Commanding Officer's conference. Companies now commanded as follows: 'A' Captain J. Marshall MC, 'B' Major D. Webster, 'C' Captain Ivor J. Wedgbury, 'D' Major R. Colville, HQ Captain L. Mawson

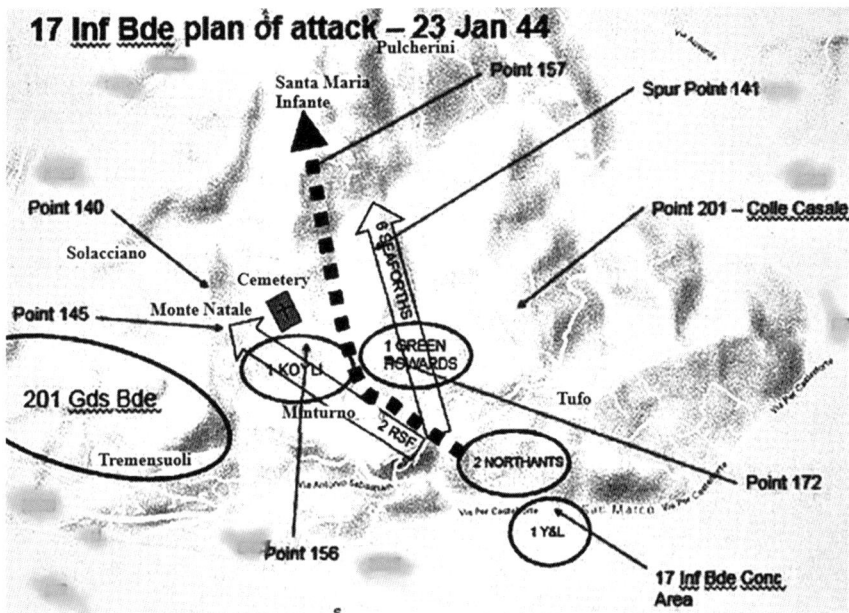

17 Infantry Brigade plan of attack – 23 Jan 44. (Map Frank de Planta)

2 Northants War Diary
23 Jan 44 – 1100

CO. went to conference at Brigade HQ where change of plan was announced. 2 Royal Scots Fusiliers and 6 Seaforth Highlanders now to attack Point 156, Monte Natale and Spur Point 141, respectively. 2 Northants to pass through at first light on the 24 Jan 44 and attack Santa Maria Infante.

Ernest Shaw 1 York & Lancs
23 Jan 44 – 1200

'We got there [rest area South-East of Minturno], in breaking light about 6.30am. I set to and dug a trench and put up a tent over it. I dug about 4 feet deep. I rigged the tent and put it up. I must have been digging about four to five hours, perhaps six. The trench was getting soggy at the bottom at that time of the year. The cooks had come up and had broken into a farmhouse about 150-200 yards down the road from where we were, so I thought I would scrounge a ration box and break it up to line the trench. Off I went. I had just got into the cook house and saw Johnny Lowd the cook. I had just scrounged a mug of tea off him, when Gerry shelled the area, so I stayed in the farmhouse with him until it was over. I set off back with this broken ration box and I ran into Bob Bowers and he gawped, glared. "Eh" he said, "They are looking for thy bits and pieces, go and have a bloody look at your tent".

The tent had taken a direct hit. My trench was almost circular. My gear had been blown about. The big ammunition pouch had been cut into two pieces, about the size

169

of a saucer, all jagged edges. There were six tommy gun pouches, and they were cut in two. I had got away with it again. I had stood there four/five hours. I had even had my breakfast before the cooks arrived besides the hole. It was as though I had been sent out of the way. I just had to be sent out of the way. It was just getting 12 o'clock. I formed the impression that I had left at five to twelve and the German stonk had been ordered at 12 o'clock. That was the end of four days when I might have been killed six or seven times. I never really worried after that.

Ted Rimmer came, and he heard what had happened and he wandered over from 11 Platoon. He viewed the damage and my gear, and he looked at me and he said "Hey Shawey, have you ever tried walking on water?" Then he disappeared.'

6 Seaforth Highlanders War Diary
23 Jan 44 – 1230
Battalion moves off through Tufo. Main HQ in area 791961 [800m East of Point 172].

5 Infantry Division War Diary
23 Jan 44 – 1300
In view of the stable situation, it was decided that the first stage of 17 Infantry Brigade operation would be carried out today and possibly the second phase as well.

Orders for this operation were dispatched as follows:

1 6 Seaforths will attack and hold Spur Point 141.
2 2 Royal Scots Fusiliers will attack, and hold Point 156, Monte Natale, 775966.
3 Zero-hour 1600 hours.
4 Tomorrow morning 2 Northants will pass through to Santa Maria Infante.

98 Field Regiment Royal Artillery War Diary
23 Jan 44 – 1340
391 Battery reports that Captain D.V. Leighton [371 Battery, 98 Field Regiment, Royal Artillery. Minturno CWGC] was killed by machine gun fire.

2 Royal Scots Fusiliers War Diary
23 Jan 44 – 1340
Recce party went forward to Start Line at Tufo; there was a coordinating conference at 791960 [1.5km East of Point 156, Monte Natale]. Only an extremely limited recce was possible as the approach to the objective was commanded completely by enemy positions.

1 York & Lancs. War Diary
23 Jan 44 – 1430
The new 15 Infantry Brigade commander, Brigadier J.Y. Whitfield, DSO addressed the Battalion. Enemy shelling decreased during the day.

17 Infantry Brigade War Diary
23 Jan 44 – 1445
General Harold Alexander, C-in-C, 15 Army Group visits Brigade HQ.

2 Royal Scots Fusiliers War Diary
23 Jan 44 – 1600
The Battalion reached Start Line which came under enemy shell fire between 1530 and 1600 and two casualties were suffered. Major F.W. Batey, 156 Field Regiment was wounded in the arm but able to carry on.

The attack went in under a barrage with 'B' Company right and 'D' Company left followed by Tactical HQ, 'C' Company in reserve and behind that Battalion HQ and Regimental Aid Post. The advance was terribly slow over thick, rough country fitted with numerous ditches and darkness was falling before the objective was reached. The axis of the attack necessitated wheeling right when under the ridge and this manoeuvre proved exceedingly difficult owing to gathering mist and darkness and the fog of gunfire in the valley.

6 Seaforth Highlanders War Diary
23 Jan 44 – 1600
Attack on Spur Point 141 starts

91 Field Regiment Royal Artillery War Diary
23 Jan 44 – 1600
Attack by 2 Royal Scots Fusiliers. Enemy Direct Fire reported exceedingly heavy – many infantry casualties including Commanding Officer 2 Royal Scots Fusiliers killed.

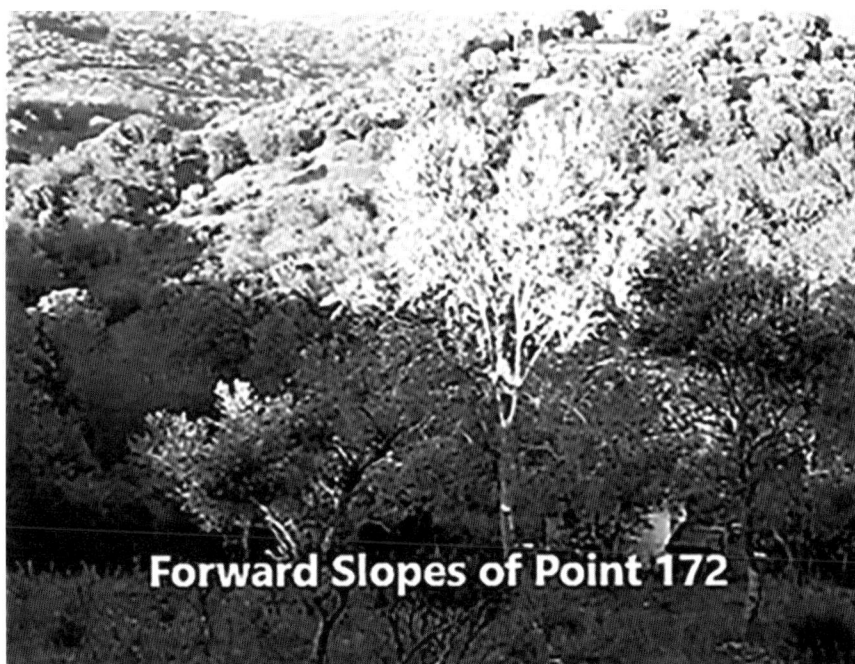

Forward slopes of Point 172. Start Line for 6 Seaforths on Point 172 looking towards Spur Point 141. (Photo C.J.M. Strafford)

2 Cameronians War Diary
23 Jan 44 – 1600
6 Seaforth Highlanders passed through 'C' Company to Point 172 and then attack Spur Point 141. Throughout the artillery barrage supporting the attack our guns kept dropping rounds on Tufo!

7 Cheshires War Diary
23 Jan 44 – 1600
Brigade attack on Point 156 [145], Monte Natale, and Spur Point 141 goes in. NOT successful.

2 Scots Guards War Diary
23 Jan 44 – 1600
German activity was confined to shelling Minturno which mattered very little in itself but a good many rounds fell on Right Flank Company, and some came over the hill into the area of Battalion Headquarters, Support Company, and 'A' Echelon. Right Flank had seven casualties during the day; Support Company had one.

An attack was put in on Monte Natale by the Brigade on our right.

Frank de Planta writes
23 Jan 44 – 1600
'5 Infantry Division could advance no further beyond Minturno because the Germans had perfect observation from Monte Petrella [1,533m high mountain, 5 miles North-West of Monte Natale], and 5 Infantry Division could not reach Monte Petrella without first seizing Monte Natale.'

17 Infantry Brigade War Diary
23 Jan 44 – 1610
3 Coldstream Guards arrange to help our attack with machine gun fire on left flank from 771960 [800m South-West of Monte Natale].

23 Jan 44 – 1625
6 Seaforths report they have reached intermediate objective 786967 (500m North of Point 172), without opposition.

98 Field Regiment Royal Artillery War Diary
23 Jan 44 – 1625
Regiment shoot on Fire Plan 787971 [400m North of 6 Seaforth's position]. Slow, stopped at 1630.

6 Grenadier Guards War Diary
23 Jan 44 – 1630
There was heavy shelling of the Company position, and Capt. Lowry-Corry, Second in Command '2' Company was wounded. Capt. M.W. Grazebrook took over command. Major P.C. Britten, '1' Company, and one other officer Lieut. A.J. Savill, had also been wounded.

The feature on our right, Monte Natale was due to be attacked and retaken by another Brigade. Unfortunately, during the attack, one of the attacking Companies [this would be a Company from 2 Royal Scots Fusiliers] lost its way and finished up by assaulting the hill which No. '2' Company was holding.

16/5 Lancers War Diary
23 Jan 44 – 1630

16/5 Lancers was to support an attack on Monte Natale and feature Spur Point 141 on the other side of the road. '3' Troop was assigned to this task and the attack went in at 1630. 2 Royal Scots Fusiliers were attacking Monte Natale on the left and 6 Seaforths Spur Point 141 on the right. '3' Troop was to advance along the road [Minturno–Santa Maria Infante road] supporting on either side as necessary, and if the attack was successful, they were to prevent an enemy counterattack coming down the road from the North. No '3' Troop formed up at Minturno and the tank commanders were shown the ground. There was a very nasty stretch of about 200 yards of open road, which we knew was covered by anti-tank fire, as 40 Royal Tank Regiment had previously lost a tank on that stretch. The plan was that each tank was to cross the open stretch singly as fast as it could and wait for the Troop to reform by a house with blue shutters. On reaching that landmark they would be hidden from view. Sergeant Ritchie was on the leading tank and set off down the road when ordered. As there was no report from him, Lieutenant Dill got out and seeing he was not on the road, proceeded to the house followed by the rest of the Troop. Luckily, there was a very heavy barrage from the artillery which kicked up a lot of dust, and they were not fired at from the left by an anti-tank gun. There was no sign of Sergeant Ritchie's tank. No '3' Troop then proceeded down the road to support the attack. 6 Seaforths got to their objective all right, but there was no wireless communication with 2 Royal Scots Fusiliers and Lieutenant Dill had no means of knowing how far they had got, and therefore could not support them satisfactorily, owing to not being able to identify friend from foe. However, he managed to get a shoot at some enemy on his right flank, which he identified by their green tracer, and silenced them killing quite a number. When night came the Troop was ordered to withdraw, as the poor light prevented them from being any further use. We learnt that the Commanding Officer of 2 Royal Scots Fusiliers had been killed and two Companies had gone the wrong way and gone too far to the left. The Reserve Company and the Second in Command and his HQ got on to Monte Natale numbering about 50 men but were driven off again by enemy counterattack. 6 Seaforths were also driven off by heavy mortar fire. Lieutenant Dill and No '3' Troop did very well indeed, considering the great difficulties under which they had to work and if the communications with 2 Royal Scots Fusiliers had been satisfactory, they could have been of far greater assistance. This action brought out the great importance of co-operation and good communications between the infantry and our-selves. No '3' Troop had to operate from the road, as the ground on either side was totally unsuitable for tanks and were fired on by machine guns, mortars, and artillery for a considerable time. There was no sign of Sergeant Ritchie's tank anywhere.

During the afternoon No '2' Troop (Lt. Bills) went to the right flank of the Division front and took over from a Troop of the 40 Royal Tank Regiment. They were in position beside 2 Inniskillings and their task was to prevent any enemy coming down the road running parallel to the River Garigliano from the East. They had fairly good positions looking down the road and covering Point 106 and the Damiano feature.

7 Cheshires War Diary

23 Jan 44 – 1630

Platoon supporting 13 Infantry Brigade fired on area map ref 797968 [600m North-West of Point 201], until 1630. This object being to neutralise enemy machine guns in this area and assist 6 Seaforths onto their object, Spur Point 141, map ref 787971.

17 Infantry Brigade War Diary

23 Jan 44 – 1640

6 Seaforths report on objective; being heavily mortared.

201 Guards Brigade War Diary

23 Jan 44 – 1640

6 Grenadier Guards report shelling and mortaring, and enemy infantry advance between them and Tremensuoli. 98 Field Regiment shoot Direct Fire.

5 Infantry Division War Diary

23 Jan 44 – 1650

6 Seaforths were reported on their objective but fifty minutes later a strong enemy counterattack had dislodged them. 'A' Squadron of 16/5 Lancers was at once put under command 17 Infantry Brigade.

17 Infantry Brigade War Diary

23 Jan 44 – 1700

Counterattack from West by enemy infantry against 6 Seaforths. Leading Company driven off objective.

92 Field Regiment Royal Artillery War Diary

HQ Royal Artillery report [incorrectly] 2 Royal Scots Fusiliers attacking Spur Point 141, 6 Seaforths will advance to Point 156 tonight [2 R.S.F were attacking Point 156 and 6 Seaforths Spur Point 141] and 2 Northants via Point 156 to Santa Maria Infante tomorrow morning. Batteries informed.

201 Guards Brigade War Diary

23 Jan 44 – 1730

Attack by 17 Infantry Brigade astride the Santa Maria Infante road met by opposition and 2 Royal Scots Fusiliers lost direction coming up to 6 Grenadier Guards instead of Monte Natale. A very quick counterattack by the enemy added to the general confusion.

2 Cameronians War Diary

23 Jan 44 – 1730

'D' Company patrol of Capt. Drummond and 15 Other Ranks left Tufo to shoot up the enemy platoon at 796976. The patrol reached 794974 [1km North of Point 201), and observed two enemy machine guns, two infantry guns and one mortar. The patrol was unable to go forward as our artillery shells were dropping short and they were caught in the enemy machine gun fire.

2 Royal Scots Fusiliers War Diary
23 Jan 44 – 1730
The leading Company and Tactical HQ came under heavy mortar direct fire on nearing the objective and the Commanding Officer who was himself controlling the advance was fatally wounded. Major MacMichael, Officer Commanding 'C' Company took command immediately and as visual contact with 'B' & 'D' Companies was lost, he pushed on with his own Company. In the bad light the leading Companies went too far West and missed the objective while 'C' Company fought on to it alone under heavy opposition from enemy automatic weapons. Major P.S. Sandilands, Second in Command who had come forward to take command, was wounded in the leg by machine gun fire, but remained in control and returned to Battalion HQ which was now just below the crest of Point 156 [145], Monte Natale, to report the situation to Brigade as he did not consider that he would be able to hold on to the objective. The wireless link to Brigade having failed, the Intelligence Officer was ordered to contact the Brigadier in the area of the Start Line and report on the situation. Meanwhile 'C' Company, twice rallied by Major MacMichael and Major F.W. Batey of 156 Field Regiment who had both been slightly wounded, continued the battle for the crest of the ridge against strong opposition, only being forced to give way to a sharp counterattack when each was practically exhausted. As wireless control with 'B' Company was lost and 'D' Company were not immediately available to restore the situation Major Sandilands was forced to give the order to withdraw before any orders could be brought back to him from the Brigade Commander.

17 Infantry Brigade War Diary
23 Jan 44 – 1735
Direct Fire put down on Spur Point 141 at request of 6 Seaforths.

23 Jan 44 – 1740
Report from 2 Royal Scots Fusiliers via 16/5 Lancers that they have encountered no difficulties so far.

23 Jan 44 – 1750
6 Seaforths ask for Carriers with ammunition. They correct previous report and state they were never on final objective, but only on intermediate objective which they still held.

1 KOYLI War Diary
23 Jan 44 – 1800
It was apparent that things were not going well. It had originally been intended that the Battalion should relieve 1 Green Howards on Point 172 after the main attack had passed through. This had always been a doubtful operation and not fancied by either of the unit commanders concerned and in view of the circumstances the change-over was cancelled.

It was learnt that 2 Royal Scots Fusiliers had walked into enemy direct fire and had considerable casualties. The order was given by the 17 Infantry Brigade Commander that the attack be withdrawn, and they came back in some disorder. It had originally been scheduled for us to relieve 1 Green Howards immediately after this attack, but by mutual agreement of the two-unit commanders this was postponed. In the meantime, 6 Seaforths had not been able to occupy Spur Point 141.

17 Infantry Brigade War Diary
23 Jan 44 – 1810
Request received from 6 Seaforths for six ambulances to be sent forward at once.

6 Seaforths War Diary
23 Jan 44 – 1815
Main HQ moves uphill to 790962 [600m East of Point 172).

17 Infantry Brigade War Diary
23 Jan 44 – 1825
Support Company ['C' Company 7 Cheshires] report 2 Royal Scots Fusiliers held up at 783963 [200m South of the Regimental Aid Post, which was now held by the Germans].

23 Jan 44 – 1827
6 Seaforths report firm on intermediate objective.

2 Northants War Diary
23 Jan 44 – 1830
Message from 17 Infantry Brigade saying not to proceed with plan as 2 Royal Scots Fusiliers and 6 Seaforth Highlanders attack not going as well as expected and being counterattacked by tanks and infantry.

17 Infantry Brigade War Diary
23 Jan 44 – 1835
6 Seaforths request Spur Point 141 to be registered as a Direct Fire.

52 Anti-Tank Regiment War Diary
23 Jan 44 – 1900
On reaching Brigade HQ. Recce Officer discovered that guns were not expected and there was no accommodation for them. As the 17 Brigade attack had failed it was decided that the guns were not needed.

5 Infantry Division War Diary
23 Jan 44 – 1935
6 Seaforths were firm on their intermediate objective in the area 785966 [300m North of Point 172] and 2 Royal Scots Fusiliers were moving back to their previous night's harbour area.

92 Field Regiment Royal Artillery War Diary
23 Jan 44 – 1935
Battery Observation Post reports 6 Seaforths at 786968 [500m North of Point 172], unable to reach final objective, but still trying. No news 2 Royal Scots Fusiliers.

Location other troops unchanged. 2 Northants still in reserve. The Guards Brigade front counterattacked unsuccessfully by enemy. Right of zone quiet. HQ Royal Artillery and Batteries informed.

X (BR) Corps History

23 Jan 44
17 Infantry Brigade having been relieved in the Monte d'Argento area [2km South of Minturno] by 23 Armoured Brigade, was to concentrate North of Minturno and launch an attack to recapture Monte Natale and secure the village of Santa Maria Infante, Both attacks were launched in the afternoon 23 Jan 44, but in both cases German opposition proved unexpectedly strong.

17 Infantry Brigade War Diary

23 Jan 44 – 1945
6 Seaforths asked urgently for ammunition.

1 KOYLI War Diary

23 Jan 44 – 2000
2 Royal Scots Fusiliers on the left were withdrawing without taking their objectives, whilst 6 Seaforths, sadly depleted were held on the ground well short of Spur Point 141. The attack had not succeeded.

17 Infantry Brigade War Diary

23 Jan 44 – 2025
2 Royal Scots Fusiliers withdrawing to harbour area on orders of 17 Brigade Commander after getting into an untenable position in low ground South of Point 156 [145] Monte Natale. Weather: Fine.

92 Field Regiment Royal Artillery War Diary

23 Jan 44 – 2030
Heavy fire required at 15-minute intervals on road Santa Maria Infante – S. Croce – Formia – message from HQ Royal Artillery. Regiment out of range.

2 Royal Scots Fusiliers War Diary

23 Jan 44 – Midnight
By 1900, the 17 Brigade Commander was on his way forward with the Intelligence Officer. The view of the Brigade Commander being to hold the position if possible, astride the road between Minturno and Point 156 [145], Monte Natale. Just North of Minturno, Brigade Commander met Major MacMichael with only a handful of his Company, which he had resolved to withdraw independently by Platoons. On receiving Major MacMichael's report on the situation Brigadier A.D. Dark gave orders to establish a collecting point on the road and withdraw the Battalion completely to the concentration area of that morning. This was done and by midnight the Battalion was complete in that area, all wounded having been successfully evacuated to 1 Kings Own Yorkshire Light Infantry Regimental Aid Post in Minturno. Total casualties were 53.

1 KOYLI War Diary
23 Jan 44 – Midnight
The night was spent with part of 6 Seaforths between Point 172 ridge and Spur Point 141, 1 Green Howards and our-selves remaining in our old positions. It was a quiet night and the following morning 6 Seaforths were withdrawn.

X (BR) Corps History Report
23 Jan 44
On 22 and 23 Jan 44 both Regiments of the 90 Panzer Grenadier Division were engaged. To hold this attack X (BR) Corps had the equivalent of two Divisions. The fighting was bitter and there were several anxious moments before the attacks subsided at the close of 22 Jan 44.

The 17 Infantry Brigade attack North to secure the high ground of Monte Natale began on a two Battalion front and 6 Seaforths on the right flank made some progress initially, but it met determined resistance. 6 Seaforths managed to get part of the way to their objective. The enemy then counterattacked in strength against both the attacking Battalions. 6 Seaforths were pinned to the ground near Point 172 North of Minturno and were not able to get forward, and 2 Royal Scots Fusiliers on their left advanced against heavy enemy resistance but owing to lack of co-ordination were unable to maintain themselves forward against enemy counterattack, became disorganised and had to be withdrawn.

5 Infantry Division History Report
23 Jan 44
On the left 2 Royal Scots Fusiliers suffered casualties on their way to the Start Line. 'A' and 'B' Companies led with a Troop of three tanks that moved forward as the barrage came down and disappeared. Thinking that 'A' and 'B' were lost, as indeed they were, 'C' Company followed, led by an exuberant young officer. Some of the men were singing but enemy machine guns took their toll. Lieut. Colonel A. MacInnes DSO the Commanding Officer [2 Royal Scots Fusiliers, Minturno CWGC] was mortally wounded by a heavy concentration of mortars and Major MacMichael ['C' Company Commander] took over. He too became wounded, and his place was temporarily taken by Major F.W. Batey – the Commander of 593 Battery of 156 Field Regiment. The Germans on the objective had an English speaker among them who shouted, 'Come on you yellow bastards and fight'. This demand was answered by a lone Fusilier who, slinging away his tommy gun, was last seen disappearing into a German slit trench armed solely with a jack knife.

Small arms ammunition began to run low and Major Batey organised a Direct Fire plan which enabled 'C' Company to withdraw towards Minturno with the minimum of casualties. 'A' and 'B' Companies had in fact completed almost a semi-circle and finished up amongst 201 Guards Brigade, too late to take any effective part in the attack. Major Batey was awarded the Military Cross for his leadership on this occasion.

6 Seaforths were unable to reach their objective in much the same circumstances, so 2 Northants remained uncommitted.

156 Field Regiment Royal Artillery, Bar to Military Cross Citation for Major F.W. Batey MC
On 23 Jan 44 Major F.W. Batey was with his affiliated Battalion – 2 Royal Scots Fusiliers during its attack on the feature Point 156 [7796]. Before moving off from

Minturno, Major Batey and two members of his Observation Post party were wounded but in spite of this he made the necessary reorganisation and went forward to join the Battalion Commander who was shortly afterwards killed. On his way up to take over, the Battalion Second in Command was wounded, leaving the Company Commander and Major Batey to carry on. They went forward together to reconnoitre the route and came under heavy machine gun fire. 13 Platoon was called forward as a fighting patrol and 14 Platoon took up position between 13 Platoon and Company HQ. By this time, the position was under heavy mortar and machine gun fire and Major Batey who had established wireless communication with his Battery ordered fire on the Defensive Fire tasks if the situation deteriorated. He stood up behind the mortars and directed fire and with his first round destroyed an enemy mortar position. He ran back to 14 Platoon and brought up more ammunition and kept up continuous fire until the ammunition was exhausted. During this time, he was again wounded but carried on. His small force almost reached its objective but because of the lack of ammunition was obliged to withdraw under cover of the defensive fire which Major Batey had previously ordered.

Throughout the whole period Major Batey was never once seen to take cover. He was twice wounded but refused to retire. His inspiring example and leadership carried 13 Platoon almost to the Battalion objective and his foresight in ordering fire on the Defensive Fire tasks enabled his small body of men to withdraw successfully.

[Major F.W. Batey had already been awarded a Military Cross for supporting 2 Royal Scots Fusiliers at Poggiofiorito in Dec 43. He was killed during the breakout from Anzio on 29 May 44, (Beachhead CWG).]

15 Infantry Brigade War Diary
23 Jan 44
An operation to secure Monte Natale and Spur Point 141, 788971 was carried out by 17 Infantry Brigade and took place during the late afternoon. The attack was not particularly successful; 2 Royal Scots Fusiliers in particular, suffering heavy casualties, though they secured a foothold on Monte Natale. They were finally withdrawn through 1 KOYLI during the night. 6 Seaforths met opposition not very far North of Point 172 and though they remained in position about half-way between 1 Green Howard's positions on Point 172 and Spur Point 141 for the next 24 hours, they were extremely weak on the ground and were finally withdrawn on the night 24-25 Jan 44. 1 KOYLI and 1 Green Howard's positions remained intact throughout this period though they were heavily shelled, 1 Green Howards in particular having an extremely uncomfortable time.

During the night 23-24 Jan 44, 1 Green Howards maintained contact to their front with 6 Seaforths. The Brigadier informed Division after 17 Infantry Brigade attack had failed that 2 Northants were available for counterattack that night if the enemy were to put in another attack counting on our dis-organisation. The Brigadier had intended to pull out 1 Green Howards and hold the Brigade front with only one Battalion on the ground. – 1 KOYLI – provided the 17 Infantry Brigade attack went OK. This relief was to start at 1800. In fact, with 17 Infantry Brigade attack not succeeding their relief was not possible and 1 Green Howards were obliged to stay in situ until finally relieved on night of 24-25 Jan 44.

1 KOYLI War Diary
23 Jan 44

A much more ambitious attack was planned with the object of capturing Monte Natale. 6 Seaforths were to occupy Spur Point 141 beyond the Point 172 ridge [1 Green Howards were holding most of the Point 172 ridge], and 2 Royal Scots Fusiliers the Monte Natale feature, recently evacuated by 1 York & Lancs. The attacks to be preceded by a heavy barrage. This attack was hastily prepared and laid on and nobody was quite sure of timings. It was not a success from the start. Both units were heavily shelled on their Start lines. The barrage came down and caused so much dust that 2 Royal Scots Fusiliers were confused.

1 KOYLI Military Medal Citation for Private David Huntrod

Throughout the battle for 172 Ridge and the defence of Minturno 20-23 January 1944, Private Huntrod who is a Stretcher Bearer with 'C' Company showed the greatest devotion to duty in continually collecting and evacuating casualties, whilst under enemy fire. On more than one occasion he went out when the Company was being heavily shelled and dug out men from collapsed slit trenches. On one occasion on 21 Jan 44 he had succeeded in extricating a man from the bottom of a house which had collapsed and was taking him to the Regimental Aid Post. Doing this he was severely wounded in the shoulder but evacuated the man to the R.A.P. and returned to his Company, without reporting his wound. He remained attending to casualties and giving treatment for several hours and then quietly collapsed and did not regain consciousness for some hours. Not only did he encourage and restore the spirits of the wounded men by his constant cheerfulness but his loyal devotion to duty and his continued indifference to his own personal safety were an inspiration to the men of his Company.

2 Scots Guards Military Medal Citation for Guardsman R. Perks

On 23 January 1944 Gdsm. Perks was a signaller attached to Right Flank Company, 2 Battalion Scots Guards. The Company was then holding the area of Point 141, West of Minturno. Throughout the day the Company was heavily shelled by the enemy. In the course of the morning the Lance Corporal in charge of the Company signallers was wounded and Gdsm. Perks took charge of the detachment. Throughout the rest of the day Gdsm. Perks worked continually on the maintenance of line communication to the Company usually under shellfire. In the evening, the line was cut by a particularly heavy enemy concentration of shell fire. Though enemy shelling was continuing, Gdsm. Perks on his own initiative left the comparative security of the Company Headquarters and proceeded to mend the line. While so engaged a further heavy enemy concentration fell on and around the place where he was working, which was devoid of cover. Gdsm. Perks not only mended his line in the midst of the heavy shelling but remained in the danger area till the shelling ceased, in order to check again that the line was intact. His devotion to duty and cheerful bearing on this and subsequent days in the line near Minturno, were an inspiration to the 'signals' detachment in particular, and the whole Company in general.

German views of 23 Jan 44
Lt. Wolfgang Wiedemann, II Battalion, 267 Panzer Grenadier Regiment

23 Jan 44

'After the morning mists had disappeared, the Company must have disappeared behind the high road that led from Santa Maria Infante to Pulcherini. Enemy sighting would have immediately triggered artillery fire. The men knew that, but I urged the Grenadiers to hurry. Our little band could not cope with any more failures. Soon we had overcome the steep slope, which was potted with many tunnels. Behind the road the exhausted men took cover.

In terms of personnel, "2" Company had reached its lowest point. The other Companies came into action one day later, they had correspondingly less losses. I divided the remaining 30 Grenadiers into 2 Platoons. König and Freigang, took over the two totally understaffed Platoons. We did not need a Company Commander. Our right Company line was the outskirts of Santa Maria Infante. "1" and "3" Companies occupied the village of Santa Maria Infante and additionally some hundred metres of terrain in direction to Solacciano.

Pulcherini belonged to the middle section. Further to the left was the section of III Battalion, 274 Grenadier Regiment. The remains of this Battalion were led by Captain Woock. His predecessor was Captain Krege, who had been killed on 18 Jan 44 in Minturno.

Soon we had explored suitable positions for our groups. North-West of the road leading to Pulcherini, we found particularly good shelters. In these desolate days this was a very pleasant surprise. These were certainly earth bunkers, which German Pioneers had built weeks ago for the "Gustav Line".

After the withdrawal of the Army Group reserves, we had to expect further attacks by the English, but also the English were uncertain, they did not know whether the Germans would lead further counterattacks. Therefore, the situation remained tense. There were still violent Artillery duels, neither side had any strength left for further attacks.

The left Company border was at the same time the border for the 274 Regimental Artillery. The communications worked again so I could contact Captain Woock.

The same day we met on a prominent point between Pulcherini and Santi Cosma at Damiano/Castelforte. Woock was already there before me. He was no longer calm. He had been with the old 94 Infantry Division so we reminisced about the campaign. "That's how much time we have to talk about the old days for a few minutes." said Woock. The boundaries were quickly established.

He was incredibly sad. His Battalion was made up of a pitiful few. The front was only a thin veil, after all, there was a continuous front.

When the Sergeant Major arrived the next night with the rations, we tried to bring order to the Company's personnel affairs. All units deployed in combat had to inform the relatives of the fallen, missing and wounded in a suitable manner. For days death had been among us. He was now to remain an unloved but faithful companion.

Lieutenant Friedenberger who was married, his fate unknown. Oberleutnant Kroner's mental and physical breakdown was a consequence of the use of drugs. Sergeant Pinkes, fallen, Sergeant Sachso, wounded. I could enumerate a long list of fates. When we moved to Pulcherini on 23 Jan 44 I had the impression that everyone thanked their Lord that they had survived the bad days'.

British Situation: Report
23 Jan 44 – Midnight
The overall position was as follows:

Spur Point 141: German held.
Point 156 [145], Monte Natale, German held.
Point 156, Hill in front of Cemetery: Held by 1 KOYLI.
Point 172: Held by 1 Green Howards.
Point 141: Held by 2 Scots Guards.
Point 141 Monte del Duca: Held by 6 Grenadier Guards.
Point 201: Held by 2 Cameronians.

1 York & Lancs. was resting just South-East of Minturno. The attack by 6 Seaforths on Spur Point 141 and the attack by 2 Royal Scots Fusiliers on Point 156, Monte Natale had failed to achieve their objectives, A new plan was needed!

Chapter 9

24 January 1944 – Change of Plan

HQ German Army
24 Jan 44
Field Marshall Albert Kesselring, Commander-in-Chief, South-West reports:

1) The enemy has landed about three Divisions South of the River Tiber to push into the rear of the 10th Army and take Rome. Other landings on the Italian West and North coasts are possible.
2) O.B. Southwest continues to defend the Central Italian area and secures the Ligurian, Tyrrhenian and Adriatic coasts against new enemy landings.
3) 10th Army defends its current position while holding the connection to the Gulf of Gaeta. The left wing of the Army, under enemy pressure, is moving to the front-line position, which is to be defended. The expansion of the present position and the front-line position is to be promoted with the greatest vigour. Likewise, the Senger Line [named after Lieutenant General Fridolin Von Senger und Etterlin, Corps Commander in charge of the defence of Monte Cassino. This Line is also known as the Hitler Line] will be further strengthened under the direction of the General of the Army Group Pioneers.
4) 14th Army will take command on the coastal front between Cecina and Terracina [both places included]. The date of taking command is still to be decided. The main task of the Army is to counterattack to throw the enemy landed South of Rome back into the sea.

X (BR) Corps History
24 Jan 44
After the failure of our attacks, it was apparent that several days must elapse before the offensive could be resumed. Neither 5 nor 56 Infantry Divisions would be ready for further operations without an interval for rest and reliefs. Almost the whole of 56 Infantry Division had now been engaged for a week without respite since the assault began on 17 Jan 44; most of the men were too exhausted to continue. The enemy too, were forced to remain on the defensive. There were even clear indications of thinning out, both at Castelforte and round Monte Natale but, as events had shown, there were still sufficient enemy troops to offer stubborn resistance to any renewed attack on our part and we could hope for little success until our troops had been adequately rested. 2 Royal Scots Fusiliers withdrew after the unsuccessful attack last night.

In the original attack on 5 Infantry Division front after we had occupied Tufo, the advance West went well on the left of the feature, but we were never able to dominate the spurs leading North from it. Monte Natale is the key to the use of the Formia-Ausonia road and this is in the hands of the enemy.

5 Infantry Division Intelligence

24 Jan 44
Enemy Situation:
After a short pause yesterday morning for reorganisation, the enemy was ready for a sudden and very sharp drive which came in from the North immediately after our thrust to Spur Point 141 and from the West against our attack on Point 156. This move is typical of 90 Division and is at least grounds for believing it still to be engaged, an important point for decision and one which cannot clearly be established until more identifications come in.

There is no doubt that although recovering all but one of his injured tanks the enemy has had heavy casualties to his armour compared with the strength believed originally to have been available. A civilian report has been received indicating that two more tanks have been knocked out, and our hurricane bursts of artillery must have shaken the tank personnel considerably. It is not known whether 90 Division brought their Tank Battalion with them, or whether being slow to move it, only got half-way before being diverted to deal with our new expedition [the landings at Anzio on the night of 22 Jan 44] against the rear of Tenth Army. The latter is probable, and as it is essential to give an estimate of the probable size of any tank threat on our front the top figure of 12 tanks is given based on the belief that 16 were at the very most originally available of which four must for the present purposes be write offs. No accurate or definite identification of the tanks themselves has yet been made.

The infantry force with which the enemy might be able to make a new thrust towards Minturno and still keep a firm base behind him is estimated to be not more than three Battalions, thus allowing a drive to Point 201 to be developed at the same time.

Information from Air Photographs:
The following new defences are shown on photos taken 22-23 Jan 44.

Area of Santa Maria Infante:

- 15 slit trenches 780967 [100m West of Cemetery).
- Fire trenches 773962 [500m South-West of Point 156].
- 10 slit trenches and military activity 768959 [1km South West of Point 156).

15 Infantry Brigade

24 Jan 44
1 KOYLI sent out a recce patrol to the Cemetery at first light and reported the area unoccupied but much enemy equipment left lying about. Later infantry and suspected tanks North of the Cemetery were engaged by artillery.

201 Guards Brigade

24 Jan 44
The night, 23-24 Jan 44 was without incident except for spasmodic shelling and mortaring of forward positions and the elimination of an enemy machine gun post

775964, (on Monte Natale). With daylight, enemy shelling increased its intensity causing more casualties and prohibiting movement by day in forward areas on Tremensuoli Ridge and Point 141. 3 Coldstreams reported enemy work in progress between their left forward Company and the railway. This was harassed by artillery.

1 KOYLI War Diary
24 Jan 44
The night 23-24 Jan 44 was fairly quiet. During 24 Jan 44 it was decided to pull out the remnants of 2 Royal Scots Fusiliers and 1 Green Howards [they were on Point 172 to the North of Minturno] and leave us to hold the whole of this front. This was done and the night was uneventful fortunately for us as we were by this time very thin on the ground.

1 KOYLI, now not more than 200-250 strong to hold the Brigade front. The takeover went without a hitch.

2 Scots Guards War Diary
24 Jan 44
Right flank was relieved of Point 141 by the Carrier Platoon. Later in the day they were given a sector between 'F' Company and the railway. A few shells landed in the Battalion Headquarters area and along the road back to the river. One of these wounded Tommy Marsham-Townsend [Capt. Thomas Marsham-Townsend. Minturno CWGC Cemetery] in the back; he died a few hours later. 'G' Company took over Point 141 from the Carrier Platoon at dusk. Owing to the lack of cover it is intended to hold the feature with as few men as possible by day and to use a different Company each night. There were eight casualties during the day.

16/5 Lancers War Diary
24 Jan 44
Shelling and mortaring near to 'A' Squadron. No news of missing tank. Patrols sent out to locate the tank, unable to find anything. Weather very windy with rain squalls.

17 Infantry Brigade War Diary
24 Jan 44 – 0038
Orders from 5 Infantry Division that 2 Northants will be made available for counterattack if enemy makes successful attack on 15 Infantry Brigade front.

141 Field Ambulance War Diary
24 Jan 44 – 0200
Advance Dressing Station established in house 783952 [600m South of Point 141, Monte del Duca].

2 Cameronians War Diary
24 Jan 44 – 0530
'D' Company sent forward a Section patrol to fire light machine guns at the enemy positioned at 796976 [1km North-West of Point 201), but they drew no return fire. Lt, Allen and six men of 'D' Company patrolled to San Vito 801975 and found it clear of enemy.

2 Northants War Diary
24 Jan 44 – 0830
CO. visited CO. 1 York & Lancs. to get information ref Point 156 and 1 York & Lancs. attack on it.

15 Infantry Brigade War Diary
24 Jan 44 – 0900
At the Divisional Command Conference, it was decided to relieve 15 Infantry Brigade less 1 KOYLI on the night 24-25 Jan 44. The plan was for 1 KOYLI to relieve 1 Green Howards on Point 172 as soon after dark as was possible passing to the Command of 17 Infantry Brigade on completing relief. 1 Green Howards, plus 15 Infantry Brigade HQ, Support Company and ADS would then move back across the River Garigliano to rest areas.

   17 Infantry Brigade would then hold the sector with 1 KOYLI forward on Point 172 and 2 Northants available for immediate counterattack. 2 Royal Scots Fusiliers were also kept forward in a bivouac area on the Lateral road. 6 Seaforths were to move back across the River Garigliano as well, coming out of their positions in front of 1 Green Howards about 1730 whilst 1 KOYLI would start taking over from 1 Green Howards at 1800.

17 Infantry Brigade War Diary
24 Jan 44 – 0900
Approximate casualties for last night's operations so far counted: 6 Seaforths, two Officers, 15 Other Ranks. Royal Scots Fusiliers, two Officers, 50 Other Ranks.

92 Field Regiment Royal Artillery War Diary
24 Jan 44 – 0945
Information from HQ Royal Artillery: 6 Seaforths on forward slopes of Point 172 at 785965. 2 Royal Scots Fusiliers 795952 [Lateral road 500m South-East of Minturno], 2 Northants 805953 [Point 102]. 6 Grenadier Guards Company areas 775958, 774958, 770958 and 770959 [a line going East to West just North of Tremensuoli]. Enemy heavily counterattacking against 56 Infantry Division front.

7 Cheshires War Diary
24 Jan 44 – 0950
Platoon established new Observation Post in area of 'A' Company, 2 Cameronians at map ref 798962 [200m East of Point 151].

98 Field Regiment Royal Artillery War Diary
24 Jan 44 – 1030
Division Ammunition Officer rang to confirm Field Regiment's ammunition expenditure. Is incredulous of our 11,300-shell expenditure during period 21-22 Jan 44.

24 Jan 44 – 1100
Air Observation Post reports three enemy tanks 780968 [300m North of Aid Post), possibly disabled.

5 Infantry Division History
24 Jan 44
Both 13 Infantry Brigade and 15 Infantry Brigade patrolled during daylight. The Cemetery was reported clear of enemy although plenty of equipment was lying about.

The attack on Monte Natale for today was called off but General Officer Commanding and Commander 17 Infantry Brigade carried out a recce.

This was a quiet day with the enemy making a big effort against 56 Infantry Division on the Division's right.

[The German attacks were on 56 Infantry Division at Monte Damiano. Pte. George Mitchell, 1 London Scottish was posthumously awarded a VC for his action on this day.]

2 Cameronians War Diary
24 Jan 44 – 1100
Major Graham Riley went forward from 'D' Company with two men to the enemy position at 796976 [1km North-West of Point 201]. He found one German whom he took prisoner, but the position was unoccupied. As the enemy had evacuated it before first light, 'C' Company sent forward a recce patrol of one Sergeant. and two men to 786982 [1km North of Spur Point 141], without meeting any enemy. Civilians, however spotted enemy in Santa Maria Infante and Pulcherini.

17 Infantry Brigade War Diary
24 Jan 44 – 1200
New orders for Brigade. 2 Northants to attack Point 156, probably night 25-26 Jan 44.

6 Grenadier Guards War Diary
24 Jan 44 – 1200
Again, more shelling. Casualties up to this time had now reached seven killed and 43 wounded.

2 Wiltshires War Diary
24 Jan 44 – 1200
The Battalion's casualties for the operation were nine Officers, 186 Other Ranks. German POWs taken by Battalion were two Officers and 115 Other Ranks.

98 Field Regiment Royal Artillery War Diary
24 Jan 44 – 1245
'D' Troop Observation Post. Enemy guns at 781967 [by Cemetery]. 392 Battery position shelled heavily by four guns. One of our guns out of action, one gun temporarily out of action. One man, light casualty.

1 York & Lancs. War Diary
24 Jan 44 – 1400
CO. saw all Company Commanders and gave orders for move to Casanova 9788. Companies would march to 792938 and then by Group Transport to new area. Battalion would leave 801952 [Lateral road just South of Point 102], at 2330.

92 Field Regiment Royal Artillery War Diary

24 Jan 44 – 1400

Commanding Officer returns from 15 Infantry Brigade HQ. 15 Infantry Brigade less 1 KOYLI being withdrawn to rest tonight. 1 KOYLI to come under command 17 Infantry Brigade. 2 Northants may attack tomorrow morning. North West corner of Minturno under constant bombardment from the enemy.

98 Field Regiment Royal Artillery War Diary

24 Jan 44 – 1415

392 Battery report that during recent shelling, ten rounds were destroyed before fire was put out – fuses were burnt off, but rounds did not explode.

3 Coldstream Guards War Diary

24 Jan 44 – 1430

Casualties to date on this front suffered by the Battalion are nine killed, one Officer and 49 Other Ranks wounded of which two died of wounds.

92 Field Regiment Royal Artillery War Diary

24 Jan 44 – 1500

Observation Post to receive fire orders from Battery Commander 368 Battery and Forward Observation Officer at present forward with 1 KOYLI.

2 Cameronians War Diary

24 Jan 44 – 1600

3-inch mortars fired at 799986 [2km North of Point 201]. 'D' Company were relieved by 'A' Company on Point 201. 'D' Company took over 'A' Company's position.

24 Jan 44 – 1630

The Carrier Platoon moved forward and occupied the position at 796976 [1km North of Point 201] as a standing patrol.

1 York & Lancs. War Diary

24 Jan 44 – 1700

Battalion left old area and were settled in billets at Casanova by 2300.

201 Guards Brigade War Diary

24 Jan 44 – 1720

16 enemy guns had been observed to the West during the day – pin pointing was difficult due to ground haze, but the centre of the gun area was estimated as 713954. This point was shelled by 102 Medium Regiment and enemy fire ceased.

1 Green Howards War Diary

24 Jan 44 – 1800

Battalion relief by 1 KOYLI commenced.

6 Grenadier Guards War Diary
24 Jan 44 – 1800
A party of Royal Engineers were sent off to lay mines on the right flank of '2' Company to close a gap. The Royal Engineer's party was fired on and only half the mines were laid. The Royal Engineers Company Commander was wounded.

6 Seaforth Highlanders War Diary
24 Jan 44 – 1815
Battalion HQ followed by 'C' Company leaves position [in front of 1 Green Howards who are on Point 172] on being relieved.

1 Green Howards War Diary
24 Jan 44 – 1930
Relief of Battalion complete.

17 Infantry Brigade War Diary
24 Jan 44 – 1945
'A' Squadron 16/5 Lancers to come under command 17 Infantry Brigade.

24 Jan 44 – 2000
Main Brigade HQ established at 795953 [500m South-East of Minturno).

2 Cameronians War Diary
24 Jan 44 – 2000
Sgt Lasity and two men patrolled to 790985 just short of Pulcherini. The patrol observed eight Germans move into Pulcherini.

17 Infantry Brigade War Diary
24 Jan 44 – 2015
Division report that 361 Grenadier Regiment considered no longer to be on 5 Infantry Division front. Grenadier Regiment 200 and remnants of 94 Infantry Division remain. Weather fine.

6 Seaforth Highlanders War Diary
24 Jan 44 – 2030
Battalion embarks on buses and leaves for Sorbello.

15 Infantry Brigade War Diary
24 Jan 44 – 2100
All moves were completed successfully without enemy interference and command of 1 KOYLI passed to 17 Infantry Brigade at 2000. 1 Green Howards, 1 York & Lancs. and 6 Seaforths all-in troop-carrying transport on Route 7 North of the river between 1800 and 2100. Unit transport followed after midnight. Traffic arrangements were very satisfactory, and the road kept well clear.

201 Guards Brigade War Diary
24 Jan 44 – 2150
Motor transport and horse transport heard on the San Croce Rd in the 'Squiggle' area. Horses were heard screaming. During the night two small anti-personnel minefields were laid in front of 6 Grenadier Guards and 3 Coldstream Guards positions. The work on 6 Grenadier Guards front was interrupted by light machine gun fire from Monte Natale.

With daylight enemy shelling increased its intensity causing more casualties and prohibiting movement by day in forward areas on Tremensuoli ridge and Point 141.

2 Northants War Diary
24 Jan 44 – 2359
Patrol on night 24-25 Jan 44. Two patrols, both recce, one to South-East end Point 156 and one to North West end Point 156. Both patrols reported that the feature was held by the enemy. No mines were found. Patrols returned without incident by 2359.

1 Green Howards War Diary
24 Jan 44
For deeds of gallantry over the past five days the Battalion received no less than seven gallantry decorations: a Military Cross, a bar to a Military Medal, and five Military Medals. Lieutenant-Colonel Patrick George Bulfin was also awarded the Distinguished Service Order for his leadership of the Battalion during those five remarkable days.

German views of 24 Jan 44
Lt. Wolfgang Wiedemann, II Battalion, 267 Grenadier Regiment
24 Jan 44
'In safe and, for us, 267 Grenadier Regiment infantrymen, unusually comfortable shelters, we had slept deeply for several hours. Very early I explored the area and controlled our groups. In Pulcherini, the village consisted almost only of ruins, a heavy fire attack surprised us. Some women and children were just stepping out of a cellar to get some air, when a shell hit the already heavily damaged roof above us. The fireball of the exploding shell, the flying roof tiles and the shrapnel caused these poor people a terrible panic. The shouting of the children and women still rings in my ears today. We were shocked, here still, after days of shellfire to meet civilians. Like a miracle, there were no casualties. Where could the Italians have gone? There was war everywhere and destruction in those days and weeks. Our compatriots had such experiences all over the front line.

On the way back [from Pulcherini] to the Company Command Post I met three men who were hurrying towards Pulcherini. It was the Regimental Commander from the front, Lieutenant Colonel Reich, with two escorts. He recognized me immediately, although we met only briefly on 19 Jan 44 in the Regimental HQ. He wanted to see Captain Woock and III Battalion, 274 Grenadier Regiment.

Apart from English reconnaissance troops, there was no contact with the enemy. The artillery on both sides was still firing at an unusual rate. When we, 267 Grenadier Regiment moved in the terrain, we looked for cover. The dangers were too great. Men moved like game, always listening, always securing, always looking for cover. The second night in the luxury bunker was a pleasant one. I came to my senses again. You had to have a hard-boiled mood to cope with these days of great fighting. Our soldiers were simply magnificent. The will of resistance was unbroken. The men showed toughness. The cohesion was stronger than ever.

Since 22 Jan 44, the day of the landing South of Rome, it rained propaganda leaflets every day. The German soldiers were ordered to desert. Not one case has come to my attention. The repeated references to "Unconditional Surrender" decided by the Allied leadership in Casablanca on 24-25 Jan 43 had no effect whatsoever. Also, the landing at Anzio had no moral consequences. The belief in the Fatherland, in the final victory was unbroken. Nobody spoke of Hitler or National Socialism. The confidence in the military leadership of Field Marshal Albert Kesselring, Gen. Vietinghoff, Lt. Gen. Fridolin Von Senger und Etterlin, and the Officers of 94 Infantry Division. was very great.

II Battalion 267 Grenadier Regiment had completely lost contact in these difficult days. Right at the beginning of the Allied offensive, the great danger of a British breakthrough was recognised quite early. Kesselring immediately personally ordered the transfer of II Battalion from the previous coastal section – Gaeta to Scauri – to the area North of the Via Appia near Tremensuoli. Our comrade, Alfred Heyn witnessed these countermeasures. II Battalion had the same fate as all other units that were spontaneously thrown into the battle. The bombardment of the land and ship artillery caused considerable losses. Heyn reported that two counterattacks from a quarry area stopped the attack of the "Tommies". Only the third counterattack, which Lieutenant Heyn led at night, was able to achieve small gains in terrain with corresponding own losses. More was simply not possible.

The relationship between Lieutenant Arno Born, Battalion Adjutant, and Major Frank was a close one, because everybody avoided the unpredictable and completely impersonal Commander. Poor Born had a hard time, even though he swallowed his anger. In the few weeks in which he was now Adjutant, he had got to know Major Frank quite well. I inquired how to apply for honours (Iron Crosses) for brave men who had distinguished themselves. There were no requests from the Battalion. Born beckoned away. "The Commander makes no further requests. This behaviour is incomprehensible" said Born.

"He has a sore throat," Born said softly. That was the ironic country expression when a superior wanted to earn the coveted "Knights Cross". Born continued: "Frank had expected his Battalion to take back Tufo and Minturno. Maybe we would have made it. If Frank had led his Battalion correctly, there was certainly a chance. By 'remote control' such an attack could not be successful". We had to accept the facts. Major Frank was with us for a long time,

All men had to endure these hard days. Hardly anyone talked about the little daily torments. Hunger and thirst, bruises and abrasions caused by flying lumps of earth or stones were accepted without much grumbling. Especially unpleasant were the disgusting spikes of prickly pears, which caused small burning injuries.

The Battalion Doctor, Dr. Hoffmann of course had other worries than to treat scratches. He survived the baptism of fire well. The First Aid Post was in a collapsed sheep pen. He had to constantly treat the wounded. Our "Doctor" had brilliantly passed his test. It was especially sad that the company had only two Platoons left, which were extremely understaffed at the time. All the other Companies had the same fate.'

Chapter 10

25 January 1944 – 150 Enemy on Point 156

X (BR) Corps History

25 Jan 44

A conference was held at X (BR) Corps Headquarters to discuss plans and timings; orders for the attack were to be issued on 26 Jan 44. Details of the plan and the forecast of timings were:

Phase 1, 29-30 Jan 44

5 Infantry Division to recapture Monte Natale. The whole X (BR) Corps Artillery would support the attacks in Phases 1 and 2. 40 Royal Marine Commando was to remain under command of 56 Infantry Division.

Operations on the left

While the 56 and 46 Infantry Divisions fought in vain to break into the enemy's main defensive position, 5 Infantry Division on the left of the bridgehead enjoyed greater success and now was to recapture Monte Natale which had been lost in a German counterattack on 22 Jan 44. Monte Natale was to be taken by 17 Infantry Brigade in a night attack while 201 Guards Brigade was to thrust forward on the left flank and clear the Western slopes of the Tremensuoli ridge.

5 Infantry Division War Diary

25 Jan 44

The night patrols contacted the enemy all along the front. Point 156 was held by the enemy in some strength. 15 Infantry Brigade less 1 KOYLI were relieved by 17 Infantry Brigade during the night and 2 Northants were now in a counterattack role on Point 172, 785964. If this counterattack is made, 2 Royal Scots Fusiliers will move into the area vacated by 2 Northants.

5 Infantry Division History

25 Jan 44

25 Jan 44 was a quiet day. X (BR) Corps warned 5 Infantry Division that they must secure Monte Natale. The build-up was now started for the Monte Natale attack which was planned for 28-29 Jan 44. [Note these dates do not match those given by X (BR) Corps shown above.]

Patrolling was active. 2 Royal Scots Fusiliers established a listening post at Point 141, and a fighting patrol to Point 172; 2 Northants found that Monte Natale was occupied by about 150 enemy in reverse slope positions by day. They also patrolled to

Point 141, Monte del Duca. Minturno on the far left, taken from South-West. (Photo John Strafford)

the Cemetery and to cover a gap in the minefields. The enemy had now amassed a great many guns, their ammunition supply, however, was considerably rationed.

Lieutenant D.H. Deane, 2 Scots Guards writes
25 Jan 44 Tuesday
'A Bloody day – very quiet in the morning with nice weather. Asked to go up to the awful cliff behind us. Go through Battalion HQ and Support to pick up Brodie Clarke. Just before we came down having finished our recce we were seen, and Peter got killed by an 88mm. Brodie and I saved ourselves by jumping into a latrine which was nasty. I was pretty shaken. We go up there tonight.'

17 Infantry Brigade War Diary
25 Jan 44
Intention: To recapture Point 172 if this point should be occupied by the enemy.

Method:
Troops: 2 Northants.
Troop 'A' Squadron 16//5 Lancers.
Platoon 'D' Company 7 Cheshires.
Field Observation Officer 156 Field Regiment RA.
2 Northants will move to assembly area 797962, *(*Point 151*)*.

Artillery: Fire on both targets 78396 [500m South of Cemetery] and 787962 [400m South of Point 172], to move forward 300 yards in lifts of 100 yards and then lift back in 100-yard lifts to original point. Programme to be continued from Zero hour plus 30 minutes. 5 Infantry Division Artillery under Command 98 Field Regiment and 102 Medium Regiment will support the attack of 2 Northants.

Tanks: To go forward so as to reach Cemetery 780966 by Zero hour plus 50 minutes.

4.2 inch Mortar Programme: Fire on area of Cemetery to Point 172, 50 rounds.

Enemy: Apart from the movement of some guns the enemy shows no signs of withdrawing on our front. The roads 776991 South to Minturno and South-West to San Croce 730958 are vital to him and he strongly resists any attempt on our part to capture Point 156 which would command both of these roads.

16/5 Lancers War Diary
25 Jan 44

During the early hours of the morning Lieutenant Dill took a small patrol up the Minturno-Natale road to try to find Sergeant Ritchie's tank but met with no success. In the morning '1' Troop [Lt. Holland], took over the positions in Minturno from 40 Royal Tank Regiment. This task was to prevent any enemy tanks coming down the road from Santa Maria Infante and entering Minturno. The positions were not particularly good and there was a considerable amount of shelling. In the late afternoon we moved off the road into an orange grove nearby to relieve the congestion of traffic. We had to have the Sappers sweep the mines away during the afternoon before we moved in.

'A' Squadron has one Troop in Minturno and one Troop at readiness to support 2 Northants if Germans attack Point 172.

7 Cheshires War Diary
25 Jan 44 – 0100

Lt. Munday's party re-join Company. Platoon now complete in Company location 795952 [Lateral road 500m Southeast of Minturno].

98 Field Regiment Royal Artillery War Diary
25 Jan 44 – 0100

Fire Plan received, to come into effect in the event of the Hun attacking and capturing Point 172. 2 Northants will counterattack. Plan in support.

40 Royal Tank Regiment War Diary
25 Jan 44 – 0600

'A' Squadron: Nos. '2' and '3' Troops were relieved by 16/5 Lancers and returned to Squadron HQ at 815955.

252 Field Co. Royal Engineers War Diary
25 Jan 44 – 0600

Clearing debris off road in Tufo area to open up road to Minturno, 7895.

2 Field Regiment Royal Artillery War Diary
25 Jan 44 – 0612

368 Battery Observation Post call for fire on enemy self-propelled gun in area Cemetery 780970. Two Batteries engage.

17 Infantry Brigade War Diary
25 Jan 44 – 0730

The ruined and empty village of Tufo, perched on top of a hill, is in the front line. Soldiers here try to clear a road through the rubble, a job made more difficult by constant enemy shellfire, 25 Jan 44. (Photo 2 AFPU, Sgt. Weber, TNA 11433)

2 Northants patrol reports little sign of enemy on South slopes of Point 156, but machine gun fire seen from top and sounds of much activity on the North slopes.

17 Infantry Brigade War Diary
25 Jan 44 – 0830
1 KOYLI report five prisoners of war captured in Cemetery area. Identification, 9 Company 200 Grenadier Regiment.

1 KOYLI History
25 Jan 44
The morning of 25 Jan 44 found us with the remnants of three companies on Point 172, with one Company and Battalion HQ in the Minturno area. It was a thoroughly uncomfortable position, and a determined enemy counterattack would have been difficult to cope with. For this phase of the battle the Battalion came under 17 Infantry Brigade. By lunch things began to look up. A most successful recce patrol by Sergeant C.E. Hall of 'C' Company had captured five Germans and two machine guns in the morning and it was with confidence that we learned that 2 Royal Scots Fusiliers were to relieve us that night. The relief proceeded quietly, and the Battalion moved into reserve South of Minturno.

1 KOYLI. Military Medal Citation for Sergeant C.E. Hall
The Battalion was holding a defensive position about Minturno on 25 Jan 44. The highest point on the 172 ridge was in 'No Man's Land'. It was known to have Germans on it during the night of 24 -25 Jan 44. It was essential to the defence that the Germans should not establish an Observation Post on the feature, and it was decided to send out a small recce patrol to search the feature. Owing to the number of Officer casualties in the Battalion this patrol had to be taken by Sgt. Hall, who took four other men with

him. Sgt. Hall decided to examine a shack on the highest point as his first objective. Having covered his approach from a flank with his Bren gun he encircled the shack. This was done in full daylight and during heavy enemy shelling and mortar fire. When he got near to this house, he found it was full of Germans. How many he did not know. Leaving his Bren to cover him in, Sgt. Hall and one other leapt into the shack covering the room with a Tommy Gun. The Germans leapt for their weapons and then Sgt. Hall discovered that his gun was jammed and could not fire. The prompt action of his number two saved the situation and Sgt. Hall took the complete German patrol of five men from the 90 Infantry Division prisoners, disabled the two machine guns that they were placing in position and returned safely to his own lines. Not only was this patrol extremely well executed but it obtained important identifications and prevented the whole Battalion positions being raked with machine gun fire.

1 York & Lancs. War Diary
25 Jan 44 – 0830
Battalion was able to get on with reorganisation. A few reinforcements received.

2 Scots Guards War Diary
25 Jan 44
The Carrier Platoon took over Point 141 – Monte del Duca from 'G' Company after morning stand to. The morning of 25 Jan 44 brought an unusual experience to the Carrier Platoon which had just taken over the position on the hill west of Minturno. A German officer appeared, walking towards them from the direction of Monte Natale. He walked into the Platoon position. With great presence of mind, they remained quiet, and waited for him. It turned out that he was from a Tank Squadron now in Formia and had just returned from a week's leave. He had been sent out to examine the country beside the road from Santa Maria Infante to Minturno with a view to a tank attack from that direction but had forgotten to ask where our respective lines were.

201 Guards Brigade War Diary
25 Jan 44 – 0930
Company 2 Scots Guards on Point 141 captured a German officer of Hermann Goering's Tank Battalion who had lost himself on recce. He was interrogated at Brigade Headquarters giving much information of tactical importance including the present whereabouts of his unit. A request was made for bombers to attack it, but the target was refused.

52 Anti-Tank Regiment War Diary
25 Jan 44 – 1100
Commanding Officer visited Battery Commander and it was decided to leave two 17 pounders North of Minturno in position, it being too risky to move them until the enemy had been driven off Point 172. Information from a Prisoner of War Officer from a squadron of the Herman Goering Tank Battalion gave enemy tank resources in the area as about 25 tanks, mostly Mark IV's. After a conversation with Commander Royal Artillery and Commander 17 Infantry Brigade it was decided to lay a minefield across the front of Minturno. Battery Commander estimated that 400 mines would be required.

It was decided to recce on 26 Jan 44 and lay the field on night of 26 – 27 Jan 44. Much decreased shelling.

2 Cameronians War Diary
25 Jan 44 – 1400
'A' Company sent a recce patrol to 803978 [2km North of Tufo], but it had nothing to report. 'A' Company sent another recce patrol of Sgt Docherty and four men to 789971 [600m North-East of Point 172], where they found many enemy dead. The patrol was fired on by an enemy machine gun at 789973, 200 metres away but suffered no casualties.

1 York & Lancs. War Diary
25 Jan 44 – 1430
CO.'s Conference. The CO. gave orders to reorganise with three Rifle Companies as follows: 'B' Company, OC. Major D. Webster, 'C' Company, OC. Capt. Ivor J. Wedgbury, 'D' Company, OC. Major R. Colville, HQ Company, OC. Captain Anderson, 'S' Company OC. Major K. Spencer, Captain J. Marshall resumes command of Mortar Platoon.

17 Infantry Brigade War Diary
25 Jan 44 – 1600
Orders issued for Operation 'Boots' – counterattack by 2 Northants in the event of enemy occupation of Point 172.

92 Field Regiment Royal Artillery War Diary
25 Jan 44 – 1625
368 Battery Observation Post calls for fire on 780970 [400m North of Cemetery]. Two Batteries engage.

Signalman testing a telephone wire on the roadside below Minturno. Photo 25 Jan 44, *2 AFPU Sgt. Weber TNA 11436*

17 Infantry Brigade War Diary
25 Jan 44 – 1730
Relief of 1 KOYLI by 2 Royal Scots Fusiliers in progress. Two Companies already relieved.

1 York & Lancs. War Diary
25 Jan 44 – 1830
Battalion in rest area, given a mobile cinema show; 'Andy Hardy's Private Secretary' with Mickey Rooney.

98 Field Regiment Royal Artillery War Diary
25 Jan 44 – 1900
392 Battery Observation Post received direct hit – Captain Stride evacuated with leg wounds. Bombardier Miller also evacuated with wounds. Battery Commander instructed Lt. Fisher to stand by as new Battery Observation Post Officer. 392 Battery: Vehicles believed to be tanks moving North-East up to Santa Maria Infante at 1750. At 1800 four tanks going same route.

6 Grenadier Guards War Diary
25 Jan 44
The mine field was completed by the Royal Engineer's party.

17 Infantry Brigade War Diary
25 Jan 44 – 1945
Relief of 1 KOYLI by 2 Royal Scots Fusiliers completed. Command has passed.

2 Royal Scots Fusiliers War Diary
25 Jan 44 – 2000
Battalion moved on orders of the Adjutant and relief of 1 KOYLI was completed without incident by 2000. In defensive positions areas of Point 172 and Point 141, North and West of Minturno. Company 2 Scots Guards to be under command of 2 Royal Scots Fusiliers. Layout of Battalion was as follows: 'B' & 'D' Companies on Point 172 at 785963, one Platoon Motor Machine Guns and two 3" Mortars in support. 'C' Company 785958 [400m South of Point 172] with two 3" mortars under command. One Company 2 Scots Guards at Point 141, Monte Del Duca 781959 with Platoon MMG in support. Anti-tank defence provided by five 6 pounder guns. Buildings in valley South of Point 172 were manned as strong points by Carrier and Mortar Platoon personnel.

1 KOYLI War Diary
25 Jan 44 – 2000
The Battalion was in reserve South of Minturno in comparative safety except for the odd shell or so. The Battalion now about 200 strong stayed for 48 hours busy reorganising and preparing for the next phase.

17 Infantry Brigade War Diary
25 Jan 44 – 2105

2 Northants patrol to Cemetery met strong enemy patrol at 782963 [300m South of Cemetery], which prevented it getting any further. Artillery shoot, on this Point arranged.

25 Jan 44 – 2130
Harassing fire for tonight arranged on North end of Point 156, 765978 and along road from Santa Maria Infante to 776991. Weather: Fine.

2 Northants War Diary
25 Jan 44 – 2130
Fighting patrol went to Cemetery area to scupper 88mm gun believed to operate in that area. They met strong enemy party, strength approx. 20 men at 783962 [400m South of Cemetery), and was forced to return after being fired on by machine guns from four different positions. There were no casualties and returned to Battalion HQ at 2130.

98 Field Regiment, Royal Artillery
25 Jan 44 – 2330
Shipwrecked mariners from stranded DUKW arrive at Regimental HQ.

2 Scots Guards. Military Cross citation for Lieutenant A. Erskine
During the Tremensuoli period [about 25 Jan 44] Lt. A. Erskine took out an ambush patrol. Halfway to their objective the patrol was surprised by a German standing patrol, in the neighbourhood of a house, being fired on by Light Machine Gun fire from several points simultaneously. Lt. Erskine immediately split his patrol into two parts, and under cover from one of these, led the other to attack the house. With great dash and total disregard to his personal safety, he and his party entered the house killing one German and wounding another with a machine gun and forcing the other Germans to leave the house. One of these was probably killed by a Bren Gun covering the back entrance. By this time, a general German alarm had been given, the patrol was subjected to more intense fire from all sides. Lt. Erskine then collected the patrol which had got split up and withdrew them with no loss. The patrol had gained valuable information regarding enemy dispositions, in addition to causing three enemy casualties.

German Announcement
25 Jan 44
Lt. Col. Reich, the Commanding Officer of the front-line 274 Grenadier Regiment is dead.

Lieutenant Wolfras Gieseler, III Battalion, 274 Grenadier Regiment
25 Jan 44
'When we were temporarily cut off from our Division and assigned to the rapidly advancing 29 Panzer Grenadier Division, Lieutenant Colonel Reich contacted the new Divisional staff in Esperia. On his return from this trip, he was fatally hit in front of our house at noon, by the splinters of an artillery shell that fell short when he got out of his car. This tragic accident was felt by all of our side. He was the soul of the resistance in the heavy battles and had just survived. He always preceded his soldiers and with his

rousing example gave his life away in this unusual way. Deeply shaken, we carry our dead comrade into the house.

In the village church of Ausonia the next night, I had our Commander, who is so revered and esteemed, laid out in a solemn ceremony. Two days later the funeral took place at the military cemetery in Monticelli, with full military honours. The Division Commanders of our 94 Infantry Division and 29 Panzer Grenadier Division are both present. Our Division band plays the song of good comrades after the Division padre, and I have said a few words of farewell. It is beneficial that on this sunny January day there was hardly any trace of flying in the air and the enemy artillery is silent.

After the funeral, General Steinmetz surprises me with his intention to transfer me to his Divisional Headquarters in the next few days. So, a few days later, I am parting from my old 274 Grenadier Regiment with whom I shared fifteen months of joys and sorrows.'

NCO of 276 Panzer Grenadiers Regiment, *Cassino. The Hollow Victory* by John Ellis
25 Jan 44

'I start becoming a pessimist. The Tommies write in their leaflet the choice is ours, Tunis, or Stalingrad . . . We are on half rations. No mail. Teddy is a prisoner. I see myself one very soon.'

The pontoon bridge South-East of Minturno could only be used by traffic at night as it was under enemy observation. Daylight was spent in repairing damage done by enemy shell fire and passing infantry over to the foothills in the background. 25 Jan 44 (Photo 2 AFPU, Sgt. Weber, TNA 10427)

Chapter 11

26 January 1944 – Preparing for Action

5 Infantry Division Intelligence
26 Jan 44
Enemy Situation:
The effect of the landing at Anzio has already been felt on our front. First of all, the German 190 Tank Battalion seems not to have been sent and now 361 Grenadier Regiment is considered to have left. Enemy counterattacks have ceased, and he is turning to the defensive. An increase of artillery has been evident.

The most important identification during the period has been an officer of '1' Squadron Herman Goering Tank Regiment who claims that 15 Mark IV special tanks of the Squadron have been lying up in the area of the Gaeta peninsular for the last fortnight at least. For an officer to make a recce without a map, without an orderly, and to get lost so that he wandered into our lines is suspicious, but our prisoner was unable to agree and his whole demeanour appeared to suggest that he was inwardly exasperated at his own blunder.

However, this may be, he had no knowledge of any other German tank squadron in this area although he admitted to seeing their tracks near the Cemetery and near the knocked-out Sherman at 7896 [Cemetery area]. There is the possibility that casualties in the other Squadron [believed to be '5' Squadron] have caused it to be withdrawn and '1' Squadron is to be committed in the same role.

The disappearance of 361 Grenadier Regiment argues the reduction of the enemy's threat and he will probably rely to a very great extent on his tanks to counter any attack we make on Monte Natale.

1 York & Lancs. War Diary
26 Jan 44
Battalion issued with new kit etc. and were busy all day preparing themselves for the next action.

2 Scots Guards War Diary
26 Jan 44
A complete Company of Welsh Guards under Raymond Buckeridge arrived to join the Battalion, as a fourth Company. They spent the night at 'A' Echelon.

2 Cameronians War Diary
26 Jan 44 – 0600
Lt. Saltman and men from the Anti-Tank Platoon relieved Capt. Macdonald at 796976 [1,400m North of Point 151). During the morning civilians reported 30 enemy in Pulcherini area and also enemy on Monte Bracchi.

17 Infantry Brigade War Diary
26 Jan 44 – 0815
2 Royal Scots Fusiliers patrol from Point 172 made no contact. Two Bren guns placed on forward slopes of Point 172 to command road in daylight.

92 Field Regiment Royal Artillery War Diary
26 Jan 44 – 0930
American personnel comprising one Officer and two Sergeants who joined Regiment at River Garigliano crossing to 'observe', re-join their own unit.

98 Field Regiment Royal Artillery War Diary
26 Jan 44 – 1030
392 Battery being shelled – four casualties on way to Medical Officer and one more.

26 Jan 44 – 1055
Batteries ordered to stop moving vehicles in area forthwith [visibility too good for any Motor Transport movement].

56 Infantry Division War Diary
26 Jan 44 – 1100
5 Infantry Division report: Six tanks 1.5 kilometres South of Santa Maria Infante. Santa Maria Infante unoccupied, enemy about 50 metres North of it.

98 Field Regiment Royal Artillery War Diary
26 Jan 44 – 1120
Two ambulances to this location [474 Battery] immediately.

26 Jan 44 – 1300
Regiment's position being shelled apparently by same guns as before. 392 Battery report situation serious – ammunition hit – 17 casualties.

26 Jan 44 – 1332
391 Battery report 12 rounds fell in their area.

26 Jan 44 – 1335
Orders received for 392 Battery to pull out.

26 Jan 44 – 1530
Information received from Battery Master Royal Artillery that Regiment is to be pulled out at dusk on 27 Jan 44.

Artillery played an important part in the recent advances, firing almost continuously. During a respite, the crew of a Priest self-propelled gun unpack ammunition ready for the next shoot. Minturno/ Garigliano area. 26 Jan 44 (Photo 2 AFPU, Sgt. Johnson. TNA 11532)

26 Jan 44 – 1600
Orders received to leave area at 1800, 27 Jan 44.

Lord Carver, *War in Italy*, 392 (Surrey Yeomanry) Battery, 98 Field Regiment Royal Artillery. J. Gascoigne-Pees writes
26 Jan 44 Wednesday
'A black day for the Surrey Battery. It was a very clear morning, and their first warning of trouble was a ranging air burst plumb over the Battery area. This was ominous and it was soon followed by a few shells straight into the area. The Command Post staff were inside "H" truck, and it seemed as though the shells whizzed just a foot above the hood. Soon the troops were reporting to Command Post that some gunners had been hit and all spare men from "K" and "Y" trucks were used as stretcher bearers to take the wounded to the Regional Aid Post. The shelling eased off for a while and then came on again very heavily. Several enemy guns must have been engaged on bombarding the position and then "C" Troop reported one ammo dump on fire and later reported it was out of control. Shortly after that "D" Troop reported the same thing and some guns had to move their position. More and more shells were pumped into the area but throughout the day the Surrey guns kept firing. The situation was reported to Regimental HQ and the CO.2 [second-in-command] ordered the Battery to evacuate the position when it became untenable. It was more than untenable and to hang on would have meant all would have been lost. Their own ammo was burning furiously and exploding, and the air was alive with schrapnel. The guns pulled out and Command Post made a rush job of packing up "H" truck and cleared off. They mustered together again by 391 Battery position, and it was a very dazed party that was left. 18 of the gunners had been hit out of about 100 men on the gun position. Luckily there were some rations on "H" truck,

Empty shell cases being stacked ready for removal. Minturno and Garigliano area. 26 Jan 44. (Photo 2 AFPU Sgt. Johnson, TNA 11533)

and they were able to have a brew up for the HQ party. A few more shells came over while they waited until dusk before they moved back to "B" echelon where they spent the night. Jack Beeby who was in charge of one of "D" troop's guns described the day in his diary: "the wind changed direction and our smoke screen became useless and at the same time the visibility became very clear. Soon after breakfast I was on the gun firing and with a sudden swish a shell burst two yards in front of our Priest [self-propelled 105mm gun]. A minute later another burst right at the side of us putting the gun out of action. Our armour saved us from injury but the schrapnel damaged a great deal of our equipment. From then on we were shelled solidly all day long. We had casualties every few minutes and to make matters worse two of our piles of ammunition were hit and started to explode all over the place. However, we continued firing until several more guns were knocked out and then we were given the order to evacuate. Shells were bursting all around us, trees came crashing down and the air was filled with that horrid acrid smell that comes from bursting shells.'"

17 Infantry Brigade War Diary
26 Jan 44 – 1600
Civilian reports enemy trenches along ridge on East side of road every 2 – 300 yards between Cemetery and Santa Maria Infante, also Self-Propelled guns in this area. 7 Cheshires Support Company 4.2 mortars shoot on Cemetery area.

7 Cheshires War Diary
26 Jan 44 – 1615
'3' Platoon carries out harassing shoot on Point 156. Observation Post report successful shoot.

2 Cameronians War Diary
26 Jan 44 – 1700

Intelligence Officer Lt. Campbell and two men patrolled to 790986 just short of Pulcherini and found the ridge unoccupied. Sgt. Allison and two men patrolled simultaneously to 793985 [1,600m North-East of Spur Point 141]. and also found that area unoccupied. Motor transport movement was heard in Santa Maria Infante.

92 Field Regiment Royal Artillery War Diary
26 Jan 44 – 1745
Message from HQ Royal Artillery. Patrols, 2 Royal Scots Fusiliers: Listening Post at Point 141 2200-0100 hours. Fighting Patrol to North-West corner of Point 172 all night. 2 Northants: Patrol to Point 156 to ascertain if still occupied by enemy. Patrol to main road Santa Maria Infante and Cemetery area, also to cover lane in minefield.

26 Jan 44 – 1830
Commander HQ Royal Artillery telephones Commanding Officer. 2 Northants will be attacking Point 156, night 28-29 Jan 44 or day 29 Jan 44. 500 rounds per gun to be available at gun positions. Battery Captains warned.

252 Field Co. Royal Engineers War Diary
26 Jan 44 – 1900
'2' Platoon laying of minefield in area 785958 [600m South of Point 172]. Worked through night till 0500 27 Jan 44. Not completed and to finish task during hours of darkness 27-28 Jan 44. Type of mine laid – Mark V.

2 Northants War Diary
26 Jan 44 – 1930
'C' Company sent a recce patrol to Point 156. They found the feature held by the enemy. Two machine guns fired on them. No signs of mines, but military activity behind hill. Patrol returned at 2330. No casualties being incurred.

17 Infantry Brigade War Diary
26 Jan 44 – 2145
2 Royal Scots Fusiliers patrol encountered enemy just East of Cemetery. Fire put down in that area.

17 Infantry Brigade War Diary
26 Jan 44 – 2315
2 Northants patrol found Point 156 still occupied by enemy with machine guns at South East and North West of feature. Sounds of activity from reverse slope.

201 Guards Brigade War Diary
26 Jan 44
As a result of the Anzio landings on 22 Jan 44 with the potential threat to his rear, the enemy by 26 Jan 44 thinned out his troops opposite the British on the Garigliano front and stopped all his counterattacks against them.

Chapter 12

27 January 1944 – 1 York & Lancs.
Prepare for the Front Line

2 Scots Guards War Diary

27 Jan 44

The Carrier Platoon took over Point 141, Monte del Duca for the day, being relieved for the night by Right Flank. The Welsh Guards Company took over from 'F' Company, so that with four Companies to occupy three positions it became possible to keep one Company out resting each day.

The enemy reduced their shelling of Minturno and deviated their energy to Tremensuoli, a change which suited us well but had unfortunate consequences for 3 Coldstream Guards and 6 Grenadier Guards, whose positions there were rather exposed.

16/5 Lancers War Diary

27 Jan 44

Minturno was noticeably quiet, and some German positions were spotted on Monte Natale. '2' Troop were relieved of their position by 40 Royal Tank Regiment during the morning.

201 Guards Brigade War Diary

27 Jan 44 – 0600

During the day, some enemy movement was observed and engaged. 3-inch and 4.2-inch mortars harassed the reverse slopes of the Monte Natale feature.

2 Northants War Diary

27 Jan 44 – 0600

Carrying and Protective party provided by 'B' Company for Sappers laying mine field between Points 141 and 172 North of Minturno returned.

1 York & Lancs. War Diary

27 Jan 44 – 0930

The Divisional Commander, Major General P.G.S. Gregson Ellis CBE. inspected the Battalion.

7 Cheshires War Diary

27 Jan 44 – 1100

'4' Platoon carries out harassing fire on Cemetery area. Observation Post report successful.

27 Jan 44 – 1615
'3' Platoon carries out harassing shoot on enemy positions on Point 156.

92 Field Regiment Royal Artillery War Diary

27 Jan 44 – 1730
Plan: 2 Northants will take Point 156 through Tremensuoli, probably night 29-30 Jan 44. 'Chinese' [a barrage put down to infer an assault in a specific area but no subsequent move by ground troops] barrage will be fired, followed by counter-battery programme. Real attack will be supported by concentrations of artillery fire. 1 York & Lancs. will occupy area Point 141, Monte Del Duca, and Cemetery.

1 York & Lancs. War Diary

27 Jan 44 – 1730
CO.'s Group. The CO. gave orders regarding the move up to Minturno 7895 to relieve 2 Royal Scots Fusiliers the following day when Battalion would come under command 17 Infantry Brigade. Armour to consist of 4-6 anti-tank guns towed by Carriers, 4 mortar carriers, one carrier per Company for some equipment, scout car with wireless set, all jeeps, including two fitted to include stretchers and limited number of admin vehicles. On night 29-30 Jan 44 2 Northants would attack Point 156, when Battalion would probably take up a position East of Point 156 and overlooking the Cemetery 781968.

Royal Scots Fusiliers War Diary

27 Jan 44 – 1800
Small patrol under Lieut. Baines set out with 18 men to establish listening post by night on forward slopes of Point 172 and to recce area of Cemetery 781967 and also to have an Observation Post by day 28 Jan 44. This patrol controlled some extraordinarily successful artillery shots on enemy dugouts during the day. 'C' Company recce patrol found Point 165 [just short of Santa Maria Infante on the road] at 782978 occupied and took one prisoner of war from 200 Panzer Grenadier Regiment.

Protective wiring and dummy minefield laid in front of 'B' & 'D' companies by Pioneer Platoon.

2 Northants War Diary

27 Jan 44 – 1830
Patrol went out from 'A' Company to rocky ledge 774965 [400m West of Point 156], and moved out from No '2' Company, 6 Grenadier Guards on feature 774958 [Point 141]. Patrol reached position 150 yards South of 774965 where they were challenged by the Bosche, one shot being fired. Two spandaus opened up from 100 yards to right rear of rocky ledge and from 400 yards approx. left of same place firing onto ledge itself. Possible ambush. Patrol returned having no casualties and finding no mines. Patrol found one position halfway down forward slope Point 156 disused and wired, otherwise no wire. Time of return 2100.

17 Infantry Brigade War Diary

27 Jan 44 – 1900
2 Royal Scots Fusiliers Observation Post reports parties of five or six enemy passing backwards and forwards between Point 156 and road to the Northeast.

17 Infantry Brigade War Diary
27 Jan 44 – 1935
2 Royal Scots Fusiliers patrol to Point 165 taken prisoner of war from '9' Company 200 Grenadier Regiment at 787970. Patrol is continuing with its task.

92 Field Regiment Royal Artillery War Diary
27 Jan 44 – 2015
Patrols tonight: 2 Northants recce patrols to Eastern end of Point 156 from 1730 and the Northwest end of Point 156 at 1830. 2 Royal Scots Fusiliers patrol to Point 165 out 1800 returning 2400; Standing patrol on Point 172; Recce patrol to 781967 [Aid Post], and completion of minefield at 784959 [Santa Maria Infante road].

17 Infantry Brigade War Diary
27 Jan 44 – 2310
Warning order from Division for night 28-29 Jan 44. 1 York & Lancs. will relieve 2 Royal Scots Fusiliers and 6 Seaforths will relieve 1 KOYLI. On arrival 1 York & Lancs. comes under command 17 Infantry Brigade. 2 Royal Scots Fusiliers on being relieved will proceed to Sorbello. 1 KOYLI reverts to command 15 Infantry Brigade on relief.

2 Northants War Diary
27 Jan 44 – 2345
Patrol by 'D' Company to roofless house on Point 156 moved out from 2 Scots Guards position on Point 141 at 1930. Reached hill without incident except for shelling in area 777962 [300m South of Point 156]. Patrol reached position near roofless house but did not see any movement and went on approx. 100 yards beyond house still going uphill. The patrol did not reach the track running along the top of Point 156. Patrol heard Spandau machine guns, probably from the same position as heard by 'A' Company patrol. Patrol heard mortar firing and saw flashes behind Point 156 on reverse slope approx. position 250 yards Northeast of rocky ledge. Patrol returned being shelled in area 778955 while returning to vehicles. Time of return 2345.

17 Infantry Brigade War Diary
27 Jan 44 – 2359
2 Royal Scots Fusiliers patrol to Point 165 reports Spur Point 141, 7897 clear of enemy but Point 165 occupied. Sounds of tracked vehicle on road between Cemetery and Santa Maria Infante. Weather: Fine.

Chapter 13

28 January 1944 – Planning the Attack on Point 156

5 Infantry Division Intelligence

Enemy Situation, Patrols combined with the views of a few prisoners show the enemy to be holding the general line Santa Maria Infante – Monte Natale and Point 156.

On the Division Front Monte Natale seems at the moment to be his most sensitive spot and elements of 200 Grenadier Regiment are expected to be holding this feature. Little is known of the enemy positions West of this Point.

A couple of prisoners from 267 Grenadier Regiment suggest '2' Company area to be around Point 156, while '3' Company is believed to be in area 778985 with outposts forward to Point 165 (783978) where there is a small house surrounded by a double apron barbed wire fence and which three men were observed by a patrol of ours last night.

Detail, Road cratered, single line traffic at: 780965 [Aid Post, Santa Maria Infante Road].

Major General Bucknall (left), outgoing Commander 5 Infantry Division and Major General P.G.S. Gregson Ellis, incoming Commander 5 Infantry Division, looking at enemy positions across the River Garigliano. 28 Jan 44 (Photo IWM)

2 Scots Guards War Diary

28 Jan 44

The Welsh Guards Company took over Point 141 for the night. There were no changes of position and no casualties.

52 Anti-Tank Regiment Royal Artillery War Diary

28 Jan 44

Battalion Commander informed of 17 Infantry Brigade attack on Point 156 on 28-29 Jan 44. After discussion with 17 Infantry Brigade Commander, it was decided not to take 17 Pounder guns up to Point 156 at first light owing to difficulties of recce and finding positions in the dark.

252 Field Co. Royal Engineers War Diary

28 Jan 44 – 0200

Minefield completed. Number of mines laid, 233 Mark V on a 250-yard frontage. Trace and minefield record proforma passed to Commander Royal Engineers, 5 Infantry Division.

17 Infantry Brigade War Diary

28 Jan 44 – 0325

2 Northants patrol to Point 156 reports two machine guns on each side of rocky ridge at 774965 [300m West of Point 156], guns fire into ridge across front of their position. There is good going between 2 Scots Guards position and Point 156 and easy to keep direction along this route. Mortar heard firing from behind Point 156. Patrol shelled on its return at 778955 [300m West of Point 141, Monte del Duca].

17 Infantry Brigade War Diary

28 Jan 44 – 0725

2 Royal Scots Fusiliers patrol lying up on forward slopes of Point 172 reports considerable noise from enemy occupying Cemetery and sound of tracked vehicle moving back along road.

15 Infantry Brigade War Diary

28 Jan 44 – 0900

A conference was held at Division HQ and the plan for the attack on Point 156 feature was outlined as follows:

On night of 28-29 Jan 44 1 York & Lancs. would relieve 2 Royal Scots Fusiliers on Point 172 feature and come under command of 17 Infantry Brigade. 1 KOYLI would be withdrawn for rest to Nicolleto. On night 29-30 Jan 44, 2 Northants would attack Point 156 feature at approx. 0200 followed up by 6 Seaforths who would occupy the Cemetery and ground East of the road North of the Point 172 feature. On night of 29-30 Jan 44 1 Green Howards would move up to concentration area South of Minturno as Divisional reserve. On night 30-31 Jan 44 1 Green Howards would relieve 2 Northants on Point 156 and Brigade HQ would move up to take over the command of 17 Infantry Brigade's sector.

7 Cheshires War Diary

28 Jan 44 – 0900

The Commanding Officer went to 'A' and 'C' Companies to plan for barrage shoot on night of 29-30 Jan 44. Recce made of area Point 65, 779949 but this Point could not be used as infantry were going to use that area for start line. Shoot would have to be done from Point 141, Monte del Duca 785956.

17 Infantry Brigade War Diary

28 Jan 44 – 1100

2 Royal Scots Fusiliers has directed fire on slit trenches at 781967, [near Aid Post]. Two direct hits scored, and further casualties inflicted on enemy running from trenches. Sounds of ammunition exploding in Cemetery area.

28 Jan 44 – 1115

Civilian reports camouflaged tanks dispersed along road between Cemetery and road junction 776991.

156 Field Regiment Royal Artillery War Diary

28 Jan 44 – 1220

Enemy position engaged by one gun. Ammunition seen to explode and Germans moving 778964 [Monte Natale].

1 York & Lancs. War Diary

28 Jan 44 – 1230

Recce parties consisting of Commanding Officer, Company Commanders and Mortar Platoon Commander, left Casanova by jeep at 1130, arriving at 17 Infantry Brigade HQ 795952 [Lateral Road] at 1230. When the CO. had seen the Brigadier, Battalion representatives recced their areas with their opposite numbers of 2 Royal Scots Fusiliers and then awaited the arrival of the Battalion who would cross the bridge at 808933 at 1830.

92 Field Regiment Royal Artillery War Diary

28 Jan 44 – 1500

1 York & Lancs. moving forward into line again tonight. Battery Commander and Forward Observation Officer accompanying.

7 Cheshires War Diary

28 Jan 44 – 1615

'3' Platoon carries out harassing fire on to Point 156.

5 Infantry Division

28 Jan 44 – 1700

5 Infantry Division is to increase the size of the bridgehead by seizing Monte Natale and the area of the Cemetery. 17 Infantry Brigade will capture the area of the Cemetery and Point 156.

LEFT: 2 Northants under command with two Platoons and 'A' Company, 7 Cheshires for consolidation. Three detachments of 38 Field Company, Royal Engineers.

RIGHT: 6 Seaforths will operate to protect the right flank of 2 Northants and deny the enemy the use of the road for a counterattack. They will establish a Company in the area of the spur about Point 172, 787966 (Grigg Hill) and, will operate to dominate the Cemetery area by 0400.

Tanks. One Troop moves on orders Brigade HQ to area of Cemetery to come under command of 6 Seaforths on arrival, primarily to deal with tank counterattack, but also available to deal with infantry counterattack.

Immediate recce will be arranged by Commander 'A' Squadron 16/5 Lancers with CO. 2 Northants to discover if the tanks can be moved from the Cemetery to Point 156 in order to come under the command of 2 Northants.

6 Seaforths will establish minimum of two anti-tank guns in the Cemetery area as soon as possible after occupation. In order to deceive the enemy as to direction of attack and to draw Direct Fire as though attack coming in along high ground from the Cemetery area, a Deception Fire Plan including barrage, directional Bofors and machine gun fire to be put into effect. [This is a 'Chinese' attack.] Separate instruction for machine gun fire given to CO. 7 Cheshires.

6 Seaforths to move initially to area around Tufo, moving thence to position on track leading to Point 172 from present 1 York & Lancs. HQ.

2 Northants HQ initially to road junction 781955 thence to 778959 [500m South of Point 156].

17 Infantry Brigade War Diary
28 Jan 44

Zero hour for attack. 30 Jan 44 – 0130. Tanks: Troop already in Minturno available to provide fire for dealing with counterattack on Point 156. Fire to be called for through Brigade HQ.

1 York & Lancs. War Diary
28 Jan 44 – 1715

Battalion left Casanova by motor transport to 782940, then by march route to new area. A2 and B Echelon transport remained at Casanova.

92 Field Regiment Royal Artillery War Diary
28 Jan 44 – 1740

Message from HQ Royal Artillery. Recce patrol leaving tonight for Point 156. Out 1800.

92 Field Regiment Royal Artillery War Diary
28 Jan 44 – 1815

Instruction from HQ Royal Artillery. No shooting in Cemetery, area 781967. 2 Royal Scots Fusiliers patrols investigating area.

2 Northants War Diary

28 Jan 44 – 1830

Recce patrol to Point 156 did not reach the hill owing to Spandau fire at head of wadi 776960 and some shelling in same area.

2 Cameronians War Diary

28 Jan 44 – 1930

'C' Company relieved 'A' Company on Point 201. 'A' Company took over 'C' Company's position at Point 151. The night was generally quiet.

2 Royal Scots Fusiliers War Diary

28 Jan 44 – 2000

Relief by 1 York & Lancs. started. Companies marched independently to Route 7 and moved from there on transport.

2 Northants War Diary

28 Jan 44 – 2130

Patrol returned reporting lack of success in reaching Point 156.

92 Field Regiment Royal Artillery War Diary

28 Jan 44 – 2215

467 Battery Commander now forward with 1 York & Lancs., reports Forward Observation Officer from 156 Field Regiment also with Battalion.

1 York &Lancs. War Diary

28 Jan 44 – 2330

The relief of 2 Royal Scots Fusiliers was completed by 2330 with the Battalion in position as follows:

'C' Company Point 141, 785958, 'B' Company Point 172, 785962, 'C' Company, Point 172, 783962, TAC HQ 788959, Rear 795953. Battalion has under command, No '1' Company 2 Scots Guards on Point 141, 782959 and 'A' Company 7 Cheshires, also one Troop of tanks 16/5 Lancers. Spasmodic shelling of area during hand over. Forward Observation Officers from 92 Field Regiment attached, and Direct Fire tasks arranged.

If Battalion is driven off its present position, artillery fire is arranged. Direct Fire on known Self-Propelled gun positions. Battalion slightly shelled at 0215, 0230, and 0305. Direct Fire called for. Night dry but cold. Battalion received 6 officers and 20 other ranks today but owing to the move up they were unable to be absorbed at present.

1 York & Lancs. Ernest Shaw

'We had three Companies, then for a while, then after we got back to normal with these reinforcements, we went back to relieve the Guards on Point 156, the Guards who had replaced us. The Major talked to us before we went because he had been sworn at in the same manner. He was in the line with us when we were coming out. He had an apology from the Colonel of the Guards Regiment over this episode. We got back to relieve them on Point 156, and they were quite apologetic to us individually. Men came to us and said how sorry they were, but at the time I could have belted some of them when we were walking out.'

2 Royal Scots Fusiliers War Diary

28 Jan 44 – Midnight

Lt. Baines reported presence of Self-Propelled gun on road North of Cemetery and set out with two men armed with PIAT to deal with it at 1800. He returned at midnight to report that the gun had withdrawn after dark and brought valuable information from his recce of the area. Lt. Baines later acted as guide to 6 Seaforths in their attack on Spur Point 141.

164 Field Ambulance War Diary

28 Jan 44

During the period 18-27 Jan 44 stretcher bearer parties went out continuously to the Regional Aid Posts to collect casualties from forward areas. On one occasion 11 civilian casualties were collected and cleared from a minefield by Captain Hill-Irving and party of one Medical Orderly and four stretcher bearers.

1 KOYLI War Diary

28 Jan 44

We were back in our original area at Noceletto where we were at once reinforced. Our total casualties in this battle were 30 killed, 10 died of wounds, 32 missing, 102 wounded.

Chapter 14

29 January 1944 – HMS *Spartan* Sunk, 31 Lives Lost

5 Division Intelligence

29 Jan 44

Our attack on Point 156 (775965) met resistance not from 200 Grenadier Regiment as had been expected but from 1 Battalion 361 Grenadier Regiment, which we had been told was not to be considered on our front any longer. When the identification came through it was some slight consolation to know that we had expected the correct Division in that sector.

‘1’ Company, ‘1’ Battalion, 361 Regiment seem to have borne the brunt of the attack. Its fighting strength was about 80 at the start. The consensus of opinion among the 27 prisoners is that some 20 were killed.

A recently captured order stated: ‘The Fuehrer orders that the Gustav Line will be held at all costs since a wholly successful defence would have important political repercussions. The Fuehrer relies on every metre of ground being contested most fiercely.’

Having issued this message some days ago, the Fuehrer must be having a restless night – or perhaps his advisers have failed to tell him that he has again lost another 100 prisoners and as many killed trying to hold this precious line.

In conclusion it is perhaps fitting to remark that the men of ‘5’ Company 267 Grenadier Regiment cheered when they saw their Company Commander arrive at the Prisoner of War collecting point. ‘How did you manage to get him out of his dug-out’ they said.

Enemy losses: The total number of prisoners and deserters collected by the Division since 2100 17 Jan 44, is seven Officers and 484 Other Ranks.

156 Field Regiment Royal Artillery War Diary

29 Jan 44

Enemy: Prisoners from 267 Regiment suggest ‘2’ Company area to be around Point 156, while ‘3’ Company is believed to be in area 778985 with outposts forward to Point 165 [783978] where there is a small house surrounded by double apron barbed wire fence at which three men were observed by a patrol of ours last night.

16/5 Lancers War Diary

29 Jan 44

The Squadron Leader told tank Commanders the plan. During the early hours of the morning 2 Northants were to make an attack on Point 156, at the same time 6 Seaforths were attacking on the right of the road, their objective being Spur Point 141. 6 Seaforths were also to occupy the Cemetery. During the night 6 Grenadier Guards and 3 Coldstream Guards were attacking the spur Northwest of Tremensuoli to cover the left flank before 2 Northants went in. '2' Troop was to be at the Cemetery at first light to guard against an enemy counterattack down the road. The Second in Command was to recce positions for '1' Troop and the track running below Point 156 with a view for dealing with an enemy counterattack on Point 156 and shooting up any infantry that came over the top.

92 Field Regiment Royal Artillery War Diary

29 Jan 44 – 0100

467 Battery Commander reports additional Direct Fires may be called for. Also new task 787966-792964 [near Point 172]. Battery Commander now in Minturno. Direct Fires passed to Batteries.

1 York & Lancs. War Diary

29 Jan 44 – 0630

'B' Company sent small patrol to Point 172 to overlook the Cemetery 781968 and observe movement of the enemy in the area.

6 Grenadier Guards War Diary

29 Jan 44 – 0745

Company Commander's conference was held at Battalion HQ. The Commanding Officer giving the outline plan of the attack on two features which were only 800 yards away. The Battalion was to attack two pimples, right '3' Company 764964, left '4' Company 762959. '1' Company to take over the Coldstream right lead Company, and '2' Company returns to its present location. 3 Coldstreams were to make a limited advance on our left at the same time.

1 York & Lancs. War Diary

29 Jan 44 – 1000

Slight enemy shelling of area. Weather fine and warm with good visibility.

29 Jan 44 – 1015

'D' Company patrol contacted 2 Cameronians on Point 201, 799966, where they have a standing patrol.

17 Infantry Brigade War Diary

29 Jan 44 – 1030

Zero hour for 2 Northants attack tonight advanced to 0130.

1 York & Lancs. War Diary

29 Jan 44 – 1030

'D' Company patrol went to area 786964 [100m East of Point 172] where they heard noises. Found Italian civilians pruning trees, who reported no enemy in that area for about ten days!

92 Field Regiment Royal Artillery War Diary
29 Jan 44 – 1030
Message from 467 Battery Commander. Observation Post now at 790963 [600m East of Point 172]. Battery Commander at 1 York & Lancs. Battalion HQ, 788960. 'C' Company at Point 141, 785958, 'B' Company at Point 172 785962, 'D' Company Point 172 783962. One Company 2 Scots Guards at Point 141 782959,Monte Del Duca. Enemy self-propelled guns at 780985, 783987, and 782982.

2 Northants War Diary
29 Jan 44 – 1045
Battalion moved off by march route to the Assembly area.

6 Seaforth Highlanders War Diary
29 Jan 44 – 1100
CO. meets Platoon Commanders at Rendezvous 788959 shows them the ground and goes over situation with them.

1 York & Lancs. War Diary
29 Jan 44 – 1250
Two Italian civilians who had come through Spigno 7901 and Santa Maria Infante 7898 passed to Brigade for interrogation.

29 Jan 44 – 1330
17 Infantry Brigade Commander visited Tactical HQ and told CO. of tonight's operation. Password for tonight 'Bitter-Sweet'.

141 Field Ambulance War Diary
29 Jan 44 – 1600
12 Sappers from Advanced Dressing Station attached to Medical Officer in charge 2 Northants to carry cases from Regimental Aid Post to be established during night area 778966 to Car Post 780966.

12 Sappers from ADS attached to Medical Officer in charge 6 Seaforths to carry cases from Regimental Aid Post to be established during the night area 798963 to Car Post 800962.

1 York & Lancs. War Diary
29 Jan 44 – 1615
Area shelled for 5 minutes. New Direct Fire tasks arranged as follows to take effect when 6 Seaforths reach Point 156.

At 0030 30 Jan 44 an artillery barrage would be laid down and at 0130 2 Northants would attack Point 156, 775966, Monte Natale, passing through Point 141, 782959, Monte Del Duca. When they are on objective 6 Seaforths would pass through the Battalion and

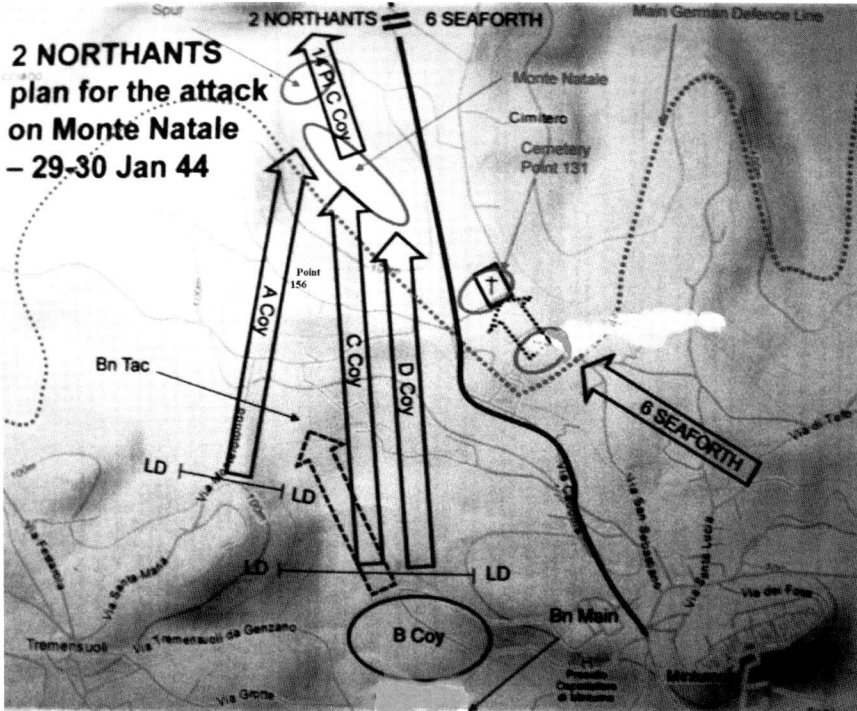

2 Northants plan for the attack on Monte Natale 29–30 Jan 44. (Map, Frank de Planta)

take the position in and around the Cemetery at 781968. When the operation for which the Battalion would hold a firm base is complete the above Direct Fire tasks come into effect.

17 Infantry Brigade War Diary
29 Jan 44 – 1635
Officer Commanding 207 Anti-Tank Battery reports he has found good position for 17 Pounder at 797962. Gun to be put in position tonight.

1 York & Lancs. War Diary
29 Jan 44 – 1715
Fairly heavy barrage laid down by own Artillery in support of 201 Guards Brigade who are carrying out small operation in area 763967.

Nicolson, Capt. Nigel, *The Grenadier Guards in the War of 1939-1945, Volume II*
29 Jan 44
'The Coldstreams were operating on the left flank and the Grenadiers on their right were ordered to capture two low hills, separated by an orange grove, eight hundred yards ahead of their present line. According to the plan, the hills were to have been captured in the evening, allowing them time to spend the night in consolidation, and be prepared to resist a counterattack at dawn. It worked out very differently.'

201 Guards Brigade War Diary
29 Jan 44 – 1730
Grenadier Guards right and 3 Coldstream Guards left got out of their slit trenches in the gathering darkness – formed up where they were – and moved forward through mortar and machine gun fire towards their objectives.

6 Grenadier Guards
29 Jan 44 1745
Zero hour. '3' and '4' Companies set off followed 15 minutes later by '1' Company.

201 Guards Brigade War Diary
29 Jan 44 – 1800
The night was pitch black and with no moon.

23 Armoured Brigade War Diary
29 Jan 44 – 1800
The presence of tanks, probably '1' Squadron Herman Goering Tank Regiment is identified by Photo Reconnaissance Unit along the roads running behind the Monte Natale feature, from San Croce – Santa Maria Infante, where they are presumably held in a counterattack role. Their presence here together with the considerable infantry concentration in front of them, indicates again that this is an essential hinge of the enemy's line. The cutting of the road in this area would not be a vital blow to the enemy but it would both complicate his supply and would reduce the mobility of his reserves to such an extent that in the long run his situation on the present line would become untenable.

1 York & Lancs. War Diary
29 Jan 44 – 1800
Area of Tactical HQ heavily shelled for 10 minutes by 105mm guns probably in reply to our barrage. Message received that hot meals are on way from Rear HQ to 'D' and 'B' Companies. 'C' Company being able to cook in their own area.

'B' Company patrol which had been overlooking the Cemetery 781968 all day, returned having seen no enemy movement throughout the whole day.

52 Anti-Tank Regiment Royal Artillery War Diary
29 Jan 44 – 1800
207 Battery: Recce made by Battery Commander and Troop Commander for 17 pounder gun positions North West of Tufo near Point 201 [798966], to fire on to road Santa Maria Infante 7898 – Cemetery 7896. Left at 0900. A position was found at 798963 but track to it unbelievably bad. Battery Commander decided to attempt it and gun was brought up at 1800. Work was started on the track and continued all night.

17 Infantry Brigade War Diary
29 Jan 44 – 1820
1 York & Lancs. report that lying up patrol overlooking Cemetery observed no movement even when our shells landed there.

1 York & Lancs. War Diary
29 Jan 44 – 1825
Area again shelled for some minutes by 88mm or 105mm guns. Verey lights seen from area Tremensuoli 7795 towards Point 172, 783982 as follows: one Green (two minutes), one Green (three minutes), red over green over red.

6 Grenadier Guards War Diary
29 Jan 44 – 1825
'3' Company reported itself about 100 yards from its objective meeting extremely heavy opposition. Further report from '3' Company that the opposition was coming from the West.

201 Guards Brigade War Diary
29 Jan 44 – 1828
6 Grenadier Guards reported right forward Company having stiff fighting on its objective. This report proved to be too optimistic as they were still 200 yards short of it.

Nicolson, Capt. Nigel, *The Grenadier Guards in the War of 1939-1945, Volume II*
29 Jan 44
'No sooner than the right-hand Company [Major H.C. Hanbury, M.C.)]moved forward from their trenches than they were caught in a crippling barrage, and twelve men arrived at the foot of the objective itself. On the left No. 3 Company [Major E. Penn M.C.] had better fortune at the start, but on approaching their hill they heard the clicking of German rifle bolts and the Platoon Commanders only had time to shout 'Down' before the first volleys crashed over their heads. Both Companies were now held up and much weakened: it was already extremely dark, and the two reserve Companies were not only beyond striking distance but had never seen the ground in day light. Nevertheless, Colonel Kingsmill decided that both reserve Companies must be employed if the hills were to be captured before day light, and they began to feel their way forward in the darkness, guided by wireless messages from behind and the sound of firing from in front.'

92 Field Regiment Royal Artillery War Diary
29 Jan 44 – 1835
467 Battery Commander: Enemy shelling 784957 [Point 141 – Monte del Duca]. Enemy machine gunning on left. Our shelling appears to be falling in correct place.

6 Grenadier Guards War Diary
29 Jan 44 – 1850
'4' Company reported that they had reached objective but that there were still Germans on it.

201 Guards Brigade War Diary
29 Jan 44 – 1855
6 Grenadier Guards report left forward Company objective captured. This proved to be optimistic. They were only 15 strong, two Platoons having lost touch in the dark and still 200 yards from the objective. The dark night and enemy fire made control almost

impossible in rocky and scrubby country. Meanwhile 3 Coldstream Guards had moved forward to their objectives with little opposition but both Company HQ wireless sets were knocked out. News came back slowly.

5 Division History
29 Jan 44 – 1900
The Guards attacked and secured their objective. 6 Grenadier Guards on the left and 3 Coldstream Guards on the right to the West of Tremensuoli. This was planned to give room for 2 Northants and 6 Seaforths to attack Monte Natale and the Cemetery, respectively. The whole of X (BR) Corps Artillery and two Cruisers were to fire in support.

6 Grenadier Guards War Diary
29 Jan 44 – 1922
3 Coldstreams on our left reported left-hand objective taken without much opposition. During the next few hours, the situation became confused and communication bad. The Intelligence Officer was sent to find out the exact situation. It was however clear that '4' Company had not captured its objective.

201 Guards Brigade War Diary
29 Jan 44 – 2045
Further Direct Fire and known mortar positions were fired in support of 6 Grenadier Guards right forward Company. Some rounds fell short on our own troops – due to fatigue both of gunners and gun barrels.

1 York & Lancs. War Diary
29 Jan 44 – 2230
2 Scots Guards under command on Point 141, Monte Del Duca, 782959 asked CO. for permission to use three-inch mortar in case of counterattack. This was granted on condition they were not used after 2 Northants attack on Point 156.

6 Grenadier Guards War Diary
29 Jan 44 – 2230
Intelligence Officer returned with the news that '3' Company were still 100 yards short of objective and that '4' Company was also slightly short of theirs, and very thin on the ground.

17 Infantry Brigade War Diary
29 Jan 44 – 2237
2 Northants new HQ established road junction 781955.

6 Grenadier Guards War Diary
29 Jan 44 – 2240
'1' Company was ordered to advance to take '3' Company's position. '3' Company can then go to help '4' Company. This would, if necessary allow '4' Company to withdraw to '1' Company's position.

29 Jan 44 – 2250
'1 Company reached '3' Company's area.

29 Jan 44 – 2255
At this point '2' Company was ordered to attack and help '4' Company. '1' Company was then ordered to stay with '3' Company.

6 Seaforth Highlanders War Diary
29 Jan 44 – 2300
Troops arrive in Tufo assembly area.

17 Infantry Brigade War Diary
29 Jan 44 – 2335
2 Northants complete in Assembly area less one Machine Gun Platoon. Weather: Fine.

HMS *Spartan* Naval History
29 Jan 44
On 29 Jan 44 in the bay at Anzio, HMS SPARTAN [which had been part of the convoy Ernest Strafford was in for his journey from Liverpool to Italy in October 1943] was hit on the port side in the stern half of the ship and after the funnel by an Hs 293 Glider, which exploded in the engine room. The compartment flooded and fire started in the after superstructure causing explosions. It capsized and was abandoned after an hour when fires could not be controlled. 31 lives were lost, 523 Survivors were rescued by HM Cruiser DIDO, HMS LAFOREY and HMS LOYAL)

38 Field Company Royal Engineers War Diary
Night 29-30 Jan 44
An officer recce party and two Sections were attached to 2 Northants for possible mine clearing in the attack on Monte Natale 7796. One Sapper admitted to hospital with shell shock.

HMS *Spartan* after being attacked, 29 Jan 44.

Chapter 15

30 January 1944 – Monte Natale Recaptured

16/5 Lancers War Diary

30 Jan 44

Weather still fine. No.2 Troop 'A' Squadron moving up towards Cemetery, 781966 in support of 6 Seaforths and 2 Northants. At first light one tank blew up on a mine but recovered, remainder in position.

17 Infantry Brigade War Diary

30 Jan 44 – 0030

Missing machine gun Platoon now in assembly area with 2 Northants. Beginning of diversionary barrage to give impression that attack is coming from the East.

1 York & Lancs. War Diary

30 Jan 44 – 0030

The new day opened noisily with the barrage laid down for the 17 Infantry Brigade attack. Enemy guns replied to our barrage trying to neutralise our Bofors anti-aircraft guns which were firing direction tracer from the area 800901. Few shells fell in the area.

2 Northants War Diary

30 Jan 44 – 0030

Assaulting Companies moved to Start Lines: 'A' Company to area 774959 [Point 141] 'C' & 'D' Companies to area 778957 [50m West of Point 141, Monte del Duca].

17 Infantry Brigade War Diary

30 Jan 44 – 0105

6 Seaforths and 156 Field Regiment Royal Artillery report enemy Direct Fire falling in Minturno area.

30 Jan 44 – 0115

Enemy Direct Fire now responding to diversionary barrage and falling near Point 172.

30 Jan 44 – 0125

6 Seaforths moving forward from Assembly Area.

7 Cheshires War Diary

30 Jan 44 – 0130

'3' & '4' Platoons firing concentrations in support of 2 Northants attack. Firing carried out without any hitch. Total of 560 rounds fired (70 rounds per gun).

2 Northants War Diary
30 Jan 44 – 0130
Companies moved off start lines. 'C' & 'D' Companies sustaining some casualties from enemy harassing fire.

6 Seaforth Highlanders War Diary
30 Jan 44 – 0130
Tufo, 8096, Battalion moved off in order: 'B' Company, Tac HQ, 'C' Company, 'A' Company Porterage Platoon, Main HQ, Regimental Aid Post.

2 Northants War Diary
30 Jan 44 – 0145

Tac Battalion HQ and reserve Company passed Start Lines and moved to position at 779959 (600m South-East of Monte Natale].

141 Field Ambulance War Diary
30 Jan 44 – 0200
2 Northants attacked Monte Natale. Casualties evacuated back to Advanced Dressing Station, 783952, by ambulance thence to Medical Centre 158.

17 Infantry Brigade War Diary
30 Jan 44 – 0220
2 Northants report all going well. 'D' Company mortared while forming up. A few casualties.

5 Infantry Division History
30 Jan 44 – 0230
The barrage opened at half an hour after midnight. The Germans immediately reacted by shelling all possible forming up places exploiting fully the fragmentation of shell on rocky ground. As a result, the attack itself started an hour late. On the left the Guards took all their objectives, with one minor exception. Some excellent and prompt wiring in conjunction with defensive fire, helped to stave off determined counterattacks.

2 Northants had much assistance for their advance over difficult ground in the shape of porters and Carriers for their ammunition and extra stretcher bearers provided by 141 Field Ambulance. The lower terraced slopes of Monte Natale with their 12-foot banks particularly caused the rate of advance to be considerably slowed down. Despite this by 0230, the attack was proceeding smoothly with 'C' and 'D' Companies on the lower slopes.

6 Seaforth Highlanders War Diary
30 Jan 44 – 0230
Tac HQ arrive at track junction 100 yards North of main Minturno Road, 786958. 'B' Company forked right, and Tac HQ waited until 'C' Company passed through. New order of march was 'C' Company, Tac HQ, 'A' Company, Stretcher bearers from 141 Field Ambulance, Porterage Platoon.

2 Cameronians War Diary
30 Jan 44 – 0230
'A' Company at Point 151 was shelled by our own artillery.

2 Northants War Diary
30 Jan 44 – 0230
'A' Company reported good progress being made. 'C' & 'D' Companies were not in contact with Battalion HQ.

17 Infantry Brigade War Diary
30 Jan 44 – 0235
Some casualties to 'C' Company, 2 Northants from mortars while on slope. Reserve Company not yet called for. Progress satisfactory.

201 Guards Brigade War Diary
30 Jan 44 – 0245
Satisfactory progress with little opposition reported by 17 Infantry Brigade attack on Monte Natale. This was a great relief to 6 Grenadier Guards whose right flank was exposed. Enemy artillery and mortar fire switched to the 17 Infantry Brigade front.

2 Northants War Diary
30 Jan 44 – 0245
Rear of Tac HQ shelled. Believed one of own guns falling short.

17 Infantry Brigade War Diary
30 Jan 44 – 0255
156 Field Regiment Royal Artillery Observation Post reports spasmodic harassing fire from '88's' and '105's' on road between Minturno and Cemetery.

15 Infantry Brigade War Diary
30 Jan 44 – 0300
1 Green Howards left their rest area and moved up to a concentration area just South of Minturno near the area of the old Brigade HQ. Nothing untoward occurred during the move. The Brigadier left early for Division Tac where he remained until the afternoon.

52 Anti-Tank Regiment Royal Artillery War Diary
30 Jan 44 – 0300
207 Battery: After working all night on track, became completely bogged and it was found to be impossible to get the gun in.

17 Infantry Brigade War Diary
30 Jan 44 – 0305
6 Seaforths starting to go forward.

6 Seaforth Highlanders War Diary
30 Jan 44 – 0310
Main HQ established at 785964 [Point 172].

17 Infantry Brigade War Diary
30 Jan 44 – 0325
2 Northants left hand 'A' Company going well. Some shelling.

30 Jan 44 – 0330
2 Northants report all companies going well, some small arms fire.

X (BR) Corps War Diary
30 Jan 44 – 0330
During the night 17 Infantry Brigade launched attacks with 6 Seaforths and 2 Northants towards Monte Natale. Our troops were established in the Cemetery and on top of Monte Natale. Enemy counterattacks which came in before first light were beaten back.

1 York & Lancs. War Diary
30 Jan 44 – 0330
Message received from 17 Infantry Brigade that 'A' Company 2 Northants on objective at 772966 [Monte Natale]. Rest going well. Night again dry and cold.

6 Seaforth Highlanders War Diary
30 Jan 44 – 0400
'C' Company clear house at 785964 [Point 172] and moved 200 yards forward to highest ground & began to dig in. 'A' Company passed through. Tac HQ established at house 785964 [Point 172].

2 Northants War Diary
30 Jan 44 – 0400
Tac HQ moved forward to area 776964 [Point 156, Monte Natale] and dug in. CO. went forward with Intelligence Officer. There was still no contact with 'C' & 'D' Companies. CO. found 'C' Company moving uphill led by Second in Command as Company Commander had been wounded on Start Line. 'D' Company could not be seen or heard on right but was making good progress.

141 Field Ambulance War Diary
30 Jan 44 – 0400
6 Seaforths attacked Spur Point 141. Casualties evacuated to Advanced Dressing Station 164 established in Quarry 803954. And thence to Medical Centre 152 by ambulance.

17 Infantry Brigade War Diary
30 Jan 44 – 0420
6 Seaforths report Company forming positions on Grigg Hill 787966 [400m East of the Cemetery and 500m North of Point 172). HQ established Point 172.

30 Jan 44 – 0435
2 Northants report 'A' Company, right, Company 'D' almost on objective.

30 Jan 44 – 0445

2 Northants report 'A' Company had no opposition. Prisoner of War total now ten. No news from 'C' Company centre, but tape seen going forward over Point 156. Officer Commanding Company wounded. 'D' Company, right, nearly on objective. No small arms fire. Some casualties from shelling. One Platoon missing.

92 Field Regiment Royal Artillery War Diary

30 Jan 44 – 0455

Information from HQ Royal Artillery re. progress of attack. Guards: all objectives taken except flank, forward Companies 6 Grenadier Guards not quite on objectives. Reserve Company working round, expect to reach objective by daylight. Unsuccessfully counterattacked, and wire erected by Guards created some confusion. 2 Northants: left Company gained 772966 at 0345. 6 Seaforths: Cemetery area occupied with little enemy opposition, few casualties, one Platoon missing, believed taken Prisoners of War by Germans.`

X (BR) Corps War Diary

30 Jan 44 – 0500

In 5 Infantry Division sector the attack of 201 Guards Brigade had been successful and all objectives except one were being consolidated. The last objective was finally captured after a final attack supported by artillery fire at first light.

16/5 Lancers War Diary

30 Jan 44 – 0500

We heard from the Squadron Leader who had spent the night at Brigade HQ that 6 Seaforths and the Guards had got their objectives and 2 Northants had got onto Point 156.

6 Seaforth Highlanders War Diary

30 Jan 44 – 0505

'C' Company reported they were in position. There were found to be mines in the area and there were some casualties while digging in.

17 Infantry Brigade War Diary

30 Jan 44 – 0515

6 Seaforths in Cemetery. No opposition.

6 Seaforth Highlanders War Diary

30 Jan 44 – 0530

After passing through 'C' Company, 'A' Company went forward and took Cemetery 781967 with little opposition.

16/5 Lancers War Diary

30 Jan 44 – 0530

The Second in Command and '2' Troop started off, but things went badly at the beginning as the Second in Command and the leading tank of '2' Troop got stuck in a ditch. Sergeant Barker's tank managed to get out, but the Scout car was firmly stuck, so the Second in Command had to travel on the back of Sergeant Barker's tank.

5 Infantry Division History

30 Jan 44 – 0545

'C' Company [Captain E.W. Kitchin] of 2 Northants had cleared the highest point and shortly afterwards, 'D' Company [Major R. Greaves] had cleared the Eastern edge of the feature. The whole position was consolidated for the inevitable counterattacks at dawn. It had been a most successful and well conducted attack.

Equally successful and without much incident was the attack of 6 Seaforths on to the Cemetery itself. By first light they were in complete control of the area with some prisoners from 301 Infantry Regiment of 90 Light Division. It was then possible to send some tanks to strengthen the position and the Battalion was able shortly afterward to patrol to Santa Maria Infante.

This was an undisputedly successful day for the Division as its objectives had been taken for less than 100 casualties and in return for at least 120 prisoners. The field guns fired over 500 rounds per gun in the attack and a further 200 rounds against the counterattack.

17 Infantry Brigade War Diary

30 Jan 44 – 0545

'C' Company, 2 Northants on top of Point 156 with one Platoon checking forward slopes and digging in. Prisoners of War now 15 including one wounded.

6 Seaforth Highlanders War Diary

30 Jan 44 – 0545

Two 6 pounder anti-tank guns reported now in position in Cemetery area.

2 Northants War Diary

30 Jan 44 – 0545

'C' Company on Point 156 and dug in. 'D' Company less one Platoon on objective and Company, 6 Seaforth Highlanders moving to Cemetery 781967.

17 Infantry Brigade War Diary

30 Jan 44 – 0550

First prisoner of war arrived at Brigade HQ. Identified as '1' Company 361 Grenadier Regiment, previously believed to have left this front.

30 Jan 44 – 0610

2 Northants report approximately 30 casualties in Regional Aid Post so far including Commanders' 'C' and 'D' Companies. 'D' Company have lost one Platoon in dark. All Companies on their objective.

2 Northants Citation: Military Cross for Captain Lamb

On the night of 29-30 Jan 44 the 2nd Battalion, Northamptonshire Regiment were ordered to seize Point 156. The Regional Aid Post under Capt. Lamb was ordered to follow the Battalion axis which ran up the slopes of a wadi.

Owing to the darkness of the night and the difficult uphill going the RAP lost contact with the move of the Battalion Tac HQ and followed the line of the wadi.

German POWs being marched to the rear near Minturno. They were captured during the bitter fighting in the hills above the town and could be from 274 Grenadier Regiment of 9' Infantry Division, which originally defended this sector, although by this date, 30 Jan 44 many other German units had arrived to reinforce the line and they had become somewhat intermingled. (Photo Sgt. Johnson AFPU, TNA 11543)

Soon after the attack began the wadi was very heavily and accurately shelled by enemy mortars and artillery. The stretcher bearers at once suffered casualties and only a limited number were available to help evacuate the casualties of the two forward Companies who had crossed the Start Line some 150 yards in the rear.

Stragglers from the two forward Companies made their way to the wadi. Capt. Lamb was the only Officer on the spot and took command over a situation which was showing signs of losing control.

He redirected the men from the forward Companies towards their objective, organised the remaining stretcher bearers, and then, himself, worked unceasingly, and with a very limited staff, in evacuating casualties from the wadi and from the start line.

It was not possible, owing to the darkness of the night and possible loss of direction to move the RAP from the line of the wadi. With a complete disregard for his own personal safety and showing gallantry of a high order, Capt. Lamb completely restored the situation. It was his presence and words of encouragement to stragglers and wounded that gave inspiration to the men with whom he came into contact in the line of the wadi now subject to very heavy artillery and mortar fire.

Throughout the night the powers of leadership shown by Capt. Lamb were of an exceedingly high order. The manner in which he completely restored a situation which showed signs of losing control at a vital time of the operation was exemplary and he quickly played a telling part in the successful advance and assault of the Battalion onto Point 156

17 Infantry Brigade War Diary
30 Jan 44 – 0615
6 Seaforths report one Company in and around Cemetery. One Company 784963 [Point 172].

6 Seaforth Highlanders War Diary
30 Jan 44 – 0615
'B' Company reported on objective having encountered little opposition. Patrol from 'A' Company went to 780973 where three enemy were seen in area Point 165, 785965.

'B' Company went to Spur Point 141 found it unoccupied and returned with enemy documents.

17 Infantry Brigade War Diary
30 Jan 44 – 0620
6 Seaforths report mines at 783969 [Santa Maria Road, North of Cemetery]. Pioneers checking road.

6 Seaforth Highlanders War Diary
30 Jan 44 – 0630
Troop of 'A' Squadron 16/5 Lancers [Sherman tanks] has one tank under command in position in Cemetery area. One tank damaged by mine.

2 Northants War Diary
30 Jan 44 – 0630
Whole Battalion dug in on objectives. 'A' Company announced they had taken approx. 30 POWs, most of POWs thoroughly demoralised by our shelling of Point 156.

30 Jan 44 – 0645
Tied up defence of Point 156. Both Machine Gun Platoons of 7 Cheshires were in position and able to cover likely enemy counterattack approaches.

'A' Squadron 16/5 Lancers War Diary
30 Jan 44 – 0645

The Troop arrived at the Cemetery. The second tank [Troop Leader's] went up on a mine and Trooper Munton was wounded in the stomach. Unfortunately, this tank completely blocked the road for another tank to get by it or for the leading tank to get back. The relief Scout car for the Second in Command came up and went past the mined tank, followed by a carrier, which also went up on a mine, and completely blocked the road. The Armoured Recovery Vehicle arrived shortly afterwards and started to remove the mined tank. Meanwhile the Second in Command returned from his recce and reported that there were no suitable positions for '1' Troop on the track. The Commanding Officer arrived at about this time having walked up from camp and looked round the positions. The two rear tanks of '2' Troop were able to fire from the road on to Point 156 very well and could therefore carry out the job originally intended for '1' Troop. The Sappers, which the Squadron Leader had sent up, arrived swept the road and reported it clear.

6 Seaforth Highlanders War Diary
30 Jan 44 – 0645
One Carrier damaged by mine in attempting to evacuate casualty from damaged tank. Driver wounded and subsequently died. Intermittent shelling of Battalion area during day.

17 Infantry Brigade War Diary
30 Jan 44 – 0650
2 Northants report Point 156 finally clear of enemy.

56 Infantry Division War Diary
30 Jan 44 – 0650
5 Infantry Division report: Guards did not clear up objectives properly. 2 Northants have captured Point 156 and 6 Seaforths are in same area – taken 25 Prisoners of War including one Officer.

52 Anti-Tank Regiment Royal Artillery War Diary
30 Jan 44 – 0700
Two 6 Pounders from 6 Seaforths sent up to Cemetery.

92 Field Regiment Royal Artillery War Diary
30 Jan 44 – 0700
HQ Royal Artillery report Guards not requiring fire on target. 6 Seaforths around Cemetery with Company areas 784963, 787966. Own tanks now moving toward Cemetery area. 15 Prisoners of War taken; all from 361 Grenadier Regiment 90 Light Division. No further news from Guards, apparently on objectives as fire cancelled.

17 Infantry Brigade War Diary
30 Jan 44 – 0720
One tank blown up by mine near Cemetery. Road now being cleared.

30 Jan 44 – 0730
6 Seaforths report no enemy bodies or equipment found in Cemetery. Estimated casualties – one killed, one wounded. 2 Northants report HQ established at 775963 [Point 156, Monte Natale].

Nicolson, Capt. Nigel, *The Grenadier Guards in the War of 1939-1945, Volume II*
30 Jan 44
'After many hours of searching, No. 2 Company [Capt. M.W. Grazebrook, MC], linked up with No. 4 Company [Major H.C. Hanbury], just as dawn was breaking, and found that they had ten minutes in which to form up for the attack. An artillery barrage came down at exactly the right place and time, and the two Companies surged up the hill together as soon as the shell fire had ceased. It was a very successful attack, in which Lieuts. V.E. Naylor-Leyland and Lt. R.O.H. Crewdson took leading parts. They cleared the hill in hand-to-hand fighting, taking thirty-seven prisoners. Meanwhile on the other flank, Nos. 1 and 3 Companies had also joined forces, and by much the same methods, led by Lieuts. H.W. Freeman-Attwood and the Master of Saltoun, they captured the other hill. The total number of prisoners was seventy-eight, and twelve German machine-guns were taken in addition. On our own side thirty-five Grenadiers were killed and one hundred and thirteen wounded. Among them were Lieut. O.M. Sainsbury, who was killed, and Major Hanbury, Capt. Grazebrook and Lieut. Crewdson, who were all wounded, the last named for the second time that day.'

6 Grenadier Guards War Diary
30 Jan 44 – 0730
It was not until 0730 that '1' and '3' Companies reported objective completely in their hands although it had been reached many hours before. At about the same time 3

Coldstreams report that our '2' Company had obviously taken its objective and quite a number of prisoners. Lt. O.M. Sainsbury was reported killed in the attack.

X (BR) Corps History
30 Jan 44 – 0730
201 Guards Brigade began its attack on 29 Jan 44 and met stiff opposition on its right flank, where the two forward Companies of 6 Grenadier Guards were still held up short of their objectives on 30 Jan 44 at 0115. A third Company was then sent to work its way around from the North, and by 30 Jan 44 – 0730, the enemy position had been turned. On the left 3 Coldstream Guards advanced quickly against light opposition, securing its objectives, and beating off an enemy counterattack during the night.

17 Infantry Brigade War Diary
30 Jan 44 – 0740
6 Seaforths patrol saw enemy on East side of road in the area of Point 165, but no enemy encountered on the way. Road blown at 781967 [just North of Cemetery], but enemy diversion on the East side passable to tanks and, with work, to vehicles. 2 Northants report they have four machine guns in position with both the left flank and the centre Companies.

1 York & Lancs. War Diary
30 Jan 44 – 0800
Message received from 17 Infantry Brigade as follows: 3 Coldstream Guards and 6 Grenadier Guards both on objectives. 6 Seaforths one Company right on Grigg Hill, 786967 and one Company in Cemetery area with two anti-tank guns in position. One tank in position, one tank blown up by mine and two waiting to go up. 2 Northants on position Point 156. One Company left with four machine guns. One Company on feature with four machine guns and one Platoon forward with two machine guns. They suffered 30 casualties but took 30 prisoners [90 Panzer Grenadiers]. Passwords for tonight 'Mother' and 'Goose'.

'A' Co. 2 Northants had taken Monte Natale. There was hand to hand fighting, so another Company was put in to restore the situation. There were 150 Germans on the reverse slopes of Monte Natale and 60 bodies were recovered. 3 Coldstream Guards and 6 Grenadier Guards on objectives and gave support.

38 Field Company Royal Engineers War Diary
30 Jan 44 – 0800
Attack on Monte Natale successful – no mines encountered. Detachment of Royal Engineers returned to Company lines. One Section mine-swept the main road to 100 yards short of the Cemetery 781960 lifting five mines. Tellermines No. 3 with Mark 1 fuses were found.

201 Guards Brigade War Diary
30 Jan 44 – 0820
68 Prisoners of War counted from '5' & '7' Companies, 267 Grenadier Regiment. The enemy laid a smoke screen between Monte Natale and Tremensuoli followed by a counterattack on Monte Natale from the North. This was easily dealt with.

92 Field Regiment Royal Artillery War Diary

30 Jan 44 – 0855

Message from HQ Royal Artillery. No shooting area of road from Cemetery to Santa Maria Infante. Patrol of 6 Seaforths now going out. Batteries informed.

52 Anti-Tank Regiment Royal Artillery War Diary

30 Jan 44 – 0900

Battery Commander made a recce of Point 156. No suitable gun positions found.

3 Coldstream Guards War Diary

30 Jan 44 – 0900

Intermittent gun and mortar fire during the morning. 74 Prisoners were brought in from 267 Panzer Grenadier Regiment and 171 Reinforcement Regiment. Their morale seemed high, and at the same time did not seem unduly depressed at the prospect of captivity. They gave us a large amount of valuable information.

6 Grenadier Guards War Diary

30 Jan 44 – 0900

The Battalion had captured 68 prisoners with the number still escalating.

6 Seaforth Highlanders War Diary

30 Jan 44 – 0935

'B' Company reported five enemy with machine gun at 778975 [1km North of Point 156, Monte Natale]. At same time a patrol reported from 2 Northants; enemy in square 7797 moving East along 100 contour & turning Southeast towards the Cemetery. This German Patrol consisted of six men together and two men detached at the rear. Same patrol was also reported on reverse slope at 768977 which was occupied by the enemy.

2 Northants War Diary

30 Jan 44 – 0945

Patrol to Rio Perligia returned reporting an enemy patrol moving East along 100 contour in square 7796. No movement seen on Rio Perligia ridge. Company, 6 Seaforths warned us of this enemy patrol.

'A' Squadron 16/5 Lancers War Diary

30 Jan 44 – 1000

The Armoured Recovery Vehicle whose crew had done a magnificent job, cleared the road and towed the tank away. Unfortunately, the Engineers had missed a mine and the relief scout car belonging to 17 Infantry Brigade HQ went up as it was turning around. The driver unfortunately was wounded. The above shows the difficulty of detecting mines when there is a lot of metal about, as arrangements had been made for the road and verges to be swept before the tanks went up the road. The leading tank [Sgt Barker] was in a position by the Cemetery to deal with any enemy counterattack coming down the road. The general situation at this point may be of some interest. 6 Seaforths on the right were in position on the Southern end of Spur Point 141 with one Company forward astride the road and just forward of the Cemetery, with 2 Northants on Point

156 on the left running somewhat back from the Cemetery. 2 Troop was confined to the road and under command 6 Seaforths. Close co-operation was difficult for several reasons – (i) the infantry was not used to operating with tanks. (ii) The Company of 6 Seaforths turned out not to be the one with whom we had been instructed to plan before the attack and knew nothing about us. (iii) We only had communications with 2 Northants on our left through 17 Infantry Brigade HQ. Our leading tanks sat just short of Cemetery corner prepared (i) to blow up any enemy tank which nosed round it, (ii) to assist the infantry if any enemy counterattack penetrated their Forward Defence Lines. Sgt Barker commanding the leading tank did very well, being on his feet by the corner all day, watching out for any attack by enemy armour or infantry. This he did, although the enemy were shelling and mortaring Cemetery corner off and on throughout the day.

2 Cameronians War Diary
30 Jan 44 – 1000
CO. attended the 'O' Group conference. Orders were given for the 17 Infantry Brigade attack to seize and hold the Bulgarini – Monte Bracchi ridge. 2 Cameronians were to attack on the left and seize Bulgarini. 2 Inniskillings were to attack and seize Monte Bracchi on the right and 2 Wiltshires to remain in reserve in Tufo. 2 Wiltshires to relieve 2 Cameronians during the night 30-31 Jan 44. 'D' Day dependent on when 56 Infantry Division on the right captured Damiano feature.

17 Infantry Brigade War Diary
30 Jan 44 – 1005
16/5 Lancers report 'Dingo' scout car borrowed from Brigade HQ blown up by mine on road 780967.

6 Seaforth Highlanders War Diary
30 Jan 44 – 1015
Enemy patrol engaged by 4.2 mortars of 17 Infantry Brigade Support Company. Observation Post report on this shoot: enemy patrol eliminated.

7 Cheshires War Diary
30 Jan 44 – 1030
Enemy machine gun post about 778975 engaged by '4' Platoon. Post neutralised – believed direct hit.

92 Field Regiment Royal Artillery War Diary
30 Jan 44 – 1030
467 Battery Commander gives location of 6 Seaforths Company areas 786967 and 781965, with patrols to Point 165, 783979 [1,200m directly North of the Cemetery]. 2 Northants Company areas Point 156, 755966 and 774966 with patrols to 777966.

6 Seaforth Highlanders War Diary
30 Jan 44 – 1140
'B' Company had four casualties due to enemy shelling.

7 Cheshires War Diary
30 Jan 44 – 1150
'A' Company fired by observation on enemy Observation Post and Motor Machine Gun post at 782971 [Santa Maria Road, 600m North of Cemetery].

5 Infantry Division History
30 Jan 44
Report: 'C' and 'D' Companies of 2 Northants ran into enemy defensive fire, while 'A' Company to their right was forming up for the final assault on the North-West end of the feature [Point 156, Monte Natale]. '8' Platoon of this Company led by Lieutenant A.C. Garner, moving down a river to take a smaller hill, met an enemy party advancing to counterattack the Battalion. Resolute action, in the form of an old-fashioned charge, gave the enemy no chance. They fled, leaving '8' Platoon with twelve prisoners and two machine guns, and 'B' Company in possession of the Western edge of the feature.

2 Northants Citation: Military Cross for Lieutenant A.C. Garner
Lieut. Garner commanded 8 Platoon of 'A' Company on the night 29-30 Jan 44 when 2 Northants were ordered to capture Point 156, the role of 'A' Company being to assault the western slopes of the feature and to protect the left flank. The Platoon objective set Lt. Garner was a ridge running East and West down the slopes of Point 156. This necessitated cool and skilful leadership to ensure this ridge was safely in our hands before daylight. The going was difficult.

Leading his Platoon with great skill down these slopes Lt. A.C. Garner met a Section of the enemy advancing up the slopes. He at once led the charge towards the enemy, and 12 Germans were made prisoners of war.

Capt. R.C. Road, Camp Commandant HQ. 5 Infantry Division, prefers to take his dinner in the open, sitting on an upturned box outside the cookhouse. Minturno area, 30 Jan 44 (Photo 2 AFPU Sgt. Weber, TNA 11639)

Lt. Garner then began to re-organise on his objective, and two enemy machine gun posts were successfully 'mopped up.'

At 1200 hours on 30 Jan 44, Lt. Garner was ordered to lead a patrol to discover if any enemy were occupying the wadi which ran at the foot of Point 156. He crossed the wadi and led his patrol a further 1,000 yards towards the enemy positions. He lay up and by his careful observation was able to bring back most valuable information that no enemy were forming up to counterattack on the left and most sensitive flank of Point 156.

Throughout the complete operation which lasted for 72 hours, and which entailed the seizing and holding of Point 156, Lt. Garner displayed powers of leadership of a high order. His Platoon position was continually subjected to heavy and accurate shell and mortar fire, throughout the three days. But by his very skilful leadership and powers of command, Lt. Garner was responsible, not only for his Platoon's very successful attack on to his objectives, but also for a thorough and complete re-organisation to resist any enemy counterattack.

15 Infantry Brigade War Diary
30 Jan 44 – 1300
2 Northants attack on Point 156 and Monte Natale had gone well on the previous night but the programme of reliefs within the Division was revised considerably. A decision about the role of 1 Green Howards and the change of command from 17 Infantry Brigade to 15 Infantry Brigade was decided on. It was then decided that 1 Green Howards should relieve 6 Seaforths who had established themselves in the Cemetery and in the area to the West of this (7896) while 15 Infantry Brigade would take over command of 17 Infantry Brigade's sector the same night.

2 Northants War Diary
30 Jan 44 – 1315
Enemy counterattack reported forming up. 'B' Company ordered to 'stand to'. '12' Platoon ordered to move in reserve behind 'C' Company on Point 156. '12' Platoon under command Lieut. S.C. Hamer MC advanced with fixed bayonets to end of Point 156 spur and restored position.

17 Infantry Brigade War Diary
30 Jan 44 – 1315
2 Northants report counterattack forming up against them. Direct Fire tasks to be fired at slow rate until further orders.

30 Jan 44 – 1330
2 Northants report situation confused. Counterattack appears concentrated on 'C' Company and the Platoon on the forward slopes is in difficulties, but no enemy has appeared over the ridge and Point 156 is still secure. One Platoon of 'B' Company (Reserve) ready for counterattack. No tanks seen. Direct Fires to be intensified.

2 Cameronians War Diary
30 Jan 44 – 1330
The CO. issued orders for the Battalion attack on Bulgarini ridge.

7 Cheshires War Diary
30 Jan 44 – 1335
Instructions received to engage target at 777976 [1km North of Point 156]. '3' Platoon put on to this and commenced firing.

2 Cameronians War Diary
30 Jan 44 – 1400
Information was received from Brigade HQ that the attack was postponed indefinitely as 56 Infantry Division had to move back to previously arranged positions. 2 Wiltshires were not now to relieve 2 Cameronians. Tufo and Point 201 were heavily shelled.

17 Infantry Brigade War Diary
30 Jan 44 – 1415
2 Northants report situation in hand. Forward Platoon was temporarily overrun, but position restored by a Platoon of 'B' Company.

30 Jan 44 – 1430
6 Seaforths report heavy shelling of Cemetery and ask if it is possible for casualties to be evacuated by day. Arrangements made with Advance Dressing Station to provide extra stretcher bearers for the purpose.

'A' Squadron 16/5 Lancers War Diary
30 Jan 44 – 1430
6 Seaforths six pounder anti-tank gun in position just forward of Cemetery corner was knocked out by a direct hit and the crew came back, as also did the forward infantry Platoon owing to the heavy shell fire on their position. Sgt Barker hearing that a 6 Seaforths Officer was lying out in front badly wounded got hold of two 6 Seaforths and went out with a stretcher and brought him in. His coolness and command of the situation at this time was exceptionally good. As soon as darkness fell '2' Troop was withdrawn back to harbour. '1' Troop being left in position at Minturno. During the day Sgt. Ritchie's tank was seen burnt out on the road about 300 yards beyond Cemetery Corner.

5 Infantry Division History
30 Jan 44 – 1430
The counterattack came in on 'C' Company of 2 Northants at 1330. For half an hour previously, the enemy had been seen coming up in strength and the forward Platoon 14 of 'C' Company was heavily shelled. The Division and Corps Artillery rose to the occasion, but the German gunners put down a very neat box barrage round the attack to isolate it from a well sited Section of 7 Cheshire machine guns and the left half of 14 Platoon. By sheer weight of numbers, the Platoon was overwhelmed, but the enemy's success was short lived. 12 Platoon of 'B' Company [Lieutenant Hamer] counterattacked and restored the position by 1430. There was no more trouble that day.

2 Northants Citation: Bar to Military Cross for Lieut. S.C. Hamer
Lieut. Hamer, MC, commanding 12 Platoon, 'B' Company, 2 Northants was at 1000 hours 30 January 1944 ordered to clear up the situation on Point 156 onto which

the enemy had launched a counterattack and had succeeded in establishing himself, following the capture of this dominating feature by the Battalion the previous night.

The ground from Lieut. Hamer's forming up place to Point 156 was incredibly open, and subject to very heavy and fully accurate mortar and shell fire. With great determination and at the head of his Platoon, Lt. Hamer led his men forward. The Germans who had managed to establish themselves on the crest of Point 156 were driven off at the point of Lt. Hamer's Thompson Sub Machine Gun.

Lt. Hamer at once began to re-organise on the feature, and to re-organise those men which remained of the leading Platoon of 'C' Company who had been overrun by the counterattack.

Due to Lt. Hamer's own personal example, his coolness and cheerfulness under difficult conditions, the men of his Platoon were able to re-organise, and later in the same afternoon to drive off a second enemy counterattack launched at this particularly bare and exposed part of the Point 156 feature.

Throughout the 36 hours which Lt. Hamer spent on Point 156, a Point very well and very accurately registered by enemy artillery his powers of leadership and command, and his complete disregard for his own personal safety under periods of very heavy shell fire, were a magnificent inspiration to all the men under his command and it was so very largely due to his fearless example, and to his determination, that throughout the period the Battalion spent on Monte Natale, this dominating feature of Point 156 always remained in the possession of 2 Northants.

1 York & Lancs. War Diary
30 Jan 44 – 1435
Message received from 17 Infantry Brigade that 2 Northants on Point 156. Right Company 6 Grenadier Guards attacked. Hand to hand fighting on Point 156. 2 Northants sent in another Company which restored the situation.

17 Infantry Brigade War Diary
30 Jan 44 – 1450
2 Northants report position completely restored on Point 156. No enemy dead or wounded found. Tanks in Cemetery area report smoke being put down about 600 yards to their right front. Smoke is drifting across their front from East to West.

30 Jan 44 – 1500
16/5 Lancers report unable to find suitable position for their Troop in 2 Northants area. Have not yet contacted Commanding Officer 2 Northants.

201 Guards Brigade War Diary
30 Jan 44 – 1500
42 Field Company Royal Engineers lifted the 'S' minefield laid in front of 6 Grenadier Guards. 2 Scots Guards withdrew its Company from Point 141, Monte Del Duca.

1 Green Howards War Diary
30 Jan 44 – 1500
Battalion ordered to take over from 6 Seaforths after dark.

1 York & Lancs. War Diary
30 Jan 44 – 1510
After enemy counterattack on Point 156 had been beaten off, Platoon of 'C' Company moved in to relieve 2 Scots Guards on Point 141, Monte Del Duca, 782959.

2 Northants War Diary
30 Jan 44 – 1530
Companies 'stood down', few Germans, if any, having reached Point 156.

7 Cheshires War Diary
30 Jan 44 – 1600
Instructions received that Company will be relieved tonight by 15 Infantry Brigade Support Company. It is noted that a total of 861 (mortar) rounds have been fired in the last 24 hours and in four hours actual firing time – a much larger task than the Company has ever carried out before. All ranks have worked well, and results have been most encouraging. 6 Seaforths report that result of this morning's shoot on enemy machine gun post five enemy killed and machine gun destroyed.

141 Field Ambulance War Diary
30 Jan 44 – 1600
Eight Sappers who had been attached to 2 Northants previous day returned to Medical Post. 12 Sappers sent up to Advanced Dressing Station from 42 Field Company. Approx. 65 battle casualties passed through 141 Field Ambulance since midnight.

6 Grenadier Guards War Diary
30 Jan 44 – 1615
Counterattack was reported coming in on '2' Company at 1315. Excellent shooting by the gunners who put down tremendous fire helped us.

The counterattack beaten off by 1615. Lt. R.P. Parr was killed and two Company Commanders wounded, Major H.C. Hanbury MC and Captain M.W. Grazebrook. By this time, '1' and '3' Companies had amalgamated and were put under command of Major E. Penn and '2' and '4' Companies under command of Captain Withins.

Capt. Nigel Nicolson, *The Grenadier Guards in the War of 1939-1945, Volume II*
30 Jan 44
'The Germans did not fail to launch their usual counterattack during the afternoon. It was beaten off by a combination of artillery fire and close shooting by the Grenadiers. When the gun barrels grew too hot for further firing a fighting patrol was led to the farther ridge by Lieut. R.P. Parr and there, he too, after successfully beating back the Germans was killed. "We managed to keep them off", wrote Capt. M.W. Grazebrook with masterly understatement, "as it is very boring to have to take a thing like that twice."'

2 Northants War Diary
30 Jan 44 – 1630
Orders: Patrols in night of 30-31 Jan 44: Fighting patrol to 766973, strength One Officer, 10 Other Ranks to try and bag prisoner.

Counterattack on Point 156 now clarified. The Platoon Commander of the Platoon on the end of Point 156 spur was at Company HQ when the attack came in. By the time he had returned to his Platoon HQ the counterattack had reached the forward slopes of Point 156 and taken 18 men of 14 Platoon Prisoner of War. Remaining troops were unable to fire for fear of hitting their own troops.

2 Northants Citation: Military Cross for Captain E.W. Kitchin
On the night of 29/30 January 1944 'C' Company of the Northants Regiment was ordered to capture Point 156, the dominating feature of M. Natale. Hardly had the Company crossed the start line, some 1000 yards from the objective when the Company Commander was wounded.

Captain Kitchin at once took control and command of the Company. He personally led and encouraged his men up to the top of Point 156. The assault had to be made up very stiff and difficult 'going' owing to the high terrace banks. 'C' Company, once they had recovered from their original disorganisation were immediately fired by a determination to reach the top.

During their assault, the Company encountered very heavy and accurate mortar fire from the enemy defensive fire which fell across the line of advance. At 1015 hours the following morning the enemy launched a counterattack against the Point 156 feature. Due to the calmness and determination of Captain Kitchin in the face of very heavy and concentrated enemy shell and mortar fire and his own personal example of leadership, 'C' Company and one reserve Platoon were able to completely restore the position.

At 1620 hours the enemy launched a second counterattack. The determination with which Captain Kitchin had inspired his two Platoons and the coolness under heavy fire which he displayed, saw the enemy again driven off.

The high powers of leadership displayed throughout the capture and re-organisation on Point 156 on M. Natale by Capt. Kitchin were an inspiration to all ranks of his Co., sadly depleted by casualties. His coolness under fire, his determination to reach his objective and his personal example throughout the complete operation were without any shadow of doubt, largely responsible for the successful seizing and holding of M. Natale.

2 Cameronians War Diary
30 Jan 44 – 1700
6 Seaforths to relieve 2 Cameronians tonight who will in turn relieve 2 Wiltshires.

6 Seaforth Highlanders War Diary
30 Jan 44 – 1800
1 Green Howards start taking over our positions.

1 York & Lancs. War Diary
30 Jan 44 – 1845
Relief of one Platoon of 'C' Company on Point 141, Monte Del Duca, by 'D' Company completed. Hot meals and tomorrow's rations brought up for the Battalion.

1 Green Howards War Diary
30 Jan 44 – 1920
Battalion HQ established in house 787961.

6 Seaforth Highlanders War Diary
30 Jan 44 – 2000
Battalion arrive in new area 8096 on West side of Tufo. Battalion HQ established in house 799962. Two Companies move into position on Point 201 and one Company on Point 151 square 7996. Battalion comes under command of 13 Infantry Brigade.

1 Green Howards War Diary
30 Jan 44 – 2015
Relief of 6 Seaforths complete. Company areas 'A' 783964, 'B' 787966, 'C' 787964, 'D' area Cemetery 781967. Local covering patrol during night.

2 Cameronians War Diary
30 Jan 44 – 2330
'A', 'C', 'D', Companies were relieved by 6 Seaforths without incident.

1 York & Lancs. War Diary
30 Jan 44 – 2340
'D' Company report a 'neberwerfur' gun firing on Tremensuoli. General line of direction East to West Point 141 to Tremensuoli. Enemy shelling during the night was very slight, only about 15-20 shells falling. None in the Battalion area. The night was very dark and seemed warmer.

The Battalion came under command of 15 Infantry Brigade who had relieved 17 Infantry Brigade.

3 Coldstream Guards War Diary
30 Jan 44 – 2400
The total casualties whilst the Battalion was in the forward area were: 20 Other Ranks killed, seven Other Ranks died of wounds, three Officers wounded, and 83 Other Ranks wounded.

2 Wiltshires War Diary
30 Jan 44
Battalion is to go out of the line for a rest. In the evening Battalion leaves Tufo for Casanova. Billets in houses in the town reasonably comfortable.

6 Grenadier Guards War Diary
30 Jan 44
A Platoon of reinforcements under Lt. Hollingsworth was sent up to strengthen '2' and '4' Companies.

X (BR) Corps
30 Jan 44

241

Report: 17 Infantry Brigade met little opposition, 2 Northants reached Monte Natale within four hours, and at the same time 6 Seaforths occupied the Cemetery 781966, so as to secure the Brigade's right flank. Both Brigades consolidated rapidly and broke up a number of enemy counterattacks that took place during the afternoon. These were mostly only in Company strength, indicating the extent to which German reserves in this sector had been thinned out since the violent battles of 20-22 Jan 44.

Fifth Army ordered X (BR) Corps to supply an extra Brigade for VI (US) Corps in the Anzio bridgehead as soon as possible. 168 Infantry Brigade who were then resting were nominated to move. With the impending removal of this Brigade, it was necessary for X (BR) Corps to postpone for some days plans for a further substantial offensive. The total of prisoners of war captured by X (BR) Corps since 17 Jan 44 reached 1070.

2 Scots Guards War Diary
30 Jan 44
Coldstream Guards having endured a long and unpleasant spell at Tremensuoli exchanged positions with this Battalion after dark last night, in collaboration of 6 Grenadiers on their right, who took 80 prisoners. They had carried out a successful advance of about 700 yards. The positions taken over were located with two companies on the forward slopes, West and below the village, with the reserve Company and Battalion HQ actually in it. 'F' Company were given the reserve position; 'G' Company and Right Flank were forward in the appropriate order, the Carrier Platoon were on the left, a short distance down the road to Minturno. Battalion HQ was in a relatively safe but very inhospitable downstairs room, in a house in the centre of the town. It opened onto a narrow street, protected on the enemy side by two rows of three storey houses, which it was hoped would stop shells coming in straight and were also high enough to catch most mortar bombs on their way. These houses which were on the forward edge of the town overlooking the Company positions, with the ground sloping down to Scauri and Formia. They gave excellent observation, and the Intelligence Section kept our post permanently manned, the gunners used another house.

Capt. Nigel Nicolson, *The Grenadier Guards in the War of 1939-1945, Volume II* '
Jan 44
'A Grenadier Officer gives a good idea of the conditions that the Guards Brigade were fighting in:

"A village street is like a row of decayed teeth. In the remains of one house, a gun team have slung a tarpaulin over the roofless walls, and they are cooking their dinner with the sticks of furniture which remain. In the next house, where only the cellar is still intact, a wretched peasant family looks up at you from the earthen floor, crouching on their haunches all day long, and refusing to leave; from any house which has a few rooms fairly water-tight there will come a glow of hurricane lamps, the buzz of telephones and officers running to and fro. Having been obliged to shell this village, and then impose ourselves piecemeal on what remains of it, one feels almost ashamed of this constant traffic of heavy lorries which is steadily grinding the decent civilian life out of the place – this constant passage of khaki, which is probably all these people have known and will ever know of the English. And when the battle passes it will be exhilarating for us, but it will mean that every village we reach will be reduced to the same state.

Perhaps the Italian civilians suffered more than any. The war which the armies had been making and following for years would suddenly burst upon them in the middle of an afternoon. The familiar names of their villages and little towns would for the space of a few hours be circled on the maps of rival commanders, mispronounced upon a score of wirelesses, lifted from obscurity into the communiques which the world would read the next day. A sloping field, which to the farmer had merely been an awkward piece of ground to plough, would be reconnoitred by a German subaltern, occupied by a tired dozen of his men, shelled, attacked, and then captured, leaving behind strips of jagged metal, and two humps, perhaps beneath a rough, wooden cross. The armies could have no respect for private property. They imposed themselves upon the country like a plague of locusts. No door was closed to them and while they brought with them every resource necessary for life and battle, the peasants in their own homes had often so little that they would dig up the empty army ration tins for scraps of food. When they were wounded (being too inexperienced to judge the risk they ran from the feathery shuffle of a falling mortar bomb), they had no other recourse than to crawl to Allied aid posts for their charity and skill. Sometimes they would take to the mountain roads, walking with bundles on their heads through the dust and look up with smiles at the troop carriers. In spite of all their hardships, the Italians remained well disposed to their liberators, quite unaffected by the German propaganda posters which represented us as rapacious brutes, mostly black. They would come forward to meet the leading troops with a basket of cherries, a bottle of wine, or a clutch of eggs in a straw hat. For them our arrival meant the end of the war. An instance of this attitude stands out in the mind of one Grenadier. His jeep happened to be the first to enter a hill-top village bypassed by the main advance. As he drove into the little piazza he was puzzled to see the children run screaming to their mother's aprons. This had never happened before. And the explanation? The children thought that he was a German officer returning to reoccupy the village. After making himself known and taking a glass of wine with the priest and mayor, he came out to find his jeep festooned with country flowers and the children dancing around it."'

Chapter 16

31 January 1944 – Enemy Counterattack

5 Infantry Division History
31 Jan 44
The enemy no longer shelled the river crossing with much vigour, his valuable ammunition being needed in the Monte Natale area where he kept up both mortaring and shelling consistently.

15 Infantry Brigade War Diary
31 Jan 44
During the night patrolling was only local and the only contact made was by 2 Northants whose standing patrol, which was on the forward edge of Monte Natale, met a small enemy patrol. Little shelling occurred.

16/5 Lancers War Diary
31 Jan 44
At first light '1' Troop moved up to the area of the Cemetery. During the night Lt. Holland had contacted 1 Green Howards Company, who had taken over from 6 Seaforths on the right. On arrival at the Cemetery, he contacted the Company Commander and established communication with an 18-radio set (strapped to the back of his tank), with that Company.

2 Cameronians War Diary
31 Jan 44 – 0100
The relief of 2 Wiltshires was completed without incident. 'A' & 'C' Companies were now in reserve positions behind Tufo at 802960 and 804958, respectively. 'D' Company was in position at the East end of Tufo with 'B' Company engaged at the West end. Battalion HQ remained in Tufo. The Battalion was now in reserve but prepared to counterattack or assist 6 Seaforths.

1 Green Howards War Diary
31 Jan 44 – 0600
Observation Posts established at Point 172 and at Spur Point 141.

15 Infantry Brigade War Diary
31 Jan 44 – 1000
2 Northants suspected the enemy of preparing to counterattack as there were signs of movement on Point 165. 4.2-inch mortars accordingly engaged for five minutes.

52 Anti-Tank Regiment Royal Artillery War Diary
31 Jan 44 – 1000
207 Battery: 2 Northants on Point 156 asked for anti-tank guns to cover their rear as enemy tanks used that approach on their last counterattack. Battery Commander went up to recce positions, found unsuitable for 17 Pounders but one 6 Pounder position at 780965 [Aid Post]. 2 Northants decided to occupy it at night.

1 York & Lancs. War Diary
31 Jan 44 – 1020
Heavy shelling of area commenced, both by 88mm and guns of larger calibre, about 25 shells falling in area. One man wounded.

31 Jan 44 – 1115
Shelling slackened. Artillery Observation Post on Point 172 reports guns firing from behind Bulgarini 7898 on bearing of 360-degree grid.

2 Northants War Diary
31 Jan 44 – 1455
Recce patrol left from 772966 [300m West of Point 156] under command Lieut. A. C. Garner along track running North-West along spur and down stream bed North-West of Point 156 at 1000. Patrol crossed stream and laid up. Patrol Commander went forward alone in scrub 200 yards Southeast of buildings at 767973. No movement seen to North. Mortar heard firing from area North part of 7596. Dugouts seen at 756970. The patrol returned to base at 1230.

Recce patrol one officer and eight Other Ranks left from 778965, Point 156, Monte Natale, and moved North-West into Rio Perlata wadi. Patrol moved up under command Lt. Gregory to 100 contour at 774975. Patrol then moved North-East across wadi being sniped at from house South of Point 165. Patrol moved back into wadi and was mortared from Colle San Martino area. Patrol saw no enemy in Rio Perlata wadi and returned without casualties at 1455.

158 Field Ambulance War Diary
31 Jan 44 – 1600
Casualties slackening off. Total to 1600 was only 63. 'B' Company attached to 15 Infantry Brigade moving up to Advanced Dressing Station, 783952.

Total casualties for period 25-31 January 1944
Casualties (Battle)   440
            (Sick)   <u>169</u>
      Total   <u>609</u>

2 Cameronians War Diary
31 Jan 44 – 1605
CO. held an 'O' Group conference at Tufo. The Battalion now at three hours-notice to cross the Start Line and Companies were placed at one hours-notice to leave Tufo.

2 Northants War Diary
31 Jan 44 – 1620
'B' Company ordered to 'stand to'. In first stages of counterattack enemy machine gun fire came on to forward positions from area road at 780970 [Santa Maria Road 500m North of Cemetery]. Direct Fire was fired by 3-inch Mortars. Enemy were seen moving South-East through trees towards Point 156 and engaged with light machine guns.

'A' Squadron 16/5 Lancers War Diary
31 Jan 44 – 1620
In the evening '3' Troop moved out to 6 Grenadier Guards and took up a position on a 'Y' road just South-East of Tremensuoli. These positions were taken over from 40 Royal Tank Regiment. That night Lt. Holland went out on patrol to Sgt. Ritchie's tank to discover what he could do. The patrol consisted of an Officer of 1 Green Howards and a few men. Lt. Holland managed to identify the body of Trooper Youster but could find no sign of anybody else. He did not climb on to the tank owing to it being a very bright moonlit night and the danger of booby traps. The tank had been hit twice by a 75mm by the co-driver's compartment. There was a dead German lying nearby; it is rather surprising that the Germans had made no effort to bury Trooper Youster or their own man, although they may have been behind their lines for several days. On the return from the patrol the 1 Green Howards Officer turned to Lt. Holland and said, 'Thank God, my last patrol.' '4' and '1' Troops returned to camp that evening and '2' Troop moved to Minturno.

15 Infantry Brigade War Diary
31 Jan 44 – 1630
2 Northants reported considerable machine gun fire on their left front and called for Direct Fire which was put down. Later a small infantry attack came in from the North and Direct Fire was again called for. The attack was apparently broken up and a patrol sent out immediately afterwards to see whether the enemy were still active and found about 30 dead Germans.

1 York & Lancs. War Diary
31 Jan 44 – 1630
Lieutenant Colonel R.F. Wilson left the Battalion and command was taken over by Lieutenant Colonel R.J.A. Kaulback

[Both the Brigade Commander and the Battalion Commander in charge of the original attack on Monte Natale had now been replaced! Lieutenant Geoffrey Winter said that when he visited Brigade HQ just after 1 York & Lancs. had been attacked and forced off Monte Natale there was an air of panic and chaos, for the fear was that the Germans would break through back to the River Garigliano and the entire advance by the British would be brought to a halt.]

2 Northants War Diary
31 Jan 44 – 1645
Some of the Direct Fire fell short into the area of a 'A' Company platoon. Some casualties (one killed and six wounded) were sustained. Enemy did not succeed in setting foot on

Point 156. The Direct Fire was stopped, and the situation quietened down allowing inter platoon reliefs to continue.

5 Infantry Division History
31 Jan 44
From first light onwards, '12' Platoon, 2 Northants, was heavily shelled on its spur position. A desperate counterattack in the afternoon was promptly despatched by well controlled small arms fire and the familiar artillery 'wall of steel'. A patrol sent out in the evening counted over sixty bodies caught in the first Direct Fire.

92 Field Regiment Royal Artillery War Diary
31 Jan 44 – 1725
Message from HQ Royal Artillery. Further patrols tonight: 2 Northants to go out at 1900 to area 772966 to spur-772980. At the same time 1 Green Howards were to send a fighting patrol to Point 165, 782978 – road junction – Santa Maria Infante. Between 1930 and 0200 6 Seaforths were to go from Tufo to Bulgarini. Between 1730 and 2100 2 Cameronians were to go to Tufo – Point 156 – road junction 804975. Artillery Batteries have been informed not to fire in these areas at these times.

5 Infantry Division War Diary
31 Jan 44 – 1730
A counterattack on 2 Northants on Point 156 was driven off by small arms fire. Direct Fire put down on the enemy as they withdrew is believed to have killed 20-30 of them; a follow up patrol found this number of bodies.

15 Infantry Brigade War Diary
31 Jan 44
During the whole of the morning and afternoon 2 Northants were worried by a gun firing from the West, from approximately 7196 and our own artillery put down three bombardments in that area. Patrol during the morning produced the information that there were enemy in the area of Point 165, 784987.

23 Armoured Brigade Intelligence War Diary
31 Jan 44 – 1800
Enemy Situation: Own Front. Our attacks on the left flank of the River Garigliano bridgehead have helped to clear up the identities of the enemy units facing us there. On Monte Natale 7796, Prisoners of War were taken from 361 Grenadier Regiment, thereby disproving the belief that this Regiment of 90 Panzer Grenadiers Division had entirely disappeared from our front. On their right were found 267 Grenadier Regiment and on their right again, according to an Officer Prisoner of War from 267 Regiment the only remaining Battalion of 267 Grenadier Regiment is in position on the coast. The other Battalion of 267 Infantry Regiment was recently located South of Santa Maria Infante 7798, and on their left, holding Monte Bracchi, 194 Alarm Battalion was yesterday identified. On the rest of the front, to the right flank of the bridgehead, the enemy order of battle remains as it was previously known to be. The mystery at the moment, therefore, is the

whereabouts of 200 Panzer Grenadier Regiment and of the remaining Battalions of 361 Panzer Grenadier Regiment.

It is noticeable that the enemy units are getting very thin on the ground; 71 Regiment, for example, is virtually eliminated. Moreover, none of the 800 and more Prisoners of War that had passed through our cages by 30 Jan 44 had heard of reinforcements reaching their formations. It is evident, then, that the enemy command must improvise some sort of a general reserve for their line since the margin of safety is now too narrow a one to work on with only those units that he has forward. The manner in which our forces on Monte Natale were counterattacked yesterday afternoon – not immediately, as if by a local reserve, but after a definite interval – suggests that such a force is in being. No identification was obtained from this counterattack, but it seems probable, now that the Herman Goering group have gone back to Rome, that elements of 90 Panzer Grenadier Division are doing their stuff for them, and possibly some of 200 Panzer Grenadier Regiment are employed on this.

15 Infantry Brigade War Diary
31 Jan 44 – 1800
A warning order was received that 1 KOYLI would relieve 2 Northants.

The Brigadier ordered Officer Commanding 1 York & Lancs. to prepare plans for a counterattack on the Monte Natale feature. Two plans were made to cover in each case, an attack by day and an attack by night. The first was to be based on an attack launched from the West in the event of Monte Natale being captured but the Cemetery still remaining in our hands and the second based on an attack from the South in the event of both Monte Natale and the Cemetery being lost to us.

Considerable enemy vehicle movement was heard after dark along the Santa Maria-San Croce Road and 4.2-inch mortars engaged the road junction 776990 with harassing fire.

A patrol furnished by 1 Green Howards which was sent to Point 165 was fired on at close range by three machine guns and engaged what it estimated to be about 30 enemy but suffered no casualties. A patrol from 2 Northants which went out later to Point 127, 773976, found it unoccupied but heard enemy moving to the West.

1 York & Lancs. War Diary
31 Jan 44 – 1800
The CO. explained that the role of the Battalion in the new area was one of counterattack against Point 156, Monte Natale, 775966 in case 2 Northants should be driven off that feature, and then proceeded to 15 Infantry Brigade HQ where he laid his plans for the operation for the Brigadier's approval. Lieutenant Colonel Osborne, 156 Field Regiment Royal Artillery also attended the conference to lay on a Divisional holding programme in support of the attack.

6 Seaforth Highlanders War Diary
31 Jan 44 – 1810
17 Infantry Brigade patrol along stream today 778979 sniped at from Point 165, 782978 and Point 127, 773976 believed clear. Direct fire brought down on enemy machine guns area 767963. Enemy gun at 7196 active.

1 Green Howards War Diary
31 Jan 44 – 2000

Fighting patrol returned having reached pimple 781975 where enemy platoon post was encountered. Three or four enemy known to have become casualties. Sgt Ware tried to bring back wounded prisoner but owing to enemy fire had to leave him. Pimple 781975 became known as 'Maria Tit'. Local patrols for remainder of night. Local patrol troop Spur Point 141, 7897 returned no enemy seen.

2 Cameronians War Diary
31 Jan 44 – 2000

Information was received from Brigade that the operation 'Witchcraft' was unlikely tonight. Companies were still at one hours-notice to leave Tufo but to stand down when preparations are complete. During the period covering the crossing of the River Garigliano to the end of January the Battalion had suffered approx. 130 casualties, a figure which exceeded the total number of casualties during the whole Sicilian campaign.

1 York & Lancs. War Diary
31 Jan 44 – 2200

Tac HQ began moving to new area at track 791957. Move worked smoothly and without a lot of interference from enemy shelling which remained fairly quiet throughout the night. HQ settled and working in new area at 0200 1 Feb 44. Night cold but dry.

2 Scots Guards War Diary
31 Jan 44

Sgt. Thomas of 'G' Company was killed in the evening when out on patrol. Another man trod on an 'S' mine, which wounded three of them, but Sgt. Thomas jumped into a slit trench to escape and set off either a booby trap or another mine.

A padre from 17 Infantry Brigade came to Battalion HQ to say that he had buried an officer and three guardsmen at Pontifiure. They were identified by documents to be Ian Tait and Guardsmen Reidy, McGee and Miller.

German views of 31 Jan 44
Lt. Wolfgang Wiedemann, II Battalion, 267 Grenadier Regiment
31 Jan 44

'So, at the end of January, beginning of Feb 44, men from 194 Fusilier Battalion took over our positions and our safe shelters. At dawn we marched through Santa Maria Infante, always seeking cover and as quiet as possible. The respect for enemy shellfire was still very great. Silence still did not penetrate in the front areas. Nervousness triggered an abundance of fire and concentrated fire on prominent points. Neither side trusted the other. The ship artillery was also still being felt. At the Southern edge of Santa Maria Infante, we would receive further orders.

The company sought cover on the North facing slope. There were a lot of small and bigger trenches. The impact of the bombs dropped by the fighter-bomber aircraft had torn considerable holes into the earth. Tanks of the "Hermann Goering Panzer Division" had been the main targets of the fighter bombers.

Bombed and shot British and German tanks testified to the violence of the fighting. We could hear the roar of the battle from the foot of Point 201 behind us, and about 10 days ago I was looking for the Regimental Command Post of Lieutenant Colonel Reich. Now I was quite familiar with the blood-soaked terrain.

"Herr Lieutenant", shouted a voice. It was one of our food carriers, "I have some food in my sacks for '2' Company; it is to be distributed!" The battle was over. Now the survivors received their rations. It seemed a bit strange, but I do not think this well-meant matter could be settled. There was no need for distribution. Since these benefits were available in the form of small packages for the Company from 19 Jan 44, everyone took as much as they could, the rest were left.

A messenger from the Battalion brought the order that "2" Company should follow a mountain range slowly descending and take up positions in the village of Solacciano, about 2 km away. The Commander expects the Company Officers in one hour about 200-300 metres North of Solacciano to give orders. Now I made sure that they were in a hurry. This place gave me the creeps, any moment shell fire raids could come down on us.

When we were relieved by 194 Fusilier Battalion we learned that the brave Regiment Commander of 274 Grenadier Regiment, Lt. Col. Reich had been promoted to Colonel. Also, the Knight's Cross was given to him after his death.

Now "2" Company moved on the Northern slope of the ridge, protected from enemy eyes. Despite limited visibility, the Gulf of Gaeta could be seen in the distance. The men were proud that they had defied a formidable superior force. With the occupation of the positions in and around Solacciano by II Battalion 267 Regiment a new phase began – for our Division, the first Cassino battle was over.

Just below the ridge, where everything was forested, the Company Commanders of I Battalion 267 Grenadier Regiment met to receive orders. Lt. Friedenberger was missing, his fate then still unknown. Captain von Schönfeldt had taken over No 1 Company – his six months as Company Commander began – one of the prerequisites for a career on the General Staff. Lieutenant Horst Castner had taken over No 3 Company. In addition, Lieutenant Dirr, Commander of No 4 Company and I were present.

Major Frank started the situation report loudly, ignoring our advice to speak a little quieter; until he came to the division of the Company limits, a sudden shell fire attack near him drowned his loud voice. He was the first to disappear into a shell hole of an abandoned grenade launch [mortar] site. All others, of course, sought shelter from the shells. After the bombardment had begun, Frank called out "All clear", then disappeared down the valley. Comrade Horst Castner remembers this typical little experience very well, that was his first impression of Major Frank.'

Capt. Nigel Nicolson, *The Grenadier Guards in the War of 1939-1945, Volume II*

'Let us examine the conditions under which the Germans fought and lived. The Germans were tired, sick and nervous. It was not only that they suffered from the psychological effects of constant retreat and the hostility of the people which grew into open partisan warfare. There was also the physical exhaustion imposed by the lack of transport and Allied air superiority which prevented the use in daylight of the few German lorries which remained. They marched by night, and it was a relief to halt at dawn to defend the slope of some rocky hill, for then they could rest, and they could hit back. Not many of them, even in the moments of greatest hopelessness, would take the final step of desertion, but their attitude when taken prisoner would often be one almost of gratitude to their captors. The Germans had been told by their officers that the British take no prisoners, or hand them over to the Russians for execution. Is it then surprising that they should have fought their hardest to evade capture, and then be overwhelmed by relief to find that they were treated no more harshly than one of our own soldiers under arrest? All they knew was that our supplies, our equipment, our morale were apparently inexhaustible, our determination inflexible, our initiative unchallengeable. On their side the advantages were few. They could leave behind mines and booby traps; and blow up the bridges. They were withdrawing back on their own supply dumps at the same time as the Allies were putting a greater distance between their front lines and their bases. But little more. They did not know what they were heading for: we knew, without a shadow of doubt.'

Chapter 17

1 February 1944 – 1 York & Lancs. Back to Point 172

2 Cameronians War Diary
1 Feb 44 – 0600
Battalion dispositions – 'A' Company in reserve at 802960, Tufo. 'B' Company in position at West end of Tufo, 'C' Company in reserve at 804958 [200m South of Tufo]. 'D' Company in position at East end of Tufo with Battalion HQ in Tufo.

1 York & Lancs. War Diary
1 Feb 44 – 0730
Battalion spent a quiet night and the first day of the new month dawned clear and bright with good visibility. The CO. and Intelligence Officer, with Lt Col. Osborne, Commanding Officer 156 Field Regiment, Royal Artillery and Major Sedgwick, Battery Commander 92 Field Regiment, RA [attached to the Battalion] went to Point 141, Monte del Duca, 782959 to carry out recce for the operation and to lay on the necessary artillery targets. Full artillery concentrations to be laid on and complete agreement was reached between both COs. Tasks were also arranged for both 3-inch and 2-inch mortars. During a quiet morning, the Battalion was able to finish settling into its new area.

[As from 1 February the York & Lancs. War Diaries were typed rather than hand-written. A sign, perhaps of more attention to administrative detail under the new Commanding Officer!]

1 York & Lancs. War Diary
1 Feb 44 – 1130
The CO. and IO. went to Tac HQ of 2 Northants. The CO. contacted Lt. Col. Stevenson DSO of 2 Northants and discussed his plans for the operation with him. Lt. Col. Stevenson was able to give some valuable information as he had attacked from a Start Line in the area in which our CO. also intended to begin one of the attacks.

2 Royal Scots Fusiliers War Diary
1 Feb 44 – 1200
Recce party arrived at HQ 201 Guards Brigade and was taken from there to HQ 6 Grenadier Guards, 777954. 'B' Company had counterattack role at 773959, Point 141, two detachments of 3-inch Mortars at 773954 and two at 778955 had defensive fire tasks only.

2 Northants War Diary
1 Feb 44 – 1245
Patrol sent out to try and locate Boche bodies lying forward of Point 156 at 0800. Patrol returned having found no bodies, only pieces of leather equipment and a German officer's pistol near some blood-stained bandages. The patrol went up the wadi Rio Perlata, keeping in riverbed to West of Point 165 at 799976. Patrol fired on by machine gun from Point 165 and from Point 127. Movement was observed in direction of Santa Maria Infante and road North-West to Pulcherini bend. The Patrol arrived back at base at 1245.

1 York & Lancs. War Diary
1 Feb 44 – 1400
The CO.'s 'O' Group conference: The CO. laid his plans for the operation before his Company Commanders and Platoon Commanders. There were two alternative plans, which were to be used in daylight or darkness making in fact four plans in all. The Start Line for one attack would be Point 172, which would be held as a firm base by our own troops and would be called 'TILDEN'. The other would commence from area 776954 [600m South-West of Point 141 Monte del Duca], and would be called 'FERRY'. In both cases 'B' Company would attack from the right and 'C' Company left with 'D' Company on Point 141 to come up onto the feature as soon as it had been captured. In daylight the rate of advance would be 100 yards in four minutes and by night 100 yards in six minutes. Tactical HQ will be established in 'D' Company's area 782959 [Point 141 Monte del Duca].

7 Cheshires War Diary
1 Feb 44 – 1420
'5' Platoon upstaged area 795960, Point 151, and laid on a short burst of fire. Three killed, Two wounded.

15 Infantry Brigade War Diary
1 Feb 44
During the day little enemy movement was observed except in the area of Point 165, in the area 7798 and on Point 127 which for the first time was found to be occupied by an enemy machine gun. Mortars from the Support Company, 7 Cheshires, harassed the road junction North-West of Santa Maria Infante in the early afternoon.

1 York & Lancs. War Diary
1 Feb 44 – 1500
Company Commanders went to 2 Northants HQ to carry out recce of approaches to Point 156, Monte Natale.

1 Feb 44 – 1600
Observation Posts established in 'D' and 'B' Company's areas to render 'situation reports' on activity along the Battalion front all 24 hours of the day.

1 Feb 44 – 1630
'C' Company shelled. One man was wounded and one suffering from shell shock.

6 Seaforth Highlanders War Diary
1 Feb 44 – 1806
6 Seaforths report booby trap across track 797978 now removed. Enemy machine gun position 791986 and movement in Pulcherini. 15 Infantry Brigade patrol fired on this afternoon Point 165, 783977 and Point 127, 773975 also mortar at 785984.

201 Guards Brigade War Diary
1 Feb 44
The outline of the new German line West of our position is now becoming apparent. A deserter said that on 30 Jan 44 his Company took over from another Company on the forward slopes of Point 201. 793995.

2 Northants War Diary
1 Feb 44 – 2100
Relief going on quietly, with two companies relieved and passing downhill from Point 156.

1 Feb 44 – 2130
Relief completed except for Platoon machine guns which were not yet relieved.

1 Feb 44 – 2145
CO. handed over Command to Commanding Officer 1 Kings Own Yorkshire Light Infantry. Battalion rested in Sorbello after being relieved on Point 156.

1 York & Lancs. War Diary
1 Feb 44 – 2200
There was a fair amount of shelling on the Battalion during the late evening and early morning, but no casualties were caused. Night again fine and cold.

6 Seaforth Highlanders War Diary
1 Feb 44 – 2200
German deserter came through our position at Point 201, 798965.

2 Royal Inniskilling Fusiliers War Diary
1 Feb 44 – 2230
Fighting patrol left for Monte Bracchi feature 779985 at 1900 to ascertain if feature was held and to get dispositions of enemy troops. Going Northwest crossing the River Dei Reali thence North to ring contour 799985. Visibility was good as there was a bright moon and objects could be discerned at 50 yds distance. Patrol reached track running Northwest at 804983 without event at 2030. Lay up on track until after artillery barrage had gone down on objective. Observed barrage which fell right on objective. At 2130 barrage lifted to peak of Bracchi feature and moved North. At this time four enemy mortar bombs fell. Mortar was fired from reverse slopes Bracchi. Patrol proceeded towards objective, when about 100 yards from crest of feature a lighted cigarette glowing in the darkness was observed and a short cough heard. Patrol got into firing positions and fired a burst of the Bren gun. This was not answered, and two bursts of

Tommy gun were then fired. A shout obviously from someone who had been hit was heard and scuffling of two or three men running back. We then fired a Bren burst to the right of the feature, hoping to draw fire. This was answered by two shots from a rifle.

Immediately the rifle fired, a short word of command was heard and more scuffling of running men. The feature was then reached, but no trace of enemy weapons, equipment etc. was found. Patrol returned to base at 2230.

'A' Squadron 16/5 Lancers War Diary
1 Feb 44
'2' Troop went to the Cemetery at first light. We had several shells land near our camp and Trooper Skinner was wounded. During the afternoon a Sapper, taking a walk in the hills behind our camp went up on an 'S' mine. We therefore decided to have the area, where 'C' Squadron were going to spend the night of the take-over, swept, just in case. 2 Royal Scots Fusiliers had taken over from 6 Grenadier Guards at '3' Troop's positions. During the evening 'B' Squadron arrived to take over from 40 Royal Tank Regiment, who were going out for a rest. '4' Troop took over from '2' Troop at night.

2 Scots Guards War Diary
1 Feb 44
The enemy shelled the Tremensuoli village a certain amount, but the Company areas were not paid much attention. The main square opens up to the West so that anyone foolish enough to walk about there is very apt to provoke hostile action; most people realise this but there is one rather lonely donkey, which sometimes wanders there and was several times the cause of shell fire. It has learnt to run to the houses for shelter when it hears shells coming, but not to avoid the square altogether.

Chapter 18

2 February 1944 – 1 York & Lancs. Recce Point 156

5 Infantry Division Intelligence
2 Feb 44
At Point 201 a deserter from the German '4' Company 267 Grenadier Regiment gave himself up. It is noteworthy that this is only the second deserter who has come into us from 94 Infantry Division since the battle began – a distinct difference from other perhaps better-known Divisions who daily produce their crop of changelings.

15 Infantry Brigade War Diary
2 Feb 44
A quiet night was enjoyed with only slight shelling. Patrols found Point 165 still occupied and Point 127 this time manned by four machine guns. It was hoped the enemy would counterattack in which event the artillery would concentrate on Point 165 and it was arranged that an Observation Post on Point 201 in 13 Infantry Brigade's area and also the Air Observation Post, which would take off at first light, should give warning of the enemy's intention to do this.

1 Green Howards War Diary
2 Feb 44 – 0315
Recce patrol from 'C' Company returned. In area Point 165 German voices and sound of digging were heard, a few bursts of machine gun fire were heard on return journey.

1 York & Lancs. War Diary
2 Feb 44 – 0530
Company Commanders went to Point 156, 775966, to recce positions they would take over.

6 Seaforth Highlanders War Diary
2 Feb 44 – 0600
Patrol to house 791986 shot up occupants with light machine gun and Vickers MMG from 7 Cheshires. Reported squealing from inside. Patrol waited but there was no retaliation.

2 Feb 44 – 0830
1 KOYLI relieved 2 Northants on Point 156, 783978 Monte Natale. Patrols reported Point 127, 773976 and Point 165 783978 held by enemy.

1 York & Lancs. War Diary

2 Feb 44 – 0830

Weather warm, with good visibility. During the day Platoon Commanders carried out recces in area Point 156. Good information passed in by Company Observation Posts re enemy shelling.

156 Field Regiment Royal Artillery War Diary

2 Feb 44 – 1000

593 Battery fired propaganda shells containing the weekly news sheet 'Frontpost'

2 Royal Inniskillings Fusiliers War Diary

2 Feb 44 – 1030

Since approx. 0900 this morning a cruiser [probably HMS *Orion*] supported by a destroyer has been shelling enemy positions. The BBC News mentioned H.M.S. Orion as shelling the coast.

2 Feb 44 – 1545

Mules loaded with cooking utensils break loose and run into a mine field. Pioneers were engaged in clearing a path for the mules when one mule exploded a mine. This caused one man killed and one man injured who afterwards died from his wounds. The mule was killed outright.

1 York & Lancs. War Diary

2 Feb 44 – 1600

The Brigadier visited the CO. and gave his permission for 'C' Company to move back to area 794948 [1km South-East of Minturno], in reserve & 'D' Company to take up position on Point 141, 785958 Monte Del Duca.

2 Feb 44 – 1700

Change-over of 'C' and 'D' Companies commenced.

'A' Squadron 16/5 Lancers War Diary

2 Feb 44 – 1830

'C' Squadron arrived and took over our positions and harboured next door to us. The Squadron Leader warned Maj. Elwes about the shelling, but Maj. Elwes said 'Oh, they won't shell at night, so I'll dig in in the morning. Alas, they were fateful words, because from 0200 nobody got any sleep, owing to the noise of all the Artillery around us firing and the enemy's replies, some of which landed very near, and one dud (luckily) shell landed in the area. We are told 'C' Squadron dug very deep the next morning! During the night, our knocked-out tank had been taken over the bridge, after some good work by Sgt. Dadford and the crew of the Armoured Recovery Vehicle to get it down to the bridge.

16/5 Lancers War Diary

2 Feb 44 – 1930

'A' (and then 'C') Squadrons had two Troops out, one at the Cemetery and back along the road between 781967 and 780966 [going North towards Santa Maria Infante], the other centred on the Y crossing 775954. [midway between Tremensuoli and Minturno]. All these Troops were in position in case of a counterattack which never materialised. Troop Leaders do night recces on their feet to get an idea of the ground they are going to have to traverse during the next phase.

2 Scots Guards War Diary

2 Feb 44

The Observation Posts have been very busy since our move up. Their position is an extremely unpleasant one, particularly that of the Intelligence Section, which is on the top floor of a three-storey building and a very obvious target. Both the gunners and our own mortar Platoon have been regularly engaging opportunity targets.

'A' Squadron 16/5 Lancers War Diary

2 Feb 44

Troop moved up to the Cemetery in the morning. In the afternoon we had a lane swept for the tanks to take up a position to fire on a house, which had been discovered to be occupied by the enemy by a patrol of 2 Scots Guards. This position was very near '3' Troop, and we hoped that they would get a shoot. Unfortunately, a counterattack came in on 2 Scots Guards during the afternoon which somewhat delayed things and we did not consider we had time to do it well, as an Observation Post would be necessary higher up the hill. So, with regret we left it to 'C' Squadron.

5 Infantry Brigade War Diary

2 Feb 44

Diversionary patrols in the direction of Point 127, 774985 were to be supplied by 1 KOYLI. The day as a whole was quiet, the only enemy movement being on Point 165 and the shelling of 1 KOYLI by a self-propelled gun which was fired from the San Croce – Santa Maria Infante Road.

Chapter 19

3 February 1944 – A Quiet Day

1 Green Howards War Diary
3 Feb 44 – 0630
'C' Company returned successfully having occupied Point 165 with very slight opposition. No counterattack was put in. 'C' Company captured three POWs belonging to '1' Company, 194 Recce Regiment.

1 York & Lancs. War Diary
3 Feb 44 – 0730
Having been warned that the Battalion may also have to take the role of counterattack on the Tremensuoli feature 7795, should the Guards be beaten off the feature, the CO. and IO. went on a recce of the area to find out possible means of approach etc. for the attack. The CO. also contacted the 201 Guards Brigade Commander, Lt. Col. Harris, 2 Scots. Guards.

92 Field Regiment Royal Artillery War Diary
3 Feb 44 – 0815
2 Royal Scots Fusiliers report area 767957 shelled by enemy at 0730.

3 Feb 44 – 0824
2 Royal Scots Fusiliers report same gun now shelling 785955 [300m East of Point 141 Monte del Duca].

6 Seaforth Highlanders War Diary
3 Feb 44 – 0845
Situation report from 13 Infantry Brigade: 2 Inniskillings raid supported by artillery chased enemy from positions 800985. Later silent patrol found positions abandoned, much ammunition and grenades lying about. 15 Infantry Brigade Company raid on Point 165 produced three prisoners of war from '1' Company 194 Recce Regiment who state that Company was weak. Torches, believed of enemy patrol, seen back on Point 165 before first light.

1 Green Howards War Diary
3 Feb 44 – 1400
'D' Company daylight patrol left for Point 165, 7897

92 Field Regiment Royal Artillery War Diary
3 Feb 44 – 1620
Further patrol details. 6 Seaforths from Tufo to North end Pulcherini 1800 – 0200. 2 Scots Guards to 760954 1800 – 2400 [1km West of Tremensuoli].

2 Cameronians War Diary
3 Feb 44 – 1730
'D' Company at East end of Tufo to be relieved by Company of 6 Seaforths.

6 Seaforth Highlanders War Diary
3 Feb 44 – 1730
Situation Report 13 Infantry Brigade: 6 Seaforths now have two Companies on Point 201, one Platoon on Point 151, 795962. One Company less one Platoon East end of Tufo.

1 York & Lancs. War Diary
3 Feb 44 – 1730
The Division Commander, Major-General P.G.S. Gregson Ellis CBE, visited the CO. at Tactical HQ.

3 Feb 44 – 1930
'D' Company now relieved moved to embarking point followed by remainder of Battalion.

92 Field Regiment Royal Artillery War Diary
3 Feb 44 – 2045
467 Battery Commander now at 2 Royal Scots Fusiliers Battalion HQ at 778955 then Forward Observation Post at 764963. 2 Scots Guards patrol killed three enemy in house within our Direct Fire line. 2 Royal Scots Fusiliers Company locations 772958,764961, 761951. Enemy heavy gun located in area 725999. Forward Observation Post ranging Medium Regiment on to it at first light. Battery Officers informed.

D. Woolard, attached to 2 Wiltshires, *My Day, 3 February*
'We were busy all morning loading the Carriers and giving a final test to the radio sets. By 3.30pm we left Casanova to take up positions again near Tufo'.

Sir David Cole, 2 Inniskillings, *The Road To Rome*
'In the evening we were relieved by 2 Northants. With the help of a little moonlight, we slung our worldly goods around our shoulders and heavy with fatigue and sleeplessness slipped and slithered down the ridge to the road below.'

2 Scots Guards War Diary
3 Feb 44
The enemy have been using a weapon which cannot be accurately identified. It appears to be a rocket propelled bomb weighing about 250 lbs. When fired the source of origin gives out a bright flash, the bomb makes a very nasty noise and can be seen in flight.

It makes a very large crater but is apparently inaccurate and has done no harm as yet. In the early hours of this morning, one landed just forward of the village, failing to explode. It will be dug up by some experts, after a discreet period has elapsed.

Eddie Crutchley took out a patrol of six men to form an ambush on a carefully chosen point on a track. They successfully intercepted a party of 10 Germans, killing two and seriously wounding a third, who escaped but could be heard screaming for several hours afterwards. There were no identifications on the bodies who were apparently also on patrol. Eddie and his men got back unscathed.

Chapter 20

4 February 1944 – Private Ernest Strafford is Buried

1 York & Lancs. War Diary
4 Feb 44 – 0700
The weather was again fine in the morning with good visibility but in the late afternoon the weather broke, and showers prevailed making visibility extremely poor.

6 Seaforth Highlanders War Diary
4 Feb 44 – 0700
15 Infantry Brigade Patrol found Point 165 held by four machine guns. Point 127 reported clear.

1 Green Howards War Diary
4 Feb 44 – 0800
Captain Parker, the Adjutant accidentally shot in the leg. Lieut. Hovington became Adjutant.

7 Cheshires War Diary
4 Feb 44 – 0900
Officer Commanding Company and Officer Commanding '4' Platoon recce area for a position for '4' Platoon move forward. Position found at 777953.

4 Feb 44 – 0930
Tac HQ And Battalion HQ established at 784943 in a house adjoining 'A' Company HQ.

156 Field Regiment Royal Artillery War Diary
4 Feb 44 – 1300
591 Battery fired special propaganda shells 'out with the secret weapons'. One shell burst immediately in front of the gun, covering the Regimental area with leaflets.

15 Infantry Brigade War Diary
4 Feb 44 – 1300
A day patrol was sent out by 1 KOYLI to observe the San Croce – Santa Maria Infante road from a vantage point on the 127 Ridge. At 1300 it reported that it had seen nothing. A patrol to Point 165 by 1 Green Howards found the enemy still there and were sniped at but without casualties. A certain amount of shelling occurred during the day, mainly

from guns sited due North of Minturno, although the heavier calibre guns seemed to be still firing from the West.

Our main offensive action during the day was a harassing shoot on Santa Maria Infante carried out by the 4.2-inch mortars of 7 Cheshires and timed on information received from Prisoners of War to coincide with what was hoped to be the ration drawing parade of the German 194 Recce Battalion. The discovery of 30 dead Germans in front of Monte Natale and their subsequent identification as '5' Company, 200 Panzer Grenadier Regiment cleared up an old mystery. These were obviously part of the unit which had counterattacked 2 Northants on 31 Jan 44.

1 Green Howards War Diary
4 Feb 44 – 1450
25 pounder propaganda shells dropped on Point 156, 7998 also Santa Maria Infante.

1 York & Lancs. War Diary
4 Feb 44 – 1530
CO. 'O' Group conference. The CO. gave details of orders for the counterattack on the Tremensuoli feature. Giving particulars of the start line, rate of advance, artillery support, etc. The operation will be called 'Willis'. The CO. also dealt with numerous other administrative points, and gave orders for the formation of the 'Tigers', a Platoon of one Officer, one Company Sergeant Major, three Sergeants and six men per Company which would be trained purely for deep patrolling and generally causing a nuisance behind enemy lines by laying mines, blowing bridges etc. The CO. also laid down plans for the formation of a Refit Company in the Battalion. Under this arrangement when the Battalion moved into the line, a number of Officers and NCOs would be left behind from the Battalion and carry out training in the Refit Company to provide a pool from which to replace casualties.

2 Scots Guards War Diary
4 Feb 44 – 1600
The enemy shelled the Battalion area intermittently all day. They used 88mm guns from quite a short range, also firing solid shot at the houses now in use as Observation Posts. In return our gunners and the mortar Platoon engaged numerous targets on observation and shelling reports.

'F' Company sent out a patrol with Hugo Charteris to a point slightly short of the scene of last night's battle. The patrol first found some holes cut in the ground to take 'S' mines and were then seen by two men who fired at them and ran. They had come upon a mine laying party, with a half-track vehicle, which immediately started up and departed with an undignified haste, but they also had a formidable covering party armed with about four 'Spandau's' and a 'Bren'. These all-opened fire in the general direction of the patrol, but apparently without being able to see them, the patrol returned individually, with the exception of one man.

1 York & Lancs. War Diary
4 Feb 44 – 1630
The CO. and Intelligence Officer again sent to Tremensuoli area on a further recce. 'D' Company area was fairly heavily shelled during the afternoon, causing three wounded.

7 Cheshires War Diary
4 Feb 44 – 1730
CO. and Officer Commanding visited '5' Platoon who were on Point 156, 7796. All was quiet.

6 Seaforth Highlanders War Diary
4 Feb 44 – 1800
Situation report: 2 Royal Scots Fusiliers Company, 773958 Battalion HQ, 777954. 15 Infantry Brigade report Boche registering forward of Point 165 this morning. Believe that Boche hold Point 165 lightly, by strength by night. 1 KOYLI now have standing patrol on Point 127, 773976.

1 York & Lancs. War Diary
4 Feb 44 – 2030
'C' Company came out of reserve at 1930 and relieved 'B' Company on Point 172, 785962 the latter Company going back into reserve. Relief completed by 2030 hours. Password for tonight – 'Fillet-Mignon'. The weather during the night was bad. High winds prevailed and there were very heavy showers. It improved as the new day drew near however, and Saturday dawned exceptionally fine and clear with good visibility.

4 Feb 44 was the day Ernest Strafford's 'Body recovered, identified and buried by British Troops'. We now know that the only British soldiers in the vicinity of the grave were soldiers from his own Regiment, 'B' Company, 1 York & Lancs. It is fitting that they buried him.

1 Green Howards War Diary
4 Feb 44 – 2030
'B' Company fighting patrol left to go to Santa Maria Infante, 7998 and back by Point 165, 7897. Object to get information and identification.

Service record. (York Record Office)

2 Wiltshires War Diary

4 Feb 44

During afternoon received warning order to be prepared to take over from 2 Royal Scots Fusiliers at Tremensuoli.

D. Woolard, attached to 2 Wiltshires, *My Day, 4 February*

'We left our new gun-pits after the Pioneer Platoon had cleared the area of mines. We worked awfully hard carrying the mortars and bombs uphill over a very rocky track and dug new gun-pits until 10pm.'

Chapter 21

5 February 1944 – The Aftermath

1 Green Howards War Diary
5 Feb 44 – 0130
'B' Company patrol returned. Patrol came under heavy mortar fire and automatic fire from spur 786982. The commander Lieut. Berny and six other ranks failed to return. One of the patrol reported that he heard a gramophone being used to give the impression of a stronger force.

2 Wiltshires War Diary
5 Feb 44 – 0200
Take over from 2 Royal Scots Fusiliers at Tremensuoli, 7695. Relief completed without incident. Battalion comes under command 17 Infantry Brigade.

15 Infantry Brigade War Diary
21 Jan 44 – 0345
The Brigadier now established himself in some buildings just South-West of Minturno. and Brigade Main HQ moved up to join him leaving at approx. 0345.

1 Green Howards War Diary
5 Feb 44 – 0630
Observation Posts in position on Points 172 and 141.

1 York & Lancs. War Diary
5 Feb 44 – 1230
'C' Company's Observation Post on Point 172, 785962 was shelled, causing three wounded, casualties including Lt. Pepys-Cockerell, who had just joined the Battalion. It was decided during the day to withdraw the Company from Point 172 to enable two Companies to have a short break.

15 Infantry Brigade War Diary
5 Feb 44
Patrols during the night 4-5 Feb 44 were uneventful. 1 KOYLI patrol to Point 127 produced two Prisoners of War who were taken from an outpost position and located an enemy strong post a little further back. When the patrol withdrew the artillery were brought down, but the shoot could not be satisfactorily observed. They were identified as '1' Company 267 Regiment and although they appeared to be uncertain of the exact dispositions of their Battalion it appeared that both '2' and '3' Companies of 267

Regiment were on the Point 127 feature to the left and right of '1' Company, whose main positions were just forward of the small track which runs like a backbone along the feature.

About dusk a heavy concentration on the right hit a Company of 1 KOYLI, just above the Cemetery, caused eight casualties, and it was thought that the enemy fire was brought down at this time because a Troop of tanks [16/5 Lancers] were heard withdrawing for the night from their day positions near the Cemetery. It was arranged in future to warn 1 KOYLI when they were going to withdraw and to vary the timings as the enemy seemed to be well aware of the tank's routine.

Scots Guards War Diary
5 Feb 44
During the last 16 days the Battalion has lost two Officers and five Other Ranks killed, 31 wounded, one missing and a miscellaneous collection of men suffering from 'bomb happiness'.

'A' Squadron 16/5 Lancers War Diary
7 Feb 44
In the evening, the Squadron Leader got a note from the Colonel that 'C' Squadron had recovered Sgt. Ritchie's tank by towing it away with two Shermans. They did this without interference from the enemy and pulled it back to the edge of Minturno.

1 York & Lancs. War Diary
7 Feb 44 – 1130
The CO. dealt with the advance on both flanks of 5 Infantry Division front but at fuller length with the 15 Infantry Brigade attack. The plan was to advance and capture Santa Maria Infante 7898, Bulgarini 7898, and Bracchi 7999 with 1 KOYLI on the left and 1 Green Howards on the right. 1 York & Lancs. would then go through these Battalions and exploit beyond Bracchi. 'C' Company would remain on Point 141 784956, and 'B' & 'D' Companies would move into a concentrated area behind Point 172, 'D' Company to move forward when called or alternatively to take up a defensive position on Point 172 if required.

Nicolson, Capt. Nigel, *The Grenadier Guards in the War of 1939-1945, Volume II*
9 Feb 44
'On 9 Feb 44, The Master of Saltoun was trapped in a minefield while on patrol. His fate has never been discovered and he is the only Grenadier officer who remains posted as "Missing". Italian civilians said that they had seen him being carried away wounded back to the German post, but thereafter news of him ceased.'

2 Scots Guards History
10 Feb 44
When 2 Scots Guards took over Monte Natale on 10 Feb 44, they described the trenches rapidly filled with water. Difficulties of feeding were added to the other discomforts, for some of the Platoons were in exposed positions on forward slopes. They arranged that in the daytime only sentries would occupy these positions.

2 Scots Guards War Diary
10 Feb 44 – 1700
As 56 Infantry Division are going to the Anzio
bridgehead the whole of our front is being
thinned out. All three Battalions of our Brigade
are remaining in the line, so instead of relieving
6 Grenadiers at Tremonsuoli we relieve 1 KOYLI
on Monte Natale (6 Grenadier Guards being on
the hill between). Heavy rain sets in and makes
the takeover depressing. 1 KOYLI prepared their
positions for fine weather (which they enjoyed
throughout) and the Platoons have no cover, and
their trenches are rapidly filling with water. Even
Battalion HQ dugout does not keep out the rain.
Left Flank placed as usual on the right, Right Flank
centre, 'G' Company on the left, 'F' Company in
reserve near Battalion HQ. The Commanding
Officer decided to move Battalion HQ down to a
house on the road. Takeover finished by 2130.

**W.A. Elliott, an Officer in 2 Scots Guards,
described Monte Natale**
'Monte Natale on the West flank was the worst
location. There was a deluge of rain when we took
over there at night. The slit trenches on a forward
slope had become filled to the top with water. We

British soldiers in Tufo playing the
bagpipes as others cleared the road.
Photo 7 Feb 44. (TNA)

bailed out these two-man trenches all through the night with our mess tins or steel helmets,
for we had to stay underground all day as we were under observation on a forward slope.
For some unaccountable reason I was forbidden to move back on to the reverse slope.

The mud was so sodden that our slit trenches soon filled up again, whilst we sat
on branches suspended halfway up the sides. The snow only came in the form of sleet
although the mountain tops in front were now covered in a white mantle. I spent three
days like this, soaked to the skin. It seemed worse than the 1914-18 war when deep
trenches were all interconnected and there were also communal dugouts.

On the third night the Germans brought up a mortar to fire harassing shots at my
Platoon, which they must have observed on our forward slope. Their shooting was
very accurate, as they put down over thirty bombs on one of my Section positions. But
fortunately, only half of them exploded in the deep mud. Two bombs landed near me in
the same slit trench as two Guardsmen. The first broke one man's leg and the next bomb
blew the other's head off. I was glad the night was dark when I removed what remained
of one man in order to get the survivor on a stretcher. He was very brave about it and
kept on telling the stretcher-bearers to leave him and take cover in a slit trench until the
mortaring was over. Our stretcher bearers were always outstanding.'

2 Scots Guards War Diary
14 Feb 44

1 York & Lancs. took over from us. The Battalion are to rest for four days. Left Flank and 'F' Company have rest billets in Minturno, Right Flank and 'G' Company in houses near the railway, Battalion HQ moves to a house on the road near Brigade HQ.

1 York & Lancs. Ernest Shaw's view of Monte Natale

'The situation on Point 156: About the same time when the Germans had done their pincer movement as we came out from Monte Natale on 22 Jan 1944, the Anzio landing took place. We had actually been pushed forward on our main front to try and draw any reserves the Germans had in the Anzio area down into our front line. I had the impression we took a bloody nose for the Fifth Army so they could walk into Anzio.

We went back on to Point 156 and relieved the Guards. While they had been there, some bureaucrat from the rear had given the orders that not 1" of ground had got to be yielded. They had two Platoons on the forward slopes of Point 156. That is the steep slope facing the enemy. The enemy could see almost into their trenches. Just over the brow of the hill, on the backside, there was one Platoon in reserve and Company HQ. The lads in the two forward Platoons were fed during the hours of darkness. Any relieving was done during the hours of darkness, and any replacing of ammunition. They were in an unenviable position and they had to lay low all day. When we took over, we naturally had to adopt the same position.

The Major was left out of the battle on this occasion. Capt. Ramsay had not come back after his injuries. Mr Corfield had been promoted to Captain. Lt. Corfield acting as the Company Commander, He was later promoted to Captain. We operated the same system, two Platoons over the front, one in reserve for 24 hours, then they swopped, and Company HQ did the guard at night. One particular night I was on the 12-2am shift, and I heard, what I imagined to be a couple of bursts of Tommy gun fire. It seemed to come from the other side of the hill, where our chaps were.

I stood Company HQ to, roused the Sergeant-Major, everyone. He sent me to see the Captain. We were in touch with the two forward Platoons with the field telephone. He rang through there and there was nothing to report, all quiet on the Western Front, sort of thing.

We were eventually stood down and it made me feel like a proper bloody idiot, scared of my own shadow. Not a soul in the Company heard it. Jacobs was due to go on guard as I came off. He was on from 2-4am, and Ted Rimmer 4-6am. I was trying to explain to Ted in the dugout. He said, "Let's get some bloody sleep, Jacobs will be waking me up in no time, gunfire carries miles at night". I went to sleep. Come 4 o'clock Jacobs woke me. Ted took over. Ted comes off at 6am, wakes me up and says "You were right Shawy. There was some gun fire." They had learned that a German patrol had been and picked up two of our lads. A Lance Corporal "Tanky" Eastwood and one of his men, Tommy Farr. We used to call him that after the heavyweight champion. Tanky and Tommy Farr had been taken prisoner. They found Tanky's Tommy Gun and it had been fired and probably knocked out of his hand. They had been taken prisoner, so in a way, I was exonerated, but I did not like the idea, having lost the two lads. Just saved my face. Ted said, "they must have all been asleep out there." I said, "everybody in the Company must have been asleep". Even the Platoon in reserve had not reported them. Eventually one lad was held responsible. I could not understand this. He was court martialled, and he went to prison. I never saw him no more. I could not understand why. There are two Platoons, and there are six Sections there and each Platoon had headquarters as well, so why only one nobbled, but that is how it happened.

It meant the Major was back mid-morning, they sent him straight back. That evening he took Joe and me again and we went to view the situation forward. Right, he saw this ridiculous position and withdrew the men. He ignored the Brigadier's general order not to give an inch. He brought the chaps behind the hill. He thought it was ridiculous. There was nothing to defend there. So, we got all the men behind the hilltop. The Germans could not come to where those trenches were, but there was another sequence to it.

Tanky's pal was a Sergeant Sutton. Sooty, as we called him. He was really upset at losing his best pal. He asked, "could he take a fighting patrol for revenge". He came to me as he was coming to see the Major and he thanked me for doing what I did. He said, "you must have been the only bugger awake in the Company". He told me he wanted to lead a fighting patrol for revenge. I told him they would be waiting for such an event. I said, "leave it a fortnight or three weeks". Major was of the same opinion. He tried to talk him out of it and Sooty asked if he could go before the Colonel. Eventually he had his way and Tanky's Section and Sooty went on this patrol, it was about 48 hours after we had lost Tanky. They got so far, and the Germans had sown mines in front of the position. We lost him and one other and the other five scrambled their way back. It was a double loss. Ironically, a few months later Tommy Farr escaped and re-joined us and Tanky was a prisoner of war. His mother had letters from him, and she contacted someone in the Company, so Tanky survived the war, but his mate did not.

That was Hill 156. We did not often get mail in the line. It happened occasionally. It was held up until you got a break, but we got some mail while we were on Point 156 and the Sergeant got this huge bar of chocolate. Nice chap, we called him "Sandy" behind his back because he had sandy hair.

"Sandy" gave everyone in Company HQ two squares of chocolate, and at the time I had gone to Company HQ with a message, and he left my two squares with company clerk, Jacobs. I knew nothing about it, but it came up some time after. Ted said, "Wasn't it good of Sandy to give us that chocolate?". I said, "What chocolate?" Then it turned out that he had left mine with Jacobs and Jacobs had eaten it. It is funny isn't it. I had a Tommy gun and I rammed it in his tummy. I could have killed him over two squares of bloody chocolate. I went for him. I have thought about it many, many times. I could have killed him over two squares of bloody chocolate. That is war for you, isn't it?

After the Minturno episode, we had been knocked about quite a lot. They had put us on Point 156 again and we had been made up to full strength, and the next thing is that we found ourselves at Anzio.'

1 York & Lancs. History

Early in February, violent German counterattacks in great strength against the Americans placed the whole Anzio bridgehead in great peril. To relieve the situation 56 Infantry Division was withdrawn from the Garigliano sector and sent to reinforce the hard-pressed garrison. In consequence the now sadly depleted British X (BR) Corps had no option but to stop all its own attacks and stand on the defensive.

When therefore 1 York & Lancs. returned to the area of Monte Natale, it found it quite quiet. For the last three weeks of February, it occupied the hills North and North-West of Minturno. Activity in the area was confined to occasional shelling, patrols, and raids to capture prisoners. These enabled the new reinforcements to gain useful battle experience.

On 1 March 44 1 York & Lancs. moved to an area West of Naples and three days later embarked in the evening in Landing Craft, destination Anzio. After an extremely rough voyage Anzio was reached the next day and 1 York & Lancs. went into a concentration area in some woods by the seashore about six miles North-West of the town.

Captain Ivor Wedgbury, later promoted to Major
Major Ivor Wedgbury who was awarded the Military Cross for his action at Monte Natale on 22 Jan 44 was killed in action at Anzio on 3 June 44.

Major Wedgbury's Military Cross was presented to his widow by H.M. King George at Buckingham Palace on 9 April 1946.

On the outbreak of the Second World War Ivor Wedgbury volunteered for active service on 20 Sept 39, and after a spell with an Officer Cadet Training Unit was commissioned in the York and Lancaster Regiment as a Second Lieutenant on 25 Feb 40. Two days later he married Miss Joan Archer in St. Albans Cathedral, and after a brief honeymoon he embarked for overseas service. He was never to see his wife again.

Posted to the Middle East Forces, he served overseas from April 1940, and was promoted Lieutenant on 15 Aug 41 and Captain on 5 Dec 41. Appointed Adjutant on 20 Dec 41, he was promoted to Major in June 1942, and took part in the invasion of Sicily, July to August 1943, and the subsequent invasion of Italy in September 1943. In January 1944 he took part in the crossing of the River Garigliano and in the heavy fighting at Minturno, for which he was awarded the Military Cross. In the words of his commanding officer, Lieutenant-Colonel R. J. A. Kaulback, his M.C. 'was one of the best Military Crosses won in this war and he deserved every bit of it'.

At the beginning of March, 1 York & Lancs. were transferred to the Anzio beachhead. On 23 May 44 operations commenced in Anzio to break out from the beachhead and to push on to Rome. On 3 June the Battalion was ordered to launch a subsidiary attack to help the main effort to be made against the enemy on the Acquabuona Ridge, just short of the River Tiber. Major Wedgbury 'was killed in our final battle before the capture of Rome, on the 3 June 44. We attacked at half past one that afternoon, and Ivor's Company, which he led magnificently as usual, quickly overran the German positions and captured a number of prisoners. However, the German resistance proved stronger than we had expected, and it was while Ivor was reorganising his men to deal with this that he was hit. He had gone forward to recce the position when he was caught by a burst of fire from an enemy machine gun and was wounded in the left leg and right shoulder. His wounds were dressed by his Company Sergeant-Major, C.S.M. Thorpe, and he had been carried back a certain distance when he told the C.S.M. to leave him and go to another Platoon to order it forward. The C.S.M. did this, but when he returned with stretcher bearers, Ivor had already been dead for some little time. The following morning, after the battle, he was taken back to Anzio and buried in the British Military Cemetery there, where he now lies with the rest of his men who died in the beachhead.

Brothers in Law
Feb 44
Ernest Strafford's wife Edith had four sisters two of whom, Gladys and Bessie, were married. Gladys was married to Pte. Arthur Townsend who served with 7 Field Company, Royal Engineers and Bessie was married to Pte. John Webb who served

with the Royal Marine Commandos and was based on the Adriatic coast of Italy. Her sister Winnie was engaged to Sgt Len Hill, who was also with 7 Field Company, Royal Engineers. Len Hill had been at Dunkirk in 1940 and both Arthur and Len had fought in the North Africa campaign. In Feb 44 they were near Minturno when they heard that Ernest Strafford was missing, believed wounded. They set out to search for him, without success, not knowing he was dead. At one point they were within five miles of where Ernest Strafford was buried. They went on to fight at Monte Casino helping to construct the bridge over the River Rapido.

In the period 17 Jan-4 Mar 44, X (BR) Corps captured 1,035 Prisoners of War but suffered 4,152 casualties.

During this same period at and around Monte Natale, 1 King's Own Yorkshire Light Infantry suffered 30 killed. 10 died later of wounds. There were also 32 missing and 102 wounded.

11 May 1944
The earlier assaults on the foothills around Minturno enabled II (US) Corps to launch with two Divisions on 11 May 44. They attacked with the French Expeditionary Corps on their right, the weight of which the enemy was totally unprepared for. At the time when X (BR) Corps was forced to abandon the offensive the Garigliano operations of January and early February seemed inconclusive and to have failed to achieve a decisive result, but the bridgehead gained provided II (US) Corps with a splendid springboard for the brilliant summer offensive.

It was not until 12 May 44 that Santa Maria Infante was attacked and overrun by the Americans. They faced great difficulties with many enemy anti-tank guns and machine

In North Africa. Sgt. Len Hill, back row holding child, Pvt. Arthur Townsend, front row first on left. (Family photo)

US soldiers with a 57mm M-1 anti-tank gun fighting during the initial assault on Santa Maria Infante, May 1944 (*United States Army in World War II: The War against Germany and Italy - Pictorial Record*, Washington, D.C. 1988)

gun nests opposing them. Several Sherman tanks ran on to mines placed along the only access road, but eliminating the town was vital to progress further into the mountains. By 14 May 44 the town or what was left of it, was taken.

On 18 May 44 Monte Casino was taken by 12 Podolski (Polish) Lancers. There had been four major battles and the Monastery had been reduced to smithereens by bombing and artillery fire. In this last successful battle, the Poles suffered 3,784 casualties, of whom more than a third were killed.

In the battle for Italy, it is estimated that between September 1943 and April 1945, 60,000–70,000 Allied and 38,805–150,660 German soldiers died in Italy. The number of Allied casualties was about 313,000 and the German figure (excluding those involved in the final surrender) was over 330,000. 153,100 Italian civilians were killed.

A German View: General Von Senger Und Etterlin, Commander XIV Panzer Corps
May 44
In his book *Neither Fear Nor Hope* Lt. General Fridolin Von Senger und Etterlin describes his view of the British crossing of the River Garigliano: 'I will give an

273

example of the right use of reserves in the Cassino battles. It was the attack on 18 Jan 44 against the right flank of XIV Panzer Corps where it rested on the Tyrrhenian Sea, which resulted in a dangerous penetration. The Army Group threw in its two Reserve Divisions, the 29 and 90 Panzer Grenadier Divisions, on the threatened flank. This was taking a risk which subsequently became obvious with the Anzio landing on 22 Jan 44. Yet here 29 Panzer Grenadier Division was quickly pulled back again and was able to help in delaying the Allied exploitation of their successful landing.

This was a truly classic example of the right use of reserves: keeping them far back, exploiting their mobility for dealing with the threatened main front and also with the invasion threat on the coast; then the definite step in committing two Divisions, accepting a great risk, and withdrawing one of them after the enemy had been halted, although this withdrawal occurred before the counter – thrust had regained the old line.'

D-Day Dodgers
Lady Nancy Astor, a Conservative MP, is alleged to have called the soldiers in Italy the 'D-Day Dodgers'. The soldiers answered back by composing a song about themselves. The first and the last verses were as below:

> We're the D-Day Dodgers, out in Italy
> Always on the vino – always on the spree
> Eighth Army scroungers with our tanks
> We live in Rome among the swanks,
> The carefree D-Day Dodgers, out in Italy
> Just look around the mountains, amid the mud and rain
> You will find those scattered crosses, some without a name,
> Heartbreak, toil, and suffering gone,
> The lads beneath them slumber on
> They are the D-Day Dodgers, who'll stay in Italy.
> **Private Ernest Strafford is one of those slumbering on in Italy.**

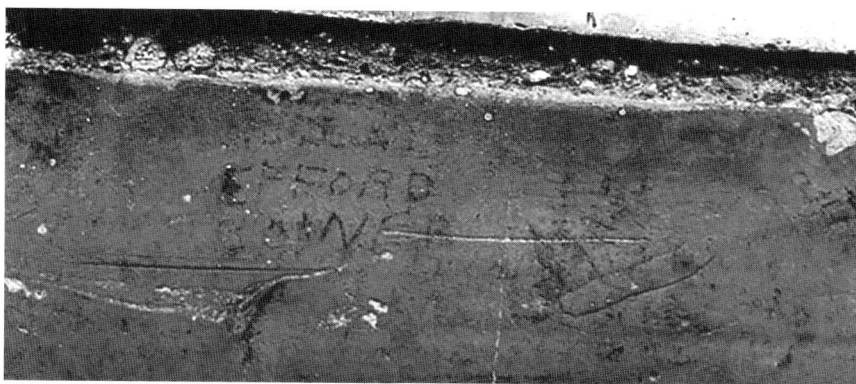

Graffiti at a house in Minturno occupied by the British in Jan 44. (Minturno Municipality)

Graffiti!

2021

In 2021 a photo was sent to me by Mario Mirco Mendico, my contact with the Municipality of Minturno in Italy. They had discovered graffiti in the basement of a house in Italy occupied by the British in the early days of January 1944. The house is on the Minturno to Castelforte road. (the Lateral road). Its address is 16 Via Per Castelforte. After crossing the River Garigliano 1 York & Lancs. arrived at this road in the early hours of 19 Jan 44 and were on it until the early hours of 20 Jan 44. Having arrived at the road 1 York & Lancs. then moved up the road until they reached their rest area. What is certain is that at some time they were within two kilometres of this house. By enlarging the photograph, you can clearly see written: 'FFORD'. Underneath it is written John ER. (my Christian names are John Ernest). I wonder if this was written by Ernest Strafford. We will never know!

Chapter 22

So, What Happened to Pvt. Ernest Strafford?

Summary of events leading up to the death of Ernest Strafford
1 York & Lancs. War Diary
20 Jan 44 – 0745
In Phase I, 1 York and Lancs. passed through Tufo and crossed the Start-line behind a barrage on time. After advancing about 800 yards, these two companies attacked the enemy with great dash and determination and, after a brief fight, the Germans surrendered.

'D' Company reported: 'have taken 50 prisoners and are on our objective'. They were held up by wire at one point and suffered about 40 casualties. 'A' Company reached their objective with little difficulty. They took 100 prisoners.

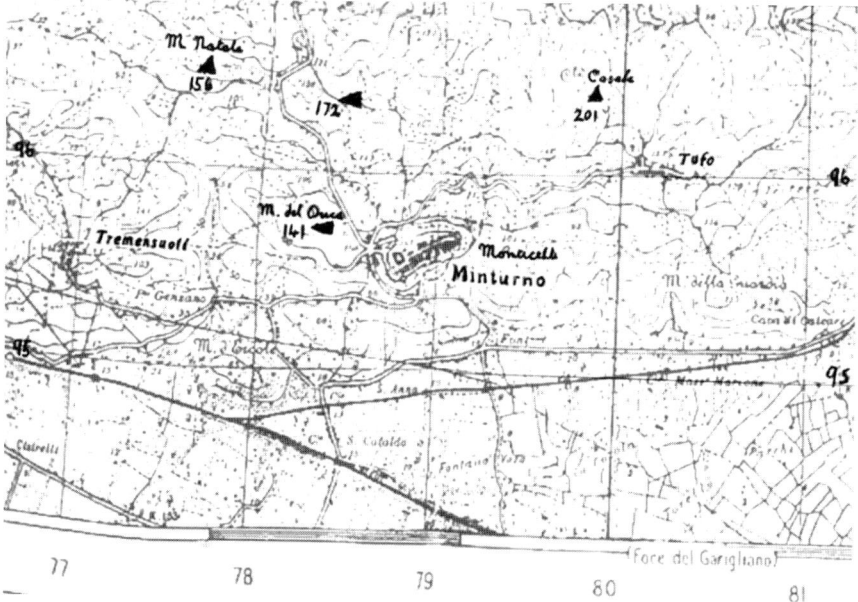

The Main Objectives – each square is 1km wide and deep.

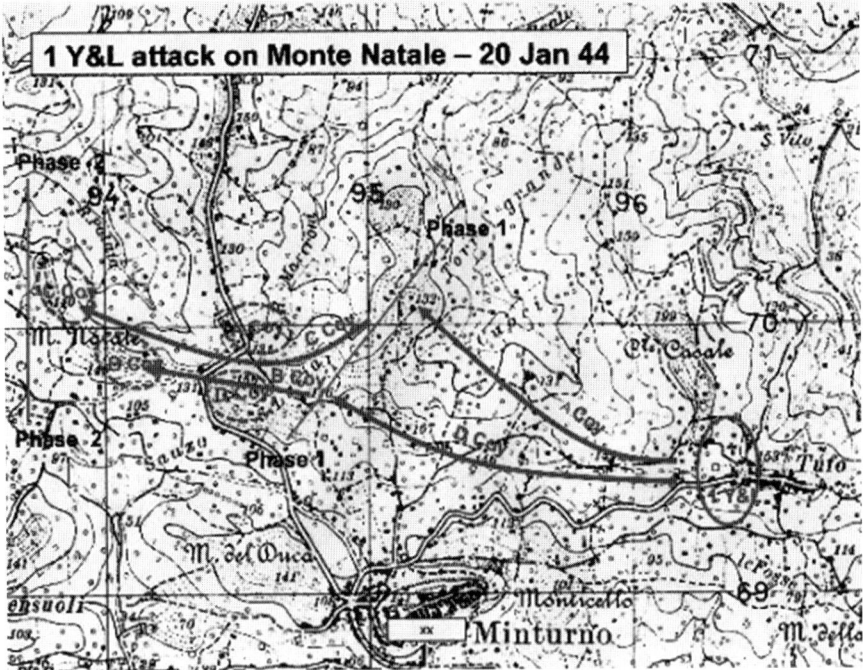

York & Lancs. actual route of attack. 'A' Co. on reaching the road turned right, in front of the Cemetery, and went around the corner to the left. (Frank de Planta)

International Red Cross
A report of an interview by the International Red Cross given by Private Thomas Pryor 5 September 1944 whilst he was a prisoner of war at Stalag IV B.

INTERNATIONAL COMMITTEE OF THE RED CROSS

CENTRAL AGENCY PRISONERS OF WAR

STALAG IV B

Concerning No. 4755938 Rank Pte. Name STRAFFORD Ernest

Regiment: York and Lancaster Regiment

Statement from Private Thomas Mills Pryor:

'I last saw Pte. Strafford wounded in the head when a mortar bomb burst among us during our attack. I believe his wounds were serious.'

Were you an eyewitness? **Yes**

Actual date of incident and place: **20 January 1944 Near Minturno**

Date: 5 Sept 1944 Signature: T M Pryor P.O.W No. 240609

International Committee of the Red Cross interview with Pvt. Thomas Pryor, 5 Sep 44.

'D' Company, 1 York & Lancs. Missing Person's Report by Sergeant Fielding
20 Jan 44

'At 7am on 21 January 1944 the Battalion, on a two Company front, "A" and "D" Companies were ordered to attack Hill Point 172, about one mile North-East of Minturno. Eventually we consolidated on Hill 172 and being then the Acting Sergeant Major of the Company I called for Platoon casualty slips and also detailed Sergeant Waddington, 18 Platoon "D" Company to gather in the dead bodies. We had 12 dead, and 33 wounded out of this action. I sent immediately for the Medical Officer of the unit to confirm the lost lives of the bodies. All personnel effects together with one identification disc was taken off, docketed, and forwarded to Battalion HQ. The Company was going to bury the men, but we had orders to move at once and on each man's body were left all particulars on a piece of paper tied to the body, plus one identity disc.'

The date of this action is 20 January, not 21 January, see War Diaries. Did Ernest Strafford die during the attack on Point 172 on 20 January 1944? Acting Sergeant Major Fielding gathered together 12 dead bodies and Ernest Strafford was not amongst them. Ernest Strafford's body was found on 4 February approx. 50m from Point 172. Ernest Strafford's body was on its own on Hill 172 when buried on 4 February. (See Grave Registration Report Form below). It is possible he was one of the 33 wounded, but unlikely as the wounded would have been taken to the Regional Aid Post and he was not amongst them. He was seriously wounded but he may have continued with 'D' Company to the slope down to the cemetery.

A cross was erected on Ernest Strafford's grave. The location is given as 786963. Point 172 location is 785963, i.e., within 100m of his body. The Graves

GRAVES REGISTRATION REPORT FORM.

Army Form W 3372

Report No. 12GRU/DRG/2059.   Schedule No. Italy 1/50,000.

Place of Burial Minturno.   Sht.171/1.

Commune 17.   Map Reference M.786963.

The following are buried here:

Regiment.	Army No.	Name and Initials.	Rank.	Date of Death.	Cross erected or G.R.U'd.	Plot, Row and Grave.
Y.& L.	4755938	*Cross* Strafford E.	Pte.	4/2/44	*6.H.H.* G.R.U.	Isolated

Particulars from Legible Cross.

It is pointed out that the 10 Graves on this Multiple 3314A. at Map. Ref. 783964, are scattered over an area of about 1,500yds. May the Burial Officer be advised of the correct Procedure please.

Lieut.
11/8/44.

Graves Registration Report Form. (Commonwealth War Graves Commission)

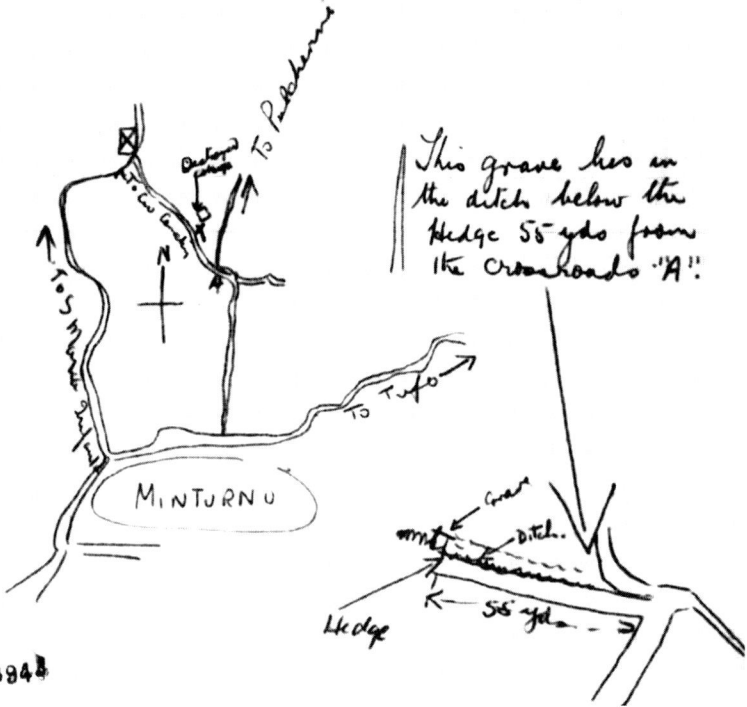

On 15 Aug 44, the Commonwealth War Graves Commission made a sketch of where Ernest Strafford was buried. (Not to scale). The destroyed cottage on the site has now been replaced by a house. (owner, Dr. Pino Russo). (Map Commonwealth War Graves Commission)

The track to the Cemetery from Tufo. Point 172 at the top. (Photo Google)

280

SO, WHAT HAPPENED TO PVT. ERNEST STRAFFORD?

Registration Report Form shows the date of death as 4 Feb 44, but this is the date he was buried. His date of death was subsequently given as 22 Jan 44.

92 Field Regiment Royal Artillery War Diary
20 Jan 44
1 York & Lancs. joined the fray and quickly captured the area of the Cemetery and the high ground Westwards. 150 prisoners of war taken for loss of two wounded in 'A' Company.

A soldier from 'A' Company 1 York & Lancs. described what happened
'Our objective was some ground outside a town called Minturno. As we were going down a muddy track a German tank was at the bottom. It let off a few shells which caused casualties, amongst them being the chap who went swimming with me at Geneiefa. I spoke to him as he was carried away on a stretcher'.

Was the swimming companion one of the two wounded in 'A' Company? If so, was Ernest Strafford the other one and still with 'A' Company?

'A' Company attacked to the right of Point 172. If Ernest Strafford had been with 'A' Company and was one of the two wounded, he would either have had to go up a steep hill to get to Point 172 where his body was found or carried on with 'A' Company towards the Cemetery.

Ernest Shaw, 1 York & Lancs
'Another lucky escape. On the same track we were going down the side of a road, up the road, perhaps 50 yards off the road on the right of the road. One of our platoons rounded the bend on the road itself and there must have been a German tank with this corner under observation and he let fly at them. There were a couple of casualties before they got off the road. While Ted and I were still behind this corner and still 30 to 40 yards short of the corner but off the road, "A" Company came marching down, a full platoon, not marching but walking in single file. Their Company Commander, I believe his name was Wilson, Major A Wilson, was not far from the front, perhaps a couple of Sections in front of him and I shouted to him "Excuse me sir watch it on the corner, you are under observation, you are better off the road". But whether he did not hear me properly, he glared and carried on. Next thing the Gerry tank sees these guys going around the corner and lets go again and they scatter. There were a few casualties. I cursed the officer. "Daft Bugger".'

If Ernest Strafford, although seriously wounded, had managed to carry on with 'D' Company or 'A' Company, he would now be in the area of the Cemetery. Was he with Major Wilson?

1 York & Lancs. War Diary
20 Jan 44 – 1750
'D' Company position on Point 172 taken over by 1 KOYLI. 'D' Company moved to area in reserve. This is remarkably close to Point 172.

If still alive Ernest Strafford may have remained at the Cemetery with 'A' Company or gone with 'D' Company back close to Point 172.

When Pat Strafford (daughter of Ernest) first enquired about Ernest Strafford's death with the York & Lancaster Regimental Museum their records showed that

he died on 21 January 1944. This was altered to 22 January 1944 after contact with the Commonwealth War Graves Commission!

1 York & Lancs. War Diary
21 Jan 44 – 1930
'A', 'B' and 'C' Companies suffered heavy casualties. 'D' Company sent up to reinforce 'A' and 'B' Companies. One Platoon being put under command 'A' Company, two Platoons under 'B' Company. Counterattack beaten off. The enemy withdrew to the reverse slope'. HQ was dive bombed during the day.

15 Infantry Brigade War Diary
21 Jan 44 – 2150
Traffic became hopelessly jammed between Point 172 and the Class 9 bridge. However, labour provided by 13 Infantry Brigade managed to clear the debris and about midnight traffic was moving round this very exposed corner OK.

With all this activity around Point 172 was Ernest Strafford there or not? If there alive, he would surely have been attended to, so he was either dead or not there.

40 Royal Tank Regiment No. 1 Troop War Diary
21 Jan 44
The disposition of No 1 Troop was as follows – Troop Leader at 781967, Cemetery, 1 disabled tank at 781968 [100m North of Cemetery corner] the third tank at 780966 [by the Aid Post on the Santa Maria road] in a counterattack role.

The Troop was dive bombed and the disabled tank was hit and set on fire, but the Troop suffered no casualties.

The fire was extinguished, and the tank abandoned. Extensive damage was caused, one engine being out of action, the radiator smashed, the left-hand sprocket smashed and the tracks and suspension damaged.

'A' Squadron of 40 Royal Tank Regiment War Diary
22 Jan 44 – 0900
One tank of No 2 Troop was shelled and set on fire, but the crew were unharmed.
Was this tank by the Cemetery when hit?

22 Jan 44 – 1000
Orders received from 5 Infantry Division to place two troops under command 15 Infantry Brigade and two under command 201 Guards Brigade. The two Troops under command 15 Infantry Brigade moved to the area of the Cemetery, 781967 and the high ground to the East of the Cemetery, at Point 172, whilst the two Troops under the command of 201 Guards Brigade took up positions at 815957 and 780954.

After Ernest Strafford was reported as killed in action, his daughter Pat recalls that an officer of 1 York & Lancs. wrote to her mother. He said that Ernest Strafford was near a tank by a Cemetery, standing near an officer when the officer was hit. Ernest Strafford went to help him when he was hit. The officer may have been either Major A. Wilson or Captain Cruickshank of 'A' Company or Major D.

Young of 'D' Company. In this case Ernest Strafford would have been either with a Platoon of 'D' Company or with 'A' Company. It is thought most likely that the Platoon of 'D' Company and 'A' Company or what was left of them retreated in the direction of Point 172 where Ernest Strafford's body was found. It is possible he was by one of these tanks when he was hit.

If the men of 'A' and 'D' Company saw the tank going to Point 172 there would have been an incentive to them to retreat that way up the track.

1 York & Lancs. War Diary
22 Jan 44 – 1030
There was a pause in the enemy counterattack. The new composite 'B/C/D' Company, although almost surrounded, still barred the way to Minturno and was prepared to fight on if need be.

The enemy were thus able to bring fire to bear behind 'A' & 'B' Company positions making a counterattack on 'A' Company's position impossible. Later in the morning enemy tanks advanced down the road to 783963, 400 metres South of the Aid Post but were held up by our tanks. Enemy machine guns were established in the houses at 778963, 500 metres to the West. Patrols were sent out to stalk the enemy tanks and to deal with their machine guns with some success.

We now know that the Germans were close to Ernest Strafford by 1030, if he was still with a Platoon of 'D' Company or 'A' Company. Did he retreat towards Tufo?

1 KOYLI War Diary
22 Jan 44 – 1200
It was not until about 1200 that Officer Commanding 'B' company was compelled to withdraw from point 172 to the next high ridge some 300 yards south. By this time, the Battalion was getting thin on the ground. At the same time the attack was developing on our right flank.

The first fierce counterattack was weakening and the Battalion although no longer holding the whole of Point 172 ridge was firmly established with its left on the high

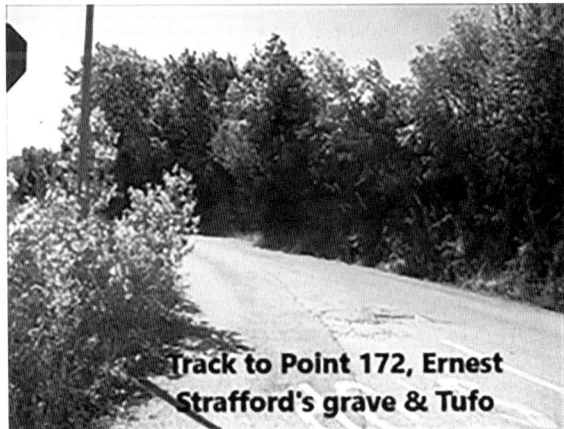

Track to Point 172, Ernest Strafford's grave and Tufo. Photo taken from Cemetery corner. (Photo John Strafford)

ridge about 784963 [100m West of Point 172] and its right 'A' company still on the Eastern ridge of the high ground. In the meantime, 1 York & Lancs. had not been able to hold the enemy and were withdrawing in fair order down the road covered by our company on the high ground at Point 141, Monte del Duca.

22 Jan 44 – 1500
The plan was made at about 1500 by the Brigade Commander for 1 Green Howards to come up from the reserve area south of Minturno and attack behind an artillery barrage, the remainder of the Point 172 ridge. In order to enable the barrage to go down the forward Companies tightened up their position and 'A' Company were withdrawn into their original area about 787960 [400m South of Point 172]. One Company of 1 Green Howards who had been attached to 1 York & Lancs. was left on the ground covering the gap between 'C' Company and the road. 'B' Company was pulled out into the same area as 'A' Company and the two Companies were amalgamated to form 'A/B' Company. The total Companies strengths at this time were believed to be 195 approx. split 'A' Company – 50, 'B' Company – 15, 'C' Company – 50, 'D' Company – 80.

In order to enable this operation to take place one Company of 2 Scots Guards was put under the command of the Battalion and occupied the high ground Point 141, Monte del Duca, 781959. 1 Green Howards attack went in, but they had not sufficient men to push home their attack with thoroughness and were not able to occupy the whole of the Point 172 feature and despite attempts by both sides this feature remained in 'No Man's Land'.

1 KOYLI held the ground where Ernest Strafford was buried and some 150m in front of him until 1200-1500. Was he there dead or did he stop there, thinking he was safe and died after 1 KOYLI withdrew? 1 KOYLI had now retreated from Ernest Strafford's burial place.

92 Field Regiment Royal Artillery War Diary
22 Jan 44 – 1530
368 Battery Commander gives 1 KOYLI Company locations:786961 (30 metres from where Ernest Strafford's body was buried) and 789963.

Could the barrage prior to 1 Green Howard's attack have killed Ernest Strafford?

So, What happened to Private Strafford?
There are several possibilities.

- During the assault on Point 172 on 20 Jan 44 he was hit by a mortar bomb and seriously wounded and died on the spot where his body was found. However, 'D' Company collected the bodies around Point 172 and his was not amongst them. Also, he was posted as missing on 22 Jan 44 and this was later given as his date of death. It is unlikely he died at this point in time.
- On 20 Jan 44 although seriously wounded he carried on to the Minturno Cemetery with either 'A' Company (unlikely as they only had one soldier wounded unaccounted for) or with 'D' Company.
- On 20 Jan 44 'D' Company having got to the Cemetery were then moved back to the area of Point 172. Ernest Strafford may have moved back with them and then

died. However, at this point in time 'D' Company could have buried him and did not, so it is unlikely that this happened.

- On 22 Jan 44 he may have been at the Cemetery with 'A' Company or joined the Platoon of 'D' Company that had been allocated to 'A' Company.

- On 22 Jan 44 'A' Company and a Platoon of 'D' Company came under strong attack by the enemy who came down the Santa Maria Infante road. There was a disabled tank on the road and Ernest Strafford could have been by it when hit. If this was the case, it is likely that they retreated up the track to Tufo. The track to Tufo is uphill to Point 172 which is where Ernest Strafford is buried. It is the highest part of the ridge. If he was weak from being wounded, it is possible that by the time he reached Point 172 he was exhausted. With the Germans getting closer by the minute his colleagues may have told him to go behind the hedge and hide. Having gone behind the hedge he might have just then died. What he would not have known is that Point 172 was the German objective for it was the high ground over-looking the valley. It is possible they may have found him and finished him off. In battle prisoners can be a problem. It is also possible that when he reached Point 172 it was still controlled by 1 KOYLI, so he may have stopped thinking he was safe.

- If he was hit when by the tank at the Aid Post, he could have passed the 6 Grenadier Guards position and taken the same route back to Point 172 which 'D' Company had taken when they had attacked the Cemetery on 20 Jan 44.

In the afternoon of the 22 Jan 44 1 Green Howards were ordered to counterattack and take Point 172 from the Germans after it had received an artillery barrage from our own side. This barrage could have hit and killed Ernest Strafford. The attack by 1 Green Howards was only partially successful in pushing the Germans back. They retreated but not very far. Point 172 and Ernest Strafford were left in no man's land. It was not until 27 Jan 44 that Point 172 was comprehensively taken by 2 Royal Scots Fusiliers. If Ernest Strafford had been alive at the end of 22 Jan 44 he would surely have died from exhaustion, lack of water and supplies by 27 Jan 44.

The sad fact is that if Ernest Strafford had been alive and had been able to go another 300 yards past Point 172 he would have possibly been safe and rescued. He would not have been reached by the Germans, he would not have been subject to an artillery barrage, he would not have been subjected to the crossfire when 1 Green Howards attacked, and he would have been able to get medical assistance, water and food.

Exactly what happened when Private Ernest Strafford died we will never know but it is possibly one of the scenarios shown above.

On 27 Jan 45 Ernest Strafford was moved to the Commonwealth War Graves Cemetery in Minturno. and buried there, once again with a wooden cross on his grave. This was subsequently changed to a regular Commonwealth War Graves Stone.

The words inscribed on the gravestone, as requested by his wife, Edith Strafford are as follows:

'Dear Lord hold him.
He is Thine
Love him as we loved him.
With Thy love divine'

GRAVES CONCENTRATION REPORT FORM

Report No. 2/31G CU/SHH/37   cont

Schedule No.   Sheet   3

Place Of Burial MINTURNO MILITARY CEMETERY

Map. Reference

The following are buried here

REGIMENT	ARMY NO.	NAME AND INITIALS	RANK	DATE OF DEATH	PREVIOUSLY BURIED AT	RE BURIED AT	DATE OF RE BURIAL	PLOT	ROW	GRAVE
1/ Y & L	4755938	STRAFFORD E	Pte	14.2.44	12GH/DRG/ 2059	Cross	27.1.45	C	H	14
Green Howards	4384613	ROBINSON GW	Pte	21.1.44	DRG/2029	Disc	-do-	C	H	15
1/ KOYLI	4695241	BROWN J	W/Cpl	21.1.44	JSA/2027	Rank	-do-	C	H	16
1/ Y & L	4754360	FORD F	W/Sgt		DRG/2054	Rank	-do-	C	H	17
Green Howards	5573694	SALTER LR	Pte	21.1.44	JSA/2034	Cross.Disc unreadable	-do-	C	H	18
7/ Cheshire	4129357	CUNCLIFFE A.E.	Sgt	28.1.44	JSA/2031	Rank -do-	-do-	C	H	19
Green Howards	4399797	MASTERS R.S.	Pte	-do-	JRS/2153	Cross.Disc unreadable	-do-	66	H	20
C/Seaforth	14350058	CHISHOLM GD	Pte	21.1.44	-do-	Unit cross	-do-	C	H	21
-do-	4805448	SHUTTLEWORTH W	Cpl	-do-	-do-	Cross.Rank	-do-	C	H	22
1/ HENLEY & L	4694394	FRANCE C	Pte	20.1.44	AKV/2389	Cross	-do-	C	H	23
1/ Y & L	4750129	LOWERY J	Pte	-do-	-do-	Cross	-do-	C	H	24
-do-	14286028	GUNN K	Pte	-do-	-do-	Cross	-do-	C	H	25
-do-	4751589	BEVAN E	L/Cpl	21.1.44	-do-	Cross	-do-	C	H	1

Certified Capt Feb 45

Graves Concentration Report Form. (Commonwealth War Graves Commission)

Ernest Strafford's grave, Minturno Commonwealth War Graves Cemetery. (Photo John Strafford)

We Will Remember Them

Commonwealth War Graves Cemetery – Minturno
Roll of Honour:

Some of those killed in the Battle of Monte Natale 18 Jan – 4 Feb 44

L/Cpl H. Bevan	20 Jan 44 1 York & Lancs.
Cpl. J. Brown	22 Jan 44 1 KOYLI
Pte. W.D. Chisholm	23 Jan 44 6 Seaforth Highlanders
Pte. W. Cooper	21 Jan 44 1 York & Lancs.
Sgt. A.E. Cuncliffe	23 Jan 44 7 Cheshires
Pte. C. Dutton	22 Jan 44 1 KOYLI
L/Cpl B. Evan	20 Jan 44 1 York & Lancs.
L/Sgt. F. Ford	22 Jan 44 1 York & Lancs.
Pte. C. France	21 Jan 44 1 York & Lancs.
Pte. J.W. Gaylard	22 Jan 44 1 York & Lancs.
Pte. T. Gilmore	4 Feb 44 6 Seaforth Highlanders
23Sgt. J. Glover	19 Jan 44 1 York & Lancs.
Pte. G. Goldthorpe	22 Jan 44 1 York & Lancs.
Lt. V. M. Gordon-Ive	22 Jan 44 2 Scots Guards.
Pte. G. Grayson	19 Jan 44 6 Seaforth Highlanders
Pte. R. Gunn	21 Jan 44 1 York & Lancs.
Pte. F. Hargreaves	22 Jan 44 1 Green Howards
Pte. S.A. Holland	21 Jan 44 1 York &Lancs.
Pte. S. Hewitt	22 Jan 44 1 York & Lancs.
Fus. W. Hudson	23 Jan 44 2 Royal Scots Fusiliers
Sgt. E. Hughes	22 Jan 44 102 Medium Regiment, Royal Artillery.
Pte. E. Laxton	30 Jan 44 2 Northants
Capt. D.V. Leighton	23 Jan 44 98 Field Regiment, Royal Artillery.
Pte. J. Lowery	20 Jan 44 1 York & Lancs.
Cpl. L. Lush	21 Jan 44 2 Wiltshires
Lt. Col. I.D. Mackinnes DSO	23 Jan 44 2 Royal Scots Fusiliers
Capt. T. Marsham-Townsend	24 Jan 44 2 Scots Guards
Pte. R.S. Masters	18 Jan 44 1 Green Howards
L/Cpl. N. Packer	22 Jan 44 1 York & Lancs.
Pte. A. Pass	20 Jan 44 6 Seaforth Highlanders

Capt. J. Power	22 Jan 44	2 Wiltshires
Lt. G. S. Roberts M.C.	22 Jan 44	6 Grenadier Guards
Pte. W. Robinson	20 Jan 44	1 Green Howards
Pte. L.A. Salter	18 Jan 44	1 Green Howards
Cpl. W. Shuttleworth	23 Jan 44	6 Seaforth Highlanders
Capt. Edward Simpson	22 Jan 44	1 KOYLI
Pte. K. Stanley	22 Jan 44	1 KOYLI
Pte. E.H. Steward	3 Feb 44	1 KOYLI
Gnr. N. Stirk	27 Jan 44	91 Field Regiment, Royal Artillery.
Lt. C.H. Stokes-Roberts MC.	22 Jan 44	6 Grenadier Guards
Gdsmn. W.T.G. Stone	28 Jan 44	3 Coldstream Guards
Gdsmn. R. Stonehouse	29 Jan 44	6 Grenadier Guards
Pte. A. Stonier	30 Jan 44	6 Seaforth Highlanders
L/Cpl. J. Stott	20 Jan 44	1 York & Lancs.

Sheffield Telegraph Roll of Honour. (Photo Peter Strafford)

Pte. J. Stott	1 Feb 44 1 KOYLI
Pte. E. Strafford	22 Jan 44 1 York & Lancs.
Fus. G.M. Straffen	18 Jan 44 2 Royal Scots Fusiliers
Lt. J. Whiteman	22 Jan 44 Attached to 1 Green Howards.
Major A.C. Wilson M.C.	22 Jan 44 1 York & Lancs.
L/CPL. J. Wilson	21 Jan 44 1 York & Lancs.

Ernest Strafford is buried in the Commonwealth War Grave Cemetery in Minturno, which is about 78km North of Naples close to the coast. The site for the Commonwealth War Graves Cemetery was chosen in January 1944, but the Allies then lost some ground, and the site came under German small arms fire. The cemetery could not be used again until May 1944 when the Allies launched their final advance on Rome and the US 85 and 88 Divisions were in this sector. The graves are mainly those of the heavy casualties incurred in crossing the River Garigliano in January 1944. Minturno War Graves Cemetery contains 2,049 Commonwealth graves of the Second World War. It was designed by Louis De Soissons and contains the graves of sixty-eight members of the York & Lancaster Regiment.

Above left: Minturno War Graves Cemetery, Jan 44. It started as a temporary cemetery! (TNA)

Above right: Minturno War Graves Cemetery, VE Day 1945. (TNA)

Minturno War Graves Cemetery today. (Photo John Strafford)

Above left: Pat Brockman (née Strafford) daughter of Ernest Strafford. (Family photo)

Above right: Son John Ernest Strafford. (Photo Caroline Strafford)

Left: Letter from the Mayor of Minturno, Gerardo Stefanelli, 15 May 2019. (Photo John Strafford)

Letter from the Mayor of Minturno
15 May 2019

Dear John,
In the name of Minturno's people I am very pleased to receive you to our land, where your father, the war hero Ernest Strafford is buried.

I hope the warmth and hospitality of our community make your visit pleasant and fill your heart with joy and happiness.

Hereafter you and your family will not be simple tourists, but very welcome guests and we wish to see you again in the future.

All the best

The Mayor
Gerardo Stefanelli

Appendix 1

The National Archives War Diaries (WO***)

I thank The National Archives for permission to use the following War Diaries:

X(BR) Corps	**170/302**
5 Infantry Division	**170/426-427-433-794**
13 Infantry Brigade	
13 Infantry Brigade Support Company	170/562
2 Cameronians	170/1372
2 Wiltshires	170/1489
2 Royal Inniskilling Fusiliers	170/8004
15 Infantry Brigade	**170/565**
15 Infantry Brigade Support Company	170/566
1 Green Howards	170/1392
1 Kings Own Yorkshire Light Infantry (1 KOYLI)	170/1411
1 York & Lancaster (1 York & Lancs.)	170/1490
1 York & Lancaster missing Persons 361/854	
17 Infantry Brigade	**170/568**
17 Infantry Brigade Support Company	170/569
2 Royal Scots Fusiliers	170/1471
2 Northamptonshire's (2 Northants.)	170/1445
6 Seaforth Highlanders (6 Seaforths)	170/1474
Royal Artillery 2 Army Group	
52 Anti-Tank Regiment	170/1033
91 Field Regiment	170/961
92 Field Regiment	170/962
98 Field Regiment	170/966
102 Medium Regiment	170/1022
56 Heavy Regiment	215/57
Heavy Anti-Aircraft Regiment	170/1178
7 Cheshires	**170/1377**
Royal Engineers	
7 Field Company	170/1605
38 Field Company	170/1617
252 Field Company	170/1684

201 Guards Brigade	**170/636**
3 Coldstream Guards	170/1348
6 Grenadier Guards	170/1351
2 Scots Guards	170/1353
2 Welsh Guards	171/1261
16/5 Lancers	**170/825-828**
	'B' Squadron
	'C' Squadron
40 Royal Tank Regiment	**170/859**
141 Field Ambulance	**222/555**
158 Field Ambulance	**222/572**
164 Field Ambulance	**222/**

Appendix 2

1 York & Lancs. – A Brief History

The York & Lancaster Regiment was created when the 65th and 84th Regiments of Foot were paired off in the Cardwell military reforms of 1881. The 65th Regiment of Foot, raised in 1758, became the 1st Battalion and the 84th Regiment of Foot, raised in 1759, became the 2nd Battalion of the York & Lancaster Regiment.

1884, Sudan

The 1st Battalion, York & Lancs. were moved to Aden to be held in reserve for the Egyptian Campaign. After 18 months, they sailed to Trinkitat, Sudan, arriving 28 February 1884. The next day they came under gun fire and made a bayonet charge, capturing two Krupp guns. Later that day seven were killed and 35 wounded at the Battle of El Teb. The 1st Battalion was reported as 421 strong when at Souakin, 14 March 1884, before losing 32 killed and 25 wounded. They embarked on the troopship HMS *Jumna* on 29 March 1884, arriving at Dover on 22 April 1884.

1889, Second Boer War

The 1st Battalion York & Lancs. embarked for South Africa as part of the reinforcements for the Second Boer War in late 1899. It took part in the Relief of Ladysmith.

1902, Service in the Empire

Following the end of the war in South Africa in 1902, the 1st Battalion was sent to British India, where it replaced the 2nd Battalion in Mhow.

1914, First World War

In total, 22 Battalions of the Regiment served during the Great War, losing 8,814 officers and men killed in action.

The 22 Battalions consisted of the two regular Battalions, the Depot Battalion, six Territorial Battalions, nine Service, two Reserve, one Transport and one Labour Battalion. Of these Battalions, 17 saw service overseas.

Men of the York & Lancaster Regiment receiving instructions in the trenches before starting out on a patrol near Roclincourt, France. Note their camouflaged outfits.12 Jan 18. (Photo TNA)

During the Battle of the Somme eight Battalions of the York & Lancs. went over the top on the first day, 1 July 16, suffering huge casualties. Nelson Waterfall, a relative of Edith Strafford (née Waterfall) was killed on this day. Eleven Battalions of the Regiment fought during the Somme offensive.

Regular Army

The regular 1st Battalion returned from service in British India to be formed up as part of 83 Infantry Brigade in 28 Infantry Division. 28 Infantry Division consisted of regular Battalions returning from overseas service and was shipped to France in January 1915. The 1st Battalion saw action in the Second Battle of Ypres and the Battle of Loos. The Battalion then went to the Balkans as part of the British Salonika Army where it would remain until the end of the war. While the Battalion was still in France Private Samuel Harvey was awarded the York & Lancs. first Victoria Cross since the regiment's creation in 1881.

Following the Armistice of 11 November 1918 troops from the York & Lancaster Regiment were involved in a mutinous riot at Clipstone Camp, Nottinghamshire, following disquiet at the slow rate of demobilisation.

Second World War

The 1st Battalion York & Lancs. was part of 15 Infantry Brigade of 5 Infantry Division and was sent to France in October 1939, a month after the outbreak of the Second World War, where it served as part of the British Expeditionary Force (BEF). The Battalion, with the rest of 15 Infantry Brigade (which was temporarily detached from 5 Infantry Division), was carried to and from Norway, where it fought briefly in the Norwegian Campaign in April 1940, by HMS *Sheffield*. This led to a bond of friendship between the Regiment and the ship, and meant that, when the *Sheffield* was adopted by her namesake city, the Regiment was awarded the freedom of Sheffield soon after. The Battalion, after evacuation to the United Kingdom in May 1940, was sent to Scotland where 15 Infantry Brigade was reunited with the rest of 5 Infantry Division, later being posted to Northern Ireland in March 1942. After leaving the United Kingdom in March 1942 and being shipped around most of the British Empire and many Middle Eastern countries, the Battalion was finally sent to the Mediterranean, where it fought in the Allied invasion of Sicily in July–August 1943, followed in early September by the Allied invasion of Italy. They then fought in the Italian Campaign, fighting, most notably, in the First Battle of Monte Cassino in January 1944 and remained there holding their objectives gained during the battle, before being sent to the Anzio beachhead in March 1944. The Battalion, as in the aftermath of Monte Cassino, remained at Anzio until late May, where it took part in Operation 'Diadem', and in June was withdrawn from the front line, returning to the Middle East in July, where the Battalion remained for the next seven months, resting, and refitting after nearly a year of continuous action in Sicily and Italy. Landing briefly in Italy in February 1945, the Battalion, with the rest of 5 Infantry Division, transferred to Belgium soon afterwards, arriving there in March, to take part in the Western Allied invasion of Germany, where the Battalion ended the war.

After the Second World War

Following the Second World War, the Regiment saw service around the world, including participation in the Suez Crisis of 1956. With the reorganisation of the army in 1968, the York & Lancaster Regiment was one of two infantry regiments that chose to be disbanded rather than amalgamated with another Regiment, the other Regiment being the Cameronians. The 1st Battalion was disbanded in 1968, with the Regimental HQ closing in 1987.

Appendix 3

Ernest Strafford's Wedding Day

The wedding of Ernest Strafford and Edith Waterfall, 28 August 1937. (Family photo)
Left to right: Eliza Strafford (Ernest's mother), Ernest Strafford (Ernest's father), Vera Waterfall (Edith's sister), Bessie Waterfall (Edith's sister), best man, Ernest, Edith Evelyn Waterfall, Gertrude Evelyn Waterfall (Edith's mother), John Frederick Waterfall (Edith's father), Winnie Waterfall (Edith's sister).

Bibliography and Sources

Avis, G., *The Fifth British Division*, Private Papers.

Ben-Arie, Katriel, *The Battle of Monte Cassino 1944*, Rombach Verlag, 1985.

Brutton, Philip, *Ensign in Italy*, Leo Cooper, London, 1992

Caddick-Adams, Peter, *Monte Cassino. Ten Armies in Hell.* Preface Publishing Ltd, London, 2012

Cartright & Taylor, Ptes, 1 York & Lancs, Private Papers.

Carver, Field Marshal Lord, *Imperial War Museum Book of the War In Italy 1943-1945*, Pan Macmillan Ltd, London, 2002.

Chapman, Roger*, Green Howard's History.* Green Howard's magazine.

Cole, Sir David, *Rough Road To Rome, A Foot-Soldier in Sicily and Italy, 1943-44*, William Kimber, 1983.

Davies, Jane, *Images of England, The York and Lancaster Regiment*, The York and Lancaster Regimental Museum, 2000.

Deane, D.H., Lieutenant 2 Scots Guards, Private Papers.

De Planta, Frank.

Doherty, Richard, *Monte Cassino: Opening the Road to Rome*, Pen & Sword Books Ltd, Barnsley, 2018.

Elliott, W.A., *Esprit de Corps. A Scots Guard Officer on Active Service 1943-1945*, Michael Russell (Publishing) Ltd. Wilby Hall, Wilby, Norwich. 1996.

Ellis, John, *Cassino. The Hollow Victory*, Andre Deutsch Ltd, London. 1984.

Gascoigne-Pees, J., Private Papers.

Giesler, Wolfras. *My Experiences in the new setup of 94 Infantry Division in Italy from August 1943 to April 1945*, Comradeship of the former 94 Infantry Division.

Hamilton, Roy, 1 Green Howards, Private Papers.

Hawtree Hitchcock, Sgt. Raymond, A Company, 164 Field Ambulance, Private Papers.

Imperial War Museum, London.

Lepone, Antonio.

Milligan, Spike, *Mussolini: His Part in My Downfall*, Penguin Books Ltd, London, 2012.

Nicolson, Nigel, *The Grenadier Guards in the War of 1939-1945, Volume Two*, Gale & Polden Ltd, Aldershot, 1949.

Parker, Mathew, *Monte Cassino*, Headline Book Publishing, London, 2003.

Prinz, Wilhelm, Pte '274' Grenadier Regiment, *My Worst Days in World War II: Have there been failures?*

Plowman, Jeffrey and Rowe, Perry, *The Battles for Monte Cassino Then and Now*, After the Battle, 2011, Battle of Britain International Ltd

Roper, Albert, 1 Green Howards, Private Diary.

Royal Inniskillings Regimental Museum.

Shaw, Ernest Walter, 1 York & Lancs. *Oral recollections of World War Two Imperial War Museum.CRM:0107000003155.*

Sheffield, O.F., *The York and Lancaster Regiment, 1919-1953, Volume III*, Gale & Polden Ltd, 1956

Sheffield Telegraph, 5 February 1944.

Sym, J., *Seaforth Highlanders*, Gale & Polden Ltd, Aldershot, 1962.

The National Archives, Kew, London.

Von Senger und Etterlin, Lt. Gen. Fridolin. *Neither Fear Nor Hope*, Macdonald & Co. (Publishers) Ltd, London, 1963.

Wiedemann, Wolfgang, II Battalion '267' Grenadier Regiment, *My experiences in the newly established 94 Infantry Division in Italy from August 1943-April 1945*, Comradeship of the former 94 Infantry Division.

Whiting, C. and Taylor, E., *Fighting Tykes*, Pen & Sword Books Ltd, Barnsley, 2008.

Winter, Geoffrey, *Winter's Tale* Sheffield 2015; *Winter's Tale,* Sheffield, 2016

Woolard, D., *My Day*, BBC WW2 People's War.

Map Main Objectives

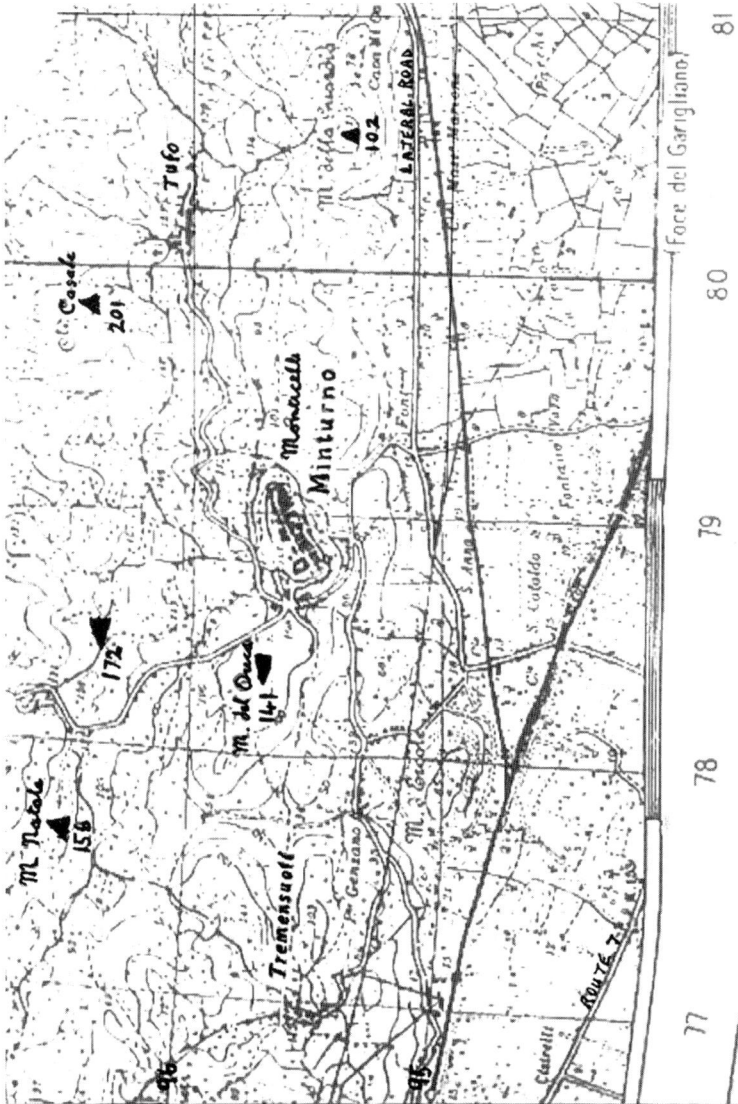